Boats, Borders, and Bases

Boats, Borders, and Bases

Race, the Cold War, and the Rise
of Migration Detention in the
United States

Jenna M. Loyd and
Alison Mountz

UNIVERSITY OF CALIFORNIA PRESS

University of California Press, one of the most distin-
guished university presses in the United States, enriches
lives around the world by advancing scholarship in the
humanities, social sciences, and natural sciences. Its
activities are supported by the UC Press Foundation and
by philanthropic contributions from individuals and
institutions. For more information, visit www.ucpress.edu.

University of California Press
Oakland, California

Library of Congress Cataloging-in-Publication Data

Names: Loyd, Jenna M., 1973– author. | Mountz,
    Alison, author.
Title: Boats, borders, and bases : race, the cold war, and
    the rise of migration detention in the United States /
    Jenna M. Loyd and Alison Mountz.
Description: Oakland, California : University of
    California Press, [2018] | Includes bibliographical
    references and index. |
Identifiers: LCCN 2017044582 (print) | LCCN 2017051141
    (ebook) | ISBN 9780520962965 (ebook) |
    ISBN 9780520287969 (cloth : alk. paper) |
    ISBN 9780520287976 (pbk. : alk. paper)
Subjects: LCSH: Alien detention centers—United States. |
    Detention of persons—United States. | Illegal
    aliens—Government policy—United States. |
    Haiti—Emigration and immigration. | Cuba—Emigra-
    tion and immigration. | Refugees—Caribbean
    Area—Social conditions. | United States—Emigration
    and immigration—Government policy. | United
    States—Race relations—History.
Classification: LCC KF4800 (ebook) | LCC KF4800 .L69
    2018 (print) | DDC 365/.4—dc23
LC record available at https://lccn.loc.gov/2017044582

Manufactured in the United States of America

26 25 24 23 22 21 20 19 18
10 9 8 7 6 5 4 3 2 1

To the many organizations and people who have survived, organized, and fought against the violence of confinement in detention and along borders, and to the memory of those who lost their lives trying

Contents

Illustrations

Acknowledgments

Research for this project took place over many years, in many places, and involved countless discussions. Thank you to Mona Lynch, Geoff Boyce, Sarah Launius, Matt Lowen, Todd Miller, Anne Bonds, Andrew Burridge, Judah Schept, Silky Shah, Bob Libal, Amy Gottlieb, David Hernández, Ethan Blue, Kelly Lytle Hernández, Nancy Hiemstra, Lydia Pelot-Hobbs, Deirdre Conlon, Lauren Martin, Mat Coleman, Niels Frenzen, Ruthie Gilmore, Craig Gilmore, Jack Norton, Naomi Paik, Brett Story, Martha Escobar, Jana Lipman, and Perla Guerrero for their work and the brilliance they have shared. They have shaped our project in all the insightful ways and none of the misguided ones.

We are grateful to Kate Coddington, Emily Mitchell-Eaton, and Tina Catania, each thoughtful scholars intimately involved as research assistants on the Island Detention Project. We also thank Laurier cartographer Trina King-Tassone for her talent and labor, and geographer Rob Fiedler for his cartography and intellectual engagement during the early parts of this research.

This work was presented at various departments, universities, and conferences where we benefited from gracious hosts and thoughtful feedback from live audiences and conversations with colleagues. We especially thank Imogen Tyler whose intellect and spirit provide inspiration and haven and Anna Secor and Patricia Ehrkamp for their scholarship and collegiality.

This book would not have been possible without the knowledge and patience of archivists and staff at the Arizona Historical Society, Arizona State University Libraries (including the now closed Arizona Historical Foundation), Chaffee Crossing, Delta State University Library Archives, the George Bush Presidential Library, the Jimmy Carter Library, the William J. Clinton Presidential Library, the Rubenstein Library at Duke University, the Genesee County History Department, the independent GovernmentAttic.org Digital Archive, Louisiana State University Libraries Special Collections, the National Archives in Washington, D.C., and College Park, MD, the Pinal County Historical Society, the Ronald Reagan Presidential Library, University of Arkansas Libraries Special Collections, the U.S. Citizenship and Immigration Services Library, and the Micronesian Area Research Center at the University of Guam.

We also thank Maura Roessner, Sabrina Robleh, and the art department at the University of California Press for their patience, support, and work on the manuscript. Additionally, we were honored to have insightful and careful reviewers.

Alison thanks comrade and co-conspirator Jenna who is an inspiration in the archive—and beyond. I've so enjoyed the days, hours, weeks, and years spent talking about ideas, unraveling mysteries, putting together pieces of an elaborate puzzle, building arguments, and meeting up in Syracuse, Toronto, Omaha, Cambridge, Waterloo, Athens, Valletta, Pavia, and other places our work brought us for seven years.

I am also grateful for the friendship, intellectual engagement, camaraderie, and support of friends, colleagues, and students, near and far, including Ishan Ashutosh, Ranu Basu, Lisa Bhungalia, Emily Billo, Alice Bloch, Kate Coddington, Mat Coleman, Deirdre Conlon, Alison Crosby, Jennifer Chun, Win Curran, Catherine Dauvergne, Judy Han, Emily Gilbert, Wenona Giles, Roberta Hawkins, Nancy Hiemstra, Jenna Hennebry, Paul Hodge, Suzan Ilcan, Loren Landau, David Ley, Audrey Macklin, Pauline Maillet, Cetta Mainwaring, Jacque Micieli-Voutsinas, Shiva Mohan, Beverley Mullings, Peter Murphy, Jackie Orr, Gerry Pratt, Monica Romero, Kim Rygiel, Mark Salter, Rachel Silvey, Rebecca Slisz, Farhana Sultana, Imogen Tyler, Tara Vinodrai, William Walters, Margaret Walton-Roberts, Celine and Helen Watkins, Kira Williams, Graham Webber, and Richard Wright. A lot of life happened as I conducted this research and wrote this book. I worked in positions at three universities in Canada and the United States: Syracuse University's Geography Department, Harvard University's Canada Program at the Weatherhead Center for International Affairs, and Wilfrid Laurier University's Geography

Department and its Balsillie School of International Affairs. I am grateful not only to colleagues but to administrative staff in each of these three places who provided important support, without which this work would not be possible. Most importantly, I thank my family. Over the course of this project, I was so fortunate to give birth to two beautiful children: Maddie Ruth and Henry. Their arrivals enhanced my life and work, intensifying my desire to better understand the past in order to work collectively for a better future. I am forever grateful to my partner, Jennifer Hyndman, for love, support, humor, and reprieve at the beginning and end of each day. We are also indebted to our extended families for tireless love and support: Bob and Henrietta Mountz, Sarah and Avery, baby Kai, Mary, Pete, and Bruce Hyndman.

For Jenna, this book invokes memories of road trips for archival and field research. On a couple of occasions, I had the great opportunity to do research with friends. Ashley Hunt and I went photographing prisons across Louisiana and found delicious peach cobbler in Jackson, Mississippi. Emily Mitchell-Eaton and I got to work at the Clinton Library together and warm ourselves from the air conditioning while watching turtles swimming in the river. More often, my days of archival work would be punctuated by sending a text message to Alison, attached with the photograph of a particularly juicy document. She has proven to be a generous and inspiring interlocutor and coauthor. I am so grateful for her expansive thought and humor at all the right moments.

This book has been my main intellectual endeavor across two states and three universities. In New York while at Syracuse University, I was sustained by the intellectual and political community shared with Lisa Bhungalia, Emily Mitchell-Eaton, Gretchen Purser, Jesse Nissim, Dana Olwan, Tod Rutherford, Don Mitchell, Aly Wane, and the Detention Task Force. My time at the University of Wisconsin-Milwaukee was made brighter by the friendships and collaborations with Anne Bonds, Lorraine Halinka Malcoe, Rob Smith, and Jenny Plevin. I am also grateful for the camaraderie and inspiration of Brian Coffey, Lane Hall, Rachel Buff, Linnea Laestadius, Ellen Velie, Richard Leson, Richard Grusin, Kristin Sziarto, Ryan Holifield, Rob Henn, Nicolas Lampert, Gloria Kim, John Fleissner, Kara Mannor, Maria Peeples, and, across the way, Karma Chávez. I finish this book as I move to Madison to join the Geography Department at the University of Wisconsin-Madison. I have already found wonderful community and engaging colleagues in Elizabeth Beardon, Michael McClure, Keith Woodward, Lisa Naughton, Morgan Robertson, Bob Kaiser, Kris Olds, Sarah Moore, Martin

Foys, Jen Plants, Kate Konkle, and Jerry Dryer. Across these spaces I am grateful for the long friendships and intellectual communities with Jenn Casolo, Laura McTighe, Micol Seigel, Shiloh Krupar, Lize Mogel, Jen Kaminsky, Paul Jackson, Nicole Pasulka, Chris Niedt, and Eddie Yuen. I have written portions of this book from the writing retreat I make in New Mexico practically every summer. While there, I enjoy spending time with my dad, Bill Loyd, and his partner, Anna Karin, and with Lorey Sebastian before heading up to Colorado to see my mom, Charlene Loyd, brothers, Nathan and Jeremy Loyd, and nieces and nephew. For the joy of making beautiful lives together—while finishing books at the same time, playing bikes, or enjoying donut-filled rambles—my love and admiration for Mark Vareschi.

Finally, last but by no means least, this material is based upon work supported by the National Science Foundation (NSF) under Award #0847133 (Principal Investigator: Alison Mountz). Any opinions, findings, and conclusions or recommendations expressed in this material are those of the authors and do not necessarily reflect the views of the National Science Foundation. NSF funding is frequently under threat, particularly when new administrations come to power. Without NSF funding, this book simply would not exist.

Abbreviations

ABC	*American Baptist Churches v. Thornburgh*
ACAP	Alien Criminal Apprehension Program
ACLU	American Civil Liberties Union
ADAA	Anti-Drug Abuse Act
AEDPA	Anti-Terrorism and Effective Death Penalty Act
AFB	Air Force base
AILA	American Immigration Lawyers Association
BAJI	Black Alliance for Just Immigration
BOP	Bureau of Prisons
BORTAC	Border Patrol Tactical Unit
BRAC	Base Realignment and Closure Commission
CAM	Central American minor
CAP	Criminal Alien Program
CAR	Criminal Alien Requirement
CBC	Congressional Black Caucus
CBP	Customs and Border Protection
CCA	Corrections Corporation of America
CHTF	Cuban-Haitian Task Force
DED	Deferred Enforced Departure
DHS	Department of Homeland Security

DOC	Department of Corrections
DOD	Department of Defense
DOJ	Department of Justice
DPC	Domestic Policy Council
EIS	environmental impact statement
EO	Executive Order
EOIR	Executive Office for Immigration Review
EU	European Union
EVD	Extended Voluntary Departure
FAA	Federal Aviation Administration
FEMA	Federal Emergency Management Agency
FHA	Federal Housing Authority
FIAC	Florida Immigrant Advocacy Center
FOIA	Freedom of Information Act
GAO	General Accounting Office
GSA	General Services Administration
GTMO	Guantánamo Bay Naval Base
HCC	Haitian Centers Council
HHS	Department of Health and Human Services
HRC	Haitian Refugee Center
HRW	Human Rights Watch
ICE	Immigration and Customs Enforcement
ICG	International Crisis Group
IGA	intergovernmental agreement
IHP	Institutional Hearing Program
IIRIRA	Illegal Immigration Reform and Immigrant Responsibility Act
IMMACT90	Immigration Act of 1990
INA	Immigration and Nationality Act
INS	Immigration and Naturalization Service
IOM	International Organization for Migration
IRCA	Immigration Reform and Control Act
JPATS	Joint Prisoner and Alien Transportation System
JTF	Joint Task Force
LPR	legal permanent resident

MLC	Minnesota Lawyers International Human Rights Committee
MPC	Migrant Processing Center
NACARA	Nicaraguan Adjustment and Central American Relief Act
NAFTA	North American Free Trade Agreement
NASA	National Air and Space Administration
NCC	National Council of Churches
NECLC	National Emergency Civil Liberties Committee
NEPA	National Environmental Policy Act
NILC	National Immigration Law Center
NGO	nongovernmental organization
NSC	National Security Council
OLA	Oakdale Legal Assistance
OMB	Office of Management and Budget
ORR	Office of Refugee Resettlement
POTUS	President of the United States
POW	prisoner of war
PTA	protection transfer agreement
REAA	Refugee Education Assistance Act
SBI	Secure Border Initiative
STCA	Safe Third Country Agreement
SWAT	Special Weapons and Tactics
TGK	Turner Guilford Knight Correctional Center
TPCR	Transition Period Custody Rules
TPS	Temporary Protected Status
UNHCR	United Nations High Commissioner for Refugees
USCG	United States Coast Guard
USCIS	United States Citizenship and Immigration Services
USMS	United States Marshals Service
USPHS	United States Public Health Service
WWII	World War II

Introduction

In December 1994, the government of Panama told the United States that it would no longer permit the U.S. government to use Howard Air Force Base (AFB) to detain Cuban asylum seekers intercepted at sea. The announcement came at the end of a series of what the Defense Department (DOD) called "disturbances" during which 2 Cubans died, 30 suffered injuries, and 221 U.S. soldiers were wounded. Even before these disturbances transpired, over thirty people held at the camp had tried to commit suicide. Attorney Harold Koh (1994a, 172) warned: "In effect, we have built offshore cities of more than 20,000 people without constructive outlets, with little to do besides getting frustrated."

Human-rights monitors who had visited earlier in the year reported in *Refugee Reports* that conditions at Howard were relaxed and welcoming for the Cubans. "The camps were spacious, set in beautiful surroundings, clean, and well-ordered" (Frelick 1994, 15). One resident of Camp One told the observers, "This is paradise. . . . Guantánamo was hell" (16). Camp One on Howard Air Force Base and Camp Bulkeley at the Guantánamo Bay Naval Base (GTMO) occupied the center of a carceral archipelago of military and civilian spaces planned, and in some cases established, as "safe havens" across the Caribbean for Haitian and Cuban asylum seekers in the early- to mid-1990s.

This Caribbean chapter of U.S. border-enforcement history remains largely forgotten. Despite important scholarship recollecting this history (Farmer 2004; Kaplan 2005; Shemak 2011; Lipman 2013; Paik

1

2013, 2016), these operations remain curiously separate from prevailing explanations for the rise of contemporary U.S. detention and deterrence policies. A central contention of this book posits that this popular forgetting is political. Political crises over migration and the nation-state repeatedly invoke "the border's" porosity, absence, or lawlessness to rationalize further fortification. Thus, there exists a strategic relationship between knowing and not knowing, between rendering bordering practices visible and strategically erasing them from public knowledge. As a result of these spectacular dynamics, attention has been focused along the historically charged United States–Mexico boundary, both naturalizing deterrence and fortification practices in this region and obscuring related U.S. policies of deterrence, detention, and exclusion in the Caribbean.

Even as the "safe haven" crisis took place in the Caribbean, the Bill Clinton administration was rolling out its new national strategy to "control the borders of the United States between the ports of entry, restoring our Nation's confidence in the integrity of the border" (U.S. Border Patrol 1994, 2). The Border Patrol strategy—called "prevention through deterrence"—was developed in consultation with the Defense Department's Center for Low Intensity Conflict and aimed to prevent unauthorized entry (Dunn 1996). The plan entailed the deployment of additional Border Patrol agents, increased fortification and surveillance of the boundary, and harsher employer sanctions. The plan focused on the U.S. Southwest, prioritizing the securing of the boundary between El Paso–Juárez and San Diego–Tijuana, before again bolstering efforts in the Tucson and South Texas sectors (U.S. Border Patrol 1994).

Borders are more than material barriers along international boundaries; border operations are performative (Andreas 2009; Mountz 2010; Nevins 2010). The Border Patrol acknowledged as much in its strategic plan when concluding that "the absolute sealing of the border is unrealistic" (1994, 1). Indeed, the plan was launched in 1994, the same year as the North American Free Trade Agreement (NAFTA) was implemented to further integrate the economies of the region. Nonetheless, the border spectacle had the immediate and enduring effect of funneling attention and anxiety over migration and national sovereignty away from the Caribbean and isolating it along the United States–Mexico boundary. In so doing, as Joe Nevins shows in *Operation Gatekeeper and Beyond,* "a semblance of control and order has replaced the image of chaos that once seemed to reign in the urbanized border region of the San Diego Sector" of the Border Patrol (2010, 7).

This spectacle builds on long colonial and imperial histories in both regions. Yet Attorney General Janet Reno's claim that the 1994 strategic plan was "necessary to establish a border for the first time" (in Nevins 2010, 115) obscures the much longer history of Border Patrol practices along the United States–Mexico boundary and their deadly consequences for border-crossers (Nevins 2003; Hernández 2010). Reno's claim also obscures the explicit development and deployment of deterrence doctrine in the Caribbean during the Cold War, designed to prevent unwanted arrivals of asylum seekers from Haiti and Cuba. This deterrence doctrine, which was firmly established by the early 1980s, made mandatory detention a central component of federal strategy and practice in the Caribbean and elsewhere.

These transnational histories of detention and migration policing are the subject of *Boats, Borders, and Bases*. We seek to explain why the U.S. detention and deportation system ballooned to the scale of its contemporary operation. In 2012, the United States made a record number of 409,849 removals, a number that dipped in 2016 to 240,255 removals (these numbers may count individuals more than once). *Removal* is the technical, legal term for *deportation;* the Department of Homeland Security (DHS) defines *removal* as "the compulsory and confirmed movement of an inadmissible or deportable alien out of the United States based on an order of removal." This number of "removals" does not count the hundreds of thousands of people whom the government "returned," unless that individual was turned over to Immigration and Customs Enforcement (ICE) for removal. DHS defines *return* as "the confirmed movement of a potentially inadmissible or deportable alien out of the United States not based on an order of removal, but through either voluntary departure, voluntary return, or withdrawal under docket control."[1] There are different categories of removal (e.g., expedited, administrative, reinstatement of prior removal order) and different legal consequences that result from a removal or return process. These distinctions matter and have political histories that are part of the vast infrastructure of carceral spaces, transportation, and surveillance that has been constructed to accomplish this scale of expulsion. For readability's sake, we sometimes use deportation, removal, and expulsion as synonyms, but we also try to take care to show how legal distinctions were developed. In 2009, Congress introduced language that would require ICE to maintain a detention capacity of at least 33,400 bed spaces, a provision that critics decry as a "bed quota," which drives aggressive migration policing and inflationary contracts with the private sector.[2]

We trace the roots of today's historically unprecedented system of confinement and removal back to the late 1970s and early 1980s when the Jimmy Carter and Ronald Reagan administrations established policies and practices to deter the arrival of Haitian and Cuban asylum seekers. Our central argument is that the U.S. Cold War response to these Caribbean migrations established the legal and institutional basis for today's migration-detention and border-deterrence regime. Indeed, we show how struggles over decidedly racialized asylum policies created the conditions for detention and border deterrence as *interrelated* practices. That is to say, efforts to prevent entry were tied to efforts to remove unwanted asylum seekers who had reached sovereign territory. The history that we trace also points to the central role that anti-Black racism and Cold War geopolitics have played in U.S. foreign and domestic policy. *Boats, Borders, and Bases* shows how anti-Black racism has worked together with anti-Asian and anti-Latinx racism to obscure the violence and geographic scope of the United States's migration policing, carceral, and deportation apparatus.

Forcible confinement has become a central element of efforts to regulate migration and migrants' lives both on mainland territory and offshore. This system was built by Democratic and Republican administrations, and popular opposition to the expansion also crossed party lines, informed by different political beliefs. In the United States, the detention of foreign nationals is a legal form of administrative confinement distinct from the rights and procedures that have been developed under criminal-justice law. The agency currently in charge of the vast detention system that fuels this expulsion is Immigration and Customs Enforcement, a department within the Department of Homeland Security (DHS), which was established in 2003. Before this time, the Immigration and Naturalization Service (INS) in the Department of Justice (DOJ) carried out this role. ICE relies on a panoply of local jails, federally owned and operated detention facilities called Service Processing Centers, and privately owned and operated facilities to carry out its operations. Customs and Border Protection (CBP) also operates facilities at ports of entry for short-term confinement.

We refer to this infrastructure as a system of *migration detention* and expulsion. There is no one commonly accepted terminology for describing and analyzing the carceral infrastructure that nation-states have developed to restrict mobility across national borders and to regulate the presence of noncitizens within national territories. Some people use the term *noncitizen detention,* or *immigrant detention*; others use *immigra-*

tion detention; still others, *migrant prisons.* The difficulty of settling on a term is multifold and brings to the fore the power of language that infuses most aspects of migration politics. First, all of these terms involve political and legal issues that are tremendously politicized. If we were to use the term *immigrant* or *immigration detention,* we would be rehearsing a commonly-told story about long-distance emigrants who want nothing more than to settle permanently in the United States. *Immigrant* erases the reality of circular migration, temporary labor migration, and asylum seeking that we center in our history. Governmental and popularly used terms like *alien* and *criminal alien* are ones that we do not use because they contribute to the overwhelming criminalization and dehumanization of people with liminal legal status. These terms do appear in our text, however, and we analyze them within the context of their use.

Our use of the term *detention* is also fraught because it can euphemize the harsh reality of coercive confinement, which is usually referenced by the term *prison.* Carceral spaces encompass more than criminal legal spaces like prisons to also include spaces of forced institutionalization, ad hoc use of hotels and military bases, jails, and temporary holding areas. There are legal distinctions between the criminal legal and the civil immigration grounds on which many migrants are confined. These criminal and civil systems are also materially and ideologically interwoven. While neither of us has formal legal training, in our collective decades of research, we have witnessed how governments use these distinctions to facilitate the expansion of carceral space and to curtail rights. We, thus, do not use the term *detention* to suggest that confinement for relatively short or indefinite periods in a jail or migration detention facility is inconsequential or less harsh than a prison. On the contrary, detention has known harmful consequences for the physical and mental health of migrants and asylum seekers. Rather, in tracing the legal, institutional, and political disputes over these distinctions—between civil and criminal, economic migrant and asylum seeker—we illustrate both their entanglements and the transnational scope of the U.S. carceral state.

Finally, our use of the term *migrant* is meant to be expansive, encompassing long-term residents who are often understood as immigrants, and asylum seekers, also referred to as asylees. Asylum seekers formally are people who have left their place of residence and have requested that they be allowed to stay in a different country owing to their well-founded fear of persecution. This term is often used interchangeably with the term *refugee,* a category of people that also has fled owing to their own well-founded fear of persecution (both terms defined by the

1951 *Convention Relating to the Status of Refugees).* In the U.S. context, refugee and asylum cases are handled by different parts of the government and have distinct legal and administrative groundings. While the experiences leading people to seek safety may be similar, the way these two groups are treated is often very different. The United States sets a quota on the numbers of refugees that it will resettle in any given year. Both the numbers and their origin in the world are the outcome of political debate and foreign-policy objectives. In the current moment, people who apply for refugee status then go through an extensive vetting process before they are authorized for admission, at which point they are connected into a formal network of voluntary organizations that does the work of resettlement. These application processes may take place in their country of origin or in a third country where they have fled in order to await a longer-term resolution to displacement. Asylum seekers also ask the government for protection, but they do so at a point of entry to the United States or after they have already been present in the country for a time (as in the case of an individual who entered on a student or tourist visa). As in our distinction between *prison* and *detention,* we make use of both *asylee* and *refugee* not because they are so different. Both groups share similar circumstances leading them to leave their homes. We attend to these terms in order to trace how governments use them in *their* efforts to thwart human mobility and the international right to asylum. As such, we often use the phrase *migrants and asylum seekers* to challenge the frequent governmental erasure of asylum seekers by classifying all international border-crossers as economic migrants. Again, our effort to draw attention to asylum seekers is not to suggest that their rights should supersede those of other long-distance migrants, but rather to show how U.S. efforts to constrain the mobility of asylees also is used to undermine freedom of movement to and from the United States in general.

We argue that border-enforcement and detention policies must be understood together and transnationally across onshore and offshore spaces where they operate. Our attention to the domestic and more distant offshore dimensions of detention and border-deterrence policies illustrates how these developments are not separate, but interrelated. The histories we tell are at once regional, highly localized, and imperial in their geopolitical configurations. As such, we build upon the insights of feminist political geographers who have developed methods for research and analysis that attend to the power and politics of the global and intimate (Pratt and Rosner 2006; Pain and Staeheli 2014; Conlon and Hiemstra 2017). Indeed, the deeply contingent and relational character of detention and border projects belies narratives of coherence and reason so often deployed by state authorities. The situated and contested outcomes offer readers a sense of futures that might be otherwise.

WHERE IS REMOTE? QUESTIONS GUIDING THIS STUDY

Our collaboration began while we were both living in the small city of Syracuse in central New York. We came to understand that this was a border city by learning about Border Patrol activity in the farmlands to our north and at the regional transportation center just on the outskirts of town. Border Patrol agents would board trains and buses in Syracuse and Rochester and ask passengers selectively for their passports and visas (Kim and Loyd 2008; NYCLU 2011; Mountz 2011b; Miller 2014). Many of these passengers were traveling to and from New York City, Boston, and Buffalo. They were not seeking to cross the international boundary into Canada, but the Border Patrol considered these transit hubs as *ports of entry,* a legal place, which they claim authorizes them to conduct stops and searches without probable cause, and to embark on some of the aggressive enforcement operations we discuss in this book.

We became involved in the local Detention Task Force that was trying to contest these practices, which appeared racially discriminatory and led to unjust confinement. The Border Patrol apprehended people who could not produce appropriate documents and detained them in local jails until they were transferred to an ICE facility, sometimes to the Buffalo Federal Detention Center about ninety miles west in Batavia, New York. Witnessing these practices and hearing stories of how activists in Rochester and Buffalo were organizing to protect migrant rights led us to question the prevailing explanations for the location and abundance of migration-detention facilities.

Questioning Border Narratives

Explanations of the large numbers of detention facilities often attribute their locations to geography, whether proximate to international boundaries or remote from migrant metropolises. Both explanations are informed by implicit narratives about the relationships among borders, detention, and exclusion. In one common narrative, movement across and/or apprehension in the United States–Mexico borderlands drives detention expansion. This explanation is understandable, given how spectacular state stories, circulated through popular media, have worked to conflate (unauthorized) migration and the United States–Mexico borderlands. Such discourses have fueled border fortification and policing in this region, but they have also fueled policing and detention throughout the country. Further, this border-centric explanation does not readily grasp how the confinement of people under ICE custody is distinct from, if related to, Border Patrol operations, which often use spaces migrants refer to as *hieleras,* or "ice boxes" (American Immigration Council 2015).

Another powerful example of the conflation between the United States–Mexico borderlands and the national landscape of detention can be seen in then ICE Commissioner Dora Schriro's (2009) study of ICE's detention system. The report was completed to inform major policy reforms to the ICE detention system. It includes a series of heat maps that depict data on detention "demand" and capacity across the country. No methods are provided for how these data were collected or mapped, leaving readers to infer their meanings. In map 1 depicting detention "demand," the blurring of apprehension and removal data creates an impression of "border-ness," even though the field offices of San Diego and El Paso, which are on the United States–Mexico boundary, are not listed among the top apprehension offices. This interpretation is strengthened by the impression of a "flood" of detention data threatening to engulf the interior of the country, as population densities uncontrollably spread out into Mexico, the Gulf of Mexico, and the Atlantic. In the original version, the data are mapped in traffic-light colors—wherein green signifies safety and red symbolizes a danger that must be stopped. The maps contribute to hysterical migration narratives that have been promulgated repeatedly by politicians and media in the United States, stoking racialized fear and xenophobia.

Another map in the same report, which depicts the ratio of regional detention capacity to apprehension numbers, suggests that many southern border sectors have more space for detention than is filled by local apprehension efforts. Los Angeles and New York City stand out boldly in red for their limited capacity, followed by Atlanta, San Francisco, and Miami. This map, then, does not so much explain apprehension and detention dynamics as create what geographer Mark Monmonier (personal communication 2012) calls a "cartographic fog." The scientific status afforded to maps lends authoritative credence to the impression of endless detention "demands," perpetuating institutional interests, but not providing an accurate depiction of detention processes. The market language of "demand" naturalizes the report's recommendation for more

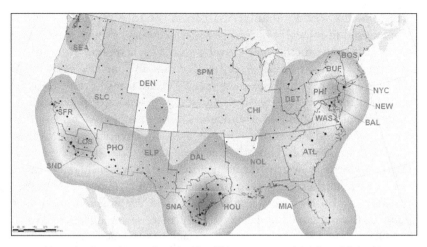

MAP 1. Hysteria along the southern border. This map was originally published in a report written by then ICE Commissioner Dora Schriro on demand for detention. The gray denotes demand, blurring apprehension and removal, and indeed, the locations of national boundaries. (Source: *Immigration Detention Overview and Recommendations.* Homeland Security: Immigration and Customs Enforcement, 2009.)

detention space by implicitly invoking its discursive twin of "supply." These visual and rhetorical moves paint expansion as inevitable.

Explanations for the geography of U.S. detention that rely on border narratives tend not to account for "interior enforcement" operations, like raids, checkpoints, and scans of federal databases, which ICE conducts, often working with other federal and local police agencies, such as county jails (Coleman 2007b). These contacts with police agents also fuel the institutional push to expand detention capacity. As we will illustrate, persistent shortages of carceral space have led to the creation of a dispersed system within which ICE routinely transfers captive people to sometimes distant facilities in order to relieve crowding, disrupt organizing efforts, and speed removal proceedings.

Questioning Privatization Narratives

Migration detention is institutionally complex. In the mid-2000s when we began this research, ICE relied on a mix of federally owned and operated facilities, contracts with private firms and local governments for its use of both privately and publicly owned facilities, and per diem arrangements with local jails. Apart from the role of private boarding houses used in the early to mid-twentieth century, private prison firms got a start in the migration-detention sector by first securitizing motels and then building "spec" facilities for the INS in the early 1980s (Hernández 2013; Shull 2014a, 2014b). Private firms have proven controversial for numerous reasons, including the ethics of profiting from confinement, the additional difficulties of oversight that private firms present, repeated allegations of abuse and incompetence, and costliness.

In the face of public concern over these issues, Schriro's review of the migrant-detention system recommended that ICE continue its operations "without the assistance of the private sector" (2009, 19). Yet federal reliance on the private sector continued, leading many critics to point to the fundamental role that the private sector has played in the expansion and location of detention facilities, particularly after Congress's so-called "bed mandate" that ICE should maintain a capacity for 33,400 individuals at any given time. Were private firms the main factor driving expansion and making decisions about where to locate facilities, or were private firms subjected to some of the same political pressures shaping the fate of federal and state prison-expansion plans? Did private firms hold the power, or were they subordinate to governmental operations and legislative decisions? These are questions we seek to answer through investigation of historical developments in specific places.

Questioning Distance Narratives

Distance opens another conundrum for explanation. The remote geographic locations of many of the facilities in the ICE archipelago *and* frequent transfers of detainees among facilities are among the most frequently criticized conditions of the U.S. detention system (Human Rights Watch 2009; National Immigrant Justice Center 2010; Hiemstra 2013). But how is remoteness measured, and can remoteness be produced? Answering these questions involves asking what constitutes remoteness: simply a place far away, a rural place, an island, a military base? And how does social distance intersect with physical distance? Does any one measure or conceptualization of remoteness inform decisions made over time about the locations of detention facilities? If so, how? Our search for answers to these questions revealed a complicated and historically contingent set of answers.

One important strand of research and advocacy concerning remoteness focuses on the role it plays in diminishing migrant rights, and especially the right to legal representation. This argument has been made by advocates since the early 1980s, and recognized by federal courts. A recent example can be seen in the 2009 Human Rights Watch report *Locked Up Far Away*. The report analyzes ICE data gleaned from a freedom-of-information request to illustrate how transfers among facilities violate migrants' access to attorneys and right to seek asylum and defend themselves from deportation. The National Immigrant Justice Center (2010) measured remoteness by calculating the mileage from a detention facility to the nearest major city, which they used as a proxy for access to legal services. They then used this driving distance to rank the geographic isolation of detention facilities. Eight of the ten most isolated facilities had no or only part-time legal-aid services that were available to people detained there. This is notable because the government is not obliged to provide legal counsel in immigration court, as compared to the criminal legal system. A 2015 study found that only 14 percent of migrants held in detention had legal representation, and migrants who had legal representation fared significantly better in receiving relief from deportation than those without representation (Eagly and Shafer 2015).

Social scientists similarly find that "remote locations create 'detached geographies' through which detainees are spatially separated from the services that guarantee their rights" (Martin and Mitchelson 2009, 466), including resources found in larger cities that offer support, advocacy, interpretation, and information (Mountz 2011a). For example, Alison's earlier work (Mountz 2011b) shows how Fujianese asylum seekers intercepted off the shores of western Canada in 1999 were detained in the interior of British Columbia. This location, remote from Vancouver, distanced them from where they would be more likely to have access to advocacy, legal representation, interpreters, and the tribunals of Canada's Immigration and Refugee Board.

Narratives of remoteness often rely on geographical imaginaries that associate isolation with rurality, provincialism, conservatism, and racism (Bonds 2009). Remoteness, thus, is discursively constructed and materially built in opposition to cosmopolitanism, connection, community, rights, and freedom. Indeed, the negative outcomes of geographic isolation are often attributed to the "backwardness" or exceptionally racist dispositions of prison towns, explanations that rely on neocolonial understandings of marginal spaces rather than explain how these places are themselves politically and economically subordinated and exploited. This narrative thereby displaces the racism and inequities of state practices that fuel carceral construction, and which often have broad popular support.

Ruth Wilson Gilmore, in her analysis of the California prison system, explains, "This apparent marginality is a trick of perspective, because, as every geographer knows, edges are also interfaces" that "connect places into relationships with each other and with non-contiguous places" (2007, 11). Far from being disconnected from, or incidental to, the vast political and economic changes that California and the United States experienced since the 1970s, prisons, jails, and migrant detention facilities prove central features of economic and state restructuring. Gilmore (2007) ties prison expansion in economically dislocated, and often isolated, places in rural California to surpluses of state capacity, finance capital, land, and labor that have been generated in the course of global economic restructuring and the political gains of the Right. Bonds (2006) examines how reliance on prisons perpetuates poverty in both the rural places where most prisons are constructed and the urban spaces from which most imprisoned people come (also see Huling 2003; Hooks et al. 2010; Norton 2015).

Other geographers, including Allspach (2010), Moran (2013), and Moran Gill, and Conlon (2013), make parallel arguments to Gilmore's observation about prisons as interfaces. They understand prisons not as Erving Goffman's (1961) "total institution" that is fully enclosed and sealed from the outside, but rather as transcarceral spaces traversed by people, information, resources, and transport systems (Moran, Piacentini and Pallot 2013). Allspach illustrates how carceral spaces extend beyond prison walls following confinement to reinforce the marginalization of formerly incarcerated women. Moran and coauthors focus on moments of state custody before formal incarceration as ones of temporal and spatial liminality to emphasize the blurring of inside and outside life.

Attention to the circulation of people, goods, and ideas through prisons reveals remoteness as relational and perspectival. If we see the detention center in Batavia, New York, like a state (Scott 1998), we see its proximity to federal courts in Buffalo (there are also courtrooms onsite in the same building as the lockdown spaces), its location on the New York State Thruway that facilitates efficient movement of imprisoned people and staff, and its location within a historic prison belt. Attica is eleven miles south, Albion is seventeen miles north, and each of these towns hosts more than one carceral facility. This example suggests that no single dynamic accounts for the dispersed geography of places where migrants are detained, whether understood through a local, regional, or national lens.

STUDYING BOATS, BORDERS, AND BASES: ON METHODS

This book began as one part of a five-year study called the Island Detention Project (Mountz 2011a; Coddington et al. 2012; Mountz and Loyd 2014), a CAREER grant funded by the National Science Foundation (with Alison as Principal Investigator and Jenna as Postdoctoral Fellow for two years). The project involved research into the use of islands to detain migrants off the shores of Australia, the southern European Union (EU), and the United States. Some of these islands, like Lampedusa in the Mediterranean and Christmas Island in the Indian Ocean, have become focal points of sharp debate over freedom of movement, rights to asylum-seeking, militarized border policy, detention, and humanitarianism. We knew that the United States had been using its naval base at Guantánamo Bay to confine so-called enemy combatants and that it had also used this base to confine tens of thousands of Haitian asylum seekers in the early to mid-1990s. Was this island base part of the broader development of the U.S. detention system? Were the remote geographies of detention crafted by design? We worked together to carve out a project that was related to, but distinct from, the research on remote islands at the heart of the larger project. Living in Syracuse, we could not help but notice the proximity of Batavia to us, the Canadian border, and miles of farm fields and rural landscapes in Western New York. We wondered how the facility came to be there, and our research began with this simple discussion. Over time, the research expanded to include case studies of three sites around the country. We were surprised to find that their histories led us back to offshore enforcement and spaces of confinement on islands and bases.

In an effort to explain how the United States came to operate a dispersed onshore and offshore carceral archipelago (cf. Foucault 1995; Gregory 2007; Stoler 2011), we conducted historical, qualitative inquiry into the political, legal, and economic dynamics responsible for the pace of expansion and locations of confinement developed since the late 1970s. Given that the U.S. government uses hundreds of jail and detention facilities to confine migrants and asylum seekers (637 different facilities in 2015[3]), we decided to develop a case-study approach that would enable us to assess competing narratives about the geography of detention: proximity to the border, remoteness, and private profit-seeking. To explore border narratives, we selected the facility in our immediate vicinity—Batavia—and those in Pinal County, Arizona, located in the towns of Florence and Eloy. In order to explore the role of privatization in the early 1980s establishment of the system, we selected Oakdale, Louisiana, as the site of the first large-scale detention facility that the INS constructed following the Mariel crisis. In the course of developing these case studies, we explored the ways in which border narratives, local politics, and subcontracting arrangements played out in these sites and elsewhere in the country. We also came to appreciate the roles that interinstitutional politics, interregional comparison and competition, and historical contingency played in siting decisions.

Because our research inquired about historical dynamics, we turned to archival records. The first obvious agency was the INS, yet when Jenna visited the U.S. Citizenship and Immigration Services (USCIS) Library in Washington, D.C., she learned that there were significant gaps in the records for the agency for the relevant period. This early setback eventually led to the development of a different archival-research strategy. By this time, we knew that records for the Cuban-Haitian Task Force (CHTF), which was responsible for responding to the arrivals, confinement, and resettlement of Haitians and Cubans in 1980, were held at the Jimmy Carter Presidential Library. This knowledge led us to pursue research at other presidential libraries covering our study period, ranging from the late 1970s to the early 2000s.

This approach involved several years of archival research beginning in 2010 in Arizona. In 2011, Jenna began a summer of research at presidential libraries beginning at the Ronald Reagan Library in Simi Valley, California, and making her way east to consult more archives in Arizona, then the George H. W. Bush Presidential Library, Louisiana State University, the Jimmy Carter Presidential Library, and finally the National Archives in Washington, D.C., and College Park, Maryland. That same year, we submitted Freedom of Information Act (FOIA) requests at the George H. W. Bush and William J. Clinton presidential libraries in order to have relevant materials processed into the public record. In the summer of 2013, Jenna consulted records at Delta State University in Mississippi, and Duke University in Durham, North Carolina, and visited Fort Chaffee, Arkansas, where she also viewed photographs and a display of memorabilia at the Chaffee Crossing museum. In addition to our analysis of these materials, we draw on legal scholarship, media coverage, and visits to each of the case-study regions. Site visits repeatedly revealed the location of detention facilities in economically depressed towns, which also had ties to existing or decommissioned carceral and military facilities.

Archival work followed a systematic routine. At each archive, Jenna would consult with the librarians and research guides to determine collections that seemed most relevant. She took notes of all collections reviewed in individual Word documents. At most archives, she was able to photograph documents herself. After a day of research, she would annotate the Word file to create a catalog linking individual documents to names of image files. At archives where Jenna made or was provided with paper copies, these were later scanned by a research assistant. All archival materials eventually were uploaded to the software Devonthink Pro, which converts images with text into searchable text. We also printed out copies of documents to read and notate. Our data analysis and writing for *Boats, Borders, and Bases* began in 2012.

This research strategy proved fruitful because the records we acquired provide insight into political negotiations among a range of government agencies and authorities from presidents and the National Security Council (NSC) advisors to local politicians and advocates. Moreover, our FOIA requests and mandatory review requests, which ask agencies to review documents that have been withheld from the public, for a variety of reasons, resulted in the release of documents on migration detention and Operation Safe Haven, which are now available for other researchers. Records of behind-the-scenes discussions within the NSC or among staff members for the White House or senators revealed frank policy-related discussions that were not always shared with the public. They also revealed discussions of strategies for informing the public and navigating difficult political situations. The combination of White House, NSC, Department of Justice, legislative, day-to-day administrative records, and available press clippings enabled us to analyze the interactions between geopolitical and domestic tensions, trace shifts in the implementation of plans over time, and map recurrent themes across different presidential administrations. These materials highlighted for us the local and historical contingency of policy development. High-level executive-branch strategies often foundered on local political pushback, just as the material limitations of logistical or organizational capacity shaped overarching strategic plans.

ANALYZING BOATS, BORDERS, AND BASES
FROM A TRANSNATIONAL PERSPECTIVE

How is remoteness produced transnationally? Much literature about transnational migration emphasizes the mobility of people and remittances across national boundaries (e.g., Rouse 1991). This definition of transnationalism remains important. We also use the term to analyze work of the state that crosses national boundaries (Mountz 2011b; Hiemstra 2013). *Transnationalism*, importantly, also refers to relationships that nonstate entities—communities, families, friends, and compatriots—maintain across national geographies. Members of the Transnational Hispaniola Collective use *transnational* to "mean the transborder and binational exchanges of people, commerce, ideas, and ecologies that have long undermined attempts by colonial powers and ruling classes to make the border a rigid, transhistorical entity" (Mayes et al. 2013, 27).

Our starting point for developing a transnational perspective on migration detention was that most accounts of the expansion of migrant detention were confined to U.S. domestic space. Such "methodological nationalism" (Wimmer and Glick Schiller 2002; also see Agnew 1994) erases extraterritorial policing and confinement, which both work to keep migrants from reaching sovereign territory and to expel them from it. Remote island detention is thereby imagined as exceptional rather than fundamental to the United States's detention and migration-deterrence regime. Accounts of migration and refugee resettlement also are often told in isolation from one another and in country-by-country accounts. This is not to say that nationality-specific or finer grained narratives of migration are unimportant. However, issues of methodological nationalism arise when the mobility of any one group of people is imagined as a discrete phenomenon unrelated to the fates and treatment of other groups. Put another way, governments have historically positioned, or triangulated (Kim 1999), groups in hierarchical relation to one another. Separate treatments of interconnected yet differentiated processes make it difficult to understand how asylum, refugee, detention, and deterrence policies are iteratively and relationally developed.

Placing Borders and the Carceral State in a Transnational World

We "scale up" the arguments on transcarceral spaces (Moran, Piacetini and Pallot 2013) to analyze transnational productions of remoteness that cross prison walls *and* national borders to create transnational carceral spaces. Our argument regarding the transnational dimensions of U.S. detention and deterrence practices may seem contradictory. How can a nation-state's bordering and detention practices be transnational? As with European Union member states' deals with some African countries or Australia's arrangements with Indonesia to deter migration to their respective territories, states try to regulate human mobility with their own transnational mobility. By referring to U.S. policies and practices as transnational, we emphasize the transnational work of the U.S. state and the mobility of its infrastructure and operations (Mountz 2011b). For the United States to operate transnationally, it has established bilateral and multilateral migration (control) efforts with other sovereign nation-states and with U.S. colonial territories. Negotiations for these agreements are not equal, given the United States's past and present imperial reach, but this does not make them inconsequential. This approach resonates with and builds on critical ethnic-studies scholar Dylan Rodríguez's (2008) contention: "The U.S. prison is a global statecraft, an arrangement and mobilization of violence that is, from its very inception, already unhinged from the delimiting 'domestic' (or 'national') sites to which it is presumptively tethered."

Border enforcement never begins or ends at national boundaries. As geographer Mat Coleman (2007a, b) argues, immigration has always blurred the imagined geographic binary dividing domestic and foreign spaces and laws. We have suggested that it can be difficult to appreciate this blurring because detention and border policies tend to be narrated apart from each other and separate from asylum and refugee policies. Breaking from histories tightly circumscribed around national origin or focused on only domestic or foreign policy reveals the deep interconnections between asylum and refugee policy and practice and legal constructs of illegality and criminality (cf. Ngai 2008). When analyzed together it becomes evident that states produce remoteness through the development of a transnational infrastructure to contain and disperse migrants in and through spaces of formal confinement and blocked migration routes in increasingly fortified and patrolled boundary spaces. State categories of "criminal," "alien," "asylee," and the like are mechanisms of sorting humans and expanding state capacities to deter.

The mid-1990s border-making stories with which we began the book emphasized the perspective of state authorities and how they explain their policy choices. Such tactical legitimation exercises have worked powerfully to concentrate migration and border issues along the United States–Mexico boundary and to funnel investments into boundary fortification and policing. While the United States–Mexico border has come to stand in for narratives about U.S. national borders and migration policies, Nevins (2010) convincingly shows how *local* political efforts proved fundamental to fueling fortification along the boundary and driving a national ideological debate.

We build on Nevins's insights about the historical and geographic specificity of national policy and practice by taking a regional approach to U.S. deterrence policies. We bring Nevins's insights together with geographic scholarship on racism and racialization. Following Gilmore, racism is the "state-sanctioned and/or extra-legal production and exploitation of group-differentiated vulnerabilities to premature death, in distinct yet densely interconnected political geographies" (2002, 261). The construction of a regionally specific yet interconnected detention and deterrence system in the United States–Mexico borderlands and Caribbean Basin is one such differentiated yet interconnected political geography. Laura Pulido (2006), Wendy Cheng (2013), and Perla Guerrero (2016) develop ideas of regionally specific racial formations, wherein racialization is both a relational and place-based set of processes whereby differently racialized groups are constructed in relation to one another. We build on their work to argue that 1) bordering and deterrence practices developed by the United States in the United States–Mexico and Caribbean border regions were developed in relationship to one another, and 2) that regionally specific deployments of racialized, gendered, and classed constructions of illegality, refugeeness, and criminality shaped the politics of policy and racial hierarchies at local, national, and international scales.

Barbadian poet Kamau Brathwaite links "the shadow of this // Coast Guard // Cutter // of blockade" to the deaths at sea of African peoples stolen across the Atlantic to work as slaves in Europe's colonies (2007, 197). Brathwaite's historical memory of race and region signals centuries-long continuities of slavery and colonialism that continue to shape the imagined geographies of, and boundaries between, the Caribbean, Latin America, and the Americas (Grosfoguel, Maldonado-Torres, and Saldívar 1995; Wynter 1995; McKittrick 2013). In considering questions of race, Claudia Milian argues that the "tendency in Latino/a studies has been to orbit around the Hispanophone Caribbean, seeking to neatly point and comprehensively index blackness in the American hemisphere through this geography" (2013, 9). Historian Ada Ferrer continues, "Historically, the boundaries of the Spanish Caribbean shifted over time, and often back and forth. If part of what characterizes the Caribbean is mobility and contact, how do we delimit the 'Spanish' Caribbean? Indeed, should we delimit it at all?" (2016, 55).

Petra Rivera-Rideau, Jennifer Jones, and Tianna Paschel suggest that a "transnational understanding of *afrolatinidade*" holds potential to move away from studies focusing either on the United States or on Latin America and the Caribbean (2016, 3). Analyzing how Africanity, Americanicity, and Latinidad have been constituted together is a decolonial project for Agustin Lao-Montes (2007; also see Grosfoguel et al. 1995). As such, Lao-Montes argues that attention to specific "diasporic-translocal" histories and perspectives "places Afro-Latina/o difference at the heart of world processes of cultural and political contestation and construction of alternative futures" (2007, 327–28).

As geographers who study state asylum- and migration-deterrence policies, our modest aim is to show the connections between the policies that the United States has deployed in the Caribbean and in the United States–Mexico borderlands. The Caribbean holds a significant place in the history of U.S. migration enforcement (Danticat 2007; Frenzen 2010; Hahamovitch 2011; Noble 2011; Shemak 2011; Lipman 2013; Paik 2016). Yet this regional history tends not to be understood in relation to the better known history of deterrence measures implemented along the United States–Mexico boundary in the early to mid-1990s (U.S. Border Patrol 1994; Dunn 1996; Nevins 2010; Hamlin 2012). Recounting this Caribbean history is important because it brings into view the relationship between asylum and detention, and allows us to historicize the criminalization of migration from a critical and overlooked vantage point, that of the Caribbean region as understood in the Cold War. Our insistence that we need to understand a longer history and different geography of deterrence and detention is not intended to minimize the fatal consequences of state and vigilante violence in the United States–Mexico borderlands. Rather, harmful practices both here and in the Caribbean have been sustained by imagined geographies that divide these places.

Deadly consequences also stem from the ways in which racialized, classed, and gendered categories of migration are deployed to subvert the mobility and undermine the lives of people from the Caribbean and Central and South America. As we detail, the concerted and creative efforts employed by the U.S. government to remove and prevent the arrivals of Haitian and Afro-Cuban people repeatedly led to the invocation of exceptional categories, the creation of new laws, and the consolidation of the tight discursive connections between Blackness and excludability, detainability, and criminality (Loyd 2015). Yet individuals targeted by these onshore-offshore logics also challenged the state's efforts to banish them. In addition to organized advocacy, we repeatedly find protests, uprisings, and escapes in the archives, disruptions that counter the erasure of racialized, remote forms of detention developed by the United States.

While the imposition of mandatory detention of Haitian asylum seekers was forcefully and persistently contested, the implications of this policy change are consistently overlooked in existing accounts of the origins of the contemporary migration-detention system. Not only do we need to attend to the role of anti-Black racism in U.S. society and the criminal legal system, but also in foreign and refugee policy.

To develop this argument, we bring critical asylum and refugee studies (Mountz 2010; Coutin 2011; Ashutosh and Mountz 2012; Nguyen 2012; Espiritu 2006, 2014; Paik 2016) together with critical carceral and criminology studies, which analyze criminalization, policing, and imprisonment as forms of racialized and gendered social control (e.g., Simon 1998, 2007; Sudbury 2005; Coleman 2007a; Gilmore 2007; Hernández 2008; Bonds 2009; Bosworth 2009; Cacho 2012; Camp and Heatherton 2016; Escobar 2016; Haley 2016). As criminologist Mary Bosworth writes, "Detention centres confound many usual categories of analysis, defying neat explanation. Prison-like yet not penal, they are filled with people recognizable but foreign" (2014, 210). Scholarship that focuses on the criminalization of migration has drawn attention to the ties between the criminal legal and migration-enforcement systems (e.g., Miller 2003; Stumpf 2006; Chacón 2007, 2009; Bosworth and Kaufman 2011; Dowling and Inda 2013; Inda 2013; Golash-Boza 2015; Escobar 2016; Macías-Rojas 2016). While there exist longer historical roots to this system (Buff 2008; Coleman 2008; Ngai 2008), it is widely accepted that these systems have grown considerably closer since the 1980s as part of the broader wave of legislating new crimes and tougher sentences and appropriating more money to policing. The well-known result was an explosive increase in jails, prisons, and people confined in them.

While we concur with the broad brushstrokes of this convergence narrative, we also build on arguments by Menjívar (2006), Chacón (2015), and Coutin (2000, 2003) that criminalization and illegalization do not result in neat categories of authorized versus unauthorized migrant, or legal permanent resident versus criminal alien. Rather, collisions of civil and criminal laws, and policing practices work to produce "legal liminality." Chacón explains:

> Liminal legality is characterized first and foremost by its inherent legal uncertainty. Individuals' legal assurances against full marginalization lack definitive temporal scope and are generally extended as privileges, not rights. The inherent fragility and the indefinite nature of the period(s) of administrative grace create instability in many aspects of the lives of liminal legal subjects (2015, 716).

We argue that state authorities deployed mechanisms of legal liminality for asylum seekers differentially in relation to the Cold War and racialized rationales. Further, we show how the detention and deterrence of asylum seekers *preceded* concerted criminalization efforts begun in the late 1980s. This argument is significant for two reasons. First, it points to a distinct genealogy of U.S. migration detention than that tethered to either United States–Mexico border narratives or domestic-crime politics. Second, it illustrates the precariousness of asylum, a possibility that can be undermined through the use of politically malleable terms like crime.

LOCATING BASES IN MIGRATION CONTROL

As with the broader scholarship on contemporary island spaces of migration control, our work on the history of detention facilities revealed the recurrent use of obsolete and active-duty military bases to deter, confine, and remove migrants within mainland territory and in offshore Caribbean locations. Site-specific histories of these facilities (e.g., Kaplan 2005; Vine 2009; Lipman 2008, 2013; Paik 2013, 2016; Espiritu 2014; Loyd et al. 2015) reveal the historical and contemporary impulse to segregate and contain by targeting and criminalizing racialized groups. It is on these racialized, colonized, and militarized grounds that we locate the United States's transnational migration-detention and -deterrence regime. We thereby shift attention from the land border to the high seas and islands at the "edges" of American empire (Burnett 2005; Davis 2015). Migration "crises" in these sites reveal the disparate treatment of Cold War refugees and the enduring legacy of empire. The use of colonial military bases provided the practical and legal basis for building up today's historically unprecedented detention, deportation, and border apparatus.

Decommissioned and active U.S. military bases in Guam, Puerto Rico, Cuba, Panama, and the U.S. mainland have served as material grounds of refugee- and migration-control operations, blurring civilian and military spaces and humanitarian and security rationales (Espiritu 2014; Loyd et al. 2015). Indeed, exceptionalist narratives of humanitarian rescue common to both the Vietnamese and Cuban refugee experiences (as explored by Bon Tempo 2008; Nguyen 2012; Espiritu 2014) obscure how racialized and militarized asylum practices created exclusionary border and detention policies. Yet the entanglements between military and carceral spaces remain virtually absent from current understandings of immigration and detention policy and operations. Recurrent productions of "emergency" also mask how the U.S. government's humanitarian and enforcement practices are symbiotic.

Beginning with the Carter administration in our narrative, political crises have resulted repeatedly in the expansion of border enforcement, detention, exclusion, and removals. While the White House looked to military bases to resolve migration crises and pursue coherent national policies, these efforts were far from certain as local communities lobbied for and fought against the opening of temporary and long-term detention facilities. Attention to the local contingency of asylum and detention practices simultaneously provides unique insight into the growth of transnational border-enforcement and detention systems.

Throughout this book, we link our analyses of enforcement activities involving boats, borders, and bases. Within this triumvirate, bases constitute a particular geographical form examined by other scholars (e.g., Davis 2011; Vine 2012). The U.S. military base infrastructure rests on and reproduces histories of empire (Gregory 2004; Kaplan 2005; Lipman 2008; Lutz 2009; Vine 2009; Davis 2011; Enloe 2014; Loyd et al. 2015). Following the seizure of Hawai'i in 1893 and the Spanish-American War in 1898, the United States would claim part or all of numerous island territories across the Pacific (including Guam, Wake Island, eastern Samoa, and the Philippines) and the Caribbean (Puerto Rico, Cuba, and, for a time, Haiti). Its "empire of military bases" in these regions would remain fundamental to its economic and political objectives in both regions (Camacho 2012).

While some locate bases on the periphery, as "edges of empire" (Burnett 2005; Davis 2015), others locate them as forward operations, as in David Vine's analysis of several waves of new U.S. bases established since the close of World War II. Vine (2009) situates the first wave as occurring during decolonization, with U.S. bases functioning as forward-looking efforts to exercise control in decolonizing regions. A more recent wave led to the proliferation of a smaller series of bases (Vine 2012) that the U.S. military calls "lily pads," platforms for military operations abroad. We also understand bases as nodes in global networks akin to Josiah Heyman's (2004) analysis of migration control operationalized through ports of entry. Whether used as platforms for military activity or militarized migration operations, bases operate as a networked archipelago for the deployment of U.S. military assets and the controlled movement of migrants (Loyd et al. 2015).

We follow scholars who demonstrate the systemic entanglement of humanitarian with military and imperial imperatives (Hyndman 2007; Fassin and Rechtman 2009; Nguyen 2012; Espiritu 2014; Williams 2014, 2015; Bryan 2015) and police and war operations (Neocleous 2014).

Rather than theorizing the blurring of civilian and military spaces and practices as exceptional, we regard efforts to draw such legal and political divisions, particularly at moments of crisis, as persistent, if contested. For example, Coleman (2007a, b) traces a history of immigration policing in Mexico intersecting with the U.S. wars on drugs and immigration across borders and jurisdictions. These "wars" utilize the same practices, strategies, tactics, and authorities, often targeting and criminalizing the same people onshore and offshore (Coutin 2010).

Like scholars of war who explain militarization as a process that relies on and recreates the material and ideological infrastructures for organizing violence, we show how efforts to create new legal geographies and categories are contingent and historically situated processes. In this effort, we are influenced and inspired by Cynthia Enloe's (2014) writing on masculinist cultures of militarism. Enloe's feminist analysis of military culture traces militarism's movement into everyday life. Our text turns to the lives of those confined in some of those actual military spaces and to those elected officials and neighboring civilians who sought to put bases to other uses. Rather than conceptualizing the frequent use of military bases in refugee and migration operations as exceptions to an abstract or established rule of law, we draw on the longer history of imperial sovereignty—traced by historian Lauren Benton (2010). She emphasizes the practical efforts of rule-making and the fraught efforts to define the relationships between military and civilian authorities in international waters and on island territories.

The militarization of migration does not just occur along the border, but has ensued in a transnational landscape of military bases and multilateral agreements. William Walters (2008) argues that scholars need to pay more attention to the material sites where land meets sea. Accordingly, we attend to the buffer zones built by the United States across the Caribbean on land and at sea. The federal government's turn to offshore migration-control efforts in the early 1980s represents a deterrence strategy through which the maritime spaces of U.S. territorial and international waters would function as a buffer zone deflecting people from U.S. shores. Not only was this strategy designed to prevent arrivals, it would also forestall the lengthy legal battles over asylum, parole, and detention concerning Haitian and Cuban people who had arrived. Transnational analysis of the U.S. carceral regime thus extends the existing conceptualization of transcarcerality in the carceral geographies literature to additional spaces of liminality (Walters 2008), where maritime spaces are constructed as sites of policing (Benton 2010; Pickering 2014).

As Walters (2008) and Benton (2010) argue, boats serve as important material—if juridically liminal—sites that connect the governance of land and sea. The erasure of such histories is part of the violence of migration detention, serving to distort and naturalize its uses. Thus, remembering the centrality of U.S. military bases and state violence to migration and detention policy means demonstrating and challenging the divisions between civilian and military domains, international asylum and domestic criminal justice. Understanding the sharp conflicts over the development of a militarized carceral asylum- and migration-control system will enable different ways of understanding and pursuing contemporary policy reform, legal advocacy, and activism.

CHAPTER OUTLINE

Throughout this book, we show how the problems associated with *remote* detention are tied to the policy of mandatory detention and to the historical *expansion* of the detention system. The expansion of onshore capacity, moreover, is deeply entangled with the rapid growth of local, state, and federal jail and prison capacity during the 1980s and 1990s (Simon 1998; Dow 2004; Welch 2004). We thus develop transnational framings of domestic carceral landscapes in order to better understand the relationship between offshore and onshore enforcement and detention regimes.

Boats, Borders, and Bases is organized chronologically and thematically into three sections with an introduction, seven chapters, and coda. Chapters in the book move between transnational and geopoliticized histories of migration and displacement and the more local, regional stories grounding them in the historical expansion of the vast U.S. detention system. Part I, Race and the Cold War Geopolitics of Migration Control, situates the emergence in the late 1970s and early 1980s of deterrence as a border-enforcement policy. We locate domestic political disputes within racialized Cold War politics and a longer colonial history of U.S. military bases spanning the Pacific to Caribbean. Part II, Building the World's Largest Detention System, examines how executive-branch decisions were implemented and how they were contested in some communities where detention facilities might have been built. The historical narratives of these chapters challenge popular explanations for the remote locations of detention facilities by drawing attention to the roles of military restructuring and locally situated carceral economies. Part III, Expanding the World's Largest Detention System, traces the culmination of 1980s deterrence policy in the creation of off-shore "safe havens" and the entrenchment of detention through increasingly severe criminal-justice legislation in the 1990s.

Part I: Race and the Cold War Geopolitics of Migration Control

Chapter 1 opens in 1980 on a desolate Bahamian atoll where 102 Haitian migrants were stranded for four weeks as the U.S. and Bahamian governments negotiated their fate. We situate this moment of exclusion on this tiny island in relation to the contemporaneous "humanitarian" responses to Vietnamese refugees. Even as the United States implemented its first comprehensive refugee policy, President Carter's exclusionary Haitian Program would plant the seeds of a racialized deterrence policy. We link these episodes to question how humanitarian and deterrence policies have come to be understood as opposing practices in the U.S. context. The history we trace shows them as simultaneous and symbiotic: U.S. foreign policy manifests in humanitarian rescue and migration control. This chapter, thus, illustrates how the racialized construction of a dichotomous discourse of rescue versus deterrence, good versus bad migrant, and bona fide versus bogus refugee animates exclusionary migration practices. These binaries were further mobilized into a relational and racialized taxonomy that categorized groups in relation to one another and Cold War geopolitics.

Chapter 2 discusses the politics of deterring asylum seekers by exploring the simultaneous efforts to find new detention space for Cubans and Haitians who had already arrived in the United States and to develop "contingency" space in the event of another mass migration. This chapter focuses on the pivotal role of military bases in the ad hoc creation of U.S. migration policy during the Carter and Reagan administrations. Haitian and Cuban asylum seekers who arrived in 1980 found themselves confined on separate military facilities from Florida to Wisconsin to Arkansas. Faced with election-year pressures, the Carter administration faced repeated pushback from local authorities and residents over the conditions and use of military bases for its migration operations. The search for and negotiations surrounding new places to site detention facilities reveal racialized imaginations and seemingly irrational commitments to expansion. This chapter explores these quixotic siting efforts: why some facilities lasted while others closed down, and still others never opened. The deeply contingent and contested use of decommissioned military bases ultimately led to the search for more permanent detention space.

Part II: Building the World's Largest Detention System

Where part I explores the White House's response to Cold War refugees and migrants, part II examines the local response to and contestations of foreign-policy decisions and the role of existing prison infrastructures in building an immigration-detention system. We question popular explanations of the role of "the border" and private prison corporations in the remote locations of immigration-detention facilities.

Chapter 3 examines how central Louisiana became the unlikely site for the Immigration and Naturalization Service's first new long-term detention facility and hub for deportation. Faced with high unemployment following the collapse of the local lumber industry, the enterprising mayor of Oakdale spearheaded a campaign to secure the new federal facility. Simultaneously, the Department of Justice debated which agency was best suited to carry out the new mandate of long-term detention of noncitizens. The INS did not have the carceral experience of the Bureau of Prisons (BOP), but because migrant detention was not a criminal-justice punishment, their imprisonment threatened to create legal liabilities for the government. These legal questions also informed jurisdictional conflict over where this new facility would be sited. Oakdale's efforts were jeopardized as Associate Attorney General Rudolph Giuliani backed the Bureau of Prisons's proposal to run a migrant-detention facility near one of its prisons in Oklahoma. The forceful backing of Louisiana politicians eventually won the facility for Oakdale.

Like Oakdale, every community has a particular history in the path to becoming a prison town. Chapter 4 examines how migrant detention became one part of the vast carceral landscape in Florence and neighboring Eloy, Arizona. Neither proximity to the border nor privatization adequately explains the patchwork of carceral facilities in this central Arizona locale. Rather, the landscape of migrant detention builds on multiple histories of confinement, including World War II (WWII) prisoner-of-war (POW) camps and Florence's status as Arizona's prison town, thereby setting the stage to examine the growing interconnections between migrant detention and the burgeoning prison system. The chapter further explores the legal histories of expulsion that form the basis for the development of "criminal alien" legislation, bolstering rationales for detention construction.

These prison towns disrupt potent and popular narratives that national land-border spaces and private industry hold a gravitational force on the expanding detention landscape. In both Florence and Oakdale, federal detention facilities are connected to a sprawling network of local jails and private facilities where the federal government contracts for detention space. Citizens and noncitizens confined in these prison belts are held on criminal and administrative grounds by multiple state authorities (federal, state, county) and their agents (public and private). The resulting interjurisdictional patchwork underscores the tight connections between migration and criminal-justice practices. Moreover, these sites illustrate the close linkages with military spaces; both Oakdale and Florence rely on nearby World War II airfields to transfer migrants within and outside U.S. territory.

Part III: Expanding the World's Largest Detention System

Part III traces the practical and legislative elaborations on the early-1980 policy of detention and offshore deterrence of migrants as they evolved into the 1990s. Second, it follows the steady push from the mid-1980s to criminalize migration and to create increasingly severe consequences for migrants convicted of felony and misdemeanor crimes. Together, these policies created a transnational infrastructure of immigration enforcement and detention and a diaspora of deported people (cf. Kanstroom 2007; De Genova and Peutz 2010; Golash-Boza 2012).

Chapter 5 tells the history of the Bush- and Clinton-era creation of an offshore detention archipelago in the Caribbean. This transnational Caribbean history is an important immediate precursor to the expansion of deterrence operations along the United States–Mexico border in the 1990s and the use of Guantánamo Naval Base (GTMO) during the War on Terror. As the numbers of Haitians and Cubans held at Guantánamo exceeded 40,000, the United States opened camps for Cubans on its military base in Panama and built additional "safe haven" sites in other countries in the Caribbean. We show how the use of offshore sites was designed to prevent the arrival of asylum seekers on U.S. shores. This moment provides a window into the insidious lengths that the executive branch traveled to redraw legal geographies and thereby separate domestic territory from international waters (and law).

Chapter 6 explores how political crises over migration and crime dovetailed to cement detention into the landscape materially and discursively. Criminal legislation passed in the mid-1980s to mid-1990s repeated the pattern earlier established in *Boats, Borders, and Bases:* asylum seekers are detained, followed by executive orders and congressional legislation authorizing these practices. Like previous efforts to deter asylum seekers and other unauthorized migrants, criminalization established far-reaching legal and institutional bases for expanding enforcement and detention. We demonstrate the many ways that asylum seekers were criminalized in legislation and policy. As with the earlier treatment of "undesirable" Cubans and "bogus" Haitian asylum seekers, the figure of the criminal alien was consolidated through its juxtaposition with notions of legal, good, and contributing refugees and immigrants. As migration and criminal-justice policy became more closely entwined, the basis for expanding detention shifted more explicitly from deterrence to a more robust tool of punishment and expulsion.

The concluding chapter 7 maps changes to detention and border-enforcement policy in recent years. We counter much contemporary scholarship that places 9/11 as a significant turning point in the securitization and criminalization of migrants and asylum seekers. While not denying the seismic securitization that followed the attacks, we place these changes in historical context to show that they continued a cycle of racialized and geopoliticized exclusions that already had been well rehearsed in U.S. border-enforcement and immigration law, and detention and deterrence policies and practices.

In the coda, we consider how more than three decades of commitment to deterrence and criminalization have led to a robust policing and detention infrastructure that harms already vulnerable groups of people and resists oversight and reform. Over three million people were removed and over two million people returned during President Barack Obama's time in office. These staggering figures follow more than 2 million removals and over 8 million returns under President George W. Bush, and 870,000 removals and over 11 million returns under President Bill Clinton (Chishti, Pierce, and Bolter 2017). Over these three presidencies, hundreds of thousands, if not millions, of people were separated from their families, and most struggled to repay debts from migration and make a living in economies that have undergone privatization and deregulation. Following deportation, many face subsequent criminalization as they are blamed for the violence and unrest fueled by decimated safety nets and economies. In this final essay, we discuss the recurrence of crisis during the Obama administration through reflection on Central American youth at the Mexico–United States border and the whole new round of crises presented in the opening months of the Donald Trump administration. We also discuss contemporary enforcement efforts in the Caribbean, noting that history continues with Haitians as a seemingly permanent exception.

PART ONE

Race and the Cold War Geopolitics of Migration Control

1

"America's 'Boat People'"

Cold War Geopolitics of Refuge

In November of 1980, an NBC television news helicopter hovers above Cayo Lobos, a tiny Bahamian atoll located just north of Cuba where over one hundred people seek shade from the lighthouse (see map 2 of Cayo Lobos). It has been almost six weeks since a U.S. Coast Guard (USCG) patrol encountered the group, whom they identified as Haitian nationals, and alerted Bahamian and American authorities. The news report cuts to the island, using a series of close-up shots to illustrate the desperate conditions faced by migrants stranded there. A pregnant woman cradles her belly, while holding a plant in her other hand. She does not speak, but the reporter explains that for food the group has been relying on "roots, leaves, anything they could find." An emaciated man standing nearby also embodies their plight.

The view shifts from the group to a small boat approaching shore. Bahamian officials, dressed in red T-shirts and white shorts, land on the island, aiming to return the stranded migrants to Haiti. The operation does not go smoothly. The Haitians resist, using what the reporter describes as rusty knives, sticks, and seashells. Reverend Gérard Jean-Juste, a Haitian Catholic priest based in Miami, has arrived on the island from Florida with a news crew and prays with a group of men gathered around him. Jean-Juste reportedly appeals for nonviolence. But an hour after his departure, Bahamian police "in battle dress" land on the beach. Holding automatic weapons, they brusquely order reporters to "pack up and get out." The broadcast cuts to an aerial view of a

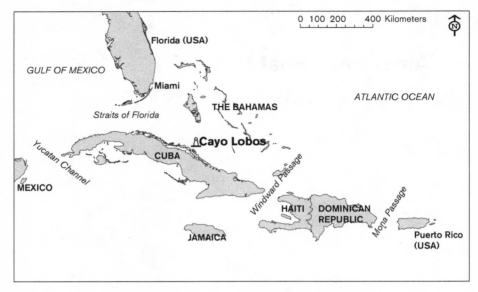

MAP 2. Location of Cayo Lobos, where Haitian migrants were stranded in 1980.

police agent shooting tear gas into the interior of the island. Another group of officers surrounds the trapped migrants, beating them with nightsticks and kicking them with their boots. Viewers do not see the migrants forced onto a boat, but we are told that they have begun their trip back to Haiti.[1] A Bahamian government spokesperson explains to a Florida newspaper, "There were some problems initially, with the Haitians refusing to go, but there was nothing physical."[2]

This scene on Cayo Lobos occurred only a few months after the spectacular Mariel Boatlift, wherein some 125,000 Cubans arrived in south Florida after Fidel Castro selectively opened travel to the United States from Cuba's Mariel Harbor. For people familiar with migration in the Caribbean at the time, this protracted crisis on Cayo Lobos was a stark—if not surprising—illustration of the racial politics and geopolitics in the region. This chapter draws out how these international political dynamics and U.S. domestic politics resulted in disparate treatment of Haitian and Cuban migrants taking to the Caribbean seas to reach U.S. shores. We further situate this crisis on Cayo Lobos, and the treatment of Haitian asylum seekers more broadly, in relation to other crises involving U.S. military authorities at sea in Southeast Asia at the same time.

The dominant telling of migration crises featuring "boat people" in this historical moment—the rescue of Vietnamese nationals, the threat of Haitian nationals, and the welcome of Cuban nationals—remembers them as unrelated events. Yet this exercise of exclusion on this tiny island was not just incidentally related to the contemporaneous "humanitarian" responses to Vietnamese refugees. Rather, U.S. officials were conscious that the United States could not condemn pushbacks of migrants in Southeast Asia and simultaneously engage in such practices with Haitian asylum seekers. Indeed, we link these episodes to question how humanitarian and deterrence policies have come to be understood and narrated as opposing practices. The history we trace in this chapter and throughout the book shows them as simultaneous and symbiotic: U.S. foreign policy manifests simultaneously in both humanitarian rescue *and* migration control.

This chapter makes a twofold argument. First, the deployment of a dichotomous migration discourse of rescue versus deterrence, good versus bad migrant, and bona fide versus bogus refugee is a well-rehearsed, racializing discourse long applied to people crossing borders. Such dichotomies of who deserves welcome and care versus who deserves punishment and exile animate differential inclusion *and* exclusionary migration practices. Analyzing how these categories work together is imperative for informing the geopolitical histories that gave rise to contemporary U.S. migration, enforcement, and detention policies. The development of offshore and onshore enforcement histories also sheds light on historic events transpiring across the Mediterranean Sea and the Indian Ocean where unprecedented numbers of crossings and deaths are taking place, and where similar debates about militarization, humanitarianism, and deterrence are unfolding (Hodge 2015; Stierl 2017).

On the Bahamian atoll in 1980, Coast Guard telephone logs and telegrams record a simultaneously intimate and international account of the prolonged crisis that these migrants endured while multilateral and interagency negotiations took place. Ten days into their time on the island, a shipping vessel told the U.S. Coast Guard that four or five people had died and that "several pregnant women were due to deliver 'at any moment.'"[3] As the days proceeded, logs report that people were "suffering from several medical problems." The U.S. Department of Justice (DOJ) had communicated to the Coast Guard that transporting the Haitians to Miami or to Haiti were both "unacceptable options."[4] The Bahamian government indicated that it "prefer that we not remove any other Haitians from the island," although it did "gratefully accept" humanitarian assistance provided by the Coast Guard.[5]

A week after the Coast Guard had made its third airdrop of food and water rations, 102 Haitian migrants remained on the island, despite assurances that the Bahamian Home Affairs office planned to charter a boat to shepherd them away. The Coast Guard alerted the State Department that the "urgent humanitarian plight" faced by "increasingly destitute" people would not be relieved by making another airdrop because of their "exposure to the elements and their lack of basic supplies."[6] By this point, the airdrop operation was so involved that the Coast Guard district operating in the area had run out of containers and parachutes.[7] As negotiations continued among U.S. embassy staff and Bahamian and Haitian officials, the United Nations High Commissioner for Refugees (UNHCR) also attempted to intervene and conduct credible fear interviews on the island.[8] Bahamian officials would not confirm that they had received the UNHCR's request.

By November 8, the crisis had begun to receive national television coverage in the United States. Three days later, Reverend Jean-Juste landed on the island with a news crew and advised the stranded group not to return to Haiti. Jean-Juste headed the Miami-based Haitian Refugee Center (HRC), which had just won a significant ruling on the discriminatory treatment of Haitians. Coast Guard logs report that the media had "informed the Haitians that the Bahamians would be returning them to Haiti and [that] the refugees not only refused to board the *Lady Moore* but attacked the vessel's crewmen."[9] The following day, the Bahamian Defense Force dispatched police to remove the stranded migrants. The Coast Guard observed that the "evacuation," contrary to Bahamian claims, "was not smooth and use of force, including small arms fire, was involved. The Haitians strenuously resisted their evacuation and it appears that several may have been injured or even shot during the melee."[10] The media reported that the migrants had locked arms to protest their removal.[11] President Jimmy Carter's Secretary of Cabinet Gene Eidenberg, meanwhile, told the press that the White House had just learned about the crisis: "I'm outraged . . . the White House is looking into the question of how this situation was allowed to occur and be known to officials of the American Government for 30 days without higher authorities being advised of the situation and action taken."[12]

An editorial in the *Miami Herald* decried all of the countries involved in the crisis for arguing over jurisdiction while people faced starvation (Miller 2006, 41). The criticism only partially identified the geopolitical conflicts at hand. The international debate buffeting Haitian lives was real, but it was also longstanding, and none of the parties could claim fully humanitarian intent. Following World War II (WWII), the Bahamas had grown increasingly reliant on Haitian labor, but by the late-1950s, the government had already begun trying to thwart Haitian migration, often through mass arrests and deportations. The government of Haiti sometimes would accept the return of its citizens, but other times it would not. When accepted, deportees were subjected routinely to interrogation and torture. Haitians, many of whom did not want to return to Haiti, often would attempt to migrate to the United States; by the early 1980s, researchers estimated that 60 percent of the Haitians living in Miami had lived in the Bahamas (Boswell 1983, 59).

Nor was the United States a disinterested party, domestically or internationally, in what was transpiring on Cayo Lobos. The highest levels of the U.S. administration—the State Department, the Department of Justice, and the National Security Council (NSC)—were aware of the effect that Bahamian deportations had on domestic migration politics (particularly in Florida), and on bilateral relations in the region. Since at least 1972, the arrivals of Haitians by boat had drawn enough political concern from Florida politicians that they began to pressure the federal government to implement practices to dissuade Haitian migration. The Carter administration had recently negotiated with the Bahamas on a series of issues, including migration and formalization of the 1964 Grey Agreement, that authorized the US Coast Guard to assist the Bahamian Coast Guard in search and rescue and law enforcement.[13] White House national security staffers had "no reason to believe that the Bahamians are not disposed to be cooperative in controlling the constant trickle of illegal Haitian immigrants."[14] With four U.S. military bases in Bahamian territory at the time, the United States valued its agreement with the Bahamas as an "integral part of the base structure in the Caribbean area," a geostrategic position that the Bahamian government sought to use in negotiating for economic assistance.[15]

All of these dynamics were at play when Bahamian officials attempted to use the forcible return of the Cayo Lobos migrants to Haiti as leverage to compel the United States or United Nations to take responsibility for *all* unauthorized Haitians living in the Bahamas.[16] At the same time, the United States was engaged in its own planning efforts to prevent Haitian migration. Mere weeks before this incident, Eidenberg had been part of discussions with the Coast Guard, the Justice Department, and the National Security Council concerning U.S. "legal authority to interdict Haitian refugee boats outside the U.S. waters for the purpose of returning the passengers to Haiti."[17]

Cayo Lobos, in short, was neither an isolated island nor incident. The waters surrounding it were subject to years of negotiations over law of the sea, bilateral policing practices, and military presence. The Haitians who had landed here were neither passive victims, nor could they fully control the economic and political forces that shaped their lives. Their faces on the nightly news could be read within a dominant U.S. (and Bahamian) narrative that they were economic migrants fleeing the poorest country in the northern hemisphere and were people whose protection was deemed humanitarian, not political. This enduring distinction between the humanitarian and the political is encapsulated in the distinction between the boatlifts of Indochinese refugees, narrated as humanitarian rescue operations, and the Haitian Program, detailed later and designed to dissuade Haitian migration to Florida. These were both racialized and geopoliticized responses, one positioning the United States as savior, the other positing the United States as enforcer, ostensibly under threat. The United States succeeded for decades in mobilizing these discourses to exclude Haitians, which is why we do not know what happened to the pregnant woman and her unborn child. They appeared fleetingly on U.S. newsreels, only to disappear from the view of an international audience once the Haitians were returned.

THE WAR IN VIETNAM AND COLD WAR MIGRATION CRISES

The fall of Saigon is remembered in U.S. narratives of the Vietnam War as the period of days in April 1975 when the U.S. military conducted a massive humanitarian airlift of refugees out of the city to begin new lives in the United States. Yến Lê Espiritu (2014, 25) argues that the "narrative of the 'good refugee' has been key in enabling the United States to turn the Vietnam War improbably into a 'good war'—an ultimately necessary and moral war." As Espiritu demonstrates compellingly in *Body Counts,* this "good-war narrative requires the production not only of the good refugee but also of a good *refuge*" (emphasis in original). In this geographical imagination, not only are refugees constructed as external and "out-of-place victims," but Americans are able to claim the identity of "magnanimous rescuers," thereby displacing U.S. military aggression (10; also see Lipman 2012; Nguyen 2012).

Indeed, the domesticating work of refugee resettlement is illustrated in the U.S. Army's *After Action Report* published in the aftermath of the fall of Saigon, which refers to the operations as "housekeeping chores" (1977, I-A-7). The cover of the report features an illustration of

FIGURE 1. The cover for the Department of the Army's *After Action Report, Operations New Life/New Arrivals* depicts a U.S. soldier extending a humanitarian welcome to a Vietnamese family. The men's handshake suggests unity or reconciliation following a destructive and divisive war. (Department of Army, 1977.)

a friendly white soldier wearing a baseball cap shaking the hand of a traditionally dressed Vietnamese man (see figure 1). The men smile at each other while a Vietnamese woman, presumably the latter's wife, stands behind the two men's clasped hands, holding a swaddled baby. The scene conveys a transparent sense of benevolence and completion, reworking masculinity from the predominance of violent conflict to a shared (though not evenly) project of masculinist protection (Young 2003). A narrative in the report describes the day-to-day process of resettlement for a "fictitious Vietnamese family," demonstrating how a

Vietnamese father is able to keep his family unified and healthy in the United States with the support of civilian government agencies, voluntary refugee organizations, and medical officials.

The U.S. war in Southeast Asia and its evacuation of some 130,000 people from Vietnam and Cambodia in 1975 relied on a much longer history of imperialism and military occupation (discussed in our introduction) there and in the region. The U.S. evacuation engaged transnational landscapes of occupation and militarization. Over 90 percent of the Vietnamese refugees who fled in 1975 were transported through U.S. bases on Guam, Wake Island, or the Philippines (Espiritu 2014, 26). Army personnel to staff these operations were transported to these sites from bases in Hawai'i, South Korea, Japan, and North America (Department of the Army 1977).

Three "refugee reception centers" were initially established on military facilities in the U.S. mainland—Camp Pendleton in California, Fort Chaffee in Arkansas, and Eglin Air Force Base (AFB) in Florida—achieving what the Army called a "practical and politically acceptable geographic distribution of sites across the country" (I-A-6-7). Overcrowding and tension at camps on Guam and the approach of typhoon season led to the establishment of a fourth site at Fort Indiantown Gap in Pennsylvania (x). American studies scholar Perla Guerrero notes that these centers also had been chosen to "disperse the refugee populations, an attempt to preemptively halt the formation of ethnic enclaves" (2016, 237).

The U.S. government's plans for resettlement onshore have been narrated in contradictory ways: as an ad hoc, last-minute response, and as a set of logical, well-executed plans (Kennedy 2014; Department of the Army 1977) (see figure 2). The long history of U.S. military activity and the scale of its capacity in the Pacific region created the conditions for a militarized operation (Davis 2011; Espiritu 2014; Loyd et al. 2015). Despite their practical power, even military records show that U.S. authorities could not act unilaterally and were forced to contend with resistance from residents living near military facilities and the independent migration of the Vietnamese civilians whom they sought to direct.

In the days before the now iconic airlift, people fleeing Cambodia and Vietnam had begun to leave their countries by boat. Many of them were picked up by U.S. Navy ships and taken to "safe havens" in the Philippines (Department of the Army 1977, I-A-3). The Philippines soon told U.S. officials that it would accept no additional refugees in transit, forcing the United States to shift its operations entirely to its territory of

FIGURE 2. A civilian federal agent explains the pace and locations of resettlement activity, including to Wake Island, Camp Pendleton, Fort Chaffee, Eglin Air Force Base, and Indiantown Gap. (Reprinted with permission of Micronesian Area Research Center, University of Guam.)

Guam (Espiritu 2014, 30). Some residents of Guam, however, were concerned about food shortages that might result from the operation, leading Governor Ricky Bordallo to reiterate the humanitarian nature of the military's activities (Loyd et al. 2015). In North America, military operations also remained reliant on local civilian infrastructure and political support. In Arkansas, officials of the city of Fort Smith threatened to turn off the base's water supply if the Army did not pay its bills for Fort Chaffee, and the local gas company informed the military that it did not have enough capacity to supply the base and local industry without rationing (Department of the Army 1977).

And finally, the people being resettled were themselves actively shaping their futures. A countermovement of over 1,500 "repatriates" who did not want to be resettled in the United States, and instead wanted to return to their home countries in Southeast Asia, developed (Lipman 2012). Nearly four hundred Vietnamese and Cambodian citizens were transported back from Fort Chaffee and Indiantown Gap through Camp Pendleton and then flown to Guam. Once there they joined another 1,400 Vietnamese repatriates, many of whom staged a series of demonstrations, including burning down at least three buildings (Department of the Army 1977, I-A-12).

Funding for the 1975 resettlement operation was authorized through the Indochina Migration and Refugee Assistance Act, which Congress passed despite polls indicating that only 36 percent of Americans thought that the refugees should be admitted (N. L. Zucker 1983). California Congressperson Burt Talcott objected to the operation, saying, "Damn it, we have too many Orientals" (Zucker and Zucker 1996, 40). Many others in Congress and the executive branch, including President Carter, NSC advisor Zbigniew Brzezinski, and the State Department, supported the ongoing resettlement of refugees from the region who had nowhere else to go or who had been associated with U.S. operations there.[18]

Ongoing violence in Laos, Cambodia, and Vietnam fueled further displacement, and by 1978 these movements constituted a massive refugee crisis across Southeast Asia. That year, over 131,000 refugees had landed by boat in or come overland to countries of first asylum, including Malaysia, Thailand, Singapore, Indonesia, and the Philippines (Stein 1979, 716). Many of the people fleeing either had been U.S. allies during the war or were trying to escape the genocide in Cambodia, or the violence and persecution by communist governments in Laos and Vietnam. President Carter, in turn, ordered American ships to rescue so-called "boat people," and promised them refuge in the United States. Canadian citizens also mobilized and resettled approximately sixty thousand Indochinese refugees (Molloy and Simeon 2016, 3).

According to refugee scholars Norman and Naomi Zucker, Carter aimed to "spur an international response to the exodus" with his announcement (1996, 40). However, a conference held by the United Nations in Geneva late in 1978 produced little change. Following the arrival of another 209,000 refugees during the first half of 1979, Thailand and Malaysia began to refuse entry to additional refugees (Stein 1979, 716). Moreover, Malaysia, Thailand, Indonesia, and the Philippines began pushing back boats, leaving thirty to forty thousand people stranded at sea (Stein 1979, 717; Frelick 1993, 682).

Carter had issued an emergency parole authorizing entry for seven thousand boat refugees in January 1978, but the scale of the ongoing crisis in the region demanded a more comprehensive response.[19] Congress, the White House, and the State and Justice Departments were keen to establish a longer-term policy for admitting refugees. In the spring of 1978, the House of Representatives had scheduled hearings on Congressperson Joshua Eilberg's (D-PA) refugee bill, which would have capped the number of refugees admitted. Meanwhile, the White House was developing its position, based on input from the State and Justice Departments. Secretary of State Cyrus Vance recommended that twenty-five thousand refugees from Southeast Asia be admitted annually, limited to those "escaping by boat and with no other offer of resettlement, and refugees escaping by land who have close relatives in this country or other close association with the United States." For Vance, "the need for such a policy is evident if we are to avoid further drowning of refugees at sea and to mitigate the suffering of land refugees in camps in Thailand."[20] Maritime migrations proved central to the early development of refugee legislation in the United States, which did not yet exist.

While Brzezinski and Vance were known to have great differences over geopolitical strategy (Bon Tempo 2008, 151; Gati 2013), they both viewed refugees in Southeast Asia as a pressing issue for which the United States had a "special responsibility," in Vance's terms.[21] The differences between their positions on this issue seem to have concerned domestic politics. Brzezinski supported Vance's proposal for parole in 1977, and again in 1978.[22] Yet following consultation with domestic-policy advisor Stu Eizenstat, he came to recommend the development of a comprehensive, joint State-Justice policy that would include "a firm recommendation on reimbursement costs to local government and a frank assessment of probable Congressional reaction."[23]

Brzezinski and Eizenstat explained to the president that while the agencies were in "considerable agreement," "the essence of the remaining disagreement between Justice and State on the overall policy question comes to whether we should support the Eilberg approach of placing some numerical limitations on the normal flow [of] refugees, or whether we should avoid numerical limits altogether." They went on to observe, "The differences within the Administration reflect those on the Hill, with the Justice Department in agreement with Eilberg and [Senator James O.] Eastland that there should be numerical limitations, and the State Department and Senator [Ted] Kennedy opposing them."[24]

Despite relatively low public support for additional resettlement for "boat people" (Bon Tempo 2008, 163), the deliberations were not about whether but how to respond to this "special responsibility." Carter was concerned that the policy not "induc[e] unnecessary suffering by encouraging refugees to leave home with no place to go."[25] Attorney General Griffin Bell opposed using the Justice Department's parole authority "for the wholesale relocation of refugees," and Congress also wanted greater oversight over this authority. Indeed, Justice was "concerned that the impact of such unilateral executive action as proposed here [by the State Department] would be devastating to their Congressional relations."[26] Carter decided to double the number of refugees admitted under the parole authorization from the 1979 figure of seven thousand per month to fourteen thousand per month. By the end of 1980, 400,000 refugees from Southeast Asia had been resettled in the United States (151), and by the mid-1990s, the number would reach 1.2 million people (Zucker and Zucker 1996, 42).

The ongoing refugee crisis in Southeast Asia and discontent over repeated parole authorizations provided the context within which Congress would pass the Refugee Act in 1979. Restrictionist Southern senator Eastland had retired, leaving Kennedy as head of the Judiciary Committee, and there was little organized opposition to the bill. When signed into law by President Carter on March 17, 1980, the bill provided the first definition of "refugee" in U.S. legislation, authorized the admission of fifty thousand refugees annually, and retained the president's authority to admit additional refugees on an emergency basis or in consultation with Congress (Bon Tempo 2008, 174–77). The new definition of *refugee* was defined with human rights principles, and represented a shift away from "its Cold War political, ideological, and geographical biases" (178). In practice, however, refugee and asylum determinations would continue to be influenced by Cold War geopolitics.

CARTER, THE DUVALIERS, AND HAITIAN EMIGRATION

Less than a month after President Carter had signed the Refugee Act into law, Congressperson Shirley Chisholm (D-NY), Senator Richard Stone (D-FL), Senator Daniel Patrick Moynihan (D-NY), and ten other members of Congress sent a letter to the president to draw his attention to "Haitian refugees [who] are America's 'boat people.' They are the survivors of a harrowing flight from oppression. Most have risked their lives to voyage 800 miles of dangerous ocean in flimsy sailboats. Many of their family and friends have drowned. All have suffered greatly." Also signing the letter were labor, religious, and civil-rights leaders, including former U.N. Ambassador Andrew Young, Bayard Rustin of the A. Philip Randolph Institute, President of the International Ladies Garment Workers Union Sol Chaikin, Miami Mayor Maurice Ferré, Executive Vice President of the Synagogue Council of America Rabbi Bernard Mandelbaum, and Haitian civil-rights leader Jean-Juste. The group expressed concern that Haitian refugees had "languished in

South Florida for 6 or 7 years" while awaiting asylum hearings, and feared their forced returns despite systematic and well-documented persecution and starvation on the island. They "fervently hope that the Attorney General will exercise his parole authority one last time to grant refuge to those Haitian refugees currently in the United States."[27]

This letter was the latest in several years of advocacy around the treatment of Haitian migrants and asylum seekers. Officials in the State Department and Immigration and Naturalization Service (INS) maintained a sharp distinction between political refugees and economic migrants, those who deserved humanitarian protection and those whose economic desperation seemingly threatened U.S. sovereignty. Even as human-rights observers continued to document political repression and systematic violence in Haiti, all but one hundred of the forty thousand asylum applications filed by Haitians in the 1970s were dismissed as "frivolous" claims (N. F. Zucker 1983, 152; Stepick 1986, 4). Critics contended that U.S. policy was based on geopolitical and racial calculations, claims that the Carter administration sought to dispel.

Haiti's history, or a version of Haiti's history, is part of how U.S. officials have defined Haitian migration as a problem (cf. Chazkel et al. 2013). James Carlin, Deputy Assistant Secretary for Refugee and Migration Affairs at the State Department, offered:

> Haiti has had a long and difficult history. It is a densely populated country without significant natural resources which has not received significant foreign investment, technological assistance, or other forms of economic stimulus until very recently. Rising directly from slavery in 1804, with no tradition of self-government, Haiti's politics have been turbulent and often chaotic in its 174 years as an independent nation.[28]

This telling narrative situates Haiti's contemporary poverty and political conflict as problems internal to the nation and its solutions as external. It isolates Haiti discursively and distorts the long history of international exploitation of its people and natural resources. Carlin also erases the U.S. government's direct and indirect involvement in Haiti's governance. In sum, this account draws an untenable distinction between the economic and political forces that U.S. officials would deploy repeatedly to categorize unauthorized migration as a domestic law-enforcement issue separate from asylum as a foreign-policy concern.

What this U.S. official's account did not tell was that Haiti had been one of France's most lucrative colonies when enslaved subjects revolted and established their independence. The government of France and business owners forced Haiti to pay for the loss of their property, an outflow of funds that amounted to 80 percent of the government's budget over a century later (Dubois 2012, 9). In 1915, the United States sent Marines to the island nation, beginning an occupation that would last twenty years. The United States rationalized its presence in the name of building up Haiti's democratic institutions and infrastructure; U.S. business had pushed for the occupation as "crucial for making Haiti attractive to foreign investors" (267). During the occupation, hundreds of thousands of Haitians were encouraged to work in U.S.-controlled sugar plantations and mills in the neighboring Dominican Republic and Cuba. These migrations would continue in subsequent decades, and would be interrupted by the Dominican massacre of Haitians under President Rafael Trujillo in the 1930s and the 1959 Cuban Revolution (Loescher and Scanlan 1984, 315; Stepick 1992, 127).

The Duvalier family rule would have significant consequences for the living conditions and political freedoms of most Haitians. François "Papa Doc" Duvalier came to power in 1958 in a contest in which he deployed hired thugs to disrupt voter registration and cultivated allegiance from the military (Dubois 2012, 328). The U.S. Marines were brought in to train the Haitian military, and Duvalier's militia, the *Tonton Macoutes,* were armed with U.S. weapons. Duvalier hired Franklin Roosevelt's son to manage Haiti's public relations. By early 1961, U.S. aid constituted 50 percent of the Haitian government's budget (334–35). Only following Duvalier's reelection in 1961, by an improbable margin of 1,320,780 to 0, did the United States shift its foreign policy. The John F. Kennedy administration began to pressure Duvalier, including supporting his opponents' efforts to overthrow his government. Duvalier tempered growing criticism by serving as a Cold War ally in U.S. attempts to isolate and invade Cuba. But after the Haitian military occupied the Dominican embassy in Port-au-Prince in 1963, Kennedy ended military and economic aid.

This cessation of formal U.S. support of Haiti's government would be short-lived. Following Kennedy's assassination, the Lyndon Johnson and the subsequent Richard Nixon administrations would prioritize Cold War imperatives over concerns regarding political repression and corruption (Loescher and Scanlan 1984, 324–25; Stepick 1992, 130–32). Duvalier's son Jean-Claude assumed the presidency following his father's death in 1971, and continued to foster strong relations with the United States. In his first four years in office, international aid to Haiti jumped tenfold; between 1972 and 1981, 80 percent of the $584 million in direct aid came from the United States (Stepick 1992, 132; Dubois 2012, 334–35, 351). But as historian Laurent Dubois observes, ironically, "It was money coming from Haitians driven into exile that in many ways propped up the economy during Jean-Claude Duvalier's rule" (2012, 353; also see Loescher and Scanlan 1984, 319).

Meanwhile, remittances from Haitians living abroad had grown from 5 percent of total national revenues in 1960 to 33 percent in the early 1980s (Dubois 2012, 353). Migration from Haiti to the United States had increased significantly following François Duvalier's assumption of the presidency. The first group that arrived beginning in the late 1950s included wealthier Haitians, followed in the mid-1960s by middle-class professionals, both groups settling primarily in New York City, Boston, and Chicago (Stepick 1992, 128). Many who entered in the 1960s arrived on and then overstayed their tourist visas, a practice that was largely tolerated.

With the Nixon administration backing Duvalier, securing visas for travel and relocation to the United States became more difficult. Haitians had been arriving in south Florida by boat for almost a decade before 1972, but a sharp decline in the number of visas issued—combined with ongoing repression under Jean-Claude Duvalier—created the conditions for increased migration by sea (Loescher and Scanlan 1984, 328; Stepick 1992, 134). As boats began arriving more frequently after 1972, local elected officials and political leaders began mobilizing for increased resources to deter and remove Haitian migrants from south Florida (Stepick 1982, 178–79).

THE HAITIAN PROGRAM

Even as the Carter White House increased pressure on Haiti to demonstrate its commitment to human rights (Dubois 2012, 355), its efforts to shift INS treatment of Haitians were contentious and uneven. At the beginning of his term, Carter's administration continued the INS's existing practice of detaining Haitians who could not post bond in jails throughout south Florida and sometimes as far away as El Paso, Texas (N. F. Zucker 1983, 154; Stepick 1992, 136). Moreover, the INS and State Department worked in tandem to deny virtually all Haitian asylum claims. Following a brief asylum interview by the INS, applications were forwarded to the State Department's Office of Refugee and Migration Affairs where reviews "were often based on the assumption that Haitian asylum claims were not valid" (Loescher and Scanlan 1984, 334).

In defending their practices, the INS and State Department maintained the distinction between economic migrants and political asylees. In 1976, the Miami INS district director, Edward Sweeney, explained, "We feel that any relaxation of the rules could produce a flood of economic refugees from all over the Caribbean, where virtually every government has serious socioeconomic and political problems" (in Loescher and Scanlan 1986, 174). A State Department official voiced the same argument one year later about a group of Haitians that was stranded at Guantánamo Naval Base (GTMO). Granting them political asylum would be a problem for relations with Haiti, but to admit them as refugees might encourage more to flee. "What do you do with the world's poor?" she lamented.[29]

By the mid-1970s, U.S. trade unions, civil-rights organizations, and faith groups vocalized their support for Haitians. Demonstrations and concerted legal advocacy would curtail the INS's exclusionary practices, introducing a new stumbling block for the Carter and subsequent Ronald Reagan administrations' responses to Haitian migration (Gollobin 1978; Kahn 2013). The National Council of Churches (NCC) brought one of the first of these lawsuits in 1974. In response, new INS Commissioner Leonel Castillo announced in 1977 that Haitians whose asylum cases were pending would be released from detention without bond and granted work authorization (N.F. Zucker 1983, 154–55; Stepick 1992, 136). Some 120 Haitians were released from jail, and within months 4,000 to 5,000 Haitians applied to the INS for work authorizations (*HRC v. Civiletti* 1980, 511–12). Deportation hearings, meanwhile, were at a virtual standstill as judges awaited word of new asylum procedures and INS attorneys declined cases, partly because of the greater due-process rights that had been won by advocates (512).

INS officials and some political figures in Miami deeply opposed the work authorizations and release of Haitians from detention, and lobbied the Attorney General to resume the INS's more exclusionary practices (Stepick 1992, 137). This pressure and the backlog of hearings led the INS in 1978 to develop the Haitian Program, an initiative designed to accelerate the removal of Haitian asylum seekers from south Florida. Mario Noto, deputy commissioner of the INS, was one of the architects of the program and coordinated efforts with the U.S. Public Health Service (USPHS), U.S. Border Patrol, and State Department. Their task, he urged, was to counter what he called the "Haitian threat," which he defined as "individuals that are threatening the community's well-being-socially *[sic]* economically" (*HRC v. Civiletti* 1980, 517).

Federal District Judge Lawrence King, who ruled on the program in the landmark *Haitian Refugee Center v. Civiletti* case, observed that two premises guided the INS's development of the program. First, it was based on the notion that Haitian nationals were migrating for economic reasons and not to seek asylum, and second, that Haitians were to be treated differently. In short, King concluded: "Underlying any attempt to discourage immigration is the assumption that none of the potential immigrants have any right to seek entry into the United States. Phrased differently, such a policy indicates a predetermination that *none* of the Haitians could deserve asylum" (514, emphasis in original). The State Department agreed to facilitate the Haitian Program by reviewing the INS's asylum decisions more quickly and by publicly urging the INS to revoke work permits (515–16).

A deeply racialized and exclusionary precedent was set in motion that would continue in U.S. immigration policy and multilateral relations. Haitian migrants would be treated uniquely. As Naomi Paik (2013, 143) notes, "Subjection to extraordinary tactics of exclusion has made the Haitian refugee an exceptional figure in US migration law and history." Their singular treatment in agreements that govern mobility would continue for decades and influence other nations' practices. Following the implementation of the Haitian Program, the number of deportation hearings held for Haitian cases jumped from approximately 6 daily to 55 in July 1978, and 150 in September 1978 (Stepick 1986, 14). To accomplish this expansion, hearings were scheduled in multiple locations, but there was no increase in the number of lawyers providing legal representation. With approximately thirteen attorneys available to represent Haitians, the INS knew that attorneys would be scheduled for multiple hearings or interviews concurrently, but decided that resolving such scheduling conflicts was "too cumbersome for us to handle" (*HRC v. Civiletti* 1980, 524). Under these conditions, lawyers often had as little as thirty minutes to prepare their cases, and hearing times were shortened from ninety to thirty minutes (Stepick 1986, 14; Paik 2013). As in more contemporary examples of the mass representation of asylum seekers (e.g., Burridge 2009; Mountz 2010; Boyce and Launius 2013), such mediated forms of access to asylum represent what has been called "thin" access to justice.

The head of the Justice Department's Civil Division in South Florida, Peter Nimkoff, who was critical of the policy of jailing Haitians, resigned from his position, citing "reasons of conscience" (N. F. Zucker 1983, 156). Nimkoff recounted a conversation he had had with INS Deputy Commissioner Noto in an interview with policy observer Naomi

Zucker. Noto had defended the Haitian Program to Nimkoff, claiming that the INS was acting in a humanitarian manner because they were not sinking Haitian boats or letting people drown (N. F. Zucker 1983, 156). This mixing of narratives of exclusion and rescue foreshadows how the U.S. treatment of Haitians would inform the subsequent treatment of other groups of asylum seekers.

Some six hundred people would be deported through the Haitian Program before it was temporarily enjoined. Judge King's 1980 ruling on the program found that the INS had created, and immigration judges had been complicit in, a program that denied Haitians the rights afforded to other migrants. "The plaintiffs charge that they faced a transparently discriminatory program designed to deport Haitian nationals and no one else. The uncontroverted evidence proves their claim" (HRC v. Civiletti 1980, 451).

While there had been programs designed to speed lawful entry, this program was unique in that there had "never before been an expedited program designed to expel applicants for asylum" (511). King continued:

> This court cannot close its eyes, however, to a possible underlying reason why these plaintiffs have been subjected to intentional "national origin" discrimination. The plaintiffs are part of the first substantial flight of *black* refugees from a repressive regime to this country. All of the plaintiffs are black. In contrast, for example, only a relatively small percent of the Cuban refugees who have fled to this country are black (451, emphasis in original).

King thus affirmed that the Haitian Program, the first of several instances of "the Haitian exception," was racialized, classed, and geopoliticized.

The contention that U.S. policy toward and treatment of Haitians was a result of anti-Black racism was a sensitive one for the Carter administration. While the political implications of such charges seem to have been important to top NSC advisors, the administration consistently would deflect, downplay, and ultimately fail to acknowledge the veracity of racism. On the one hand, the White House and State Department would concede that Haiti had human-rights problems, which United Nations Ambassador Young had criticized in his 1977 visit to the country (Loescher and Scanlan 1986, 173). Yet both the White House and State Department nonetheless would assert the primacy of economic "push" factors or emphasize similarities with the U.S. treatment of other nationalities.[30]

The Carter administration's response to criticism from the Congressional Black Caucus (CBC) illustrates this dynamic of containing the suggestion of racism while simultaneously dismissing its reality. New York Congressperson Chisholm chaired the CBC's Task Force on Haitian Refugees. In December 1979, she called for a meeting with the White House. Brzezinski conferred with NSC staffers Madeline Albright and Robert Pastor. Pastor, the NSC advisor who coordinated Caribbean and Latin American policy, concurred with the State Department's recommendation that the White House meet with Chisholm "because of the increasing sensitivity of the problem, particularly the political implications." Namely, "there is a strong implication in her letter that the Administration is treating Haitians less favorably than refugees from other areas because they are black and poorly educated." One recipient of the memo penned a sarcastic response in the margin: "as opposed to the Cambodians who are white and well-educated!"[31]

Brzezinski wrote to Chisholm that she should arrange to meet with Henry Owen, a former State Department policy coordinator, who now had "primary responsibility" for the issue in the White House.[32] After the meeting, Owen followed up with a letter to Chisholm, attaching documents that "demonstrate unquestionably the high priority the Carter Administration has given to human rights in Haiti."[33] Among these were the State Department's recent reports on human rights in Haiti and on the treatment of Haitians who had been returned to Haiti. Owen emphasized that he had confirmed the credibility of the State Department's reports with the UNHCR, which indicated that it was "unable to assert there was sufficient evidence to justify the definition" of most Haitians as political refugees.[34] Considering that the caucus had already publicly condemned the findings of the State Department's study team on Haitian returnees, this letter was unlikely to have won much confidence from the CBC and, rather, suggests White House disregard for the issue.[35] (Judge King later called the State Department's report "unworthy of belief" [HRC v. Civiletti 1980, 477].)

Indeed, even as the treatment of Haitians drew steady criticism into 1980, some in the White House continued to express incredulity at charges of racism. Pastor, in a declassified memo to Brzezinski, reiterated the distinction between economic and political migration to explain differential treatment, defended the State Department's controversial findings, and expressed frustration that the administration nonetheless needed to respond as if racism were a real issue:

> The black community in the U.S. refuses to accept the argument that we will treat the Haitians according to the same criteria as the Cubans. The group under DPS [White House Domestic Policy Staff] will try to wrestle with a

number of real options (like amnesty for the 10,000 in Florida) and damage-limiting ideas (like sending another group to Haiti to rediscover that those who have been deported are not subject to persecution). I doubt anything will come out of the exercise, except to show the black community that we care, and we are not racists. The problem is that the Haitians are like the Mexicans (undocumented workers) rather than the Cubans (political refugees), but they come by boat to Florida rather than overland to the southwest.[36]

Pastor's taxonomy by race, ethnicity, country of origin, and mode of travel was simultaneously classed, racialized, and geopolitical. Cubans were positioned as a wealthier class of asylum seekers, and as people *in need* of protection due to their flight from a communist regime. In contrast, Mexican and Haitian migrants were fleeing noncommunist regimes with whom the United States supported diplomatic relations, and they were less wealthy. An intersectional analysis of this historical moment shows how these interlocking subject positions informed vastly different responses to different groups of people arriving around the same time.

With uncertainty over Judge King's ruling, a new political crisis was brewing that would soon consume the White House and public attention. The Mariel crisis unfolded between April and September of 1980, even as approximately thirty-five thousand Haitians also arrived in Florida by boat. The question of how to manage the existing backlog of Haitian asylum claims would be part of resolving this and future mass migrations. NSC staffer Lincoln Bloomfield wrote a memo to Brzezinski, urging a policy decision on Haitians. The issues were threefold: 1) "intense" domestic political concern regarding the discriminatory treatment of Haitians as compared to Cubans; 2) "whether or not Haitians fall under the definition of refugees"; and 3) the "possibly 1-200,000 more Haitians illegally in the New York area whose status would be affected by a decision." Among the problems was "how to align our Cuban and Haitian policies to avoid the reality and appearance of discrimination." Brzezinski, presumably, penned a note in the corner of the memo, perhaps addressed to Pastor: "Plse fit into the Cuban problem."[37]

Brzezinski's note suggests a liberalization of a sort, but the Mariel crisis would soon result in a historic shift in the U.S. treatment of Cubans, and Haitians would continue to be subject to exclusionary treatment. The Carter administration developed a multi-agency Cuban-Haitian Task Force (CHTF) to respond to these mass migrations, which we explore more fully in chapter 2. Roger Adams, general counsel for the CHTF, suggested that the White House could offer to resettle Haitians already involved in INS proceedings by June 19, 1980, and issue a statement that Haitians arriving illegally after that date would be subject to exclusion and deportation. He reasoned that this dual approach would demonstrate that

> the post-June 19 Haitians risk exclusion and deportation and may discourage more from coming. It simply puts future Haitian arrivals on notice that in the future they will be treated like other illegal aliens such as Mexicans, Nicaraguans, etc., and is a declaration that our immigration laws mean something.[38]

Repeated attempts to deflect the substance of racial discrimination would be made through false comparison. Such comparisons were not merely reflections of racial-ethnic, class, and nationality hierarchies, but were part of a process of differential racialization that "affects how each group is treated legally, socially, and economically and can even determine life and death" (Pulido 2006, 25). For example, one INS official stated publicly, "It's a simple issue as to whether they are being persecuted in Haiti. . . . Clearly they are not. They are just poor people coming here to work—just like the Mexicans" (in Stepick 1986, 13). Likewise, Deputy Associate Attorney General Doris Meissner explained, "In case-by-case determinations, State has found evidence of persecution in a small number of Haitian cases. As a group, State does not believe those fleeing Haiti are political refugees. Rather they liken them to Mexicans who cross the border seeking a better life."[39] These comparisons referenced, relied upon, and advanced the commonly accepted policing of one group (Mexicans) to justify the exclusion of another (Haitians). This policing of people, categories, and exclusions transpired in ways that downplayed the coercive treatment of Mexican nationals, and obscured that Haitians routinely were held in jail without bond, unlike most Mexican border crossers. The comparison to Nicaraguans, moreover, was misleading in that Nicaraguan asylum seekers were permitted to work while their cases were pending, unlike Haitians (*HRC v. Civiletti* 1980, 519), and at least twenty thousand Nicaraguans were given relief from deportation (Loescher and Scanlan 1986, 171).

These comparisons did not so much refute the role played by race, but racially differentiate and arrange groups in relation to one another—a taxonomy that emerges in careful reading of memos among authorities located across various federal agencies. This relational racialization also can be seen with the flippant comparison to Cambodian refugees we noted earlier in the chapter, which tried to deflect racism by deploying the "good refugee" trope (Espiritu 2014). In this trope, extending welcome to one group of nonwhite people serves to indicate that all others are similarly—or fairly—treated. The rhetoric not only valorizes and naturalizes U.S. humanitarianism, but distorts the divergent trajectories of violent displacement and relocation that different groups faced even while driven by the same Cold War foreign-policy objectives.

THE RECURRENCE OF CRISES

In this chapter, we have shown the differential response and treatment of concurrent movements of racialized, classed, and geopoliticized people traveling by boat in the late 1970s and 1980. Among these crises-riddled migrations by sea, Indochinese voyages were narrated as humanitarian rescue, a redemptive account that the United States could tell about itself in the wake of its extended, controversial, and catastrophically failed military intervention in the region. Nicaraguan and Cuban arrivals had better chances than other Caribbean and Central American nationals, as we detail in subsequent chapters, because they too were deserving of some degree of geopolitical rescue in their flight from communist regimes. Haitians, meanwhile, were positioned as racialized threats, and the state response to their boat migrations planted seeds of externalization that would continue for decades in immigration, enforcement, and asylum policy implemented at sea and on land. Archival records evidence the development of racialized discourses that accompanied these enforcement responses. These discourses located groups by national origin in interlocking geopoliticized, racialized, and classed matrices of good or bad, deserving or not deserving of protection, economic or political migrants.

The crises at sea endured by Indochinese and Haitian nationals were the immediate context for a new mass migration that came to be known as the Mariel Crisis. Policy critic Naomi Zucker, writing soon after the 1980 Mariel crisis, observes:

> It is undoubtedly ironic that it was the Cubans, not the Haitians, who breached our defenses, but when the flow from Mariel was finally staunched, a trickle of Haitians still flowed, reinforcing the belief of the previous 10 years that the Haitians posed a major threat to the American community and that our only protection was their swift and unimpeded removal (1983, 154).

Even though the State and Justice Departments upheld the distinction between economic and political migration, they also would make the contradictory contention that granting asylum emboldened economic migrants. To that end, Judge King observed, "It also appears that the struggle of the Haitians in Miami to have their claims heard was perceived as part of the Haitian problem" (*HRC v. Civiletti* 1980, 512).

Indeed, this view that rights of asylum served as a magnet for migration also could be found in National Security Council deliberations. In preparation for a meeting with Bahamian officials during which bilateral cooperation to prevent Haitian migration would be discussed, NSC staffer Lauralee Peters wrote to Pastor:

> A fundamental problem in this issue is our own immigration procedures. The Haitians are attracted to Florida because our judicial decisions prevent deportation without due process and because of an INS decision (currently under review) to grant work permits to them while their cases are pending.[40]

The push and pull factors that have long structured research on mass-migration movements need to be contextualized in their historic geopolitical contexts. U.S. State Department officials acted on their own understandings of push and pull, imagining push as political threat and mobilizing political will to enhance enforcement in response to racialized migration crises. In what follows, we examine how the recurrent invocation of crisis resulted in the development of an onshore deterrence infrastructure.

Militarizing Migration

The Politics of Asylum and Deterrence

The sheer number of boats arriving on south Florida shores from Cuba during a relatively short period of 168 days created a visual spectacle that informed perceptions of crisis (Noble 2011, 41). While aspects of the boatlift and the departures were organized, many elements were chaotic and rumor-filled. Traffic was moving in two directions at once: boats departing from Cuba to Florida and charter boats departing from Florida to Cuba to bring residents' families to the United States (48). While U.S. and Cuban coast guard authorities tried to maintain a semblance of order, the volume of people and ships in need of assistance caused the U.S. Coast Guard (USCG) to abandon some standard operating procedures, such as paperwork completion and exchange of details between crews and commanding officers (49). An untold and surely undercounted number of travelers also died at sea. Political rumors abounded in both countries about migration policies and Castro's political motivations for allowing the mass departure. Among the most lasting of these rumors was that Castro was ridding his country of political opponents and other "undesirables" by emptying prisons and mental hospitals (Hawk et al. 2014, 32–33).

Cold War geopolitics informed Jimmy Carter's first public response to the events on May 5, 1980 nearly two weeks into the boatlift. By this time, some ten thousand Cubans had arrived, and the United States was opening a staging area on Eglin Air Force Base (AFB) in northwest Florida

(187). During a question-and-answer period following a speech he delivered to the Biennial National Convention of the League of Women Voters, Carter applauded the state of Florida for its contributions, and explained that he had formed a multi-agency response. "We'll continue to provide an open heart and open arms to refugees seeking freedom from Communist domination and from economic deprivation, brought about primarily by Fidel Castro and his government" (in Noble 2011, 53). His statement was interpreted widely as indicating an open-door policy to Cubans seeking to leave. Jack Watson, a presidential assistant in the Carter White House, observed that the remarks were not meant to signal "go ahead and break our laws," but the statement of welcome nonetheless "caused us problems" (Hawk et al. 2014, 188).

This chapter shows how deterrence was consolidated as a cornerstone of American asylum and migration policy in order to prevent another Mariel crisis. As discussed in the introduction, U.S. deterrence operations have not been isolated to the United States–Mexico boundary. Rather, we trace how a coordinated transnational, onshore-offshore deterrence policy evolved as a response to the 1980 "Cuban-Haitian crisis," which White House policy staffer Donna Alvarado regarded as "a precedent for the U.S. as a country of mass first asylum."[1] We focus on the centrality of military base infrastructure to this mass asylum moment and subsequent development of detention. Military bases were used for immediate confinement purposes, considered in planning exercises to develop contingency space in the event of another mass migration, and maintained for longer-term detention facilities. The search for active-duty and mothballed military bases that might be used immediately and in the future began during the Mariel crisis, led first by the Federal Emergency Management Agency (FEMA) and then by the joint military-civilian Cuban-Haitian Task Force (CHTF) established on July 15, 1980.[2]

THE MARIEL CRISIS ENSUES

Ambassador Vince Palmieri called Carter's open arms remarks a "disaster because it showed how much confusion there was" (Hawk et al. 2014, 188). Indeed, as arrivals continued, the administration's response was increasingly characterized by confusion, indecision, and—eventually—reversal. White House staff, the National Security Council (NSC), Coast Guard first responders, and the Departments of State, Justice (DOJ), and

Treasury were all upset (Noble 2011, 43). As historian Dennis L. Noble observes, "The Carter administration seemed to throw one federal agency after another at the problem . . . yet there seemed no clear lines of cooperation or reporting between agencies, groups, or the White House" (73). One day after his May 5 luncheon statement, Carter declared a state of emergency in southern Florida (Shull 2014a, 14). The political situation in the state was volatile. A plane circled Eglin AFB towing a banner warning, "The KKK is here," and the Klan rallied soon thereafter (Hawk et al. 2014, 183, 227).

On May 14, Carter shifted policy and issued a "five-point plan," which was intended to bring order to the mass migration by regulating the boatlift and instituting an airlift. The plan involved screening potential emigrants in Cuba—with special preference given to those with family members in the United States, former political prisoners, and those who had already sought refuge from the Peruvian embassy in Havana. The plan also proposed criminal and civil sanctions on boat operators (228). The USCG operationalized this plan with the design and coordination of fifteen boarding teams to meet incoming vessels. It also began a public-relations effort encouraging all U.S. citizens, many of whom were Cuban Americans using their boats to transport Cubans to the United States, to return to Florida from Cuban ports (Noble 2011, 62). (Carter had lifted travel restrictions on U.S. citizens in 1977.) Carter stepped up these efforts on May 15 by issuing an announcement that the United States would begin blockading the Florida coast (Hawk et al. 2014, 228). On June 3, Carter called up six hundred Coast Guard reservists (Noble 2011, 71). In early June, a volunteer force of private citizens entered the fray, patrolling in small private boats as a U.S. Coast Guard auxiliary (69–70). By mid-June, the acute crisis had subsided and arrivals largely ended by October. What happened to the people who were on those boats, and how did the legacy of this moment inform government planning?

Once the Mariel crisis appeared to be under control at sea, the crisis continued to unfold on land, as depicted in the provisional shelter under a highway overpass in downtown Miami in figure 3. The punctuated moment would also extend for years to come—what we refer to as the Long Mariel crisis—and continue to inform policy-making, administrative planning, and political decision-making. The United States had been welcoming Cubans taking flight from Castro's communist regime since the diplomatic break between the two countries in 1961. Yet the

FIGURE 3. "Mariel refugees in downtown Miami." This is the title that photographer Michael Carlebach gave to this image of an ad hoc encampment beneath a freeway overpass that was used to house people arriving from the Mariel Boatlift. Other civilian spaces in Miami that were used included hotels and a football stadium. The image depicts several tents with cots, a row of portable toilets, and a truck that appears to be delivering items to people living onsite. (Copyright Michael L. Carlebach, 1980. Reprinted with permission of Michael L. Carlebach. Courtesy of University of Miami Library Special Collections.)

Marielitos, as this group came to be known, were different in ways that led to their being broadly categorized as "undesirable." Not only did this group comprise more Afro-Cubans and working-class people than earlier arrivals, the presence of so many young, single men was often noted (Shull 2014a, 14). As were women sex workers who became "very actively engaged in their profession" upon arriving in the United States (Hawk et al. 2014, 186). Many of the people arriving were gay. While the INS had issued a policy guideline in 1979 stating that homosexuality should no longer be used as the only grounds of exclusion, it was not until 1990 that "sexual deviation" was removed from the Immigration and Nationality Act (INA) as a medical ground for exclusion.[3]

The Long Mariel crisis would continue to be shaped by these discourses. White House staffer Eugene Eidenberg attributed the cool welcome that many new arrivals received to the existing Cuban American community:

FIGURE 4. The Ku Klux Klan gathered outside Fort Chaffee to protest the presence of Cubans whom the U.S. government was holding on the base. This image shows several people wearing Klan hoods and robes. In the foreground, a woman holds a large U.S. flag. Behind her, a boy carries what appears to be a Confederate flag and in the other hand a bunch of newspapers with a headline reading, "White people wake up!" (Reprinted with permission of Museum of Chaffee History.)

> Initially, the first boats, as far as I can tell, were just families. . . . It was not the prostitutes and homosexuals that turned the tide—it was the young black ones. There was a deep-seated racial tension in the Cuban community, which was basically an Anglo-Cuban community (Hawk et al. 2014, 188).

It is clear that these sentiments were not isolated to the Cuban American community. The Mariel arrivals challenged the neatly drawn and geopoliticized categories of refugees into which U.S. immigration and refugee policies sorted populations. On the one hand, they were victims fleeing communism and thereby welcomed by the United States. At the same time, they were quickly cast as unruly, racialized, unexpected, and undesirable migrants whose arrivals resulted in costly expenditures of resources and political will.

The Mariel Cubans' fate once within the United States reflected the blurring between humanitarianism and militarism evident with the

FIGURE 5. The Ku Klux Klan protest outside Fort Chaffee echoed those held earlier in Florida. This image shows a line of people, some of whom are wearing Klan garb, standing evenly spaced along a road. Each person is holding a handwritten sign with different messages, including, "We do not support communist criminals," "Send them to peanuts," "Carter you want the Cubans you take them," "Fight Jewish communism," "Will it be Christ or Anti-Christ," "Today Miami, tomorrow U.S.A.," and "Ku Klux Klan pride of the land." (Reprinted with permission of Museum of Chaffee History.)

resettlement of Southeast Asian refugees. Many of the Cubans who arrived in 1980 were placed with families or resettled in Florida, while those who could not be resettled immediately were sent to military bases: Eglin Air Force Base in Florida, Fort Chaffee in Arkansas, Fort Indiantown Gap in Pennsylvania, and Fort McCoy in Wisconsin. These remaining individuals would soon be consolidated at Fort Chaffee, which previously had been used in the resettlement of Vietnamese refugees.

This group of Cubans would not receive the same welcome, however. As the first flight of Cubans arrived, a retired Marine dressed in full Klan garb ran onto the tarmac to protest their arrival (Lipman 2014, 72). The Klan later staged a demonstration on the perimeter of the base (see figures 4 and 5). Arkansas state representative Carolyn Pollan sent a mailgram to President Carter, reading, "Keep your word. No more Cuban refugees at Fort Chaffee Arkansas. Thousands in area angry."[4] Governor Bill Clinton activated sixty-five members of the state's National Guard to patrol Chaffee following a series of demonstrations by the Cubans held there (Department of the Army 1982, III-I-A-I).

RESOLVING POLITICAL CRISES THROUGH CONTINGENCY PLANNING

The Long Mariel crisis consumed the 1980 presidential and Arkansas gubernatorial elections. Candidate Ronald Reagan criticized Carter for failing to respond quickly enough, and amplified the American exceptionalist narrative of the United States as a nation of refuge in his GOP nomination speech:

> Can we doubt that only a Divine Providence placed this land, this island of freedom here as a refuge for all those people who yearn to breathe free? Jews and Christians enduring persecution behind the Iron Curtain; the boat people of Southeast Asia, Cuba, and of Haiti; the victims of drought and famine in Africa; the freedom fighters of Afghanistan (in Loescher and Scanlan 1986, 188).

Interestingly, this campaign statement flagged Haitians as among other persecuted groups that the United States would welcome. Despite this equalizing rhetoric, his speech also signaled the Cold War framing that would inform Reagan's approach to refugee and asylum issues. It soon became evident that his administration would not open doors equally to all groups.

Policy aide in the Reagan White House, Joe Ghougassian, believed that the Carter administration had "made a grave error" in having White House staff rather than the Coordinator for Refugee Affairs handle the crisis: "Refugee issues are politically explosive; it is best if the burst occurs miles away from the President's office."[5] The explosiveness of the Cuban refugee issue was underscored by the election in Arkansas where Clinton lost the governorship to Republican Frank White, who ran on closing Fort Chaffee (Maddux 2005; Sartori 2001). Once in office, White maintained close contact with the White House, reminding the president that the situation at Chaffee was "seriously damaging my political credibility and future."[6]

The need for contingency planning was an immediate lesson that the Reagan administration drew from Mariel. In assembling a team to develop refugee and immigration policy, Frank Hodsoll, a member of

Reagan's transition staff in the Office of the Chief of Staff, identified a list of issues that would need immediate decisions and action. Among these were solutions to the five thousand to six thousand Cubans still confined at Fort Chaffee, considered "largely criminals and emotionally malad-justed," the "several hundred Haitians (433) still in camps on former NIKE bases in Florida," "negotiations with the Cubans to prevent further 'Freedom Flotillas' and repatriate Cuban criminals," and the possibility that the Bahamas may expel fifteen thousand Haitians, who would then "likely try to come to Florida." The National Security Council would continue to play a role in the development of policy, but Hodsoll, like Ghougassian, did not believe that such guidance should "come (as it did in the Carter Administration) directly from the West Wing."[7]

ENTRY AND EXCLUDABILITY

In the final days of the Carter administration, Attorney General Benjamin Civiletti informed the president that legal injunctions from the *HRC v. Civiletti* case preventing exclusion hearings for Haitians had been lifted, and that the INS (Immigration and Naturalization Service) intended to resume them.[8] As William French Smith assumed duties as Attorney General, his assistant Charles Renfrew advised him that resuming the hearings would undoubtedly engender criticism and new litigation. Because of expected delays to an already lengthy hearing process, a backlog of four thousand cases since October 1980, and arrivals of approximately three hundred Haitians weekly, Renfrew concluded, "It is highly questionable whether the above exclusion program can be truly effective even with substantially increased resources." He advised that three additional measures should be considered: legislation authorizing Coast Guard interdictions, emergency waivers of the "normal exclusion process," and the construction of more detention space. "[F]or any exclusion program to have significant deterrent effect, the illegal aliens must be held in custody during the exclusion process."[9]

This memo includes the basic ingredients of the two-pronged deterrence program that the Reagan administration would roll out in his first year in office: mandatory detention and interception at sea. The premise that detention would serve as a deterrent relied on funneling entrants into exclusion proceedings, rather than paroling entrants based upon determination of status. The distinction at the time within immigration law between exclusion and deportation rests on a dubious legal geography over "entry" to the United States, over which the executive branch exercises tremendous authority under the plenary power doctrine. According to the INA, an "excludable alien" is one who seeks to enter, but has not yet entered, the United States, whereas a "deportable alien" has already entered U.S. territory. The question becomes where and what constitute "entry," answers that are neither obvious nor as simple as they might seem (Weinberg 1984–1985, 582). Legal scholar Margaret Taylor (1995, 1096) explains: "Neither parole nor detention within the United States counts as an 'entry' under immigration law. Instead, under a legal fiction sometimes known as the 'entry doctrine,' excludable aliens are 'treated as if stopped at the border.'" This legal distinction was deeply consequential. Described as possessing "virtually no constitutional rights," excludable aliens could not petition an immigration judge for release and faced indefinite detention (1098).

Cuban and Haitian people who came to the United States in 1980 were classified as "Cuban-Haitian entrants (status pending)." This legal designation built on country-specific legislation designed for Cuban nationals, beginning in 1966 with the Cuban Adjustment Act (Rusin et al. 2015, 1). While distinct from the definition of refugees provided under the 1980 Refugee Act, this group was in some ways treated like refugees, but in others more like migrants seeking entry. Under Carter's Executive Order 12251, Health and Human Services (HHS) was tasked with housing and resettling "Cuban-Haitian entrants (status-pending)." But as historian Jana Lipman explains, Cuban-Haitian entrants who were still being held in refugee camps were

> legally equivalent to being stopped at border control or an immigration checkpoint in an airport. This doublespeak created a material contradiction between Cubans and Haitians' *legal* status and their *physical* status. Even if they waited for weeks or months on US soil, legally, Cubans and Haitians were not *in* the United States until they were paroled with a sponsor (hence the "status pending" designation) (2013, 123, emphasis in original).

This liminal administrative and legal category blurred the line between refugee and unauthorized migrant, and hence the roles of HHS and the INS.[10] The designation also blurred the legal geography of status and access to rights; although people were physically on sovereign territory, their legal designation as not yet having "entered" sovereign territory mediates access to asylum. The search for space to house, detain, process, and resettle these migrants reveals the nebulous quality of the category and also the growing power of the Justice Department's (DOJ) definition of the situation.

CLOSING FORT CHAFFEE

In July 1981, Attorney General Smith sent President Reagan a memo with recommendations from the President's Task Force on Immigration and Refugee Policy, which was investigating options for resolving three interrelated issues: detention and housing for Cubans still held at Fort Chaffee; planning for an "immigration emergency (e.g., Mariel boatlift)," and establishing detention as a removal and deterrent policy. Smith wrote, "All 950 Cubans remaining at Fort Chaffee have problems that prevent their release into the community (250 mentally ill and retarded; 400 antisocial; 100 homosexual; 100 alcoholics or drug users; 100 women, babies, elderly, and handicapped)."[11] Over the coming months and years, this group of Cubans—whom the Carter and Reagan administrations referred to privately and publicly as *undesirables, excludables,* and *incorrigibles*—would be moved to federal prisons and to state and federal health-care facilities.[12] The State Department, meanwhile, was tasked with negotiating with Cuba for their return.

In the immediate term, three facilities had been identified for both detention and hospitalization: a Naval Training Center in Bainbridge, Maryland; the Port Isabel Service Processing Center in Los Fresnos, Texas, which was operated by the Immigration and Naturalization Service; and Ellington Air Force Base, a facility near Houston, Texas, that was partially used by the National Air and Space Administration (NASA), the Texas National Guard, the Coast Guard, and the U.S. Army Reserve. The Bainbridge and Port Isabel sites also had the space necessary for detaining ten thousand to twenty thousand people on an emergency or long-term basis. These two sites were located in "relatively isolated areas, but the costs of providing services would not be prohibitive." And unlike Ellington, a suburban location where community opposition "would be considerable," only limited objection was expected.[13]

The Attorney General's memo listed another eleven civilian and military facilities across the country that had been "considered and found inadequate." Below, we quote the list directly from this memo, which names the sites and provides notes for consideration on their suitability (or lack thereof) as potential sites for detention:

1. Matagorda Island Air Force Range

   Five miles off Gulf Coast of Texas, near Port O'Connor. Barrier island with significant environmental/legal problems; high cost of transporting services.

2. Hamilton Air Force Base

    Marin County, California. Suburban residential area. Litigation pending involving legal title, environmental questions, and planned conflicting local use.

3. Almaden Air Force Station

    Santa Clara County, California. Existing structures in disrepair and unsuitable (single-family units). Mountain-top site with severely limited capacity for expansion.

4. V.A. Medical Center, Augusta

    Outside Augusta, Georgia. Located in suburban residential area.

5. Highlands Air Defense Site

    Highlands, New Jersey (60 miles from New York City). Capacity limited to less than 500.

6. Roanoke Rapids Air Force Station

    Roanoke Rapids, North Carolina. Limited capacity; extensive improvements in sewage and water plant necessary.

7. U.S. Naval Home

    Downtown Philadelphia, Pennsylvania. Limited capacity; concentrated urban environment.

8. Sault St. Marie Air Force Station, Minnesota

    Small facility; extreme climate; structures unsuitable for detention.

9. Fort Jefferson National Monument, Florida

    Sixty-eight miles west of Key West. Historic structure; no other facilities; environmental/legal challenges likely; high cost.

10. Ellis Island, New York

    New York Harbor, one mile from Manhattan. No utilities; structures in bad repair; historic site.

11. Alcatraz, California

    San Francisco Bay, one and one-half miles from mainland. Essentially no utilities; historic site; popular tourist attraction.[14]

The geographical and jurisdictional span of surveyed spaces is vast and includes several sites that seem patently improbable, save for being islands. The reasons cited for their rejection hint at the operational and political categories informing the search for detention space: federal property, capacity for detention, location, and viability (political, legal, and logistical).

But this list is also far from complete, and does not include many spaces that had been considered or were concurrently being negotiated (see map 3). Within weeks, Bainbridge, Ellington, and Port Isabel would be rejected on "political or cost grounds," and new sites would be at the top of the list.[15] Defense Department (DOD) objectives and "domestic politics" alike would influence site decisions. Objections from military officials, local elected officials, and the latter's constituents would prove decisive in eliminating a site from further consideration. In the case of Ellington outside of Houston, community opposition was considerable indeed. Congressperson Ron Paul held a hearing attended by two hundred people who overwhelmingly opposed the facility. One woman reiterated several of the common tropes circulating about Mariel Cubans: "I don't want to see my house robbed or homosexuality brought in."[16] She further predicted, "If you bring them in here you're opening a can of worms. I don't want to see my children or my neighbors raped or murdered." The mayor of Pasadena, Texas, wrote to the White House that the city was "vehemently opposed to any conversion of Ellington Air Force Base to a refugee detention center." He invoked damage to Pasadena's tax base that he anticipated from the "negative values" of a refugee camp, Ellington's "very vital contribution to NASA operations," and national defense as the reasons for the city's opposition.[17]

In the case of Bainbridge, Maryland Governor Harry Hughes and Congressperson Roy Dyson sent a letter to the Office of Refugee Resettlement (ORR) with several questions about the legality of transferring Cuban and Haitian refugees to Bainbridge: "What is the projected role for Bainbridge in the refugee program? Will it be a holding center? a processing center?" The officials were aware of the legal and political conflicts that surrounded the use of Fort Allen, Puerto Rico, which we will discuss later in the chapter. Given the "apparent parallel" between Fort Allen and the plan for Bainbridge, they asked for information about assessments of the refugees' needs, availability of other facilities, efficiency of relocation from Chaffee, improvements that would need to be made to the water supply and sewage systems at Bainbridge, and compliance with the Coastal Zone Management Act. They requested a prompt reply with documentation, which they intended to "examine and copy the evaluations and analyses."[18] While the letter did not directly refuse the project, it did make clear that the state would fully vet a facility, a process that would delay resolution of an urgent problem.

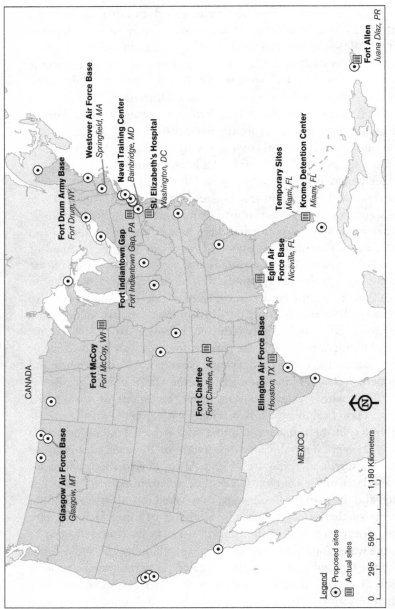

MAP 3. Sites used and proposed for detention expansion. Based on archival data, this map shows all sites under discussion and ultimately used as sites of detention in 1980 and 1981. (Sources: Attorney General to the President, 6 July 1981, Box 51, "INS—Detention Facilities" Folder, AG, NARAII. Caspar Weinberger to James Baker III, 7 July 1981, Box 8, "Detention Center and Chaffee Working (2)" Folder, PTFIRP, RRPL. Kate Moore to Frank Hodsoll, 23 July 1981, Box 8, "Detention Center and Chaffee Working (4)" Folder, PTFIRP, RRPL. Immigration Detention Policy [n.a], 14 September 1981, Box 2, "Cuban-Haitian [5]" Folder, KM, RRPL. Kate Moore to James Baker III, 6 November 1981, Box 8, "Detention Center and Chaffee Working (9)" Folder, PTFIRP, RRPL.)

Caption for map 3 continues: In addition to the sites included in the previous list, the following proposed sites are depicted but *not labeled* on the map.

Alamaden Air Force Station, Santa Clara County, CA

Alcatraz, CA

Camp Atterbury, near Edinburgh, IN

Camp Parks, Dublin, CA

Caswell Air Force Station, Limestone, ME

Ellis Island, NY

Fort Dix, New Hanover Township, NJ

Fort Jefferson National Monument, 68 miles west of Key West, FL

Fort Leonard Wood Army base, near Waynesville, MO

Hamilton Air Force Base, Marin County, CA

Havre Air Force Station, Havre, MT

Highlands Air Defense Site, Highlands, NJ

Lockport Air Force Station, Lockport, NY

Matagorda Island Air Force Range, Port O'Connor, TX

Minot Air Force Station, Minot, ND

Naval Hospital, Philadelphia, PN

Navy base, Imperial Beach, CA

Navy complex, Portsmouth, NH

Opheim Air Force Station, Opheim, MT

Port Isabel Service Processing Center, Los Fresnos, TX

Ramey Air Force Base, Aguadilla, Puerto Rico

Richards-Gebaur Air Reserve Station, Kansas City, MO

Rickenbacker Air Force Base, Columbus, OH

Roanoke Rapids Air Force Station, Roanoke Rapids, NC

Sault St. Marie Air Force Station, Sault St. Marie, MI

U.S. Naval Home, Downtown Philadelphia, PN

V.A. Medical Center, Augusta, GA

The shifting set of sites considered by the Reagan administration provides insight into the political forces shaping the options the government weighed. Electoral politics was a clear factor in decision-making. Following two cabinet meetings in July 1981 at which relocating the Cubans at Chaffee was discussed, President Reagan expressed support for using Bainbridge and "interest in exploring the use of Guantanamo" for this purpose.[19] Bainbridge, described in a local newspaper as a "crumbling, rotting, and overgrown reservation," would require complete rebuilding, with projected construction costs of $40,000/person and operations costs of $40,000/person annually.[20] While expensive, they were consistent with Bureau of Prisons (BOP) construction costs and approved by the Office of Management and Budget (OMB). However, Hodsoll noted that "moving the Ft. Chaffee population on a temporary basis to Bainbridge could be dangerous (they could tear down the buildings; and we would not have adequate medical facilities) and would be very adverse from a political view (clearly favoring Arkansas over Maryland)."[21] Indeed, the Maryland congressional delegation publicly opposed the project, and its members were insulted that local officials had not been consulted.[22]

Hodsoll consulted with the Department of Defense and informed the President's Counselor Ed Meese III, Chief of Staff Jim Baker, and Deputy Chief of Staff Mike Deaver that Defense considered Guantánamo to be "unsuitable."

Virtually all of its physical plant suitable for housing is being utilized; DOD states that the treaty leasing Guantanamo to the U.S. provides that it can be used only as a coaling station. Detention of the Chaffee population here could be used by the Cubans as a reason for cancelling the agreement, and forcing us out. DOD is also worried that Castro might turn loose additional Cubans at Guantanamo if we housed these Cubans there. . . .

While undesirable from the point of view of Guantanamo's status in relation to Cuba and of similar (but somewhat greater) difficulties to Bainbridge in terms of construction, domestic politics would be best served by putting these people in Guantanamo. But we would still have an at least 6-9 month wait and at least $40 million in construction. State will have a view on use of Guantanamo by Friday.[23]

The irony that the detention of Cubans on Guantánamo threatened the U.S. Navy's lease of a refueling station (and not its military uses) speaks to the political contingency of this imperial site, or the appearance of contingency, that Defense advanced to decline it being used to confine migrants. By November 1981, the State Department still had not produced its views, and the question remained as to the Navy's authority to detain civilians—a haunting foreshadowing of legal battles to come years later. An attorney in the Department of Justice had concluded that he did not believe that the base at Guantánamo was part of the United States for the purposes of the Immigration and Nationality Act.[24]

Even before Guantánamo was floated as a potential site for detention, Defense Secretary Caspar Weinberger had informed the Attorney General, as chair of the President's Task Force on Immigration and Refugee Policy, that as "a matter of policy, we should not plan to use Defense Department resources to handle illegal entrants."[25] While Weinberger recognized the difficulties other agencies faced, he asserted that "it would not be in the national interest to divert Department of Defense personnel and facilities from their primary purpose, nor would it be consistent with the traditional practice of avoiding the assignment of military resources to civilian functions."[26] Although Guantánamo would not be used systematically until years later, a development that we discuss in chapter 5, Hodsoll's concern regarding domestic politics suggests that these implications actually would outweigh Defense objections.

Glasgow, Montana

When inquiring about Guantánamo, Hodsoll learned about an entirely different set of decommissioned U.S. Air Force radar stations located throughout the continental United States that were available for use. A table on the second page of the memo lists the location of the radar stations together with information about the sites' congressional districts, congresspersons, and other comments. Representatives Don Clausen (R-California) and Clair Burgener (R-California) were each noted as a "good friend," and Olympia Snowe (R-Maine) and Jim Jeffords (R-Vermont) represented swing votes.[27] In short, "Legislative Affairs indicated that all of the locations present political problems. Virtually all are located in Republican Congressional districts—districts where there are critical swing votes, or good friends who would feel 'stabbed in the back.'"[28]

In addition to these political considerations, the Department of Health and Human Services assessed the operational viability of the decommissioned radar stations. Bright yellow highlighter was used to demarcate the locations of these obsolete facilities on a map of the continental United States. Most were located along the United States–Canada boundary. They had been part of an array of Air Force radar stations comprising the Air Defense Command built at the outset of the Korean War. The HHS review concluded that the two sites in California (Klamath and Mount Laguna) would be suitable, but "properties on the northern border all have the basic problem of climate, logistical support and staff availability."[29] (California and Maine had begun converting such sites into detention facilities, and New York was considering doing the same.)[30]

Despite these issues of cold winters and availability of staff, another former Air Force facility near the Canadian border in Glasgow, Montana, would become the "only one viable option" for immediate use.[31] Hodsoll described Glasgow as a "boom town with temporary construction workers for a natural gas pipeline currently being constructed." A private contractor (based in Washington, D.C.) was "prepared to take on and try to rehabilitate the worst half of the Chaffee population (450 anti-socials)."[32] The Air Force base had been converted into an industrial park. Negotiations over its use involved HHS's Office of Refugee Resettlement and the INS, and would stretch well over a year. During this time, the rationale for the facility shifted from resolving the Chaffee crisis to operating a detention facility for Haitians held at Krome. To secure this site, administration officials made efforts to lobby members of Congress to remove known opposition. Republican Representative Ron Marlenee, who lived fifty miles away, had threatened to "write us a letter 'putting a hold on the matter' no matter how the Glasgow City Council comes out."[33] Hodsoll suggested that the administration "should be prepared to sweeten the pot for Glasgow."[34] A few days later, following discussions, Marlenee had a "change of heart" and dropped his opposition.[35]

News that the industrial park would be used as an INS detention center created a new opponent. Local Native American tribes (not named in the correspondence) raised concerns about the legality of the facility under the National Environmental Policy Act (NEPA), signed into law by President Richard Nixon in 1970.[36] To prepare for such a lawsuit, Kathryn Oberly, special litigation counsel for the Land and Natural Resources Division at the Department of Justice, wrote David Crosland, General Counsel for the INS, with two recommendations:

> First, the initial population to be housed at Glasgow should be limited to "Cuban/Haitian Entrants" as defined in the Refugee Education Assistance Act of 1980. If it is, we can avail ourselves of the NEPA exemption contained in that statute. If, at a later date, INS wants to introduce other nationalities into the facility, it would be relatively easy to argue that the environmental impact of substituting, say, a Nicaraguan for a Haitian is zero, and thus no EIS would be required for a change in nationalities once the facility is operational. If, however, the facility starts off as a multi-national operation, the REAA exemption will be unavailable.
>
> Second, I strongly recommend that INS quickly prepare an environmental assessment and a "negative declaration," in which you determine, if feasible, that the Glasgow project is not a major action significantly affecting the quality of the human environment and hence no EIS is required. This should be done regardless of the initial make-up of the population, as extra insurance against the possibility that a court will find the REAA exemption inapplicable.[37]

This memo is revealing in its candid assessment of how the INS could use refugee and environmental legislation to avoid litigation and advance its detention objectives. If this strategy had been pursued, and it does not appear to have been, forms of protection offered through refugee and environmental regulations would be twisted into the means for expanding carceral space ("substituting, say, a Nicaraguan for a Haitian"). This breezy interchangeability of people suggests the overriding presumption of detention for asylees. Positing detention as "not a major action affecting the quality of the human environment" would render the carceral space and people held within it as unhuman.

As of October 1981, Glasgow remained the preferable site, but a series of developments would diminish its desirability in the coming months. These included the continued "outplacing" of the Chaffee population, including to Atlanta Federal Correctional Institution and state hospitals, and new demands from the Glasgow industrial park for a

Federal Housing Administration (FHA) loan to finance a drug and alco-hol treatment center.[38] Perhaps most importantly, at some point in late 1981, the INS took over negotiations for the Glasgow site from HHS.[39] Given Attorney General Smith's commitment to constructing more detention space for deterrence, the Glasgow site was less than ideal. Ongoing crises over Krome and Haitian migration to Florida provided him with additional rationales to push for new facilities "in the south-ern part of the country."[40] In the meantime, Hodsoll explained that the Attorney General regarded Fort Chaffee as "the ideal place for both Cubans and Haitians, and that moving Cubans to Glasgow will be expensive and could be criticized."[41]

Of course, keeping Chaffee open was not viable because President Reagan had assured Governor White of his intention to close the facil-ity.[42] But Smith was correct that the Glasgow proposal would be criti-cized. Michael Horowitz, general counsel in the OMB, wrote in Sep-tember 1981 that the "decision to build a new detention facility in Glasgow, Montana may have been made (at an annual cost of over $36 million, and in the face of charges that exposure of tropical dwellers to the freezing temperatures of Montana is literally brutal), but it is a tem-porary solution at best."[43] The *Miami Herald* compared the proposal to the cruelty of the Soviet gulag: "In the Soviet Union, criminals and political dissidents are sent to the Arctic zone, where they are put to hard labor as punishment. The Government's consideration of Mon-tana smacks of a send-them-to-Siberia attitude" (Miller 1984, 133).

NEGOTIATING FORT ALLEN

In the midst of efforts to negotiate the Glasgow, Montana, site and close the refugee camp at Fort Chaffee, the Department of Justice had resumed efforts begun under the Carter administration to open a detention facil-ity at Fort Allen, a former military base near Ponce, Puerto Rico. After the Cuban-Haitian Task Force announced in September 1980 that the administration would relocate Cuban-Haitian entrants, and soon only Haitians, to the base, the Commonwealth of Puerto Rico and its munic-ipalities successfully sued to block the fort's use on environmental grounds. The next day, Carter issued Executive Order 12244, which exempted the base from the Federal Water Pollution Control, Clean Air, Noise Control, and Solid Waste Disposal Acts.[44] Preparations to activate the site continued in anticipation of a legal resolution, but the restraining order remained in effect when Reagan took office.

A series of developments in the spring and summer of 1981 prompted a renewed effort to open Fort Allen for detention purposes. In late May 1981, the INS in south Florida began detaining Haitians seeking entry without authorization, a new policy of detention for deterrence that President Reagan would not announce until July 31, 1981 (Weinberg 1984–1985, 577; Helton 1986, 358). In articulating the objective of the policy, Attorney General Smith explained to President Reagan that "the Administration [should] detain rather than release illegals pending exclusion hearings. This is now the policy in the southwest (e.g., Mexicans) and was the policy in Florida (e.g., Haitians) until 1977."[45]

Smith downplayed the scope of his policy change, while also touting it as the tough new measure needed to restore integrity to the border. Yet legal advocates and scholars have interpreted the Reagan administration's revival of mandatory detention as a significant historical departure. The INS had ended its policy of mass detention (as at Ellis and Angel Islands) in 1954 (Gwynn 1986; Helton 1986; Simon 1998). To then Attorney General Herbert Brownell Jr., his new parole policy represented "one more step forward toward a humane administration of the immigration laws." In 1958, the Supreme Court underscored Brownell's statement: "The parole of aliens seeking admission is simply a device through which needless confinement is avoided while administrative proceedings are conducted. . . . Physical detention of aliens is now the exception, not the rule, and is generally employed only as to security risks or those likely to abscond" (in Helton 1986, 355).

Given this renewed commitment to detention, the numbers of people held by the INS rapidly outstripped its infrastructure. While Attorney General Smith often cited the steady arrivals of Haitians as a rationale for more detention space, his choice of examples is telling; equating Haitian and Mexican migrants obscures asylum rights by invoking the common sense of Mexican excludability, naturalizing detention as a tool of border control. Moreover, he also sidestepped the reality that the lengthy periods that Haitians spent in detention as asylum seekers contributed to soaring confinement numbers and times. Smith's comparison to the situation in the southwest for Mexican nationals, moreover, obfuscates another legal category: that of "voluntary departure." An artful legal term, "voluntary departure" refers to the "departure of an alien from the United States without an order of removal." A person who is "allowed to voluntarily depart concedes removability but does not have a bar to seeking admission at a port-of-entry at any time."[46] For people in deportation or removal proceedings or held in detention, the possibility of accepting a "voluntary departure" can result in less time in detention and in not having a removal or deportation record, which would result in a ban on entry that lasts for some period of time. The voluntariness of electing this form of return is, of course, questionable in carceral conditions, but the prevalence of "voluntary departure" makes the comparison between Mexican and Haitian nationals deeply misleading. In 1975, 92 percent of the people held in detention were Mexican, and 84 percent of people detained elected voluntary departure, with the average time in detention being 3.2 days (Taylor 1995, 1099). In contrast, the General Accounting Office (GAO) (1983, 6) found that between May 1981, when the new detention policy was instituted, and June 1982, 1,300 of the 2,700 Haitians were held at Krome for nine to twelve months. Smith and others in the administration blamed legal advocates for this situation, assiduously avoiding the reality that the detention policy itself undermined asylum rights.

Because the legal injunction preventing exclusion hearings for Haitians had been lifted in December 1980, the INS incredibly began to conduct mass exclusion proceedings, and brazenly refused to allow attorneys to be present. On June 11, 1981, the Haitian Refugee Center (HRC), along with the National Emergency Civil Liberties Committee (NECLC), the National Council of Churches (NCC), and the American Civil Liberties Union (ACLU), sued, in *Marie Lucie Jean v. Meissner,* to halt the hearings and prevent the deportations of ninety Haitians who had been ordered deported (Kurzban 1983–1984, 41). The government removed eleven people to Haiti by the time advocates won a temporary restraining order preventing further deportations and requiring new hearings (Gwynn 1986, 343).

The next significant development prompting action on Fort Allen came two months after the implementation of mandatory detention. On July 17, 1981, Florida Governor Bob Graham sued the INS over conditions at Krome. In a letter to Attorney General Smith sent two days before filing suit, Graham wrote:

> An emergency situation exists at the Krome North facility for Haitian entrants in Dade County, Florida. The current population is in excess of 1,600. An unknown number of additional Haitian refugees is expected within 24 hours. The water and sewer systems are not functioning, creating extremely unsanitary conditions and a public health hazard to the Haitian population and staff within the Krome Center, as well as the general South Florida community.[47]

His letter further detailed a series of demands concerning Krome and migration facilities in Florida that Graham had been raising for months.[48] First, the Krome facility must meet the state of Florida's public health standards. Second, a plan should be made to transfer detainees out of Florida to reduce Krome to the "design capacity" of 524 people. Third, no one detained at Krome should be released into Florida except for those reuniting with family members. Fourth, no new resettlement or detention facilities should be placed in Florida. Fifth, all entrants should continue to be screened medically. Finally, Graham called for the U.S. Coast Guard to increase its patrols and share information with the state regarding potential arrivals.

Governor Graham's lawsuit citing poor health conditions at Krome was not the first. Weeks before the Cuban-Haitian Task Force announced that it planned to use Fort Allen, the Dade County Department of Public Health had ordered a series of immediate improvements to the Krome South refugee camp.[49] At the time, Haitians were being held at Krome South and Cubans at Krome North, where conditions were only marginally better. Following the 1980 lawsuit, the Cuban-Haitian Task Force spent $5 million to improve Krome North as an INS "turnaround" site (Lipman 2013). The INS subsequently confined Haitian adults at Krome North and used Krome South, where conditions also continued to deteriorate, to confine unaccompanied Haitian minors (see figure 6).[50] Images of the Krome camp taken by photographer Michael Carlebach show sparse interior and exterior spaces surrounded by barbed wire where adults tried to find shade and children made play spaces.

On the same day that the state of Florida sued the Justice Department, the INS began moving Haitians out of Krome to federal prisons and INS facilities scattered across the country. This led to further overcrowding within these systems and efforts to construct new detention facilities, developments that we detail in chapter 3. Associate Attorney General Rudolph Giuliani, meanwhile, traveled to Puerto Rico to negotiate an agreement to use Fort Allen. The Reagan White House believed that Carter's failure to consult with the Puerto Rican government had produced "a severe backlash," which became a political issue in the commonwealth's gubernatorial race.[51] Talks with Puerto Rican officials Governor Carlos Romero Barceló, Secretary of State Carlos Quirós, and San Juan Mayor Hernán Padilla would result in an agreement that reduced the number of people who could be confined there to eight hundred for no more than one year. Further, no Haitians would be resettled in Puerto Rico unless they had family members in the commonwealth.[52] In exchange for this "important favor," the Reagan administration appointed several people to ambassador positions.[53]

FIGURE 6. "Haitian refugee children playing soccer at Krome detention center." This is the title that photographer Michael Carlebach gave to this image of four Haitian children who managed to play within the sparse confines of Krome. (Copyright Michael L. Carlebach, 1980. Reprinted with permission of Michael L. Carlebach. Courtesy of University of Miami Library Special Collections.)

Since the administration had removed the major objections to the site, the circuit court judge lifted the injunction; the administration began transferring Haitians from Krome to Fort Allen on August 12.[54] The legal aid group near Ponce, meanwhile, refused to participate in hearings because they did not believe the federal government had authority to hold them and felt that "participation in INS hearings would be tantamount to recognition."[55]

Soon after the government's mass dispersal, the Haitians remaining in Krome engaged in a hunger strike. When INS officials attempted to remove the people they thought were leading the strike, Haitians resisted by throwing food and rocks, and shouting chants of "liberty or death" and "Miami is our country." They tore down the fence, and nearly one hundred people escaped from the facility. They were soon recaptured. Guards used tear gas to quell the unrest and transferred the people they named as "instigators" to a federal prison in Otisville, New York.[56] The Haitian community and their supporters in Miami mobilized a demonstration outside of the facility (see figure 7), led by Reverend Gérard Jean-Juste, to draw attention to the transfers, and "reports of beating

FIGURE 7. This photograph of a large demonstration outside of Krome organized by the Haitian community living in Miami connects the lives of people confined at Krome to U.S. foreign policy toward Haiti. Signs read, "Fight Racism Justice for Haitians," "US Hands Off Haiti," and "Freedom for Haitian Refugees in Louisiana." (Reprinted with permission of Americans for Immigrant Justice. Courtesy of Duke University, Rubenstein Library, Human Rights Archive.)

by guards, poor medical treatment for camp inmates [sic], assaults against women inmates [sic], and the imprisonment of children," the *Miami Herald* reported (Miller 1984, 129).

INTERDICTION POLICY

Soon after the first group of Haitians was transferred to Fort Allen, President Reagan announced his interdiction policy,[57] the second prong in the administration's deterrent policy. On September 29, 1981, he issued Executive Order 12324 authorizing the Coast Guard to intercept boats suspected of transporting Haitians who intended to enter the United States without authorization and return them to Port au Prince. That day, President Jean-Claude Duvalier had signed an agreement with the United States, authorizing the returns, and made assurances that people would not be subject to harm on their return. The first patrols by Coast Guard cutters in the Windward Passage between Haiti and Cuba began on October 10, and drew immediate criticism (see map 4). The *New York Times* derisively called the onboard hearings to assess fear of persecution "walrus courts" (Loescher and Scanlan 1984, 346). "The Administration resorts to walrus courts at sea because the Haitian cases have become a legal morass on land. About 2,500 are already backed up and, pending appeals, none can be concluded."[58]

Considerations for an interdiction plan had begun during the Carter administration. Arkansas Governor Clinton suggested that the departures of Cubans from Mariel could be curtailed "by stationing an aircraft carrier between Miami and Cuba and then processing the refugees before they ever get to Florida."[59] Carter also was interested in intercepting Haitians. In a previously confidential memo, Zbigniew Brzezinski and Eidenberg asked the State Department to explore the feasibility of establishing agreements with the governments of Haiti and the Bahamas to interdict and return boats transporting unauthorized Haitian migrants. "Our objective," they explained, "is simply to try to terminate the illegal flow of Haitians to the United States."[60]

The question of interdiction was a political and legal one. In addition to immediate issues of sovereignty over territory and territorial waters, the 1951 United Nations *Convention Relating to the Status of Refugees* and its 1967 Protocol prevents *non-refoulement*: forcible return to a country where someone has established a "well-founded fear" of persecution. The United States already had an agreement with the Bahamas for joint police operations in Bahamian waters, and had negotiated its earliest bilateral agreement with Haiti in 1981 (Paik 2013, 149). As the State Department negotiated with Haitian officials, the ambassador in Haiti emphasized that "we need to stress as much as possible that this is a joint effort and not simply a unilateral US interdiction of Haitin [sic] boat people."[61] The government of Haiti, for its part, "hoped that this cooperation would later extend to drug trafficking and contraband merchandise as well." The embassy also confirmed that Haiti's Interior Minister would arrange for Radio Haiti to "make broadcasts in Creole concerning interdiction efforts and the intended prosecution of trafficers [sic]."[62]

In advance of issuing the executive order, the Justice Department and White House counsel analyzed the legal authority for the president to direct the Coast Guard to interdict vessels. Fred Fielding, the Counsel to the President, concluded that "while the President's authority in this area is neither well-defined nor free from question," it appeared that existing statutes gave him the "requisite legal authority to initiate the proposed interdiction operation."[63] Fielding found principal authority through

MAP 4. Caribbean chokepoints (Yucatan Channel, Windward Passage, Mona Passage). Reproduced from the archives, this map illustrates authorities' geographical imagination of the Caribbean, amid conversations about operations to thwart boat migration from the region to the United States. [Courtesy of Ronald Reagan Presidential Library.]

8 U.S.C. §1182(f), which authorizes the president to "suspend the entry of all aliens or any class of aliens as immigrants or non-immigrants, or impose on the entry of aliens any restrictions he may deem to be appropriate."[64] In Fielding's reading, the class of subjects and geographic purview of the statute was murky: "There is some question whether this statute was intended to apply to illegal aliens, given that their entry by definition already is 'suspended,' and if it was so intended, whether it can be construed to authorize interdiction at as great a distance from the United States as the Windward Passage, some 500–600 miles from the U.S. border."[65] While concerned about the litigation that was certain to come, he nonetheless concluded that the president did have legal authority.

The Attorney General's announcement of the interdiction plan, which coincided with the announcement of the administration's detention policy, drew immediate and sharp criticism from the Congressional Black Caucus (CBC). As Fielding had expected, Chairperson Walter E.

Fauntroy questioned whether the president did have authority to order such an "unconscionable" policy. He also raised questions of international law; even with a bilateral agreement, Fauntroy warned that returns would violate the principle of *non-refoulement*. The most significant issue to CBC members was an apparent "double standard regarding first asylum issues." Fauntroy continued in his memo to Reagan:

> It seems hypocritical to urge Southeast Asian nations to fulfill their commitments as countries of first asylum while the U.S. justifies an interdiction policy on the grounds that the government of Haiti "says" that it is willing to accept the return of its citizens. . . . Interdiction, then[,] could result in the United States being directly responsible for the persecution and/or death of legitimate Haitian asylum claimants.[66]

A tragic event on October 26, 1981, brought into stark relief the politics and human consequences of deterrence when a boat capsized just off the coast of Hillsboro Beach, Florida. Thirty-three Haitians onboard drowned (nineteen men and fourteen women, one of whom was pregnant), and the remaining thirty-four were apprehended and detained at Krome. Governor Graham called it "a human tragedy which has been waiting to happen," and used the occasion to push for greater federal cooperation with the government of Haiti.[67] The Coast Guard echoed the governor, stating, "It's what we were hoping to avoid" with its patrols. The White House underscored that the interdiction program also served to save lives by halting the transit of unseaworthy vessels.[68] Critics would contest the claims that the program was humanitarian and effective. "They're still coming," Reverend Jean-Juste retorted. "They're just not caught. They drift in and I meet them every day myself."[69]

CONSIDERING FORT DRUM, NEW YORK

It was within this context that the administration tried to use yet another military base to detain Haitians and Cubans. While still in the midst of negotiations over Glasgow in November 1981, the White House announced that it would use the Army base at Fort Drum as a "temporary holding facility for aliens arriving illegally in this country."[70] Drum was about eight miles from the economically depressed city of Watertown, New York, about thirty miles south of the Canadian border. This placed the base at the heart of brutal winters where lake-effect snow routinely blankets this part of central New York. Critics, therefore, immediately compared the announcement to the harsh and remote conditions at Glasgow, Montana. Ira Kurzban, attorney at the Haitian Refugee Center in Miami, told the *New York Times,* "It's the closest thing we have in the United States to Siberia—except for the President's first choice, Glasgow, Mont."[71] Dorothy Samuels, executive director of the New York Civil Liberties Union, called on the government to "reverse the decision to put Haitian and Cuban refugees in cold storage," noting that "the Army itself describes Fort Drum as having climatic conditions unsurpassed in the continental United States for cold weather training."[72]

Arkansas Governor White expressed surprise at the announcement, and observed approvingly that the federal government had "pretty well got them [Cubans] located around the country now."[73] Fort Drum was a curious selection. Defense Secretary Weinberger seems to have softened his hard line against using military facilities for civilian migration operations, but he favored the use of Westover Air Force Base in Massachusetts, which had been identified earlier that summer.[74] However, neither HHS nor the DOJ supported using Westover, and the White House viewed it as "unacceptable because it is located in the midst of suburban Chicopee, MA (Democrat Ed Boland's district, directly next to Sylvio *[sic]* Conte's district; redistricting may place it in Conte's district; Conte opposes the use of Westover)."[75] (Apparently, both Conte and Boland were "livid at the very thought of Cubans and Haitians at Westover."[76]) Health and Human Services favored using Fort Drum, but Republican Congressperson Dave Martin strongly opposed the plan, "citing concerns over humane treatment of the Haitians, given severe weather conditions in Watertown" and the problem that detaining Haitians may pose to future military investments.[77]

Before making the announcement, the White House set about diminishing Representative Martin's opposition, whom White House staffer Kate Moore regarded as the "lynchpin" in securing use of the site. House minority whip Trent Lott (R-Mississippi) had also phoned the White House to express his opposition and support for Martin.[78] Moore suggested a strategy to assuage Martin's concerns that emphasized the humane treatment that would be provided at Drum and the economic benefits to neighboring Watertown. Chief of Staff Baker arranged for a meeting with Martin at the Oval Office, where the president was to assure Martin this was a temporary, but necessary, measure to solve a problem that he had inherited from Carter. Moreover, the White House promised to help in any way, and had already spoken to Weinberger who "indicated . . . that he will work to build up further Defense activity at Fort Drum."[79]

Although the *Times* reported that the Glasgow site had been dropped from consideration due to cost, it would actually remain in the mix for the next several months. Local opposition to relocating Cuban mental-health patients from the St. Elizabeth's facility to Fort Drum meant that Glasgow was the only viable option. The Montana congressional delegation and local residents supported its use, but the *Missoulian* had editorialized that moving Haitians there would be "brutal."[80] Anticipating further criticisms over the weather, INS Commissioner Alan Nelson and ORR Director Philip Hawkes offered, "While the climate in the winter is quite cold, there is considerably less snowfall at Glasgow than at Fort Drum. Furthermore, the buildings at Glasgow, a former SAC [Strategic Air Command] base, are far superior and much better insulated than those at the Fort Drum facility." Drum would be kept as an "additional overflow site for Haitians" if space outside of Florida or Puerto Rico were needed, which they assured was not as pressing a concern at the moment.[81]

Soon after Health and Human Services and the Justice Department had come to this understanding, the Attorney General announced that he would *not* be sending detained Haitians to Fort Drum. The *New York Times* published a sarcastic editorial praising his decision:

> A Christmas plum to Attorney General William French Smith. His Justice Department has not abandoned the idea of sending illegal immigrants who have fled Haiti to detention at icy Fort Drum, N.Y. But now it says it won't do so, at least not during the dead of winter.
>
> To hold poor, desperate people from the tropics in a camp near the Canadian border, where the temperature yesterday morning was 12 degrees, would be callous. "Siberia," some people say. So we're all for Mr. Smith's conclusion, even though we don't exactly follow his logic.[82]

The *Times* offered a different analysis than Smith's explanation that his deterrent policy was working to diminish the numbers of Haitians held in detention: "But the numbers can also be read another way—not as a sign that the fear of freezing deters migration but that illegal Haitian entrants are struggling much harder to avoid capture."[83] And given the small numbers of Haitians as compared to other groups, "Why make such a fuss over only a few hundred black Haitians, especially when doing so is sure to engender accusations of racism?"[84]

The questions that the *Times* posed were timely and pointed, but also implied that detention in a "tropical" climate like Florida or Puerto Rico was not cruel. Moreover, the editorial failed to question the premise that detention worked to deter migration, and offered a fanciful explanation that Haitians were held in detention longer than others because they, unlike other asylum seekers, had entered illegally. While advocating for "less of a fuss over Haitians," the *Times* editorial largely accepted the administration's terms of debate (illegal migration versus legitimate asylum seekers), and hence obscured that Haitians as a group faced lengthy times in detention *because* they were pursuing asylum claims that the INS (and State Department) was reluctant to hear. By focusing on icy winters, the *Times* failed to criticize the administration's systematic efforts to deter rights to asylum in the name of border control. Further, the newspaper missed the opportunity to criticize how the government's production of isolation through the use of remote sites was the key issue. For example, lawyers had criticized the isolation of even Krome, which is less than thirty miles from downtown Miami. "We said Krome is Nome. . . . It's like Nome, Alaska. If you're going to have hearings out there, the private bar will not make the trip. This has pretty much been the case."[85]

CONCLUSION

As we have shown in this chapter, deterrence took many forms, from interception and return of migrants at sea, to mass detention in remote and hostile locations across the United States. From islands to bases, authorities overlooked no corner of mainland territory in their efforts to deter through detention. In spite of harsh criticism and references to Siberian, gulag geographies, the government pursued remote geography as a deterrence strategy. Remoteness came into play repeatedly and carried with it creative legal geographies—such as declarations of nonentry—with clear consequences for detained asylum seekers and their advocates and legal counsel.

Deterrence policy developed out of a desire to prevent future arrivals of asylum seekers from Cuba and Haiti. This would not, however, be the explanation given by the Carter or Reagan White House, both of which emphasized state sovereignty over border control and the sharp distinction between political refugees or asylum seekers and economic migrants. Some members of the Reagan administration viewed the Mariel event as a "deliberate, unfriendly act by a foreign power," and, therefore, engaged in contingency planning that involved military and civilian branches of the government.[86] A previously classified report entitled "Preventing Another Mariel" drafted by an interagency task force, including Associate Attorney General Giuliani and Assistant Secretary of State for Inter-American Affairs Tom Enders, further illustrates the tight connections between geopolitical and law-enforcement definitions of problems whose resolutions may call for new legislation. Enders advised Secretary of State Alexander Haig that all of the agencies involved in the planning "agree that interdiction will not prevent all the boats from getting through; some argue that most will get through. Therefore it is important that illegal migrants not be welcomed and resettled, but rather detained and as quickly as possible deported. Such a policy will have a major deterrent effect in Cuba."[87]

This planning converged with longstanding efforts to prevent the migration of Haitians in the form of a cohesive deterrence policy comprising interception (and return) at sea and detention.[88] The imperative of detention as a deterrent both grew out of and was undone by the lack of detention space available to authorities and consistent, high-profile legal battles over its use. The facilities that would never be in Glasgow, Montana, and Fort Drum, New York, represent more than operational decisions, but rather decisive moments when the institutional commitments of the Justice Department to detention prevailed over resettlement as a project rooted in refugee law and run by Health and Human Services. In the span of a few months, the political and logistical crisis of Fort Chaffee, while not over, was diminishing. The Attorney General repeatedly praised his interdiction program for reducing arrivals of Haitians, and received a boost on November 17, 1981, when a civil suit challenging the interdiction program was dismissed.[89] Yet repeated opposition to the use of military facilities from local politicians and the ongoing objective to find a large facility in the event of a mass migration soon cohered into efforts to construct dedicated detention facilities.

By February 1982, all of the Cubans remaining in Chaffee had been transferred to federal prisons. Justice officials explained that this was both an "interim solution" and "cheaper to keep them there" as opposed to establishing a new facility (Shull 2014a, 35). But as with the use of decommissioned military bases, the executive branch did not exert limitless power to detain. Already by the outset of Reagan's presidency, legal challenges had been made to the transfer and continued confinement of Cuban nationals in the Atlanta federal prison and mental facilities. Meanwhile, Haitians vocally protested their confinement at Fort Allen and at Krome. At the same time, mayors and local officials in the Dade County, Florida, area urged the administration to release Haitians confined at Krome, fearing a repeat of the unrest of two years earlier. Given the "extremely high unemployment rate, particularly among minority youth, and the impending 'long hot summer,'" the Mayors believe Krome is a symbol which could touch off a series of riots, violence, etc. Forty-one women in Krome are holding a hunger strike."[90]

In the establishment of detention as a deterrent policy, the GAO concluded, "Cost was not an overriding consideration in the decision to detain" (1983, 28). Indeed, as this chapter shows, the primary objective was deterring Haitian migration and preventing another mass-asylum situation. The commitment to building new carceral space was rooted in the belief that detention to effect deportation, combined with interdiction at sea, would effectively deter unauthorized migration. The new policy of detention as a deterrent made asylum, a relatively rightless legal category, all the more vulnerable by backing it with carceral space. The INS sought to downplay the objective of its detention policy by focusing on weather: "A side effect may well be that there has been so much press about it [Fort Drum] being Siberia that it may have caused people to think twice. But it was not an intentional deterrent."[91] The climate is a side note in the administration's commitment to detention and to isolating asylum seekers and detainees from legal services and community and family ties.

Preventing another Mariel, relocating the Cubans from Fort Chaffee, and relieving the overcrowding of Haitians at Krome and elsewhere were intertwined projects. Reagan's staff continued with the contingency planning begun by Carter even as they sought to resolve the situation at Fort Chaffee, which continued to generate a political firestorm. Despite the repeated pushback from base communities that the Reagan administration encountered, the Department of Justice's position that detention would deter migration received White House backing. As INS's institutional power to define issues of asylum together with that of unauthorized migration was consolidated, the view that detention was a tool for *preventing* migration quickly became entrenched, as did the commitment to expand detention space. The practices established to prevent Caribbean Basin migrations would inform subsequent mass-asylum crises involving Salvadorans and Guatemalans who sought entry and protection after crossing primarily from Mexico into Texas and California. By the mid-1990s, the practices of detention and interception of migrants before reaching U.S. territory (either directly or through bilateral agreements) had already become tightly interwoven policies designed to deter migrants and asylum seekers. We discuss conflicts over where the INS would build its first new long-term detention facility and the ongoing legal and jurisdictional disputes over detention in the next chapter.

PART TWO

Building the World's Largest Detention System

3

"Not a Prison"

Building a Deportation Hub in Oakdale, Louisiana

Despite the Ronald Reagan administration's acknowledgment that the long-term detention of asylum seekers "could create an appearance of 'concentration camps' filled largely by blacks" (a charge leveled by Haitian asylum seekers to *Newsweek*), in the spring of 1982 the president requested supplemental appropriations from Congress to establish permanent long-term detention space (US Congress 1982, 227, 253). The $35 million proposal to build two 1,000-person detention facilities would more than double the detention capacity of the Immigration and Naturalization Service's (INS) existing five Service Processing Centers (SPCs).

The fragility of this moment in the history of migration imprisonment cannot be overstated. The administration's mandatory detention policy was not even one year old. Concerns over racism expanded into broad questions about the ethics and legality of long-term detention for asylum seekers. In addition to significant legal challenges that threatened to stymie the detention policy, the administration also faced pragmatic questions about which agency would run long-term facilities and where they would be located. The Office of Management and Budget (OMB) questioned the administration's detention policy on fiscal and procedural grounds. The OMB contended that "an Immigration and Naturalization (INS) detention center, which offers neither community resettlement nor institutional care is not an efficient long-term custody solution."[1] The sheer scope of ethical, legal, political, and logistical issues made it far from certain that the United States would embark on a new, permanent system of long-term confinement for migrants.

In fact, a ruling by Florida Judge Eugene Spellman on June 18, 1982, found that the administration had violated the Administrative Procedures Act. That ruling and the House Judiciary Committee's hearing on detention a few days later illustrate the tenuousness of the new policy. Robert Kastenmeier, a liberal Democrat from Wisconsin who chaired the committee, began the hearing by stating, "I seriously question the need to incarcerate Haitians or any other immigrant group pending resolution of their immigration status, particularly where claims for political asylum are made" (US Congress 1982a, 2). At the hearing, Associate Attorney General Rudolph Giuliani and INS commissioner Alan Nelson defended the administration's policy and repeatedly rejected charges of racism. Giuliani also floated two sites in Oklahoma and Virginia adjacent to active Bureau of Prisons (BOP) facilities as potential locations for new migration detention facilities that would be run by the BOP. More privately, the INS looked for ways to respond to Spellman's ruling, which had rendered their detention policy "null and void."[2]

By 1985, construction of a new detention facility had begun, but in neither Oklahoma nor Virginia. This chapter traces the unexpected story of how Oakdale, Louisiana, came to host the new facility and how the Bureau of Prisons helped to establish the INS's long-term detention infrastructure. Conflicts among federal agencies, the White House, congressional representatives, and local communities over where to locate facilities plagued this particular historical moment. Resolution of these tensions contributed to the production of remoteness across the entire system. The use and construction of remote facilities, in turn, effectively diminished detainees' access to legal representation and support, contributing to longer times within detention. Longer periods in confinement further fueled the pressure for space and led to further construction, reliance on subcontracting arrangements, and the routine use of transfers within the network of facilities. In short, decisions made at this particular moment in the early 1980s led to many of the problems that remain with the current—now vastly expanded—detention system: lack of access to legal representation, geographical remoteness, transfers, and length of time in confinement.

CONFINEMENT CAPACITY AND THE MAKING OF REMOTENESS

The Reagan administration's commitment to detention as an element of its deterrence strategy created a series of contradictions for the government. First, while long-term detention (defined as longer than thirty days) had been named as policy, federal agencies did not have the infrastructure to carry out this new mandate.[3] In the immediate term, this conflict led to a frenetic search for space to confine, which gradually solidified the belief that the government needed to expand its capacity. As our previous chapter demonstrates, military facilities were not generally available for use or repurposing. Further, the INS had neither the capacity in its short-term facilities nor the experience with long-term confinement held by the Bureau of Prisons. Mayors in Dade County, Florida, for example, believed that Haitians should be released from Krome so that Mariel Cubans could be transferred there from the county jail.[4] These factors made the BOP an appealing option for some; however, the federal prison system was also overcrowded. Additionally, there was concern about the agency's legal authority to confine people who had not been charged or convicted with a criminal offense in the U.S. criminal legal system.

The question of whether the remote geographies were by design or incidental to the system's operation was contentious even before the administration set out to build new facilities. As noted in the previous chapter, the day that the state of Florida sued the Justice Department over conditions of confinement at Krome in June 1981, the INS began moving Haitians to federal facilities scattered across the eastern half of the United States. (Justice officials told the media that the transfers had not been prompted by Governor Bob Graham's lawsuit, but later told the courts that they had.)[5] One of the destinations was the INS Service Processing Center in Brooklyn, New York, but most were Bureau of Prisons facilities spread from La Tuna and Big Spring in Texas, to the coalmining town of Morgantown, West Virginia, to Alderson, West Virginia, Lexington, Kentucky, and up to Otisville and Lake Placid, New York.

The distance of the prisons from Florida and other places where Haitian people and Creole speakers lived drew immediate criticism (see map 5). The same attorneys who had brought suit against the mass deportation hearings for Haitians in *Jean v. Meissner* now sued over the transfers.[6] This series of lawsuits, culminating in the Supreme Court ruling *Louis v. Nelson,* would become some of the most important cases concerning U.S. detention practices and policy (Gwynn 1986). Advocates contended that the transfers to distant facilities effectively denied counsel and asylum rights to detainees. Church groups who sought to visit people held in detention documented how the long distances compounded the difficulty of arranging visits with facility administrators. The lack of information, prolonged detention, and conditions of confinement created physical and mental-health problems for detainees (US Congress 1982a, 62). One woman held in Alderson told the *Washington Post,* "Here in West Virginia, we now face a very bleak life. They treat us like animals for no reason at all. They give more importance to a garbage can than they do to us." As a result, "We feel crazy. This place is too much for us" (377).

On September 30, 1981, Miami District Court Judge Alcee Hastings issued an injunction preventing the government from continuing to hold exclusion proceedings for Haitians who had been transferred from Krome and did not have legal representation (Kurzban 1983–1984, 41). The ruling's use of *refugees* not only challenged the government's contention that Haitians were economic migrants, but also situated Haitians within the dominant narrative of the United States as a nation of immigrants. Hastings rebuked the federal government for unjustly exercising power over territory to thwart the rights of brave, freedom-loving Haitians:

> Having made a long and perilous journey on the seas to Southern Florida, these refugees, seeking the promised land, have instead been subjected to a human shell game in which the arbitrary Immigration and Naturalization Service has sought to scatter them to locations that, with the exception of Brooklyn are all in desolate, remote, hostile, culturally diverse areas, containing a paucity of available legal support and few, if any, Creole interpreters. In this regard, INS officials have acted as haphazard as the rolling seas that brought these boat people to this great country's shores. Indeed, even though INS officials have been rudderless in the enunciation and application of an immigration policy, when they decided to move the Haitians to these remote areas, they acted with laser-like precision (*Louis v. Meissner* 1981, 926).

Judge Hastings's ruling has been widely cited by advocates for articulating the relationship between migrants' rights and geography (see, e.g., Kurzban 1983–1984; MLIHRC & PSR 1991; Koh 1994b; García Hernández 2011). Yet it also suggests that the government's policy was more coherent in its implementation than it was. The appearance of "laser-like precision" had more to do with the administration's relentless commitment to confinement than with the perfect execution of a

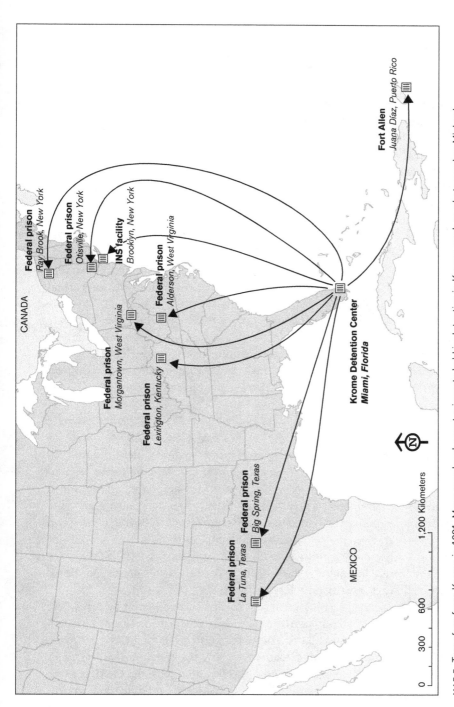

MAP 5. Transfers from Krome in 1981. Many people who met migrants held in detention in Krome, such as photographer Michael Carlebach, witnessed their forced departure to other parts of the country, but never knew where they ended up. This map shows the locations of those transfers and the range of possible destinations.

detailed plan. If anything, the obstacles that the Department of Justice (DOJ) repeatedly encountered while trying to achieve its objectives of deterrence and removal led the agency to pursue short-term solutions and draft contingency plans that resulted in a flexible, patchwork system. While this pragmatic approach appeared flawed in terms of rational planning criteria like efficiency or fiscal prudence, its very malleability worked to build remoteness into the operations of the system. The result proved very effective in diminishing migrants' rights, and is consistent with contemporary forms of ad hoc, crisis-driven enforcement strategies that favor government flexibility over migrants' freedoms.

"INS HAS NO EXPERTISE IN THIS AREA": NEGOTIATING JURISDICTION FOR LONG-TERM CONFINEMENT

In order to resolve the immediate crises over the remaining Cubans at Fort Chaffee and Haitians at Krome, the Reagan administration turned to the Bureau of Prisons. The question became whether the BOP or the INS would be best suited to run a long-term detention regime. This was not simply a logistical question of available space, though this practical issue was significant, but also one of administrative experience and legal authority. The administration's push for new detention space remained uncertain, and debate over construction proved tightly connected to the debate over jurisdiction.

The Office of Management and Budget issued one of the first barriers to the expansion of the detention system. Edwin Harper wrote to Stanley Morris at the Justice Department that while Chief of Staff "Jim Baker recalls agreement to a new detention center," the OMB wanted the Department of Justice to "rejustify its 1982 supplemental request to fund a new detention facility."[7] The OMB contended that because the remaining Cubans at Chaffee had been transferred to BOP facilities and "the Haitian flow is dramatically reduced," an INS facility would not be an "efficient long-term custody solution. Moreover, INS has not demonstrated, in our view, the ability to operate a well-managed detention facility, especially on a large scale."[8]

The Department of Justice wrote to Baker, expressing "distress" at the OMB's letter. Deputy Attorney General Edward Schmults explained that because moving Cubans from Chaffee to BOP facilities "put great additional pressure on our already overcrowded federal prison system," Justice thought there had been an understanding with the OMB regarding the need for construction.[9] Thus, Justice wanted to construct a federal prison in Phoenix, and the president had requested funds for a new migration-detention facility in McAlester, Oklahoma. Harper countered that "Jim Baker and I do not recall agreeing to the approval of this project."[10] Before the OMB would move forward, it asked for an "in-depth analysis from the Department [of Justice] demonstrating the need for a new prison, especially a facility in Arizona as opposed to other sites, such as Florida."[11]

The OMB's points of opposition did not simply concern immediate logistical issues, but questioned the very need for detention in refugee policy and interior migration policing. The OMB indicated that it "disagree[d] with the [Justice] Department's view that the transfer of Cubans to BoP facilities should be an interim step pending establishment of a permanent detention facility."[12] The OMB viewed the apparent effectiveness of interception as a deterrent and the post-*Louis* asylum-hearing process for Haitians as evidence that "Haitian detention needs in the future are unlikely to require long-term custody."[13] More broadly, they argued that a "detention facility does not bear on potential refugee flows." The OMB rejected the administration's hypothesis that detention worked to deter asylum seekers, yet the letter took an understated tone: "It should be noted that U.S. refugee and immigration policy is oriented to orderly entry processes from refugee camps or Consular Offices overseas not to housing entrants here in detention centers."[14] Finally, the OMB took a similarly critical stance on the "role of detention facilities as enforcement support." Anticipating objections that advocates would invoke in subsequent decades about how filling prison cells can become its own overriding logic, the OMB contended that additional detention capacity "may encourage INS to detain aliens longer in order to justify the facility's need—often entailing deportation proceedings—when voluntary departure would be simpler."[15] This was a significant rebuff to the administration from within the government. The OMB flatly questioned the reliance on detention as a cornerstone of U.S. migration policy, suggesting that detention did not itself represent order nor have a place in refugee policy.

By the spring of 1982, there was still no resolution to the questions of whether a long-term detention facility would be built or where it would be located. Congress had removed the line item for the McAlester, Oklahoma, site during budget reconciliation, and the Justice Department was still debating whether the BOP or the INS was the agency most suited for the task.[16] Renee Szybala, special aide to Associate Attorney General Giuliani, delivered to him a seventeen-page policy-options paper that had been prepared by a Justice Department task force, which outlined the advantages and disadvantages for four alternatives: 1) continue INS management of its facilities; 2) continue INS management of its facilities with consultation from the BOP; 3) transfer long-term INS detention functions to the BOP; and 4) transfer short- and long-term INS detention functions to the BOP. Szybala found the report "extremely disappointing. It contains no recommendations and little helpful guidance on implementation."[17] She wrote:

> All people familiar with the issue believe that responsibility for long-term detention of aliens should be transferred to BOP. Chairman [Romano] Mazzoli [D-Kentucky], for example, recently wrote to the Attorney General suggesting this be done. INS has no expertise in this area and has housed long-term detainees in sub-standard conditions. Until BOP was requested by you to provide assistance to INS at Krome, the facility was a disgrace. BOP, on the other hand, has proven ability and is the Department's expert in this field.[18]

The report was not as feckless as Szybala's memo suggests. Unlike the OMB's pointed questioning of the renewed reliance on detention, the DOJ task force clearly supported the administration's views, indicating "there is a need for a centrally located multipurpose permanent detention facility."[19] Further, the task force indicated that "it would be reasonable to have BOP either, assume responsibility for such a permanent facility, or, at a minimum, advise and assist the I&NS in the planning, design, and programs of the proposed facility. . . ."[20] Given this, it seems that Szybala's disappointment issued from the perception that the paper did not definitively support shifting responsibility for long-term detention to the BOP, as favored by Giuliani and others.

One of the disadvantages that the report identified to using BOP facilities to confine migrants was "the stigma of 'criminalization' of the alien detention function."[21] Szybala brushed aside this concern, stating:

> This may be true to some extent. On the other hand, the change may be publically viewed as a positive step motivated by concern for the aliens' welfare, which is what it is. Many alien detainees are currently housed in actual penal institutions without any great public outcry. Any stigma would actually be reduced after the transfer of responsibility because those in BOP facilities would no longer be housed in "penal" institutions but rather in facilities called something like "Immigration Detention Service Centers" managed by a separate section of BOP.[22]

Szybala's reasoning captures two recurring elements of argumentation that work simultaneously to deny and facilitate the connections between penal institutions and migrant-detention facilities. First, she contrasted the disgraceful state of INS operations to BOP-run facilities, which she lauded as rationally planned and humanely run institutions. At the same time, she sidestepped the criminalization question by invoking the legal and political conceit that migration detention was merely administrative and not punitive. Accordingly, the BOP could run detention facilities under a euphemistic title, suggesting that confinement provided a welfare "service" for migrants.

Advocates also routinely challenged the legality of detaining migrants within punitive facilities, and there was concern within the Department of Justice over this issue. In 1981, BOP Director Norman Carlson indicated that the BOP lacked the legal authority to hold Cubans who were diagnosed with mental illnesses. Moreover, he objected to an expansion of the agency's jurisdiction, which he viewed as "very inappropriate" and one that "invites court challenge."[23] INS Acting Commissioner David Crosland wrote an eight-page memo detailing legal, ethical, and jurisdictional issues. First, it was "problematical as to how much law enforcement efforts can do to stem the tide of future arrivals."[24] Second, "the legal authority of INS to detain Cubans in mental facilities or federal correctional institutions has been challenged."[25] There remained a question

> as to whether the Government has legal authority under the immigration laws for indeterminate, perhaps lifetime, detention of potentially dangerous criminals and mentally ill individuals (who do not meet standards for involuntary commitment) when there is no hope of ever executing exclusion orders to Cuba. . . . [A] decision will have to be made whether to: (1) continue to rely on INS authority and risk possible adverse court decisions; (2) release individuals notwithstanding possible dangers to themselves and/ or society; or (3) seek specific statutory authority for such custody.[26]

In June 1982, these issues of legal authority, jurisdiction, and carceral capacity were debated at Congressperson Kastenmeier's hearing on the detention of migrants in federal prisons. By this time, the majority of Cuban detainees at Chaffee had been transferred to a maximum-security federal prison in Atlanta, against the strong objection of BOP Director Carlson.[27] While the prison, built in 1902, had been slated for closure, the majority of people held there were Cuban detainees, and 150 to 200 convicted U.S. citizens remained to "do the maintenance work in the institution" (US Congress 1982a, 28). In questioning from Kastenmeier, Carlson explained, "We try to keep them [Cubans] separate from convicted felons, for obvious legal reasons. That presents a problem to us in our institutions in terms of logistics of the operation of the facilities. But we do keep them separate in terms of housing and movement around the institution." Kastenmeier continued, "So the only real difference is that they are separated or segregated from your prison populations in these facilities?" Carlson replied, "Insofar as possible, that's right." Kastenmeier pressed, "So in all other respects, they are prisoners just like the other prisoners?" To which Carlson answered, "That is correct" (22). The architecture of shared prison space continued to blur the distinction between administrative and punitive confinement.

GEOGRAPHY GETS MORE POLITICAL IN SITE-SPECIFIC BATTLES

The proposal that Giuliani presented to the Kastenmeier committee asked for $35 million to construct two 1,000-person migration-detention facilities that would be run by the Bureau of Prisons. "BOP is the Attorney General's detention expert. It is experienced in both short- and long-term detention, while the INS experience, until recently, has been with short-term cases only" (US Congress 1982a, 15). The sites he proposed next to existing BOP facilities in Petersburg, Virginia, and El Reno, Oklahoma, would provide detention space for the Northeast and Atlantic seaboard and the Southwest, respectively. The advantage of the proposed facility in El Reno, a town just west of Oklahoma City on I-40, was that the "southwestern border's SPCs could be utilized primarily for normal border apprehensions as longer term cases were shifted to the El Reno facility allowing INS to maximize its enforcement efforts in the southern border area" (5).

Giuliani invoked narratives of the lawless southern border to normalize the significant shift to long-term detention in deterrence policy. The dual rationale that Giuliani provided for the new facilities—fulfilling President Reagan's and the Attorney General's commitments to "regain control of our Nation's borders" and "strengthen and increase INS enforcement activities"—elided "normal" border-control practices with the administration's efforts to deter asylum claims (US Congress 1982, 4). Long-term detention was analogized to the established practice of short-term detention and invoked as a measure of effective migration policing. Regaining control through detention was necessary, in Giuliani's telling, to respond to, and hopefully prevent, "sudden mass influxes." He proceeded to note that in addition to Cuban and Haitian nationals were "Salvadorans, many of whom have filed for asylum, [and] have accounted for approximately 30% of the space available at the Port Isabel, El Paso, and El Centro SPCs." "These special problems," Giuliani advanced, "have merely highlighted our critical lack of space, they have not created it" (10–11).

By invoking the normalcy of Latinx apprehensions in the United States–Mexico borderlands, Giuliani both naturalized those longstanding practices (Hernández 2010) and minimized the administration's historic shift in policy. In equating asylum seekers with disorderliness, he named detention as a means to restore order. Yet he evaded the fact that the Reagan administration's foreign policy and reliance on detention (as opposed to parole) drove the "need" for detention space. This commitment to confinement, nonetheless, was evident in his justification for turning authority for long-term detention over to the Bureau of Prisons and constructing separate confinement spaces. The INS's use of BOP space "although necessary in the short term, is undesirable as a general policy. While aliens who await processing in BOP facilities are segregated from the general inmate population, we do not believe it is advisable to house administrative detainees in correctional facilities with those convicted or accused of crimes" (US Congress 1982a, 8). The push for new facilities would rest, then, on the claim that construction was necessary to resolve overcrowding and the appearance of legal disorder. While the standards for confinement that the INS presented at the hearing were "drawn heavily from the standards developed by the DOJ and the ACA [American Correctional Association]," the long-term confinement of legally distinct populations in virtually interchangeable facilities would serve to create the appearance of distinct objectives, even though both "detention" facilities and "prisons" would be run by the BOP (101).

The legal and administrative muddle of this moment is illustrated by the rapidly changing landscape of proposed facility locations. Local opposition had developed to the use of the McAlester, Oklahoma, site, and plans for the El Reno and Petersburg, Virginia, sites that Giuliani presented at the House hearing were not as certain as they seemed. Less than two months earlier, Carlson and Nelson had jointly prepared a site-selection paper for Giuliani, which sidestepped BOP–INS jurisdictional disputes to focus on location, recommending La Tuna, Texas, and Petersburg, Virginia. Given their recommendations, why didn't Giuliani suggest La Tuna in his testimony? While Carlson and Nelson backed the site, the site selection report noted that there "may be significant opposition to the establishment of another alien detention facility in the State of Texas."[28]

The concern over Texas may have been referencing the controversy that had ensued a year earlier when the INS moved Haitians from

Krome following Governor Graham's lawsuit. Texas Republican Senator John Tower contacted the White House, livid about the transfer: "You have tripled the black population of Big Springs [sic], Texas, and not even advised me in advance." White House legislative affairs staffer Max Friedersdorf characterized the situation as a "monumental disaster" for congressional relations, and not only with this Republican ally. The "problem," Friedersdorf wrote, "is compounded because Big Springs [sic], Texas, is in the District of Congressman Charles Stenholm (D-Tex), leader of the boll weevils."[29]

The worry was that neither conservative Democrats (colloquially known as "boll weevils") nor Republican allies would reliably implement the administration's plans. A similar political conundrum would ensue shortly thereafter with the Petersburg, Virginia, site. While Giuliani had successfully negotiated with Puerto Rican allies to remove their opposition to Fort Allen, the same could not be said for appealing to elected officials from Virginia. Senator John W. Warner, Jr., Senator Harry F. Byrd, Jr., and Congressperson Robert W. Daniel, Jr. wrote a letter to Attorney General William French Smith that expressed incredulity at the administration's claim that the facility would be used for two to three days prior to deportation. "Based upon the real experience of other detention centers," they anticipated much lengthier periods of confinement, and expected that "relatives or friends of the detainees [would] move to close proximity of the center."[30] As a result, they expected "an additional financial and social burden to the community" in an area that was already "hard-pressed to provide these services to their own citizens."[31] The representatives pointed to the fiscal and social burden that *Plyler v. Doe,* a Supreme Court decision that held that undocumented children have the right to K–12 public education, would have on citizen residents. This "'free' public (possibly bilingual) education—free, that is, except to the taxpayers of the community who will have to bear the cost of this education through increased property tax payments."[32] As in McAlester, Oklahoma, and Houston, Texas, elected officials and local residents in Virginia deployed a mix of xenophobic arguments (communicable diseases, requirement to teach in a foreign language) and economic reasons (welfare costs, overreliance on the federal government, or unwanted federal function) for their opposition to a detention facility in their districts.[33]

In contrast, the proposed construction at El Reno seemed welcome and viable. Despite well-organized and vehement opposition elsewhere, Carlson and Nelson did not anticipate any significant resistance here.[34]

El Reno already hosted a Bureau of Prisons facility, and Republican Senator Don Nickles supported the project.[35] Oklahoma Democrat Glenn English, chair of the House Government and Individual Rights Subcommittee, called for a hearing for the proposed site. The situation changed rather rapidly when the first resident to speak at the hearing appeared with a petition opposing the construction. He told the chair, "Now, we've got only 1,700 signers on that petition but since this time, our figure of people who are opposing it exceeds 4,000, and we can still get more." He then appealed to English: "If we can't get the appropriation stopped with your help, we will give it a try in court and see if we can't tie it up there for a couple of years. We're not through with this at all, Congressman. We're serious about it" (US Congress 1982b, 19).

Regional Siting Battle: El Reno versus Oakdale

By January 1983, El Reno was still being considered and continued to have Senator Nickles's backing, but a site in Oakdale, Louisiana, now appeared as a serious contender.[36] The mayor of Oakdale, George Mowad, had been lobbying the Justice Department for the detention facility since early 1982. In addition to organizing backing from residents, businesses, chambers of commerce, faith communities, and civic associations, Mowad had gathered support from both Louisiana senators, six of eight congressional representatives, the governor, and Allen Parish officials.[37] This level of support did not indicate a foregone outcome. Governor David Treen asked for supportive letters from Senators J. Bennett Johnston and Russell Long and Congresspersons John Breaux and Gillis William Long before he endorsed the project. An aide to Senator Long ventured that Treen's reluctance to support the facility issued from concern over potential political fallout, as encountered by Arkansas Governor Bill Clinton after riots at Chaffee.[38]

Mayor Mowad was a tireless backer of the project, repeatedly invoking the high unemployment in the area—with figures cited ranging between 25 percent and 31 percent—as a rationale for the federal project. Mowad cultivated relationships in order to generate action by congressional representatives. In testimony to the Lower Mississippi Delta Development Commission, Mowad explained:

> When we heard about the fact that the detention center was going to be built by the Immigration Naturalization Center [sic], we came back home and looked at it and looked at the economic impact. And rather than saying, "Hey, we don't want it," as most places had done, one place in north

Louisiana had done, and the more we looked into it, the more obvious the economic advantages. It is a recession proof industry, unlike the timber industry which we had been faced with for so many years exclusively. It made a higher pay scale available. . . .[39]

In March 1982, Oakdale hosted a visit from the INS during which eight hundred people attended a public meeting in support of the project.[40] The two local newspapers were running a series of stories about what the facility would mean for the parish, and at least one church was actively urging support from its congregants.[41] Hopes and confidence were high. When Mowad and Holman Jones (former congressperson and well-connected Oakdale booster) learned in April 1982 that Giuliani had decided to turn long-term detention operations over to the BOP, they asked Senator Johnston to speak with him. An aide to Johnston explained the situation: "As you know, Oakdale was competing with El Reno, OK and because there is a current prison facility at El Reno, they feel El Reno now has the edge."[42] Mowad had also ascertained that the Justice Department was not considering Oakdale's unemployment rate in their decision-making. He again contacted Johnston's office, this time imploring the senator to bring the issue directly to the White House.[43]

Despite this public support, and unbeknownst to Mowad, Carlson and Nelson had completed a site-selection analysis and rejected Oakdale. They cited its relative remoteness, higher construction costs, limited ability to serve as a multi-use facility, and potential delay in construction due to time needed to acquire land.[44] In making his recommendation to the Attorney General, Giuliani affirmed Carlson and Nelson's support for El Reno (and rejected their preference for La Tuna, Texas, for reasons previously discussed). While Senator Johnston's phone call had not swayed Giuliani, Giuliani did note that Oakdale might be a good "fall-back" in light of "extremely strong congressional and community support."[45]

In early June 1982, Giuliani wrote to Johnston, explaining the Justice Department's decision to proceed with the El Reno site. He described the efficiencies that would result from co-locating the facility, and the relatively faster construction time on federal land. Moreover, the DOJ "had to consider the relative remoteness of this location, 160 miles northwest of New Orleans and 210 miles northeast of Houston. A large portion of the operating costs at any INS facility consists of alien transportation expenses. Oakdale, at this time, lacks major highways and proximity to major airports."[46] He also addressed unemployment as the key motivating factor for Oakdale to pursue the facility. As Mowad suspected, however, it did not rank as a significant factor: "While there is undeniably a large and willing workforce available in this area, we believe that recruitment of needed bi-lingual staff would prove difficult."[47]

When Mowad learned that Oakdale was no longer under consideration, he again reached out to congressional representatives. An aide to Johnston penned a memo to the senator, relaying that Mowad had been "very upset" when he called the office. Mowad had said he "smells a rat," and wanted the senator once again to "go to the White House" and to "really look close at the appropriations."[48] Johnston's position on the Senate Appropriations Committee was widely understood as the "important key to funding."[49] Earlier in the year, for example, the Justice Department had appealed to Johnston to support the president's budget amendment to fund a permanent detention facility.[50] The mayor urged Johnston to play hardball: "Tell Justice that if Oakdale cannot be considered, the appropriations for the Center will be taken out of the bill legislatively."[51]

HOW DOES THE BORDER STRETCH TO OKLAHOMA OR LOUISIANA, AND WITH WHAT RATIONALE?

Following Giuliani's decision, opposition to the Petersburg, Virginia, and El Reno sites grew, and Louisiana officials continued to organize. In late May, the Louisiana delegation sent a letter to the White House, asking President Reagan to overturn the Justice Department's decision.[52] Senator Johnston used his position on the Senate Appropriations Committee to write language into a supplemental appropriations bill that required that a detention facility could not be built within a prison and that Allen Parish must be considered in the site-selection process. Johnston took aim at the efficiency-through-proximity rationale that Giuliani had offered for the El Reno site by invoking a different set of geographic rationales. He cited Giuliani's June testimony to the House— in Johnston's words, "it is bad policy to locate one of these prisons as part of a Federal prison facility"—to undercut the BOP's primary rationale for co-location and thereby advance the Oakdale location.[53]

In efforts to justify the location of proposed detention facilities, narratives detached "the border" from its commonsense reference in the geographical imagination—the United States–Mexico boundary regions— and relocated it in new places. Stretching and shifting border logics and locations enabled federal and local officials to use commonsense understandings of border-enforcement operations and targets to rationalize the expansion of detention infrastructure and diminish the significance of the long-term detention policy shift. In his testimony to Congress, for example, Giuliani minimized this departure by collapsing all government functions to law enforcement:

> The capacities of the INS special processing centers and contract space available have largely dictated the level at which the INS apprehension program, both at the borders and in the interior, can function. Those capacities have been inadequate. In some areas, this has resulted in less use of the INS enforcement branches. In others, it has resulted in relaxed policies of bond or release on personal recognizance. As a result, enforcement of final orders of deportation remains low due to the failure of many aliens to appear for deportation. This situation can no longer be tolerated (US Congress 1982a, 3).

The assertion that detention capacity drove enforcement, meant that *only* the expansion of carceral space would enable the government to abide by its own laws. This posture effectively turned parole, which had been used by Attorneys General for decades as a vehicle for asylum, and discretion, into indicators of lawlessness. He thereby preempted the question of whether the laws and confinement were just.

The shifting, or flexible, rationales for expansion are evident in local discussions of detention. When the INS visited Oakdale in March 1982, the INS representative appealed to local residents concerned about unemployment by invoking border and migration policing as functions to "protect U.S. citizens' employment rights."[54] Following apprehension, the INS official explained that a migrant would be held for an average of three to five days before a hearing, telling the story of short-term detention as a seamless process of removal that involved no substantive legal, logistical, or ethical questions. This narrative was repeated in reporting on the facility. A news clipping in Senator Johnston's files reports that Mowad had been told that 95 percent of the facility would be filled by Mexican nationals, and quotes the police chief as saying, "We don't see any problems. We pick up illegal aliens here all the time, mostly Mexicans. . . . They come in here to plant trees (for the timber industry) and never present a problem."[55]

The geographic imagination of the border as a site of convenient entry and efficient exit informed the myth of detention facilities as part of a seamless border wherever they were located. Mowad, for example, explained that Oakdale's facility would confine people who had been apprehended in Midwestern cities like Chicago or Kansas City and that a "selling point" for Oakdale was that it was a "convenient mid-point on the trip back to Mexico."[56] The lengthy zigzag across space that this scenario would entail was obscured by the imaginary of a flexible border. Indeed, Senator Johnston explained to constituents that Oakdale's location should be considered because "it was close to the area where aliens would come from."[57] This rationale was underscored by Virginia Senator Warner, an opponent of the Petersburg site, who told the press that he supported Johnston's amendment, noting, "Oakdale is centrally located between two areas where illegal aliens are apprehended—Texas and Florida."[58]

The detachability of the border as a commonsense logic of frictionless apprehension and expulsion also becomes evident in efforts to distinguish administrative detention from criminal legal imprisonment. The objective of long-term confinement was advanced through rhetorics of temporariness and nonbelonging. A Catholic church in Allen Parish, for example, used a page of its Sunday bulletin to articulate reasons for parishioners to accept the new facility. It began by discussing unemployment figures of 26 percent as "cold realities that we must face. Those who can say: 'we don't want that kind of thing here' without knowing what that 'thing' is, have not yet hear [sic] their little ones cry for hunger. Or they are so smug in their own personal financial security that they do not care about their neighbor."[59]

The minimization of long-term detention as a project rested on and reproduced commonsense ideas of "the Southern border" and *who* was subject to migration policing. Residents also used familiarity to minimize commonly voiced fears of prisons, evident in the remainder of the bulletin's text:

> We must not panic—this facility is a type of industry that could be the "boom" that Allen parish needs—WITH VERY LITTLE PROBLEM, if any. Even if you build a college you are inviting a problem—many problems. This would have far less tha[n] a college. This facility is <u>NOT A PRISON</u>. Persons caught in norther [sic] U.S. as being unlawful in the U.S.—without permission to be here, are <u>detained</u>, processed, and then deported back to Mexico. (most of those this center would handle would be from Mexico.) There would be no way that they could "take jobs"—fact [sic] this is to keep them from taking jobs. They could in no way be on our streets—they would be behind a double 12 foot fence with guards. They are not criminals—those who are caught and found to be criminal are sent to a prison detention center—not here. They are family people looking for a better life. This center would give immediate jobs—for construction about 350 jobs—a little later about [600] to 700 jobs with a payroll of about 18 million dollars. We might can get it—if the community does a great big welcome to it.[60]

The message tried to assuage concerns by noting that this facility would be filled with other family people, who then would be unable to compete for work, and also would be less troublesome than partying college students. This narrative offers competing reasons to explain the seemingly natural suitability of detaining noncitizens in close proximity. Those who would be detained are presented as "not criminals," but similarly as "family people looking for a better life." This positioning then enables justification of the role the facility would play in meeting the employment needs of local residents. One group's insecurity through detention ensures another group's economic security through proximity.

Lengthening Distance from the Border

The Justice Department's push for more detention space emerged from the Reagan administration's policy of mandatory detention, which ensnared Haitians, Cubans, and now, moving through the 1980s, asylum seekers from Central America. The United States had long been involved in supporting governments friendly to its interests in the region. A Central Intelligence Agency (CIA)–backed military coup in Guatemala in 1954, for one example, was accompanied by military aid, training, and advising. While President Jimmy Carter had stopped military aid (though not counterinsurgency training) to Guatemala, Reagan resumed military aid, even as the U.S. media published reports about assassinations and political violence in the region. The Reagan administration also increased its arms shipments to Honduras, which served as a base for U.S. military operations in neighboring countries (Golden and McConell 1986, 24–25).

Salvadoran and Guatemalan nationals fleeing United States–backed dirty wars encountered hostile landscapes for asylum-seeking and few chances for protection. Only 1 percent of Guatemalan asylum applications and 3 percent of Salvadoran asylum applications were approved in the 1980s (Villiers 1994, 902). Once again, there were conflicts among different parts of the government as to whether to grant extended voluntary departure (EVD) status to Salvadorans—as then applied to all nationals from Uganda, Afghanistan, and Poland (nationals from Nicaragua, Ethiopia, Lebanon, Hungary, Romania, Iran, and Czechoslovakia were granted individualized hearings). EVD was a temporary, liminal status: neither asylum nor refugee status, it temporarily suspended deportation and detention, and granted authority for people to work on renewable work permits.

The House passed a resolution on December 15, 1981, calling for EVD status for Salvadorans, but the State Department did not support extending this protection.[61] Elliot Abrams, Assistant Secretary of State for Human Rights and Humanitarian Affairs, testified to the Senate in 1985:

> If you look at the four countries for which there is EVD today, one thing in common with them is they are far away, and that is not a coincidence. That is, we are extremely reluctant to grant EVD to any country which is nearby and has had a long history of massive illegal immigration to the United States for economic reasons (Zucker and Zucker 1996, 93).

The assertion that Central Americans have a "natural history" of extended migration for economic reasons defied historical fact (Schoultz 1992). Only after the Salvadoran and Guatemalan governments escalated attacks on their own citizens, respectively in 1980 and 1981, did people from these countries flee to the United States in significant numbers (Schoultz 1992, 165). Abrams, meanwhile, was actively supporting the dictatorship of General Efrain Ríos Montt, who was carrying out acts of genocide against indigenous people in Guatemala.[62]

The Reagan and George H.W. Bush administrations rationalized their refusal to extend EVD to Salvadorans and Guatemalans on anti-communist foreign-policy grounds and on the geographic reasoning that temporary protection for people fleeing from nearby countries would promote unlawful migration (Fitzpatrick 1994, 45). President Reagan animated Cold War geopolitics with Red Scourge fears, painting people fleeing Central America as an unstoppable force. If the United States did not win its fight there, he warned, "the result could be a tidal wave of refugees . . . —swarming into our country seeking a safe haven from communist repression to our south" (in Zucker and Zucker 1996, 84).

Meanwhile, the INS claimed that it treated Salvadorans "as it treats other aliens," and processed them on a "case-by-case basis, relying largely on State Department advice that few if any have a well-founded fear of persecution if returned to El Salvador."[63] The INS apprehended some 15,900 Salvadorans in fiscal year 1981 alone, and this group comprised 30 percent of the people being held in INS facilities in Port Isabel, Texas; El Paso, Texas; and El Centro, California (US Congress 1982a, 10–11). Most of the Salvadorans confined by the INS forewent deportation hearings by signing voluntary departure papers, which sped the return process. While a favorable outcome for the INS, this situation did not reflect Salvadorans' preferences to return so much as the use of detention as a coercive deterrent to asylum.

Two court cases in April 1982 shifted this inherently coercive situation. First, the Southern District Court for Texas-Brownsville in *Nuñez v. Boldin* ruled that the INS was obliged to advise Salvadorans and Guatemalans of their right to seek asylum. The second case concerned a Salvadoran man named Crosby Wilfredo Orantes-Hernández, the named plaintiff in a class-action suit who was apprehended by INS agents at a bus stop in Culver City, California, beaten, and then taken to detention. While in detention, he was urged to sign voluntary departure documents, but was not notified of his rights to counsel, asylum, or a deportation hearing. The Central District Court for California in *Orantes-Hernández v. Smith* found:

> Salvadorans are frequently arrested, deposited in waiting rooms, interrogated, put onto buses, and flown back to El Salvador all in a matter of hours. Often the aliens do not understand the language in which they are addressed, much less the chain of events which has been set in motion. In this environment, "coercion" is not limited to physical force or outright threats (Zucker and Zucker 1996, 91).

The court issued a preliminary injunction requiring the INS to refrain from deporting any class member (Salvadoran nationals) without providing them with a notice of the right to asylum.

The courts's affirmation of rights to asylum together with the administration's carceral resolve created additional pressure on the existing detention infrastructure and underscored the administration's ongoing search for space. In the process, the Justice Department sought to maintain a distinction between short- and long-term detention objectives: "It is important to note that short term/quickly processed Mexican nationals apprehended in the immediate border should not be linked with the longer term individuals to be detained in the proposed centers."[64] Ostensibly, making clear distinctions between facilities' uses would enable both the INS and the Border Patrol to increase their apprehension, detention, and removal rates. Whereas new detention facilities brought "the border" into closer proximity with local communities across the United States, those seeking protection in the form of political asylum found themselves distanced from their rights.

BUILDING PROXIMITY

In light of the Fort Allen debacle and the *Nunez* and *Orantes* decisions, the Justice Department continued its search for contingency space that would be available in case of a "mass illegal immigration emergency."[65] Concern centered on the "overall instability of the Caribbean Basin, and the many thousands of El Salvadorans in refugee camps in Mexico and other countries. . . ."[66] This contingency space, distinct from long-term detention, would soon enter the deliberations between Oakdale and El Reno. In the fall of 1982, Oakdale leaders hosted another site visit, this time attended by Attorney General Smith. With El Reno still in the running, Oakdale backers refined their lobbying efforts to respond to the concerns raised in Giuliani's June decision letter. First, they offered to provide the federal government a deal on real estate and utilities. The city of Oakdale "guarantees the land costs will not exceed $1,200 per acre," and offered $150,000 in cash or land for the site.[67] The city promised to install water, electricity, and gas lines to the property at no cost to the government.[68] The feds would also be charged commercial rates for utilities and only $125 monthly for sewerage service. Second, backers identified members of the "Hispanic speaking population" and involved them in the site visit.[69] Third, they challenged the perception that Oakdale was remote, identifying its proximity to state and U.S. highways and to several commercial and military airfields (see map 6).

By January 1983, the INS would come to be swayed by this proximity argument, now noting that Oakdale was closer to more consular offices (located in Houston, Texas) than El Reno was to embassies (in Dallas, Texas).[70] Despite the higher cost and distance from a BOP facility, the INS now preferred Oakdale because it had "community acceptance," which the agency identified as

> an extremely important ingredient in site selection. Over the past few years, lack of community acceptance and community opposition was instrumental in INS being denied or delayed access to several suitable potential sites to house alien detainees. This, coupled with the opposition leader's avowed determination to block completion of the facility at El Reno through litigation or other means, should be given careful consideration in arriving at a decision.[71]

It was at this moment that the search for contingency space entered decisively into the ongoing debate between El Reno and Oakdale. The amount of space that the Justice Department had in mind for a contingency site would provide temporary quarters (tents) for two thousand to five thousand people on short notice. The BOP remained concerned that building a new facility so far from an existing prison would prove to be a "white elephant" if the INS did not continue to require space, but agreed that El Reno residents were unlikely to accept the contingency site.[72]

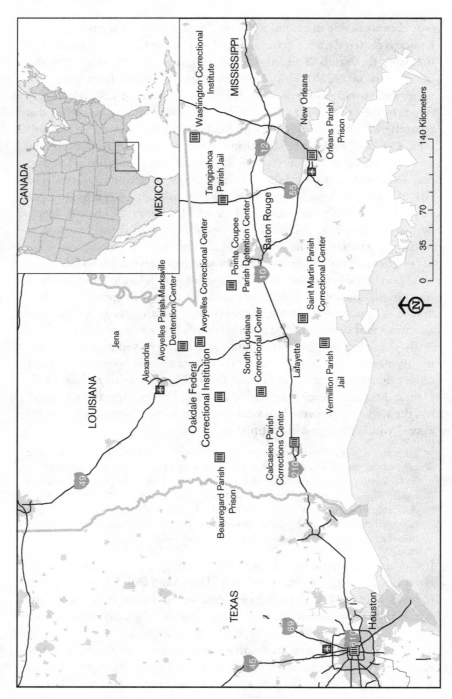

MAP 6. Situating Oakdale, Louisiana. This map situates Oakdale within a broader regional prison economy and regional transportation infrastructure.

Giuliani wrote to the Attorney General, saying, "This is a close call. I recommend that the proper officials in Oakdale be approached to determine whether they are actually receptive to use of the site for contingency purposes."[73] In early February, BOP and INS representatives met with Oakdale officials to discuss the town's openness to the contingency option and the possibility of the facility's being used to confine people convicted of federal offenses. Mayor Mowad and the alderpersons for Oakdale supported the flexible use of the space and unanimously passed a resolution that Mowad had prepared, endorsing a one hundred–acre contingency site.[74]

These commitments secured the deal for Oakdale. The Bureau of Prisons would lead the process, "with the help of INS," of acquiring land and completing the environmental review process.[75] The BOP identified a three hundred–acre parcel of undeveloped timberland owned by a lumber company and zoned as rural, as their site.[76] The "terrain and timber growing features" in the area "would allow a low profile facility, not readily visible to area traffic."[77] Attorney General Smith approved construction on the site on December 10, 1983, in order for the "open, campus-like" facility to be operational in 1985.[78]

FIGHTING REMOTENESS: RIOTS, REBUILDING, AND EXPANSION

A group of immigration attorneys, including the American Civil Liberties Union (ACLU) and Lawyers Committee for International Rights, made a last-ditch effort to prevent the construction of the facility in *Roshan v. Smith*. They invoked the location of Oakdale and the National Environmental Policy Act (NEPA) in their suit. Remoteness was their fundamental concern. They argued that the capacity and rural location of the facility would jeopardize detainees' rights to counsel and due process. They also contended that the environmental impact statement had failed to consider the social and health effects of the facility or the contingency site.

Similar concerns had been recognized by Judge Hastings in 1981 and upheld by the Supreme Court in *Jean v. Nelson* regarding the transfer of Haitians to facilities across the Eastern Seaboard. In this case, however, Washington, D.C., District Court Judge Thomas Hogan summarily dismissed *Roshan v. Smith,* ruling that the plaintiffs did not have standing to sue because the facility was not yet open and people were not yet confined there. Thus, he concluded the attorneys' argument regarding "the threat of injury [was] too conjectural" (1985, 906). Hogan continued, "The

Court is left to hypothesize as to what degree of distance between the location of [pro bono] lawyers and the ADC [alien detention center] will serve as a prohibitive factor." The possible "inconvenience arising from the mere distance between themselves and clients they represent or claim they wish to represent, with the complete absence of any claim of affirmative interference with their ability to do so," meant that they had no First Amendment claim (907).

While Judge Hogan minimized distance as an "inconvenience," almost immediately upon the opening of Oakdale, the transfer of detainees would present problems for migrants and their attorneys. The first people to be held at Oakdale were transferred in from El Centro, California, in April 1986 (Kahn 1996, 151). A couple of months later, workplace raids at two Long Island factories just before the July 4 holiday resulted in the apprehension of forty-seven people, forty-three of whom were Salvadoran. A group of forty individuals apprehended in the raid was handcuffed together and flown to Oakdale without being allowed to contact their family members or attorneys. At the time, there was no prohibition in New York against hiring undocumented migrants, and the factory owner posted some of the bail money that enabled them to return to Long Island. Oakdale was now on the map as a place that epitomized the production of remoteness: designed to be far from attorneys, and thereby to "increase the speed and number of deportations."[79]

In the spring of 1984, even before construction had commenced, Mayor Mowad embarked on efforts to expand the capacity of the municipal airport in order to improve the connectivity of the site. The Allen Parish Airport Commission and Allen Parish Police Jury began working to purchase land in order to extend the runway and add a terminal so that the INS would have closer access to an airfield.[80] The immediate objective was to secure $2,475,000 in funding from the Federal Aviation Administration (FAA). Senators Long and Johnston and Congresspersons Breaux and Long once again proved themselves active supporters of the efforts, and Governor Treen committed $600,000 for the required local matching funds.[81] Airport authorities in nearby Alexandria and Lake Charles, however, opposed the expansion, prompting the FAA to ask for more information on expected traffic.[82] Unsurprisingly, given his previous efforts, Mowad collected data from the INS, letters from private firms committing to use the facility, and support from Louisiana's Secretary of Public Safety and Corrections, who indicated that the new state prison slated for Allen Parish would rely on the Oakdale airport if it were expanded.[83]

On this matter, Mayor Mowad would not be successful. When Oakdale opened, the INS began using Esler Airfield in Alexandria, Louisiana, some forty miles away, and expanded operations there into a "satellite office" in 1990. Nevertheless, the new federal facilities in Oakdale had set in motion a longer-term dynamic involving local and regional competition to secure INS revenue. Oakdale would become a fundamental and long-lasting node in a broader carceral and legal infrastructure in which different state and private actors would vie to provide the transportation facilities and services and to contract detention space that the INS relied upon to conduct its operations. The construction of centralizing infrastructures (agglomeration) for government operations facilitated the expansion of carceral institutions and deportations, while maintaining Oakdale's relative remoteness for migrants and their advocates.

A delegation from the group called Minnesota Lawyers International Human Rights Committee (MLC) visited Oakdale soon after the detention facility had opened in 1986. Notably, the complex had been constructed with eight courtrooms for holding immigration hearings, which meant that detainees would not need to be shuttled back and forth to federal courts in New Orleans or Houston. As would be repeated in facilities constructed after this time (and at the site of the large-scale raid in Postville, Iowa, in 2008), the government moved court infrastructure and personnel to sites of confinement to facilitate the removal process (Stumpf 2013). In the first six months of operations, three immigration judges with the Executive Office for Immigration Review (EOIR) and three INS attorneys saw five thousand cases, most of which resulted in deportations (Minnesota Lawyers International Human Rights Committee 1987, 11). The Ecumenical Immigration Service, based in New Orleans, created Oakdale Legal Assistance (OLA) to provide *pro bono* legal services to people confined at the facility. Because of the sheer number of people detained, they focused on asylum cases; in the first five months of their operations, they filed 120 asylum cases and offered legal assistance to another 675 people. Their efforts are impressive considering the hostility toward OLA from the BOP, INS, and EOIR that the Minnesota delegation documented. MLC learned from an EOIR employee that "EOIR support staff had discussed setting a policy allowing them to help other legal representatives but not OLA" attorneys, whom they regarded "as political activists" (14–15). An OLA paralegal, Robert Kahn, would publish one of the first book-length exposés of migration detention, *Other People's Blood,* in 1996.

Only a few months into operations at Oakdale, the INS announced that as of November 1986 it would use the facility exclusively to confine Mariel Cubans. Most of the Cubans would be transferred to Oakdale from the federal prison in Atlanta, where they had been living on lockdown for two years following a riot in 1984 (Nacci 1988, 5). While some would remain in Atlanta, the ostensible objective of this centralization was to facilitate their release into halfway houses, given that Cuba would not accept their return (Minnesota Lawyers International Human Rights Committee 1987, 29–36). Kahn contends that the "change of mission" was intended to disrupt legal services being provided to Central American asylum seekers being held there (1996, 169).

In 1981, the Justice Department had implemented a status review plan to assess who among the Cubans held in BOP facilities might be eligible for release.[84] The State Department had also been in talks with Cuba since 1981, while Carter was still in office, to negotiate the return of so-called "undesirables."[85] In 1984, Cuba and the United States signed the "Repatriation List" agreement, naming 2,746 individuals in U.S. custody whom Cuba would repatriate. In exchange, the United States would resume the issuance of visas in Havana. Under this agreement, some 201 people were returned before Cuba halted the agreement to protest the commencement of Radio Martí broadcasts in 1985.[86]

News of this deal drew ire from Republicans and Democrats. Governor Graham, a Democrat, pressed the administration to learn if Marielitos confined in Florida prisons were part of the negotiated list; they were not.[87] Jeb Bush, then chair of the Dade County Republican Party, wrote to Edwin Meese III, who succeeded Smith as Attorney General in 1985, urging him to intervene in the State Department's decision: "That statement has done more damage to the Administration's support in the Cuban American community than anything else in the last six years."[88] Referring to the bargaining chip of entry visas, Bush continued, "To me and to many others, it is unconscionable to use as a tool of negotiating with Castro the one group of people who have consistently fought the communist dictatorship in Cuba." Another Democrat, South Carolina Comptroller General Earle Morris Jr., exclaimed to Vice President Bush, "I never cease to be amazed, astounded, agitated, alarmed and aggravated by some of the stupidity of our federal government. The most recent decision of absurdity totally without merit is the decision to return 2,500 Cuban undesirables and to admit 25,000 more Cubans in annual perpetuity. How silly can we get?"[89]

The uncertainty of indefinite detention, release, or forcible repatriation was the context within which the Cubans detained in Oakdale and Atlanta learned that the Cuban government had again agreed to resume repatriations in November 1987. Officials in neither facility knew how many people were on the list for deportation, and put staff on alert for disturbances. Two days after the news, two hundred to three hundred Cubans attempted to storm the front entrance building at Oakdale, and fighting ensued between a growing group of Cubans and INS and BOP guards. In a few hours, ten of fourteen buildings in the Oakdale complex had been destroyed and twenty-eight people were being held hostage.[90] Local law enforcement, the Louisiana National Guard, and INS's newly established SWAT team, Border Patrol Tactical Unit (BORTAC), arrived on the scene that day, and soon were joined by FBI and BOP hostage negotiators. A couple of days later, detainees held in Atlanta also staged a revolt, taking seventy-five hostages and burning three buildings.[91] In the early days of the uprisings, which would continue for several days, Attorney General Meese announced that he would extend a moratorium on deportations and hearings for those being held, but did not offer a permanent right to remain in the United States.[92]

The takeovers would be called "unique in the history of the federal correctional system, in terms of their sheer magnitude, origin and complexity."[93] They were among at least twenty-five other major "disturbances" (including riots, food strikes, fights, and demonstrations) involving INS detainees in fiscal years 1985, 1987, and 1988 (Karacki 1989, 32). Cubans held at the Krome facility had burned down a dormitory in 1986 and then were transferred to other federal prisons (Kahn 1996, 152). The media referred to the events as riots, but the chief researcher for the Bureau of Prisons, Peter Nacci, characterized the "disturbances [as] more closely related to what we commonly refer to as an insurrection—an act of open rebellion against an established government or authority—than to a riot" (1988, 3).

Criticism of the State and Justice Departments' operations, federal intergovernmental relationships, and the handling of Mariel Cubans' indefinite detention, and migrant detention more broadly, began in the midst of the uprisings. Senator Breaux told the press that the State Department had made "a disastrous mistake" in not notifying the Justice Department about the resumption of returns to Cuba: "It was handled very poorly and that's pretty mild."[94] A second set of circumstances that drew scrutiny was the overcrowding in each of these facilities and the broader federal prison system. The New York Times reported that

1,039 people were confined at Oakdale, "81 percent more than the number for which it was designed. The Atlanta prison held 1,591, or 47 percent more than its supposed capacity."[95]

The after-action report produced for the Attorney General deflected criticism of prison conditions and the BOP and attributed the disturbances to the "nettlesome problem of Cuban nationals being held in federal custody."[96] It noted that in response to the BOP's "overall overcrowding rate" of 156 percent, the mission of the facility at Oakdale had been "re-designated" to confine solely Cubans, a fix that would shift their location, but not magically create more space. Even more than the policies and conditions of potential indefinite confinement, the Attorney General affixed the problem firmly to the Cubans themselves. This shift is evident in Acting Associate Attorney General Thomas Boyd's report to Congressperson Kastenmeier, explaining the immediate precursors to the riots:

> Its complexity flowed both from the fact that the underlying reason for the riots was unrelated to anything under BOP control, and because those responsible represented a completely unique population: they were foreign-born; many spoke little or no English; most were not serving time for federal offenses and had already completed serving state or local sentences; and their immediate goal was to be allowed to remain in U.S. detention facilities (and ultimately, to remain in the United States).[97]

Boyd's mix of individual factors and governmental policy flattened distinctions between culture, language, and governmental power, effectively shifting the blame for the uprising from problematic policies to the group with least control over their lives.

While preventing another Mariel had been the impetus to construct Oakdale, this transfer of Mariel Cubans represented another ricochet of the long Mariel crisis. Resistance to confinement on the part of Cubans would manifest most volatilely in riots, and result in their transfers to facilities across the country, spurring the push for expansion in Oakdale and elsewhere. The destruction of Oakdale was followed by the fairly immediate reconstruction of the complex. Expansion plans had already been under way for Oakdale II, which was to be the federal deportation center whose first phase of construction was slated to include 350 new bed spaces. With the riots, Mayor Mowad saw the opportunity to secure funds for immediate construction of the entire one thousand–bed facility, in addition to the reconstruction of what was then known as Oakdale I. "It is important that we push to expand now since the memories of the riot is [sic] so front in everybodys [sic] mind," he wrote to Senator Breaux.[98]

The expansion of Oakdale made the complex an even more central element of the Justice Department's efforts to confine and expel migrants. The Oakdale I complex destroyed in the uprising would resume operations in January 1989 as a federal detention facility. Oakdale II would become a deportation center once opened in March 1990. Finally, an 80,000-square-foot administrative building would host offices for Executive Office of Immigration Review courts for the eastern portion of the United States.[99] Rather than concentrating Cubans here, upon reopening, Oakdale I was used to confine men who were not Cuban or Mexican and who were convicted of federal offenses. Oakdale II centralized so-called "criminal aliens" who had been released from state and local facilities.[100] Mariel Cubans would once again be dispersed to facilities across the country, according to the BOP's post-uprising policy of confining thirty or fewer individuals from this group in any one prison (Welch 2000, 79).

POLITICIZING GEOGRAPHICAL REMOTENESS AND CONTINGENCY

While criteria such as proximity to migrant population centers and existing Bureau of Prisons facilities entered into decision-making about where to build new permanent detention capacity, ultimately these criteria did not determine where facilities were built. As with attempts to use military bases, the construction of new detention facilities proved to be politically charged, repeatedly catalyzing communities that would contest or—conversely—advocate for facility construction. Opposition from local constituencies quickly sank some proposed sites, just as motivated constituencies and elected officials could successfully lobby for a facility.

This contingent set of place-based and intergovernmental dynamics, together with the Reagan administration's resolute commitment to incarceration, entrenched the trend toward remote locations of facilities. At the same time, local and federal actors worked to minimize the remoteness of Oakdale by constructing the infrastructures for confinement and deportation operations to function. These included building courts directly adjacent to the detention facilities, expanding transportation networks, and leveraging crisis to push for more rapid expansion. The result was the creation of a central node of U.S. detention and deportation infrastructure in the middle of Louisiana that persists today. The scope of site battles on display in this chapter, and their resolution, dispels any one rationale applied to the historical geographic expansion of the U.S. detention system. This carceral geography is not a history attached to any one border or region, but instead a story of dynamic political and legal contexts and contingent geographical reasoning and rationales.

The sustained and well-resourced commitment to deter asylum seekers meant that the lines between administrative and punitive confinement blurred, even as legal precedence and authority and distinct jurisdictional and institutional legacies remained salient. As this chapter illustrates, debates over whether new long-term detention capacity would be developed also involved deliberation over which agency would be charged with running any new facilities. This, too, was a contingent outcome, given lingering questions about whether the government would continue to confine unauthorized migrants and asylum seekers for long periods, and given concerted migrant self-organizing and advocacy efforts. Even as standards for confinement for INS and BOP facilities converged, the legal distinction between administrative and criminal legal confinement (and the conceit that "administrative" meant "temporary") was invoked repeatedly to rationalize carceral expansion, curtail migrants' rights, and refute charges of racism and abuse.

Finally, the normalcy (which is not to say acceptability or justness) of the oppressive treatment of Mexican migrants by border and immigration police together (Hernández 2010), coupled with anti-Black racism, naturalized and fueled the expansion of long-term detention. The minimization of racism through an appeal to "natural" proclivities to migrate or objective foreign-policy objectives did not lessen the racialized targeting of migration policing or deterrence policy. Indeed, efforts to deter asylum seekers through detention would collide with the politics of law and order to embed carceral logics into migration policy as much as local livelihoods, even before formal criminalization legislation was passed. In the midst of the bipartisan law-and-order turn, the next chapter examines how crime became a new tool in legislative and administrative efforts to expel unwanted migrants.

4

"Uncle Sam Has a Long Arm"

War and the Making of Deterrent Landscapes

In 1983, the Immigration and Naturalization Service (INS) assumed jurisdiction over a minimum-security Bureau of Prisons (BOP) facility in Florence, Arizona. This central Arizona town in Pinal County sits between Phoenix and Tucson and near the Gila River Indian Community. Florence had hosted the state's largest prison since the early 1900s. When Florence incorporated the state prison into the city limits in 1982, it immediately doubled the city's population. The town's reliance on unfreedom, and the incorporation of confinement into the fabric of daily life, informed popular narratives. A booster document reported residents joking, "Half the population of Florence is behind bars, and the rest are in the bars."[1]

Arizona's Department of Corrections (DOC) had been under court order to relieve the overcrowding of its Florence prison since 1977, which led to a series of state-level sentencing reforms and expansion plans. In *Sunbelt Justice,* legal scholar Mona Lynch details how opposition to the proposed construction of a new prison in the Phoenix suburb of Litchfield Park to relieve overcrowding eventually failed. The process, however, politicized the geography of prison siting in the state. While Republican leaders favored expansion, they were also able to paint proponents of urban construction as arrogant for "forcing the prison on a community that did not want it, especially when Florence was willing to take it" (2010, 109). Such political pressures within the state resulted in further concentration of state and federal carceral institutions in Florence and Pinal County in the decades that followed.

The state of Arizona had hoped that it could use the federal prison site for decades, but federal dynamics conflicted with the state's designs for this facility. State and federal prison overcrowding were significant, and interconnected, issues across the country. With forty-one states under court order to relieve the dire conditions of their prison systems, the localized politics of prison expansion soon collided with the politics of migration deterrence and expulsion.[2] The result would be legislation and administrative procedures that would facilitate the deportation of migrants enmeshed in the criminal legal system. The BOP was poised to transfer its Florence facility to the INS, which was also searching desperately for space. In its efforts to expand capacity, the BOP had already opened a new Metropolitan Correctional Center in Tucson, and was building another facility in Phoenix.[3]

Florence and neighboring Eloy currently host one of the more significant agglomerations of carceral facilities in the contemporary landscape across the United States. This chapter examines how this concentration of prisons, jails, and detention facilities came into existence, tracing site battles as detailed in the previous chapter, and placing them in longer historical and geographic context. During and immediately following World War II (WWII), the carceral landscape of Florence and Eloy was fortified by the War Department, the INS, and Border Patrol. We explore how this potent martial and carceral mix developed in central Arizona to contribute to the formation of landscapes of deterrence. Popular understandings of the location of migration-detention facilities imagine their locations along the United States–Mexico boundary as a response to unauthorized border crossers and to speed deportations across the same boundary (conceptualized as "demand" in map 1). While border imaginaries and migration politics have certainly shaped Arizona's politics, our analysis of Florence's carceral landscape reveals shifting federal and state-level political forces underscoring the use of carceral space for different, sometimes overlapping, rationales: security, labor, criminal justice, and deterrence.

Contrary to "Southern border" narratives that assume the relation between detention and the boundary, Florence's location in a border state and its proximity to the border, over two hours' drive from Nogales, has little to do with how it became a major site of migration detention (see map 7). Rather, we explore overlapping rationales for the intensification of incarceration in Florence and the flexibility of border narratives to illustrate how criminalization and carcerality have been transnational since at least the Cold War. This analysis aligns with

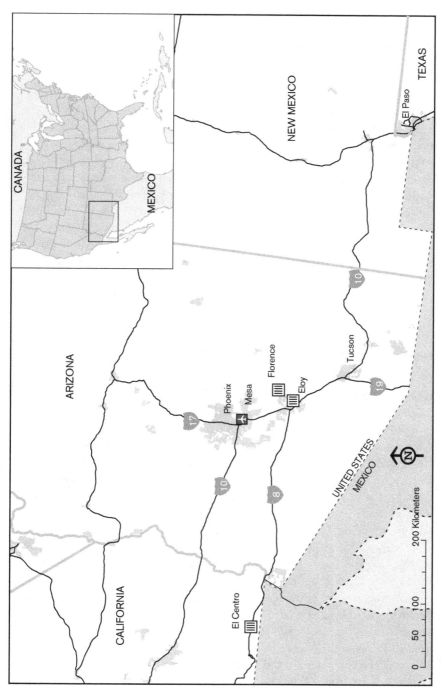

MAP 7. Situating Florence, Arizona. This map situates Florence within the regional prison economy and transportation infrastructure in Arizona.

Jennifer Chacón's (2015) call to more accurately attend to processes of criminalization. We find that Florence has been enmeshed in producing not only a variety of legally liminal statuses, but also longer histories of federal efforts to criminalize migrants.

This chapter further chronicles how national-level efforts to expel migrants grew ideological and administrative legs between the mid-1980s and mid-1990s by connecting new criminal sanctions to new mandates for state-federal collaboration. In this process, legislators sought to remedy the failure of deterrence both through continued detention and criminalization efforts that were concerned explicitly with rendering Afro-Caribbean people as a problem. The salience of deterrence would continue with Central American asylum seekers fleeing conflict in their countries. We trace how detention and efforts to contain mobility to south Texas replicated the ongoing, hotly contested treatment of Haitian asylum seekers. The emergence of the sanctuary movement in the early 1980s would challenge deterrence strategies at the scale of detention and regional INS efforts to confine asylum seekers to south Texas.

WORLD WAR II WORK FORCES IN CENTRAL ARIZONA

Florence was the site of one among the hundreds of prisoner-of-war (POW) camps operated by the War Department between 1942 and 1946 (Spidle 1975, 64). By the end of the war, some 425,000 German and Italian soldiers captured by Allied Forces in Europe and North Africa had been transported to the United States and confined in large bases and smaller branch camps in rural sites scattered mainly throughout the U.S. South and Southwest (Spidle 1975, 61; Krammer 1996, 28). At 640-acres, "Camp Florence would be the War Department's shining model," with a large hospital, swimming pool, twenty theaters, and sports fields (Hamann 2005, 9).

Florence's location on rail lines, proximity to a large expanse of federal land reserved for National Guard use, and warm climate contributed to the site's selection; but this use did not go uncontested. Members of the Rotary Club in the nearby town of Superior objected to Senator Carl Hayden that while "such camps are essential," this one would cause "unnecessary jeopardy to the largest copper producing area in the country," and hence they argued for the site to be used for soldiers.[4] The president of the Magma Copper Company drew on popular knowledge about the state's prison, objecting to the possibility that a large "floating population" of relatives and friends would gather. "I feel sure a lot of those people would be potential saboteurs and, therefore, a menace to any and all defense industries in this locality."[5]

While it is evident that family members would not be relocating from Italy or Germany to be near their loved ones, comparisons to other "floating" and migrant populations living in the area would continue. During their confinement at the Florence camp, most of the prisoners of war engaged in activities similar to those at the state prison: day-to-day operations for the facility and agricultural labor. Florence was surrounded by cotton, grain, and vegetable fields. Wartime demand for crops, combined with labor shortages caused by the war effort, meant that prisoners were contracted out to do agricultural work throughout the county.[6] In May 1945, some 85,000 prisoners of war were working in agriculture, a labor force even greater than the better-known Bracero Work Program, through which 58,000 Mexican workers had contracts (Heisler 2007, 241). Newspaper articles recollect "fond memories" of the POWs, in sharp contrast to the "influx of blacks, Mexicans and Anglo refugees from the American Dust Bowl" who arrived to harvest the fields.[7] These latter workers were characterized as "illiterates, accustomed to a hand-to-mouth existence, a people without home ties of any kind, a violent people particularly violent when in drink, who lived for today with no thought of the future."[8] The oppressive and exploitative treatment that migratory workers experienced contrasted with the "casual, friendly, and fleeting to personal and lasting" relationships that German prisoners established with Americans through their work (260).

The discourse of migrant labor as a natural condition of life for people who did not demonstrate qualities of established society was clearly racialized. Agricultural workers, of course, maintained important and enduring familial, community, and place-based ties, despite government policies that produced and policed their dislocation. The Border Patrol, established in 1924, was part of this labor management. Historian Kelly Lytle Hernández argues in *Migra!* that the Border Patrol was developed "within the bi-national context of migration control between the United States and Mexico" (2010, 7). Growers in both the United States and Mexico wanted abundant, flexible labor. During WWII, "shifts in U.S. global power and claims by the Mexican political and economic elite forced U.S. imperialism in Mexico to operate with the support and collaboration of Mexican economic and political elites" (8). Accordingly, the Bracero Program, housed in the Department of Labor, was brokered between the United States and Mexico to enable men to work in the United States on a temporary basis. While growers in the U.S. Southwest in particular lobbied the Department of Labor over wage rates, the Mexican foreign minister, too, weighed in to ban Texas from receiving Bracero workers in order to contest de jure racial segregation in the state (Calavita 1992; Foley 2007). The bilateral work program effectively "formalized the corridors of mass migration between Mexico and the United States" through strengthening ties between U.S. and Mexican authorities (Hernández 2010, 109).

The introduction of outsiders to constitute work forces was thus historically well established in this part of Arizona by the time lengthy battles ensued over the use of the Florence POW camp. Outside workers were considered highly precarious laborers, whether due to their confinement or their temporary status as noncitizen laborers on short-term contracts. These forms of precarity would continue during, and also be transformed by, World War II.

INCARCERATING FLORENCE'S MARTIAL ECONOMY DURING THE COLD WAR

Following World War II, Florence residents expected that they might acquire the POW camp from the War Assets Administration (later the General Services Administration [GSA]). A protracted dispute over who owned the land and who was authorized to utilize or dispose of the surplus property and facilities continued for the next twenty-five years. Over this time, portions of the site would be used by several state and federal agencies. In 1951, for example, a local educator sent a telegram to Senator Hayden: "For the educational well being of our children it is imperative that the prisoner of war buildings at Florence be released to the public schools."[9] A year earlier, the GSA had transferred nearly 734 acres to the state of Arizona for "educational and health purposes," and withheld another 5,700 acres next to the camp, which had been established for the National Guard by executive order in 1912.[10] Following a strike by prisoners at the state prison, the state established an Institute for Educational Rehabilitation for young first-time offenders, who would be transferred there from the adult facility.[11] The state also assumed use of the hospital on the site to relieve overcrowding at the state's mental hospital.

These local developments would not alter the decisions being made about Florence by the federal government. Florence would soon become part of Cold War efforts to rid the country of people thought to be communists or subversives. In 1952, the Bureau of Prisons began operating a prison camp on a portion of the Florence POW camp under provisions of the Internal Security Act of 1950. This legislation, introduced by Senator Pat McCarran (D-Nevada), was followed by the better-known McCarran-Walter Act of 1952. Both acts built on legislation passed in the 1910s targeting immigrants with anarchist politics and the 1940 Smith Act, which required the registration of noncitizens and enabled the deportation of individuals who belonged to organizations that advocated the violent overthrow of the government (Buff 2008, 528). The 1950 act required registration for communist or communist-front organizations and authorized administrative detention "in a time of internal security emergency."[12] The following year, Congress appropriated funds for the repurposing of six surplus WWII facilities, including former POW camps in Florence, Arizona, and El Reno, Oklahoma; a War Relocation Authority internment camp at Tule Lake, California; and surplus military facilities in Wickenburg, Arizona; Avon Park, Florida; and Allenwood, Pennsylvania (Cotter and Smith 1957). According to historian Rachel Buff (2008), these Cold War internal-security provisions resulted in a "deportation terror" that targeted, but extended beyond, immigrants with radical politics.

Indeed, the expansiveness of the internal-security rationale became evident at the Florence camp. A 1952 *Arizona Republic* story reported that Florence was being operationalized under the McCarran Act as a "stockade for dangerous subversives," in addition to serving as "a sort of second 'Ellis Island' to house immigration law cases."[13] The newspaper was referring to the practice of indefinitely detaining noncitizens suspected of radicalism on Ellis Island (Schrecker 1996). Historian Ellen Schrecker explains that the Internal Security Act enabled the INS to round up and confine more people whom they had already identified for deportation. In 1953, the *Arizona Republic* followed up and found that Florence was now being run as "an honor system camp" for "125 men convicted of crimes against the U.S. Government."[14] While there, they performed maintenance duties and grew crops for themselves and other facilities. "There is little difficulty with escapees," the newspaper noted, "for the inmates realize Uncle Sam has a long arm even though most of them are Mexican Nationals."[15] The legal geography of this "long arm" resonates with our earlier discussion of the flexibility of border enforcement in Oakdale and demonstrates the intersection of historical carceral landscapes with contemporary forms of criminalization of noncitizens.

In 1954, the state of Arizona learned that the Department of Health, Education, and Welfare had revoked the title to the property because the state had not complied with the federal terms of transfer.[16] This action occurred in the midst of what the press described as a "long-standing rhubarb" over who owned the property (the federal government under the GSA or the state of Arizona for the National Guard), the size of the property, which improvements had been transferred to whom, and how much of the property was surplus.[17] Arizona's adjutant general, who oversaw the National Guard in the state, wrote to Senator Barry Goldwater with a possible resolution to "this mess of messes."[18] He urged Goldwater to lend his support to Senator Hayden's proposal that the GSA transfer the buildings and improvements to the state, which would then renegotiate lease terms with federal agencies.

As this dispute continued, various government parties asserted their claims to or desires for the space. Hayden continued to negotiate authorization for the Institution for Educational Rehabilitation, even as he inquired about use of the site on behalf of the state prison, "and in the alternative some have suggested setting up a Veterans' Home at the site."[19] The Bureau of Prisons, however, soon contacted Senator Hayden, announcing their intentions for the site. In 1956, James Bennett, director of the BOP, explained that he had established the camp under the 1950 Internal Security Act. Moreover, "we have continued to operate this camp as a place for detention of Mexican 'wetbacks.'"[20]

Newspaper reports suggest that the Florence BOP camp was integrated into the infrastructure supporting raids of factories, agricultural fields, and Mexican neighborhoods. These raids were conducted by the INS and Border Patrol across the United States between the late 1940s and mid-1950s. Historian Jeffrey Garcilazo recounts how these sweeps, culminating in 1954 in Operation Wetback, focused on California and were fueled by a mix of anti-communist and anti-Mexican animus. One southern California newspaper exclaimed in 1950 that among the "wetbacks" were "Communists, taught in party cells south of the border to hate the Yanquis [sic]" (2001, 276). The scale of policing in the late 1940s to early 1950s resulted in approximately five hundred thousand apprehensions each year (Garcilazo 2001, 292; Hernández 2010, 143). The INS, in turn, sought funds to build two new detention facilities in El Centro, California, and Brownsville, Texas, and at a former military base at Port Isabel, Texas, and contracted with local jails for space (Hernández 2010, 143). These facilities, the latter of which became known colloquially as *El Corralón* (the big corral), would become infamous for their harsh conditions and hostility toward Central American asylum seekers in the 1980s.

The Contested Future of Florence's Martial-Carceral Economy

Following Operation Wetback, the Border Patrol remained focused on the United States–Mexico borderlands and the apprehension of men thought to be unauthorized migrants from Mexico. By the mid-1960s, although apparently no longer used for this purpose, the role of the Florence site was again disputed. The Bureau of Prisons had been using the site as a prison camp and detention center for people whose cases were to be heard at the federal court in Phoenix. The acting director of the Bureau of Prisons explained to Arizona Senator Paul Fannin, "In recent years the population of the Federal Prison Service has decreased sharply and it has become apparent to us that we cannot sustain, at their present levels, our camps at Florence and Safford, Arizona."[21] With this reduction, the BOP indicated that "a substantial portion" of the 456.5 acres it currently maintained would become available for other users.[22] Interestingly, given the disputes of two decades earlier, the letter indicated that the "land is now in the Public Domain and is used by us under a permit from the Bureau of Land Management."[23]

News of the BOP's imminent camp closure prompted two distinct responses from residents. Some opposed the shutdown, citing its rehabilitative or economic value for Pinal County and the state. A Florence-based dentist explained that the employees, their families, and the town would "be especially hard hit economically. As you know, this community is almost solely dependant [sic] on the income from services provided to the families of Federal and State Prison employees."[24] Yet a prison future was not the only vision that residents had for the city of Florence. The city attorney Robert Bean wrote to Senator Fannin on behalf of the town council, seeking help to turn the property into an industrial park. Bean wanted a full closure of the BOP camp because "the slow downgrading and removal of personnel is more disastrous to the economy of Florence than if there were an immediate removal."[25] Another resident wrote to the governor, "upset" that the National Guard, with its "vast resources," sought to maintain a claim on the space: "Historical Florence will die and be just another ghost town . . . if the towns [sic] people are not permitted to improve their economy by use of this facility."[26]

For the city, transfer and use of the property would allow it to help establish "private industry, [in which] lie the salvation of the economy of

Florence."[27] Florence's development commission created a proposal for uses of the space that would depart from the carceral economy. The report began by noting that "the condition of the camp has deteriorated to the point where all buildings should be removed and replaced with permanent structures, conforming to modern architecture."[28] The five proposed prongs for repurposing represented a mutually supporting set of economic and residential uses. First, light industry and warehousing would take advantage of Florence's location on rail lines and proximity to major Arizona cities. Second, a technical training center would prepare workers "(both men and women)" for "Arizona's expediting industry," which would complement the first use.[29] Third, the property was well suited to commuter aircraft landing and maintenance, which was "a 'must' for businessmen" in "this jet age."[30] The fourth focus would develop low-cost housing, which would support the mission of the technical training school. Fifth, the property would provide recreational and community space for the area. In addition to these civilian uses, the committee suggested that the site remained "exceptionally ideal" for civil-defense operations, including air-raid shelters.[31] The final proposed use would link the city's plan to Cold War imaginaries. "In the event of local and national emergencies, a Civil Defense Distribution Center could be set up for the dispersal of goods, foods and medical supplies. The location would be particularly suitable inasmuch as highways would be less congested than those in the densely populated areas of Phoenix, Scottsdale, Mesa and Tempe."[32]

The newly formed Florence Industrial Commission appears to have won its request as the Bureau of Prisons transferred at least a portion of the property to the commission. The state and relevant federal agencies seem to have worked out an agreement that the city would acquire the property and lease portions of it to the Arizona DOC and National Guard as needed.[33] The exact terms of the transfer are unknown, but it is clear that the transfer roiled Arizona's Department of Corrections and National Guard. (The poor quality of the microfilmed documents in Senator Goldwater's archives leaves holes in the historical record.) The DOC had been in talks with the Bureau of Prisons to lease the BOP facility, and in turn provide contract services to the BOP when it had no available space in Maricopa County.[34] In early 1969, representatives from the Arizona National Guard and Arizona DOC met with the state's attorney general at the "behest" of Governor Jack Williams to determine a course of action.[35] Among the options they considered were 1) pursuing a federal lawsuit to "rescind the conveyance"; 2) filing a state lawsuit; 3) condemning the property; or 4) maintaining the status quo.[36] The group decided that the federal lawsuit was the preferable course "because it would not directly involve the state as a party plaintiff, and would most likely produce immediate concessions on the part of the Florence Industrial Commission."[37]

The status quo option was rejected because "this would be to allow manifest injustice and a direct affront to the executive authority of the State of Arizona."[38] What was this "manifest injustice"? The answer is unclear, but the outrage suggests that state agencies bristled at a municipality having sidelined them in their negotiations with the federal government. What is clear is that the Arizona Department of Corrections did not expand to the site, and the Bureau of Prisons continued its use until its transfer to the INS in 1983. According to newspaper reports, Florence's industrial-development commission raised funds to purchase the surplus property. It rehabbed some of the residences for rental units and began operating the citrus grove. The mayor, who was also a realtor, showed the property to a land developer, who established the Western American Land & Cattle Company to develop the plot as a "mobile and modular-home community."[39] The developer would also build condominiums on site, marketed principally to snowbirds. Other dreams for the site would remain unrealized. Today, these carceral and residential uses abut each other, producing a geographical juxtaposition of free and unfree neighbors.

COLD WAR DEPLOYMENTS OF CRIMINALIZATION

By the time Bennett wrote to Senator Hayden in 1956 to explain that he was using the facility for "wetbacks," at least some Border Patrol officials were advocating a shift away from this term. Kelly Lytle Hernández recounts that the chief enforcement officer for the Southwest Region told his officers in 1956 that "the word 'wetback' . . . should be deleted from the vocabulary of all Immigration officers" because the term painted a sympathetic image of a poor, hardworking Mexican man who only sought to feed his family (2010, 205). He asserted that the agency more often was confronting "criminals, often vicious in type, and of hardened and defiant repeaters." Thus, he advised, "whenever a criminal record exists, we use the words, 'criminal alien', and when no criminal record exists, the words, 'deportable alien'" (206). These instructions corresponded with the Border Patrol's attempts to narrate its mission as "a more generalized objective of crime control" (205).

The irony that the Border Patrol would be inching away from the use of "wetback" even as the head of the Bureau of Prisons used the term to describe the people he confined at Florence underscores how the legal grounds and rationales for confinement were fluid, interlocking, and mutually reinforcing. The intertwined histories of migration and crime control at the Florence site would continue into the 1980s and 1990s as administrators and legislators looked for ways to resolve what they painted increasingly as interlocking issues. Among the first people who would be transferred to the new INS facility at Florence were Cubans, stretching the long Mariel crisis even further across space. Prefiguring the uprisings to come at Atlanta and Oakdale, Cubans sent to the Florence INS facility grew increasingly distressed at their confinement. A hunger strike they commenced early in the summer of 1985 escalated into a riot weeks later, with participants demanding, "Send us home or set us free!"[40] One cellblock in the INS facility was largely destroyed.

The events also fueled the ideological melding of immigrants with criminality and disorder. Florence's chief of police told the press that he had "never even seen a Cuban" before their transfer to the INS facility, but after spending time working with police agencies in Los Angeles and Las Vegas, he warned, "We have to remember these Cubans are felons."[41] "Knowing what I know of them, I approach them in the same way I would a rabid dog."[42] The INS also emphasized a frame of danger and disorder for the United States. The Western District Director for the INS, Howard Ezell, told the press, "They are real problems; they are people who have committed felonies—hardened street criminals."[43] He explained that all of the Cubans at the Florence facility had been convicted of crimes since arriving in the United States. "Those that we have in custody are people that I don't imagine you'd want living next door to you."[44]

This relatively small number of Cubans facing indefinite imprisonment would come to stand in for a communist menace that could not be contained. According to Joe Nevins in *Operation Gatekeeper,* Ezell was engaged simultaneously in a multipronged effort to create a moral panic about an imminent invasion in the Southwest border region. To do this Ezell employed both his post at the INS and at Americans for Border Control, a nonprofit anti-immigrant group that he established (2010, 98). One result would be the expansion of boundary fortification and policing measures. A less-recognized result involved deeper connections between the criminal legal and immigration systems—the early roots of criminalization and detention in the United States.

The Long Mariel Crisis and Criminalization for Expulsion

Legislative efforts to more closely align state corrections and federal migration authorities began far from Arizona, and were closely tied with efforts to resolve the long Mariel crisis. They were led by Democratic Florida Governor Bob Graham, who joined the Senate in 1987, and Republican New York Senator Alfonse D'Amato. The state of Florida sued the Ronald Reagan administration in 1981, contending that the overcrowding of Dade County's jails was "a direct result" of the federal government's admittance into the country of Haitians and Cubans who "were of a criminal character."[45] The suit demanded that the federal government take custody of these individuals. Senator D'Amato, similarly, began to attribute the overcrowding of state and federal prisons to noncitizens after the New York State Department of Corrections contacted him about its overcrowding problem. In both cases, animus was directed at the legislated category of "criminal aliens," noncitizens who had been convicted of particular crimes, with the objective of removing them not just from jails and prisons, but from the country.

This was a distinctly racialized effort wherein disorder in cities was linked discursively to crime, drugs, and immigrants (Simon 1998; Miller 2003; Yates, Collins, and Chin 2005). Miami became the apocryphal site for this story. The Liberty City uprising in 1980 was sparked by the acquittal of four police officers in the killing of a Black motorist in 1979. With a new president in power, the events brought national attention to deep racial segregation and worsening poverty for Black residents of Miami.

This moment collided with the government's "process of stigmatizing and criminalizing the Mariels," many of whom were poor and Afro-Cuban (Welch 2000, 79). Legal scholar Teresa Miller explains, "The imposition of criminal sanctions for conduct that previously amounted to civil violations—in other words, the creation of new categories of criminal offenses—was not the inevitable consequence of compassion fatigue," as the powerful Republican Senator Alan Simpson (Wyoming) would contend. (Simpson with Romano Mazzoli would pass the 1986 IRCA.). Rather, "the legislative will to criminalize certain kinds of immigration-related conduct correlates closely to a crisis of legitimacy that immigration policy experienced after 1975—acutely so after the 1980 Mariel Boatlift—as well as the popularity of 'tough on crime' measures already well underway in the same legislative arena" (Miller 2003, 626).

Laws pertaining to the deportation of noncitizens for convictions of certain crimes committed after their arrival in the United States have been on the books since 1917 (Schuck 2013). These laws underwent major shifts in the Immigration and Nationality Act (INA) of 1952 (McCarran-Walter Act), which broadened grounds for exclusion and deportation and established due-process rights in deportation procedures (Feldman 1993, 203). The INA legislated three principal categories of convictions that could result in the deportation of noncitizens, or "criminal aliens": 1) a "crime involving moral turpitude" committed within five years of entry to the United States, and that resulted in a one-year or longer sentence, or two separate crimes involving moral turpitude; 2) illicit drug use or violation of illicit drug laws; and 3) violation of gun laws regulating automatic and semi-automatic weapons (204). *Moral turpitude* is a notoriously undefined term, typically including murder, rape, and burglary, and also activities and identities that do not accord with heteronormative, racist, ableist, and antipoor ideologies. At various times, these have included unmarried women's sexual activity, homosexuality, consensual sodomy, and same-sex activity (Coleman 2008; Canaday 2009; Moloney 2012; Luibhéid 2015). As geographer Mat Coleman explains, the INA marked "the consolidation in US immigration law of modes of 'bio' surveillance at US borders as well as . . . postentry social control" (2008, 1099).

Migration and crime scholars have highlighted the pivotal role that policy entrepreneurs and government officials have played in fomenting moral panics, or crises, over lawlessness. Together with the media, they create the political conditions for drafting new criminal offenses and administrative procedures and implementing increased border fortification and migration-enforcement measures (Hall et al. 1978; Gilmore 2007; Simon 2007; Mountz 2010; Nevins 2010; Murakawa 2014). The renewed crisis regarding so-called "criminal aliens," which culminated in the harsh 1996 legislation that we detail in chapter 6, began to be shaped in the early 1980s, building on largely forgotten roots in the INA and previous Border Patrol practices.

The regional and racial dimensions of this push focused on discursively linking foreign nationals who had migrated from the Caribbean with criminality. Governor Graham had been insistent that "Castro's criminals do not belong in Florida's communities. They belong in the same jail cells they left in Cuba."[46] After his 1981 suit over "undesirable Cuban and Haitian refugees who are overcrowding Dade County jails," Graham pressed the issue of Cubans with President Reagan.[47] He wrote,

More than two years ago, I proposed a plan to return these criminals and other undesirables through the gates at our Naval base at Guantanamo Bay. This would show that our country is serious and tough with Castro in finding a resolution to a major problem. By taking action on the matter of these criminals, you would show all Floridians of your concern.[48]

D'Amato also involved himself in the "emergency" of "aliens in prison" as a rookie senator (1983). He was among the first congresspersons to push new legislative and administrative mechanisms, including formal collaboration between state and federal agencies, to control an ever-expanding category of "criminal aliens." This is perhaps ironic given that he had written, but does not appear to have introduced, a Senate resolution opposing the "blatant discrimination against Haitians," who were being "quartered in eight separate states, from my own state of New York to Florida to Texas" (US Congress 1982a, 219). Upon learning of noncitizens serving time in New York state prisons, D'Amato recounts that he began looking for ways to transfer them into federal custody. However, he learned that there were neither systematic administrative mechanisms nor federal prison capacity for continued confinement pending deportation.

What to do next? D'Amato narrates:

At the same time that it became apparent that transfer of aliens to the INS or the Bureau of Prisons was not practicable, I chaired an important hearing on the crime problem in New York City. The hearing examined, in detail, the national prison overcrowding crisis and the role of alien felons in exacerbating this crisis in several states (1983, 1165).

States found to have "significant" numbers of noncitizens imprisoned included New York (832), Florida (750), Texas (627), New Jersey (259), Pennsylvania (200), New Mexico (144), and Arizona (111). In short, D'Amato concluded, "what had at first appeared to be a problem for one state was, in fact, a national problem, and one that could be expected to worsen in the near future" (1166).

This jump in scale from apparently "significant" numbers in seven states to a wholesale national crisis attributed impending catastrophe to "criminal aliens." Further, D'Amato's rhetorical move tethered this abstract category explicitly to Mariel Cubans as "a sizeable criminal class" that was also involved in the "smuggling of narcotics" (1166). Following Stuart Hall and colleagues in *Policing the Crisis*, "The use of convergences and thresholds together in the ideological signification of societal conflict has the intrinsic function of *escalation*. One kind of threat or challenge to society seems larger, more menacing, if it can be mapped together with other, apparently similar, phenomena . . ." (1978, 225–26, emphasis in original). Such escalation did not guarantee results. It would take time and effort to translate ideological work into concrete governmental action.

LEGISLATING DEPORTATION SOLUTIONS TO THE DRUG WAR AND PRISON OVERCROWDING

For his first legislative move, D'Amato attached an amendment to the 1983 Immigration Reform and Control Act (IRCA), which would require the federal government to reimburse states for imprisoning non-citizens who had been convicted of felony offenses. The amendment had the support of fellow Republican Senator Paula Hawkins from Florida, who sat down with Attorney General Edwin Meese III to "explore the feasibility of returning Cuban criminals to Cuba or, in the alternative, of deporting them to some third country such as Honduras or Belize."[49] In a memo briefing Meese for the meeting, an aide noted that the Justice Department "strongly opposed" D'Amato's amendment, and that Simpson "also opposes and has indicated privately that he will not support it in conference."[50]

While IRCA did not pass that year, Senator D'Amato continued to rail against the INS, asserting that criminal aliens were "savaging our society" (Schuck and Williams 1999, 426). His efforts generated a good deal of press coverage, but the provisions he sought were included only partially in the Immigration Reform and Control Act that was signed into law by President Reagan in 1986. The act is most often remembered for three elements. First, IRCA enabled nearly 2.7 million undocumented residents, including agricultural workers, to legalize their status. Second, it created employer sanctions, which made it illegal for businesses to knowingly hire unauthorized workers. Third, the act increased funding for border policing. Less remembered elements of the act are that it barred people who had submitted their permanent residency application from applying for federal social welfare and health benefits for five years, and it required the Attorney General to begin deportation proceedings against noncitizens who had been convicted of crimes that carried deportation consequences (Feldman 1993, 207).

The latter provision was accompanied by a new program that the INS launched in response to D'Amato's overtures. The INS piloted the Alien Criminal Apprehension Program (ACAP) in Miami, New York

City, Chicago, and Denver. The aim of ACAP was twofold: 1) improving local and federal coordination, and 2) urging the "cooperation" of immigration judges in holding deportation hearings for imprisoned noncitizens (GAO 1989, 8; Schuck and Williams 1999, 370).

The war on drugs provided an important ideological and legislative opening to accelerate criminalization and associated efforts to expel noncitizens convicted of crimes (Yates et al. 2005; Hernández 2008; Escobar 2016). Scholars have shown how the conceit of combating drug trafficking served as the basis for the expansion of a transnational policing and military project. The result would be further fortification of the United States–Mexico boundary and increased transnational coordination and funding of enforcement efforts (Dunn 1996; Nevins 2010; Boyce, Bannister, and Slack 2015). The drug war also would have far-reaching implications for noncitizens on U.S. territory. Legislators, prison officials, and the press latched onto data showing drug offenses by noncitizens to frame the issue as one of immigrant criminality, not law-enforcement strategies. For example, when Florida Governor Graham ran against Republican Hawkins for her Senate seat, they both foregrounded drugs. Hawkins referred to herself as "General," while Graham posed in front of an airplane seized for drug smuggling and called for a greater military role in interdictions (Murakawa 2014, 118). Besides domestic gangs, this appeal to militarism also named entire nationalities and regions, including the Caribbean, and as targets. Democratic New York Senator Daniel Patrick Moynihan, for example, blamed crack on the Bahamas, while Republican North Carolina Senator Jesse Helms pointed a finger at a "Jamaican posse" (243).

Legislators on both sides of the aisle amplified the nexus of crime and (im)migrant status by dramatically increasing the number of offenses that would carry deportation consequences and by requiring executive branch officials to develop institutional mechanisms to speed deportation hearings and expulsion efforts. Most significantly, the Anti-Drug Abuse Act (ADAA) of 1988 created a brand new category called the *aggravated felony* that applied solely to noncitizens. The aggravated felony is not one offense, but rather was created as an umbrella category that initially combined several offenses that were already part of the INA, including crimes involving moral turpitude and drug and gun trafficking. It also named murder as an aggravated felony (Feldman 1993, 205–6; Schuck and Williams 1999, 387–88). Finally, the ADAA ended the Attorney General's discretionary authority to parole an individual convicted of an aggravated felony; struck the possibility of taking a "voluntary departure," which virtually ensured a deportation record; and prohibited people with aggravated felonies who were deported from applying for entry to the United States for ten years (Feldman 1993, 207–8).

Graham, now senator, called the provisions of the ADAA "important steps toward solving a major problem faced by Federal and State criminal justice systems—the problem of how to expeditiously remove from our streets those aliens who are convicted of murder, or trafficking in drugs and weapons" (202). The ADAA provided for the establishment of the Institutional Hearing Program (IHP), which built on the ACAP program that had been piloted in four major cities. Like ACAP, IHP aimed to provide means for deportation hearings to be conducted before release from prison (Schuck and Williams 1999, 407). The ADAA stipulated that hearings were to be held directly at prison settings, which also created the possibilities of more efficient inter- and intra-agency cooperation (GAO 1989, 9; Schuck and Williams 1999, 416).

Senator D'Amato continued his legislative efforts with the introduction of the Criminal Alien Deportation and Exclusion Act of 1990, which did not get out of subcommittee. However, the Immigration Act of 1990 (IMMACT90) continued to expand the exclusion net and refine procedures for more efficient removals. The act featured some reforms called for by immigrant groups, as discussed below. But these reforms were tied with another round of criminalization, including the addition of more offenses classified as aggravated felonies and a toughening of penalties for migrants convicted of committing them (Schuck and Williams 1999, 438). Offenses now considered aggravated felonies included another vague class called "crimes of violence" and drug trafficking (Feldman 1993, 217–18). The geography of offenses now considered aggravated felonies was also deepened and stretched to include both state- and federal-level convictions as well as convictions for offenses committed outside of the United States that are similar to those classified as aggravated felonies in U.S. law (218).

In addition to expanding the net of offenses, IMMACT90, like the ADAA, shrank the avenues for relief by shortening the time available to petition for judicial review of deportation orders; eliminating "judicial recommendations against deportation" and barring aggravated felons from demonstrating "good moral character," which was necessary to establish a case for a suspension of deportation or a voluntary departure (222–23). Before this law, there had been a six-month limit on detention for people with a final order of deportation. Congress removed this provision for aggravated-felony convictions.[51]

Simultaneously, the act reestablished the Attorney General's parole authority, some of which had been stripped in the ADAA.

For immigration attorneys, IMMACT90 "added critical spikes to a coffin" for noncitizens convicted with a growing number of offenses (Feldman 1993, 216). For critics, the act showed that once again "legislators preferred procedural reform to adequately funding the removal system" (Schuck and Williams 1999, 439). Legal scholar Peter Schuck, who supported the more efficient removal of criminal aliens, contended that the "surprising modesty of INS budget requests" in the early 1990s may have stemmed from the "agency's poor relationship with the Department of Justice. . . . Although INS management enjoyed support from OMB throughout most of this period, it was often at odds with DOJ. Throughout the early years of the Bush Administration, DOJ managers displayed little faith in INS management, sometimes sparking open confrontation" (440).

D'Amato continued his pressure to gain federal reimbursement for state incarceration costs and was joined by other local politicians, including California Governor Pete Wilson and Florida Governor Lawton Chiles, both Republicans (445). By the mid-1990s, these efforts had resulted in considerable results. The "Clinton Administration focused more closely on criminal-alien removal" than had the George H. W. Bush administration, and Congress readily supported these efforts (447). We detail the resulting expansion of detention more fully in chapter 6.

SHIFTING BORDERS AND LEGAL GEOGRAPHIES: PRODUCING LANDSCAPES OF DETERRENCE

Even as legislators were busy tightening the links between crime and migrants, an asylum crisis was brewing in the south Texas borderlands that would expose the limits of using contingency space, such as had been built in Oakdale, to respond to large numbers of people on the move. By the mid-1980s, some five hundred thousand Salvadorans were living in Mexico, and forty thousand Guatemalan refugees were living in southern Mexico (Schoultz 1992, 182–83). Refugees from Central America who sought to cross the Rio Grande into Texas encountered an already policed landscape. Kelly Lytle Hernández explains that the Border Patrol's fortification and expulsion practices had "structured a system of violence without perpetrators" (2010, 132). Migrants, in turn, relied upon their social networks to create more safety for themselves and to cross without apprehension. The Border Patrol attempted to disrupt these networks by modifying its practices, including implementation of a system of airlifts and bus-return routes for deporting people far from their point of apprehension.

The sanctuary movement can be understood within this border landscape made deadly by design. In 1982, on the second anniversary of the assassination of Salvadoran Archbishop Oscar Romero, the sanctuary movement publicly announced itself from a church in Tucson, Arizona (Golden and McConell 1986, 14). Sanctuary was by no means isolated to the borderlands; the church in Tucson was joined immediately by churches in cities from New York to Los Angeles. Tucson was part of a rapidly expanding network of churches across the United States that became the backbone of efforts to provide material protection for Salvadoran and later Guatemalan asylum seekers making their way north in search of safe haven from ongoing violence at home. By the end of 1987, there were some 448 sanctuary locations, and over 20 sanctuary declarations passed by city councils and by the states of New Mexico and New York (Zucker and Zucker 1996, 90).

The U.S. government responded to the sanctuary movement by attempting to break the safety network, through prosecution of activists and attempts to thwart and contain the movement of asylum seekers farther into U.S. territory. By the mid-1980s, Chicago-based sanctuary activists Renny Golden and Michael McConnell reported that

> "escaping" from Casa Romero [a sanctuary site in south Texas] became more difficult than crossing the Rio Grande. Reconnaissance flights began over the Texas border, with a beef-up of a thousand border guards, over half of whom cover the Texas border. INS officers raid Greyhound buses in the Rio Grande valley, demanding that every Hispanic-looking person show identification. The border patrol [sic] has placed electronic sensors in the grass in the areas surrounding San Benito to detect footsteps (1986, 69).

Salvadorans whom the INS returned from El Corralón were sent by plane to El Salvador. Sanctuary-movement activists, in turn, filed a class-action lawsuit, *American Baptist Churches v. Thornburgh* (hereafter "ABC case"), to challenge the criminalization of sanctuary activities and the denial of equal treatment under the law for Salvadoran and Guatemalan asylum seekers (Coutin 2011, 578).

The asylum crisis in south Texas had its immediate roots in Cold War asylum politics and electoral political cycles. As described in chapter 3, the United States had direct and indirect ties to the violence driving displacement and refugee migration from Central America.

Not all Central Americans fleeing persecution were treated the same way. In 1987, Reagan's Attorney General Meese had told the INS not to deport any Nicaraguans who had a well-founded fear of persecution and to authorize work authorization for these applicants. Meese was expanding the unilateral action of a Miami-based district director who also opposed the socialist Sandinista government. During the 1988 presidential election season, Republicans demonstrated their support of the Contras (Schoultz 1992, 213; Kahn 1996, 191; Zucker and Zucker 1996, 96). Between May and early December 1988, some 27,000 asylum applications were submitted to one INS office in south Texas; approximately half were from Nicaraguans, a quarter from Salvadorans, and one-eighth each from Guatemalans and Hondurans (Zucker and Zucker 1996, 94–95).

Despite election-season rhetoric favoring Nicaraguans, President Bush's administration also intensified measures to deter asylum seekers. By April 1988, with asylum applications increasing, the Harlingen, Texas, INS office instituted an expedited hearing process, which led to a further increase in applications. In December 1988, the office tightened procedures. Asylum seekers now were required to submit their claims at the Harlingen office, and they were forbidden from traveling outside of the district. The new protocol effectively trapped asylum seekers within one part of the south Texas borderlands.

Immigrant advocates and the U.S. government alike recognized that a humanitarian catastrophe was ensuing in the Rio Grande Valley. "By Christmas," the immigrant advocate Robert Kahn writes, "thousands of refugees were sleeping on the streets of Brownsville. More than 300 slept under plastic bags or pieces of garbage and in holes in the ground in a brushy field across a dirt road from Casa Romero" (1996, 192). Hundreds more found space in an abandoned motel with no running water or electricity, and several hundred people stayed on the sidewalk and parking lot outside of the Harlingen INS office.

A judge issued a restraining order on January 9, 1989, enjoining the INS from instituting these restrictions. The INS viewed this ruling as an "intervention in INS operations [that] resulted in an unprecedented influx of Central American asylum applications through South Texas and on to other destinations across the United States."[52] The INS also contended that increases in asylum seekers following the judge's order

> further outrag[ed] the residents of Cameron County as these illegal entrants camped in local fields and waited for processing in the parking lots of local businesses. Resident outrage peaked on February 10 when the City of

Harlingen sent police and fire officials to close the INS Legalization Office where the Service was also preprocessing Central American asylum applicants before allowing them to travel to their intended destinations.[53]

From the INS's telling, the judiciary was responsible for both migration and Texas residents' "outrage," dismissing the legitimacy of the courts and dismissing the possibility of residents' criticism of the INS itself.

In January 1989, INS Commissioner Alan Nelson wrote to Attorney General Dick Thornburgh to brief him about procedures that had been developed and to ask him to pursue foreign-policy measures through the State Department. Namely, Nelson wanted the administration to "press the Mexicans to shore up their border and interior enforcement. The second is a suggested effort between the U.S. and Mexico to jointly pursue an overall policy solution to Central American problems."[54] Nelson attached a memo from the U.S. consular office in Mexico City, reporting on a meeting with Mexico's interior secretary:

> The Secretary was informed that the current major immigration problem was the influx of Central Americans into south Texas, transitting [sic] Mexico, then filing for political asylum in large numbers. He agreed with the seriousness of the problem, and alluded to Mexico's problem with Central American refugees, particularly the Guatemalans in southern Mexico. He expressed a generalized strong willingness to work together on such problems.[55]

Of course, the United States and Mexico already had bilateral arrangements regarding migration, but the United States sought more concerted efforts on the part of the Mexican government.

While the Mexican government did step up border patrol and deportation efforts (Schoultz 1992, 182–83), the United States made its own spectacular efforts to deter asylum seekers from making their way to the United States. After the temporary restraining order against the INS was lifted on February 20, the INS moved quickly to launch Operation Hold the Line. (This is distinct from the operation by the same name instituted by the Border Patrol in 1993 to divide El Paso, Texas, from Ciudad Juárez, Chihuahua.) The month-long operation was "intended to deal humanely, but assertively with new flows of Central American migrants," and expressly included the deportation of Nicaraguans, once again signaling the limits of Cold War foreign-policy commitments. Operation Hold the Line was "predicated on a three-faceted strategy of aggressive enforcement of immigration laws and detention for violators, thorough but expedited adjudications of asylum claims by qualified examiners, and a media campaign to ensure public understanding and acceptance of the steps being taken by the U.S. Government in South Texas."[56]

The Acting Associate Attorney General, Joe Whitley, explained to Attorney General Thornburgh that

> we do not represent this plan to be a "fail-safe" plan which guarantees success in curbing the influx of Central Americans into the United States. I believe, however, that it is a sophisticated, humane, and reasonable approach to an exceedingly difficult situation. The ultimate goal of the plan is the deportation of large numbers of Central Americans as only deportation can deter the northward migration.[57]

Whitley's letter underscores how detention tightly linked to deportation was imagined as a deterrent. Moreover, his use of the apparently neutral language of "migration" obscured the violent conditions Central American asylum seekers were fleeing and the policing efforts they already had encountered in Mexico.

To staff Operation Hold the Line, the INS detailed five hundred more agents to support operations in south Texas, which included the resumption of one-day processing of asylum applications and detention of "unsuccessful" asylum cases at Port Isabel (El Corralón). Many other asylum seekers found themselves detained at the Webb County Detention Center outside of Laredo (Frelick 1989, 8–10). The plan called for "'soft' detention for families, women, and children" through contracts with "the Red Cross or similar organization."[58] Additional Border Patrol agents were deployed along the Rio Grande boundary with Mexico and at inland checkpoints to prevent movement farther inland. Finally, the INS deployed agents to Mexico and Guatemala as part of intelligence efforts, and to improve cooperation with the Mexican government.[59] Anticipated costs for the month-long operation reflected deterrence objectives. The budget included over $1 million for additional Border Patrol activity, between $1.37 million and $2.5 million in detention (excluding contracts for "soft detention"), and $443,410 for asylum processing.[60] Calculated with even the low end of detention costs, asylum processing would amount to less than 19 percent of the budgeted costs.

Despite the *Orantes-Hernández* injunction, which—as discussed in chapter 3—prohibited the INS from deporting Salvadorans held in detention without providing them information about their right to seek asylum, Salvadoran asylum seekers detained at Port Isabel and Webb

County did not have access to telephones or to information on their rights to attorneys. The judge issued another injunction to prohibit the INS from moving forward on deportations of Salvadorans until showing the court that INS staff had provided them with information on their legal rights (Frelick 1989, 11).

The INS's restriction on the movement of asylum seekers in south Texas created a new legal geography of deterrence. While asylum seekers were physically present on U.S. territory, they effectively were confined to a single arbitrary INS jurisdiction if they wanted to apply for asylum, or did not want to risk apprehension by the Border Patrol while attempting to travel to common destinations such as Miami and Los Angeles. Advocates characterized the resulting circumstances in south Texas as an open-air prison and war zone (Kahn 1986). This situation resonates with the persistent movement of asylum seekers from Central America through zones of confinement where geography, legal status, and enforcement infrastructure converge to make them present but absent, and excluded within sovereign territory (Coutin 2011).

Once internal procedural and policing boundaries were lessened and asylum seekers were again allowed to leave south Texas after filing their applications, they soon departed. Their arrival in Miami on Greyhound buses was widely publicized. The media again invoked classic immigration tropes, including water metaphors, characterizing "droplets of Nicaraguans" forming a "rivulet" that "probably will become a flood" (Frelick 1989, 4). The image of an uncontrollable surge of people streaming across the border sidestepped the fact that the U.S. and Mexican governments had created routes for movement by flooding far more resources into deterrence than into asylum claims and visa processing.

In fact, the image of a dam or wall was selectively applied. The sharp contrast between the relatively favorable treatment that Nicaraguans had received, until this time, and the treatment of Haitians was itself a cause of conflict in Miami and continued to fuel advocacy to prevent the deportation of Salvadorans and Guatemalans. Deterrence efforts in the Caribbean and directed at Haitians detained in the United States had not ended. As we will discuss more fully in chapter 5, another onshore-offshore asylum crisis was developing as Haitians once again left their country by boat and encountered U.S. Coast Guard (USCG) cutters while seeking safety in the United States (12).

Months after the conclusion of Operation Hold the Line, and in the midst of discovery in the ABC case, the INS issued new asylum rules that created a specialized set of asylum officers (Blum 1991). Congress, moreover, passed the Immigration Act of 1990 at a moment in which discovery in the ABC class action, anthropologist Susan Coutin contends, "was likely to prove embarrassing to the US government" (2011, 580). As discussed earlier in the chapter, IMMACT90 expanded the scope and consequences of aggravated felonies, but it also created a new temporary refuge authorization called Temporary Protected Status (TPS), which replaced the Extended Voluntary Departure (EVD) status. Congress granted TPS to Salvadorans who had been in the United States before September 19, 1990, for a window of eighteen months. The settlement of the ABC case in 1991 enabled Salvadorans and Guatemalans to reopen or file their asylum cases, resulting in three hundred thousand cases to be heard (580). Given the existing court backlog, they would not be heard for another seven years, following peace accords signed in El Salvador in 1992 and in Guatemala in 1996, and the enactment of still more legislation criminalizing migrants. These shifts in the landscapes of legal possibility and the fight for status and protection amounted to prolonged periods of temporal and spatial limbo (Mountz et al. 2002). The number of asylum applicants holding TPS grew, eventually exceeding three hundred thousand. TPS-holders had no rights to family reunification or to leave the country. New landscapes of deterrence amounted to new forms of confinement in the interior. These new carceral forms and the dynamic legal geographies upon which they were built shifted continually, in law, in the courts, and in geographies between the borderlands and the interior.

CONCLUSION: LANDSCAPES OF MILITARIZATION, CARCERALITY, AND EXPULSION

This chapter disrupts popular narratives about detention in the United States in two ways. First, we challenge easy narratives that attach carceral landscapes to their proximity to the border and its association with unauthorized entry and deportation. While Arizona is a border state, the presence and location of the U.S. nation-state boundary cannot fully explain its prison landscape. As detailed earlier, migration-detention facilities in Arizona are rooted historically in wartime and criminal imprisonment. In questioning the popular narrative of detention being driven by border crossers and of seamless borderlands removal, this chapter illustrates the leading role that the politics of expulsion and criminalization played in the expansion and operations of a nationwide detention and deportation system.

Second, we demonstrate that processes of criminalization were not new to the 1990s. Rather, this chapter broadens the picture historically (showing the roots of imprisonment in the area) and geographically (showing the broader network of facilities and movements of captive people that federal authorities moved from place to place). Like Oakdale, every prison town has a circuitous, and contested, history. Florence's wartime history of POW imprisonment, Bracero labor, and Cold War confinement illustrates the tight linkages between the material and ideological means of war-making and imprisonment. The standard narrative on the criminalization of migrants in the 1980s to 1990s tends to view the process as another instance of the era's tough-on-crime turn. While not disputing the intensification of criminalization efforts, the glaring problem with such sweeping accounts is that they overattribute agency to abstract processes (such as neoliberalism) and fail to situate them in longer-term histories and the contingent interplay of politics at multiple geographic scales. The roots of criminalizing migrants, or using criminal legal tools to expel migrants, should not be found in the 1990s or even 1980s. Rather, these legislative and detention-expansion efforts also built on earlier rounds of Red Scare xenophobia from the 1910s and 1940s.[61]

The renewal of federal criminalization efforts in the 1980s links two Cold War moments: mid-1950s efforts to expel people thought to be subversives and later efforts to expel Mariel Cubans. In both moments, criminalization was pursued as a means to resolve geopolitical issues. Incarceration and deportation became the tools for framing and managing people as national-security issues. Foreign policy and militarization dynamics converged in the construction of military spaces designed for confinement in Arizona. This carceral landscape would eventually be put to other uses. In the 1990s and 2000s, Florence and Oakdale would become increasingly stitched into the nationwide network of federal facilities designed to accelerate the removal of criminal aliens. While another piece of legislation that Senator D'Amato introduced in 1992 calling for the reuse of military facilities for criminal aliens failed, military facilities nonetheless would be repurposed for imprisonment. As we describe more fully in chapter 6, WWII airfields in Mesa, Arizona, and Alexandria, Louisiana, became the backbone for coordinating the transfer of people in federal custody within the continental United States and transnationally for deportation.

There is an important regional specificity to how the connections between the Caribbean and United States–Mexico borderlands were being reworked. Government efforts to enlarge detention capacity increasingly appealed to the drug war and expulsion as a solution to domestic prison overcrowding, but continued to maintain that detention was a fundamental deterrent for asylum seekers from both the Caribbean and Central America. The growing transnational system of deterrence in the Caribbean and Americas and fortification of the United States–Mexico borderlands, then, were interlinked politically. Efforts to deter migration through detention and to manage the long Mariel crisis resulted in the dispersal of Cubans in detention and prison facilities across the country. Racialized geographic imaginaries of the Caribbean drug trade and Afro-Caribbean criminality, likewise, fueled criminalization efforts in the legislature, which fostered detention expansion.

Detention facilities do not magically appear at sites where the government seeks to prevent entry. Rather, as illustrated by Operation Hold the Line in south Texas, the U.S. government created a transnational sieve of interception and intelligence points in concert with Mexico. The politics driving the decision to attempt to confine Central American asylum seekers to south Texas were partially rooted in Miami and the racialized conflicts over asylum in that region. The invention and targeting of the criminal alien also illustrate how migration detention became an interlinked system. With the ADAA requiring immigration hearings prior to release, federal officials struggled to determine where federal felons would be held. The plan was "to incarcerate all male, non-Cuban [and non-Mexican] federal alien felons at the Oakdale Detention Center" in Louisiana.[62] This process would involve sorting people by nationality and assigned sex. As we show in chapter 6, this program would also create a network of facilities across the nation through which to conduct the work of deportation.

PART THREE

Expanding the World's Largest Detention System

5

Safe Haven

The Creation of an Offshore Detention Archipelago

As we have shown in previous chapters, deterrence efforts to prevent asylum seekers from reaching U.S. sovereign territory resulted in a scramble to build onshore carceral spaces. The expansion of migration detention then became increasingly entangled with the growth of the broader prison system. While criminalization played a substantial role in this expansion, the *ways* in which asylum seekers became subjects of and subjected to confinement have not been amply explored. Asylum seekers and migrants increasingly found themselves confined in a network of administrative detention facilities and jails. Affidavits from Haitian asylum seekers were collected by the Florida Immigrant Advocacy Center (FIAC). These documents show a blurring of civil and criminal spaces of confinement onshore. They also show how confinement would be extended offshore.

One of the men that FIAC represented, whom we'll refer to as B. P., said that he had fled Haiti by boat because, as he explained, his "life was cheap" due to his political commitments:

> I am an honest man, and have never done anything wrong, but I have been in different cages since last winter. Here at Krome, they started the bad treatment right away. They would make us run to the cafeteria to eat, and then they'd give us five minutes and make us run back. If you'd eaten anything at all, you'd want to throw it up. Now, after I came back from Texas, it's worse: they don't even give you that long.[1]

B. P. went on to describe how after being held at Krome, he was transferred 1,500 miles away to a jail in Webb, Texas, just outside of Laredo:

They had a list of people they were sending to Texas, and I wasn't on it. So I was shocked when they pulled me wet and naked from the shower and ordered me to get dressed. They said, "You're going to Texas." I started to cry. Someone offered me some food. I was so upset I threw it down. That's when they chained me up and nearly broke my arms. I got sent to Texas like that—chained. The guards at Webb were surprised to find out we weren't some kind of big crooks.[2]

B. P.'s description of being chained while being transferred between facilities and of the guard's cruel exercise of authority during mealtimes illustrates the *punitive* function of confinement experienced by B. P. and many other asylum seekers. The frequency of transfers (besides their use as disciplinary measures) also demonstrates how persistent problems with overcrowding remained, despite the rapid expansion of carceral spaces at this time. This crisis of carceral space onshore, we contend, created the conditions for the United States to expand its targeted confinement of asylum seekers offshore in the early to mid-1990s.

During the early to mid-1990s, the George H. W. Bush and Bill Clinton administrations built on existing practices of boat interceptions to consolidate a transnational deterrence infrastructure in the Caribbean, centering on the U.S. naval base at Guantánamo Bay (GTMO). Culminating in what became known as Operation Safe Haven, both administrations secured agreements from countries in the region—including Panama, Dominica, Suriname, Grenada, St. Lucia, the United Kingdom for the Turks and Caicos, and the Bahamas—to provide temporary sanctuary to people fleeing political repression in Haiti and Cuba. Harold Koh, an attorney representing Haitians detained at Guantánamo, sought to alert the U.S. public to what was transpiring in the nation's "back yard":

> Since 1991, our Government has almost continuously maintained tent cities holding thousands of men, women, and children, surrounded by rolls of razor-barbed wire, amid the sweltering heat of the U.S. Naval Base at Guantanamo Bay, Cuba, and the former Panama Canal Zone. Those incarcerated have witnessed birth and death, hope and despair, and untold waves of frustration and tedium (1994a, 139).

In this chapter, we narrate a "prehistory" of post-9/11 uses of the U.S. naval base at Guantánamo Bay and its role within a regional deterrence network of refugee camps. Additionally, we situate this massive Caribbean enforcement project within the context of the spectacular buildup of deterrence measures along the United States–Mexico boundary in the mid-1990s. We render mappable what Koh then called camps that "rank among the most startling, yet invisible, features of United

States foreign policy in the post-Cold War era" (139). Although significant for myriad reasons, this history has been largely erased from public memory (for notable exceptions see Farmer 2004; Chávez 2012; Lipman 2013; Paik 2016), and from histories of U.S. border enforcement. The absence of the Caribbean in understandings of "the border" is evident in its virtual erasure from the Border Patrol's 1994 strategic plan. We show how the tactical erasure of the Caribbean as a policed borderland—and concerted efforts to exclude Haitian and some Cuban asylum seekers—has helped to consolidate the United States–Mexico borderlands and Latinx migration from the south as lawless threats in the popular geographical imagination.

The U.S. government's transnational expansion of detention and deterrence on land and at sea underscores the argument we introduced in our opening chapter: we need transnational framings to understand national histories of migration control. In this chapter, we develop our analysis by turning our attention to what was happening beyond U.S. national boundaries in the Caribbean Basin. As with "processing" and confinement spaces onshore, the offshore archipelago under development relied on military infrastructure. This archipelago also relied on negotiations with foreign governments and the deployment of euphemistic terms, such as "safe haven," to sidestep legal obligations and political scrutiny.

We begin with the development of this offshore archipelago, then proceed to a discussion of the role of GTMO as a place where Haitians with HIV were detained. We then delve more deeply into the creation of "safe havens," Operation Sea Signal, and "wet foot, dry foot," all at the heart of U.S. enforcement strategy in the Caribbean at this time. Next, we resume discussions begun in the introduction about state productions of border enforcement as spectacle. We illustrate how these operations fueled the state's performance of the spectacular United States–Mexico border, which in turn obscured enforcement in other regions. The historical narrative in this chapter moves on- and offshore repeatedly. In the conclusions, we explore the implications of Haitians' transnational encounters with anti-Blackness, which suggest that the geopolitics of containment found expression as a transnational practice of anti-Black racism.

BASES AND BUFFER ZONES: THE OFFSHORE ARCHIPELAGO QUIETLY DEVELOPS

While the United States–Mexico border—spectacular in its narration, from walling to crossing—has come to stand in for narratives about

U.S. national borders and migration policies, geographer Joe Nevins (2010) convincingly shows how local efforts proved fundamental to fueling fortification along the boundary and driving a national ideological debate supporting ever more enforcement. We build on these insights about the historical and geographic specificity of national policy and practice by drawing attention to the important place of the Caribbean in the history of U.S. migration enforcement (Noble 2011).

Legal Geographies of Indefinite Detention and Return

Jean-Claude Duvalier's dictatorship of Haiti ended in 1986, followed by a series of leaders and eventually the overwhelming majority election of popular Left president Jean-Bertrand Aristide in 1990. Emigration from the island then declined significantly, but following the September 1991 ouster of Aristide by a military coup, large numbers of Haitians again departed in search of asylum in the United States. President Bush initially indicated that Haitians should not be returned to Haiti. This seemed like a promising announcement considering that in the 1980s, only 11 of the 22,000 Haitians who were intercepted at sea were found to have "credible fear," and hence allowed to enter the United States as asylees (Koh 1994a, 142). However, instead of permitting asylum seekers to enter the United States, Bush created temporary "safe havens" outside of U.S. sovereign territory, onboard Coast Guard (USCG) cutters and at the Guantánamo Bay Naval Base.

Election-year politics once again became part of the policy-making context. Winning Florida's electoral-college votes—where contenders Pat Buchanan and former Ku Klux Klan leader David Duke were deploying anti-immigrant speech—was imperative for Bush's reelection bid. Bush issued a statement conveying the paternalistic message that government policies dissuaded migration: "I don't want to have a policy that acts as a magnet to risk these people's lives" (Frelick 1993, 680). While migration was not a major focus of Clinton's campaign, condemning Bush administration practices would curry favor with many Democratic voters (Nevins 2010, 104–9). Clinton took a sharp dig at his opponent:

> I am appalled by the decision of the Bush Administration to pick up fleeing Haitians on the high seas and forcibly return them to Haiti before considering their claim to political asylum. . . . This process must not stand. It is a blow to the principle of first asylum and to America's moral authority in defending the rights of refugees around the world (Frelick 1993, 688).

Non-refoulement is an important aspect of international refugee law; it prevents the forcible return of foreign nationals if this return places them in danger of physical harm. This means that the United States has an obligation to not return people who express a credible fear, even if they have not been granted asylum status.

Some 36,000 Haitians were interviewed by the Immigration and Naturalization Service (INS) at Guantánamo during an 18-month period in 1991 and 1992 (Koh 1994a, 142). As the number of Haitians confined at Guantánamo grew and the U.S. government anticipated still more departures from Haiti, Bush looked to shift the border even farther offshore. The use of GTMO was the first in a series of legal geographical maneuvers that would create tiers of asylum-seeking on boats and bases across the Caribbean, restricting access among those distanced through detention offshore. Bush also sought to establish additional "safe havens" across the region. While the Bahamas and Dominican Republic refused, Honduras, Belize, and Venezuela agreed (Frelick 1993).

Several organizations worked in tandem to bring a series of legal challenges to the practice of detaining Haitians at Guantánamo Bay, the screening procedures, and the practices of returning asylum seekers to Haiti. These included the Miami-based Haitian Refugee Center (HRC), national and university-based legal advocacy organizations, and the Brooklyn-based Haitian Centers Council (HCC). In 1991, the HRC sued Secretary of State James Baker (*HRC v. Baker*), challenging the insufficiency of process in the screening and return of Haitians. They won several appeals in lower courts, but eventually lost at the Supreme Court (Koh and Wishnie 2009). By then, "some 3000 Haitians were being held incommunicado at Guantánamo. Virtually all had been found to have credible fears of political persecution." In March 1992, the INS decided to re-interview detainees, without lawyers present, and return those who "failed the test of political asylum" (Koh 1994b, 2394). The HCC brought suit against INS Director Gene McNary in March 1992, challenging the Haitians' indefinite detention at Guantánamo (the case would be renamed *HCC v. Sale* when Clinton's acting director for the INS came into office, and is referred to as *HCC-I*).

As legal challenges made their way through the U.S. courts, another significant number of Haitians left Hispaniola by boat in May 1992. In the first three weeks of that month, the U.S. Coast Guard intercepted over ten thousand Haitians (Frenzen 2010, 380–82). Over 12,500 refugees were already confined at GTMO when President Bush issued

Executive Order 12807 from his Maine summer home on May 24, 1992 (Paik 2013, 150). What became known as the Kennebunkport Order asserted that U.S. legal obligations to *non-refoulement* did not extend to persons outside the territory and territorial waters of the United States. The numbers of Haitians attempting to depart dropped following announcement of the order, but it also raised a host of questions about U.S. legal obligations under international law (Frenzen 2010, 383).

The Haitian Centers Council brought another suit to challenge the Kennebunkport Order and direct returns of Haitians (*Sale v. Haitian Centers Council,* or *HCC-II*). A circuit court ruling found that their *refoulement* "violated the plain language" of U.S. law (section 1253(h)(1) of the Immigration and Nationality Act [INA]), but the Bush administration quickly won a stay of this ruling (Koh and Wishnie 2009, 395; Koh 1994c, 9). Advocates appealed, and this case also would make its way to the Supreme Court. The legal team in the *HCC* cases based part of their strategy on the hope that the Clinton administration would change the government's policy (Koh 1994c, 10). Given Clinton's campaign statements that Bush had a "cruel policy of returning Haitian refugees to a brutal dictatorship without hearing," this was not an unwarranted assumption.[3] Indeed, soon after his victory, Clinton reiterated this stance: "I think that the blanket [policy of] sending them back to Haiti under the circumstances which have prevailed for the last year was an error *and so I will modify that process*" (10, emphasis in original).

However, in a sharp turn that stunned refugee advocates, Clinton reversed his position days before he took office (Koh 1994a, 149). "Leaving by boat is not the route to freedom," he warned in a radio broadcast (Mitchell 1994, 75). Long-time refugee advocate Bill Frelick bitterly observed that Clinton would continue to carry out a "warmed-over" Bush administration policy (1993, 688). These practices were put to work by rationalizing interdiction and offshore detention on military bases as part of a humanitarian effort. "Of course, it isn't," Frelick countered. "The United States 'rescues' boats that are not in distress and detains their occupants, even against their will" (687).

The treacherous conditions at sea that many endured underscored the dangers people faced if they remained in Haiti. When the Supreme Court ruled on *HCC-II* following Clinton's inauguration, the court made a discursive move common in narrations of border enforcement about boat arrivals: it shifted from "rescue" in the name of safety for existing migrants at sea to "return" in the name of the safety for future, imagined migrants. As Naomi Paik observes, the ruling invoked the hazards of the sea journey "to justify repatriating refugees to their persecutors. It claimed that 'the safety of Haitians is best assured by their remaining in their country'" (2013, 151).

The *HCC-II* ruling not only upheld executive claims that U.S. international and domestic obligations to refugee rights did not extend beyond the land borders of the United States, but also asserted that the English translation of the French verb *refouler* means "to reject" not "to return." Justice Harry Blackmun, the lone dissenter, retorted that these twists of reasoning meant that "the word 'return' does not mean return . . . [that] the opposite of 'within the United States' is not outside the United States" (Koh 1994b, 2414). The Supreme Court had ruled that the U.S. obligations did *not* extend extraterritorially to international waters. It thereby upheld a Bush-era legal opinion issued by the Department of Justice (DOJ) indicating that migrants intercepted in U.S. territorial waters were not entitled to protections against return (Frenzen 2010, 386). That is, the ruling crafted a legal geography in which the high court ruled that the United States was not obliged to respect refugees' rights to not be returned to a situation where they might face persecution (Dastyari 2015, 108).

Koh called the court's decision a "profound disappointment" that continued a "disturbing pattern of reflexive deference to presidential powers in foreign affairs and hostility toward both aliens and international law" (1994c, 1–2). Perhaps more disturbing is that the case had been brought on already-narrow legal grounds. The suit was not even claiming the right to asylum, but merely the right to not be returned (Frelick 1993, 677; Koh 1994c, 18–19). For refugee advocate Frelick, this diminished legal terrain represented a setback to gains made globally:

> The draconian measures taken by the United States have changed the parameters of what is considered acceptable. We have become minimalist in our demands, not because we are any less committed to advocating for a range of rights and benefits for refugees and asylum seekers, but because the violations committed by our government deny even minimum standards of refugee protection that we had thought were no longer open to question (1993, 678).

The Supreme Court ruling on *HCC-II* effectively shrank the spaces of access to asylum to mainland territorial boundaries (Frenzen 2010, 386). The decision provided the political and legal basis for the U.S. government to continue its regional deterrence strategy, including extraterritorial and third-country safe-haven policies. By setting its own legal geographic terms, the United States ostensibly could abide by international principles of *non-refoulement* even as it denied the right to asylum. Ultimately, the United States implemented a form of *neo-refoulement:* "a geographically based strategy of preventing the possibility of asylum through a new form of forced return different from *non-refoulement*" (Hyndman and Mountz 2008, 250). Koh was unconvinced by the court, and labeled the U.S. tactics a form of "deliberate refoulement" (1994a, 146).

Contesting HIV Exclusion

When Clinton took office, and as the HCC cases were still being decided, some 310 Haitian refugees—all of whom had passed credible-fear interviews and most of whom were HIV positive—remained confined at Guantánamo. Because GTMO remained an active naval base, only a portion of the facility was used to confine asylum seekers, in an unused air base called McCalla Airfield and in unused housing for Marine training at Camp Bulkeley. Group-specific detention practices had evolved on the naval station with specific camps designated for particular groups. Haitian persons were confined in a series of segregated camps across these spaces. In addition to sex-segregated adult camps, Camp 5 held families; Camp 9 was for unaccompanied minors (also known as "orphan camp"); Camp 10 was an administrative segregation (solitary confinement) unit, which young people called the "kid jail"; and Camp Bulkeley confined HIV-positive persons (Pearcy and Little 1996; Joint Task Force 160, 1996).

Camp Bulkeley was in operation from 1991 to 1993. The confinement of people who had been recognized legally as refugees, but whom the U.S. government refused to admit, represents a form of imprisonment that consolidated a racialized health panic with the U.S. government's existing pattern of exclusion of Haitian asylum seekers. In the early 1980s, the Center for Disease Control named Haitians as among the "4-H" groups that it considered at-risk (and to blame) for HIV: homosexual men, haemophiliacs, heroin users, and Haitians (Farmer 2004, 2006; Chávez 2012, 64; Paik 2016, 100).

As Paik (2016) describes in *Rightlessness,* the conditions of their indefinite confinement at Bulkeley were poor. Housing was shoddily constructed of plywood and open to the elements with open-air vents in the ceilings and floors and windows that were barred, but did not have glass (105). Food was inedible and often spoiled, and the sanitation procedures the military maintained for the camp were so terrible that a

Doctors of the World physician called "the conditions there a disgrace" (106). In July 1992, the *Association des Refugies Politiques Hatienes* (ARPH), formed by Haitians confined at GTMO earlier in the year, held a protest march on the camp's soccer field. The military responded with force, deploying soldiers in riot gear and placing over thirty Haitians in isolation for punishment (122). While negotiations ensued over the next several months between ARPH and the authorities, the latter ultimately did not end Haitians' confinement.

Just before officially assuming his presidency in January 1993, Clinton announced that he would maintain his predecessor's policies. In response, the ARPH began a hunger strike on January 29. Given the prolonged nature and unknown outcome of their confinement, the commitment to the strike was high. One strike leader, Claude Laguerre, explained, "Everyone here [is involved with the strike]; children, pregnant women. We all either sacrifice ourselves, or we know we'll never get out of here" (137).

The strike generated significant media attention and solidarity actions in the United States. Law students working on the *HCC* cases staged a hunger strike, an action that soon spread to other college campuses. Jesse Jackson and other civil-rights leaders organized mass civil-disobedience actions; Hollywood luminaries and sports legend Arthur Ashe spoke out (Koh 1994a, 149). When Reverend Jackson and a group of journalists and lawyers attempted to visit Camp Bulkeley in March 1993, none were allowed to enter but Jackson, who was accompanied by an interpreter from the HRC. Jackson reported, "It is clearly a camp now, not for rescue, but for repression."[4]

The queer health-activist group ACT-UP held a major civil-disobedience action in New York City that resulted in the arrest of more than twenty people (Chávez 2012, 65); this followed a demonstration the group had held outside of the Varick Street INS facility where two Haitians, who were HIV-positive, had been transferred, ostensibly for medical reasons. This demonstration would be particularly important in light of the abusive treatment that Haitian detainees had experienced at Krome the previous year. According to depositions taken by the Haitian Refugee Center, guards at Krome told the Haitian men "incorrectly" that they were HIV positive. They were then "commanded to clean the toilets with their bare hands because 'you are all HIV Positive anyway.'"[5]

When a higher court returned the HCC case on the legality of indefinite confinement at Guantánamo to a lower court, attorneys amended their claim to directly challenge the base's use as "America's first HIV concentration camp" (Koh 1994b, 2397). The trial for this case (known as *HCC-III*) would begin in March 1993. By this time, approximately eighty Haitians had been admitted to the United States to pursue their asylum claims, including people who could not get adequate medical diagnoses or treatment and women who were far along in their pregnancies. On March 26, New York District Court Judge Sterling Johnson issued an interim ruling that Haitians with AIDS, a diagnosis based on T cell counts, "were being denied 'adequate' medical care on Guantanamo."[6] Johnson ordered that the U.S. government must medically evacuate refugees who had a T cell count below two hundred (Paik 2016, 145).

In April 1993, the president's national security advisors Anthony Lake and Samuel Berger sent Clinton a decision memo on the ongoing litigation and what to do about the remaining 187 HIV-positive Haitians held at Guantánamo Bay. In addition to the group subject to litigation, the memo set out to explore whether to admit additional groups of detainees to U.S. mainland territory and how this would take place. These groups included people whose T cell counts were below five hundred (forty-nine people), children of HIV-positive Haitians (twenty-five), spouses of Haitians who had already been granted entry who were HIV positive (fourteen), women who were in the early stages of their pregnancies and HIV positive (four), and unaccompanied minors (two) (some people were counted in more than one of these categories). Lake and Berger observed that "there has been no adverse reaction from conservatives in Congress, from the press or from the public" following the administration's decision to comply with Judge Johnson's order.[7] Given ongoing litigation, they suggested that permitting entry for people on medical grounds could amount to an admission that care was inadequate at Guantánamo. Yet if the administration were to permit entry for these groups before the final ruling, it would also "avoid adverse findings of fact (i.e., about conditions on Guantanamo) from a hostile judge which could not be reversed on appeal, and would not imply Government admissions on any of the legal issues in the case."[8]

As detainees' bodies were sorted into tiers of confinement associated with need, care, and politics, the decision to permit entry was made potentially moot by the Supreme Court's decision pending in *HCC-II* about whether returns of Haitians without interviews would be deemed illegal.[9] Judge Johnson ordered the remaining HIV-positive detainees to be released, extending his previous ruling stipulating that the government must either release the refugees or provide them with adequate living conditions and medical care at GTMO. The ruling found that Haitian refugees held at GTMO did have constitutional rights; otherwise, the government would "have discretion deliberately to starve or beat them, to deprive them of medical attention, to return them without process to their persecutors, or to discriminate among them based on the color of their skin" (Koh 1994a, 151). Yet "release" did not necessarily mean that the U.S. government must admit them to the U.S. mainland. As Paik concludes, "Because the U.S. government could not perform the seemingly impossible—transforming the camp into a space of living—it had to free the refugees. But it could not send the refugees back to Haiti, and no other country would accept them. The government therefore had no choice but to bring the refugees into the United States" (2016, 145). Rather than diminish the strength of the onshore and offshore carceral regime, this decision further entrenched it.

The Clinton administration would comply with the *HCC-III* ruling on the same day that the *HCC-II* ruling was issued (Koh 1994a, 139). In this case, the Supreme Court ruled against Haitians' being returned, finding that the *non-refoulement* obligations in neither the INA nor Article 33 in the 1951 *Convention Relating to the Status of Refugees* applied to Haitians who had been intercepted in international waters (Koh 1994b, 2397). This case would underscore Bush's Kennebunkport Order and create the domestic legal basis for buffering U.S. territory and expanding a transnational carceral archipelago.

OPERATION SEA SIGNAL AND THE CREATION OF OFFSHORE "SAFE HAVENS"

U.S. politicians pressed the Clinton administration to escalate pressure on the military government of Haiti. Officials in Florida emphasized how restoring stability in Haiti was needed to slow migration. Governor Lawton Chiles wrote to Attorney General Janet Reno in early December 1993, expressing concerns about the state's ability to care for "would-be-refugees," particularly following Hurricane Andrew.[10] He noted that the existing "blockade appears to be discouraging Haitians from leaving Haiti," but that "many of the 25,000 to 40,000 Haitians who have taken up residence in the Bahamas are now seeking entry into the U.S. through Florida."[11] Chiles also had written to Secretary of State Warren Christopher, urging him to consider discussion of the ongoing "protection" of Haitians with Bahamian officials. Congressperson Porter Goss (R-Florida) offered his own "safe haven" proposal of "immediately relocating President Aristide by helping him establish a secure base on

Haitian soil," by which he was referring to the Haitian island of Île de la Gonâve.[12] Goss contended that the appeal of his proposal was that Aristide's presence would offer a "psychological boost for the vast majority of the populace who supported him and 'demagnetizes' Florida as the destination of last resort for despairing Haitians."[13]

In May 1994, National Security Council (NSC) deputies met in the situation room for one hour to discuss how the administration could increase pressure on the Haitian military. According to a declassified document, the State Department would work to push its perspective at the U.N. Security Council, and a series of financial and travel sanctions would be planned.[14] As with Florida officials, migration was a major item of concern on the NSC's agenda. The NSC decided to pursue a two-pronged plan of establishing a Migrant Processing Center (MPC) and third-country resettlement arrangements for Haitian refugees. The council created a priority list of sites for locating the MPC: 1) "ashore (in the Dominican Republic, Turks and Caicos, or Jamacia [sic]"; 2) "at a dock in these locations"; or 3) "at sea (although there are logistical problems that the Haiti Migrant Task Force might examine)."[15] In this archipelago of sites that they envisioned, the Department of Defense (DOD) would be the "'landlord' for the MPC and will contract with a commercial cruise ship immediately."[16] The INS would be charged with processing and the Coast Guard with transporting migrants. Efforts to establish MPC sites and agreements with resettlement countries would be pursued diplomatically.

The National Security Council's plans proved reminiscent of federal, interagency responses to earlier Haitian and Cuban migrations. As we have recounted in previous chapters, the first of these was the Mass Immigration Emergency Plan from 1983. The plan, updated in 1993 with the name Operation Distant Shore, provided for interagency collaboration and allocated a portion of funds to states in the case of an immigration emergency.[17] The second was Operation Sea Signal, which the Chairman of the Joint Chiefs of Staff began planning immediately after the 1992 presidential elections. Operation Sea Signal was a joint military operation between the U.S. Coast Guard, the U.S. Navy, and the U.S. Marine Corps, which also had a prominent role for international nongovernmental organizations (NGOs). It was designed to respond to an expected increase in the migration of people from Haiti (JTF-160 1996, EXSUM-1). The sum of these efforts would be offshore solutions to keep people close to home and far from U.S. mainland territory (see figure 8).

FIGURE 8. Photograph of a U.S. Coast Guard cutter that was taken by a legal advocate for Haitian asylum seekers confined on Guantánamo. The U.S. government used these ships to patrol the waters and also conducted credible-fear interviews onboard. (Reprinted with permission of Americans for Immigrant Justice. Courtesy of Duke University, Rubenstein Library, Human Rights Archive.)

In June 1994, as the administration moved forward with plans to reinstate Aristide in Operation Restore Democracy, the United States also resumed onboard screening of refugees. Restore Democracy would ostensibly restore safety to Haiti, and thereby facilitate returns and slow departures (EXSUM-3). Sea Signal, a self-described "chameleon-like operation whose character changed constantly," would intercept migrants at sea and carry out "migrant humanitarian operations" from May 1994 until January 1996 (EXSUM-1). By July 1994, over 16,000 Haitians had been offered "safe haven" at Guantánamo; by September the population of Haitians and Cubans at GTMO peaked at 47,809 (EXSUM-2). Meanwhile, the National Security Council had plans to "examine North Coast sites [in Haiti] for returning migrants and expansion of in-country processing, including a possible additional in-country processing center."[18] Despite the name, "safe haven" would amount to confinement and virtually no chance of making an asylum claim in the United States.

The U.S. government's approach to creating offshore safe havens was part of a post–Cold War trend. As geographers have shown (Chimni

1995; Hyndman 2000, 2003), these new geopolitical dynamics contributed to dramatic shifts in refugee "management" worldwide wherein efforts were made to provide displaced people with provisional protection in third countries in the same region where they had been displaced. Far from being a project that the United States could accomplish alone, the Clinton administration had to work to create bilateral arrangements with countries in the region. "A Presidential envoy will go to the Dominican Republic next week to discuss sanctions enforcement, citing the MPC, and US assistance programs. A senior level approach will be made to the UK regarding Turks and Caicos as a site for the MPC."[19] Likewise, diplomatic efforts to involve third countries in resettlement involved geoeconomic incentives: "For the less wealthy countries, we will note that funds for resettlement will be available to the UNHCR for this purpose."[20]

By the National Security Council's meeting in July 1994, these coordinated regional efforts were referred to as the "Safehaven plan." Even though the United States was already intercepting and confining asylum seekers, the plan's official launch was to be held on July 5 and announced on Voice of America and on Haitian commercial radio stations through the United States Information Service.[21] American Immigration Lawyers Association (AILA) staff that met with officials from the INS and State Department soon thereafter learned that "during the first week of shipboard screening, numbers were running about 100 per day (week of June 15). This increased dramatically the week of July 4, where numbers reached 1000 per day, and 4000 over 4th of July weekend."[22] U.S. officials stated that this uptick "provoked change to safe haven," but this statement defies the reality that plans for Sea Signal and other resettlement arrangements had been in the works for some time.[23] Indeed, government officials also revealed during this briefing that "safe haven country agreements have been concluded with Antigua, Grenada, Dominica, St. Lucia, Suriname, Panama (after Sept. 1), etc. Most will take limited numbers, 1000 or less."[24]

"WET FOOT, DRY FOOT"

As the Haitian refugee crisis continued, Fidel Castro announced that he would allow Cubans to leave the country in July 1994. Some thirty thousand Cuban asylum seekers departed by boat, expecting to reach U.S. shores. In a dramatic reversal of its longstanding, Cold War–motivated reception of Cuban refugees, the United States announced that it

FIGURE 9. Photograph of rafters after interception. Migrants are being transported by authorities from a small ship en route to a larger ship. Here, authorities stand over medicalized migrants, processing their interception. (Courtesy of U.S. Coast Guard, dvidshub.net.)

would intercept boats (many of which were rafts, or *balsas,* and those onboard were known as *balseros,* rafters) and confine Cuban asylum seekers at Guantánamo (see figure 9). On August 19, Clinton announced the notorious "wet foot, dry foot policy," which would allow those who made it onto dry (main)land to receive status in the United States, while those intercepted at sea would be returned. Within the week, talks with Castro on migration were under way (Noble 2011, 186). By the end of the month, the United States and Cuba had signed an agreement providing for the return of Cubans who did not meet credible-fear standards, following the precedent set with Haiti a decade earlier.

For the military task force running Sea Signal, the new surge of migrants represented an "entirely new stage" for the operation, as "its mission expanded and reoriented to a new reality" (JTF-160 1996, EXSUM-2). The U.S. Coast Guard increased patrols and resources in the Florida Straits on August 12, and Operation Able Vigil officially began the week of August 22 (Noble 2011, 189–90). During this first week, 10,190 Cubans were intercepted, including 3,253 in one day alone. They were then transported to Guantánamo where the Joint Task Force (JTF) ran camps at four locations: McCalla Field (17,000

Haitians and 18,000 Cubans), the Rifle Range (4,000 Cubans), Radio Range (17,000 Cubans), and the Golf Course (9,000 Cubans) (JTF-160 1996, EXSUM-3). Crowding in these spaces led the United States to enter into an agreement with Panama to allow the U.S. government to use its Howard Air Force Base to confine nine thousand Cubans (Koh 1994a, 155; Noble 2011, 190).

A seventeen-person team of NGOs coordinated by WORLD RELIEF under the auspices of the United Nations High Commissioner for Refugees (UNHCR) had been working at Guantánamo for a month when they issued a press release on September 1, 1994. By this time, over fourteen thousand Haitians and fifteen thousand Cubans were being held at Guantánamo. "Ongoing logistical problems including personnel security clearance, and shipment of supplies and donations continue to plague the program," they announced. The public health team, which would have sixteen additional staff members, had not yet been approved, and the NGOs had concerns about the lack of communication with the outside world, poor living conditions for those who were confined there, and inadequate medical and psychosocial care, including counseling for "the many who feel isolated and abandoned."[25] Indeed, they worried "that there will be additional suicide attempts . . . triggered by the anxiety and depression of the detainee, unless the voluntary agencies who [sic] are used to working with these people are given freedom to do so."[26] The humanitarian team was grappling with the constraints placed on their work, restrictions that were much more severe for asylum seekers who were confined there. Within such circumstances, "We continue to be concerned that Guantanamo is visibly more of a detention center than a safe haven."[27]

Cuba and the United States reached an agreement on September 9 that included 20,000 visas per year for Cubans to enter the United States, plus an additional 4,500 to 6,500 visas during the first year, and cessation of the hijacking of planes and boats. In exchange, Cuba would do its part "to stop the exodus" and accept direct repatriations (Noble 2011, 186). Cubans and Haitians responded immediately to this development by staging coordinated demonstrations the next day in all four main areas of the camp. As with earlier demonstrations, these were met with force (JTF-160 1996, EXSUM-3).

Tensions would ease for the Cubans in October when the U.S. government began admitting defined groups under "parole protocols": 1) elderly and necessary caregivers; 2) serious medical cases; and 3) unaccompanied children. Clinton announced in a press conference that the Cubans detained at Guantánamo would be moved to safe havens in other countries. Attorney General Reno allowed Cubans (with the exception of convicted criminals) to enter the United States under the Cuban Adjustment Act of 1966 (Noble 2011, 187–88). On May 2, 1995, Reno affirmed "that Cuban migrants not paroled under the original four protocols would be eligible for entry into the US on a case-by-case basis" (JTF-160 1996, EXSUM-4). In July 1995, the International Organization for Migration moved migrants to Bolivia, Venezuela, and Spain (Agency Summary-IOM-7).

Yet this relaxation of entry restrictions would not be extended to Haitians. Repeating the racialized and geopoliticized segregation at Krome, Haitians and Cubans were held in separate camps, with conditions in some of the Haitian camps especially poor.[28] A medical doctor who provided care to the Haitians on the base told attorney Cheryl Little that "the general attitude of the military personnel," including military doctors, "was that they did not want to look after the Haitians."[29] The doctor did not have food to provide for her patients living with tuberculosis, and was told "if the military gave them extra food it would cause a riot," a claim she disputed.[30]

Military personnel broadcast information about "voluntary repatriation" to Haitian camp residents by megaphone, and this information was posted "in the shower area, as well as in the camp newspaper."[31] The issue of "voluntary repatriation" became particularly charged. Military personnel responded defensively when advocates confronted them with detainee reports of being pressured to accept voluntary repatriation every morning at 6:00 a.m. and after each nightfall.[32] Frelick wrote a report about his site visit and weighed into the debate. While the information the government provided was factually correct, he argued that its frequent dissemination to a group of people who had already been found to have a well-founded fear of persecution upon return was unacceptable.[33] Confinement created conditions that undermined meaningful consent to voluntary repatriation: "*The isolation of the GTMO population from the outside world—and especially from their families in Haiti—creates a coercive backdrop for the decision to repatriate. . . . This isolation must be rectified immediately by establishing mail and phone links to the outside world.*"[34] By creating the GTMO camp for HIV-positive Haitians as an island (detention facilities) within an island (the naval base) within an island (Cuba), U.S. authorities further foreclosed any path out of confinement. Although monitors and advocates such as Frelick protested the situation, those detained remained largely out of view of the public, obscured by their confinement and the narrative of crisis and spectacle of border enforcement playing out elsewhere.

BUILDING THE SPECTACULAR BORDER

In contrast to the invisible dimensions of detention at Guantánamo Bay, more spectacular forms of enforcement were being developed elsewhere, specifically along the United States–Mexico border. A central contention of our book is that the buildup of deterrence efforts in the Caribbean and the United States–Mexico borderlands is interconnected. The tactical erasure of fortification and policing practices is part of statecraft. Claims of lawlessness or governmental absence provide the rationale for further state action in places where state agents are already at work. Given the scale of the Safe Haven operations in the Caribbean and the high pitch of concern over migration in 1994, it is notable that the *ongoing* Safe Haven operations remain absent from the Border Patrol's July 1994 strategic plan (see map 8). This plan received substantial criticism because it established the "prevention through deterrence" doctrine of funneling border crossers away from established migration routes to more treacherous places. As we have shown, decades' long efforts in the Caribbean to address migration were explicitly deterrent operations, so why did they not figure in this report?

To answer the question of why Safe Haven was obscured, we turn briefly to theories of spectacle and then complicate them with theories of regional racial formation. In *Border Games,* Peter Andreas argues that strategic images and symbols of the border "are part of a public performance for which the border functions as a political stage" (2009, 9). Alison Mountz writes in *Seeking Asylum,* "Visuality is an affective register through which sovereignty is secured" (2010, 23). The border as a performative space produces not only a sense of beleaguered nationhood on the part of some U.S. citizens, but it positions the state as a protector of the nation and, contradictorily, as the protector of migrants who themselves are endangered by increasingly fortified borders and classed and racialized migration laws (Walters 2010a; Williams 2014, 2015).

To call the border a performance or spectacle is not to say that it is unreal or that its effects are not deadly. Spectacles, following Guy Debord (1994) and Nicholas De Genova (2002, 436), are not false distortions of reality. Rather, they are "a worldview transformed into an objective force" that shapes what is seen and unseen (Debord 1994, 13).

ILLEGAL ENTRY CORRIDORS

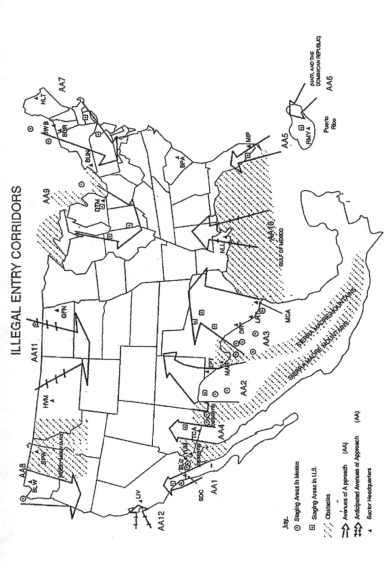

Key:

⊙ Staging Areas In Mexico

□ Staging Areas In U.S.

∕∕∕ Obstacles

⇨ Avenues of A Approach   (AA)

⇉⇨ Anticipated Avenues of Approach   (AA)

▲ Sector Headquarters

MAP 8. This U.S. Border Patrol map entitled "Illegal Entry Corridors" is from the *Border Patrol Strategic Plan 1994 and Beyond*, which elaborated the "prevention through deterrence" doctrine. This map is notable visually for using arrows to depict and rank the importance of so-called "avenues of approach." Large arrows over the United States–Mexico borderlands suggest that these are significant pathways, while arrows from Haiti and the Dominican Republic into Florida are much smaller. The map also depicts natural features such as deserts, mountains, and water bodies as obstacles to migration. The plan calls for an increase in policing in major entry corridors, which the plan proposes will have a deterrent effect in which migrants will be "forced over more hostile terrain, less suited for crossing and more suited for enforcement." [U.S. Border Patrol 1994.]

Geographer Shiloh Krupar usefully conceptualizes spectacle as "a tactical ontology—meaning a truth-telling, world-making strategy" (2013,
10) that creates powerful symbolic divisions between people and places
that are actually deeply intertwined.

As the map included in the 1994 Border Patrol plan illustrates, the
United States–Mexico borderlands are depicted with prominent arrows
sweeping northward. South Florida and Puerto Rico are listed as fifth-
and sixth-priority regions, just ahead of the northern border states of
Washington and New York (see map 8). Yet at that very moment the
scale of the Safe Haven operations was substantial; costs had reached
$30 million monthly, nearly 45,000 asylum seekers were confined, and
3,800 military troops deployed to the island base's migrant operations
(Koh 1994a).

The erasure of the Caribbean border operations and the simultaneous direction of attention to the United States–Mexico borderlands
enacted a spectacular separation of regionally specific operations that
would also discursively divide refugees and asylum seekers from economic migrants. These distinctions, as we have seen, were geopolitical
and racialized. Forgetting the anti-Black animus driving Caribbean
deterrence and detention operations would ideologically fortify the
imagined geography of "the border" as one isolated to the United
States–Mexico borderlands. This set of recursive processes would serve
to naturalize and legitimize coercive policies directed at Latinx people
while obscuring the role of anti-Black racism also driving the expansion
of detention and deterrence there and nationwide.

The deflection from ongoing Safe Haven operations amidst the launch
of Operation Gatekeeper hinged on regional racial politics, which were
playing out in the context of heated midterm elections. In California,
Pete Wilson was clamoring for the declaration of an immigration emergency and campaigning behind the anti-immigrant ballot initiative,
Proposition 187, which would bar undocumented migrants from attending public school or receiving emergency medical care. This proposition
hitched nativism to fiscal concerns, positioning Latinas as the source of
budget woes and population increases (Calavita 1996; Escobar 2016).

In Florida, the racialized geopolitical context was somewhat different. Democratic Governor Chiles was seeking reelection against Republican Jeb Bush. Governor Chiles, one aide told the *New York Times,*
"made every effort at preventing Mariel II" (in Fitzpatrick 1994, 407).
He appealed to Attorney General Reno in May 1994 for reimbursement
of law-enforcement and public-health costs resulting from the arrivals

of Haitian and Cuban migrants.[35] Later that summer, Chiles declared a state of emergency in response to the Cuban migration in order to access funds from the Immigration Emergency Fund.[36] Even though Chiles called for federal support to reimburse the state for continued arrivals, an appeal that was not successful, the Cuban-American electorate was split on the migration crisis and the regularization of relations with Cuba. Candidate Bush aligned himself with other conservative governors pushing for tougher federal law enforcement, supporting the ongoing detention and return of Cubans.[37]

Regularizing relations with Castro was politically delicate. The September 1994 arrangement that the Clinton administration made with the Cuban government allowing the United States to return intercepted Cubans was controversial. President Clinton defended his decisions in a letter to Simon Ferro, a Cuban-American and former chair of the Florida Democratic Party, who had complained about the agreement. Chillingly, Clinton echoed prior rationales for why people may be detained indefinitely at Guantánamo Bay:

> Last October, you suggested to me that we allow migrants at Guantanamo into the United States. While I agree that was the preferable, humane solution, standing alone it may well have triggered another massive outflow of Cubans, endangering their lives and defying our ability to control our borders.[38]

The president proceeded to explain his decision to return people: "Because the United States cannot admit all Cubans who seek to come here, and because we know that Guantanamo should not be used as an indefinite safehaven [sic], I concluded that the only way to forestall a massive and dangerous exodus was to signal our determination to put an end to illegal migration from Cuba."[39]

Clinton's letter rationalized deterrence in humanitarian and sovereign terms at the same time as he foreshadowed the unknown future of indefinite detention at the base that became notorious during the United States–led "War on Terror" (Butler 2004). Ending boat migrations was about restoring the rule of law and preserving life. His decision had been made as a result of "our long-standing objectives . . . to regularize migration relations with Cuba. This is important not only to guarantee the integrity of our national borders, but also to ensure that Cubans do not take to the sea in unseaworthy rafts at great peril to their lives."[40]

It was amidst the controversy over Safe Haven and the election-year call for tougher migration controls that Reno launched Operation Gatekeeper in October 1994. We suggest that the plan was positioned both to defuse California Governor Wilson's restrictionist stance and to deflect attention from the Safe Haven operation. The Clinton administration depicted Gatekeeper as a means to "reinstitute the rule of law at the border," establishing a bright line where before "the border was dark, violent, anonymous, and largely unregulated" (Bersin 1996, 254).

Following the 1996 elections, in which Prop. 187 in California passed overwhelmingly and Governor Chiles narrowly defeated Bush, ideological efforts to promote Gatekeeper and deflect Safe Haven continued. Following what the Defense Department called "disturbances"—during which 2 Cubans died, 30 suffered injuries, and 221 U.S. soldiers were wounded—the government of Panama told the United States in December 1994 that it would no longer permit the United States to use Howard Air Force Base for Cuban asylum seekers. The United States ended its confinement of Cubans in Panama a few months later, in March 1995, yet Clinton continued to defuse criticism of the operations. That June, the president delivered remarks to the "Cuban-American Community," which reiterated the rationalization he had provided to Ferro:

> In the summer of 1994, thousands took to treacherous waters in unseaworthy rafts, seeking to reach our shores; an undetermined number actually lost their lives. In response, I ordered Cubans rescued at sea to be taken to safe haven at our naval base at Guantanamo and, for a time, in Panama. ...Senior United States military officials warned me that unrest and violence this summer were likely, threatening both those in the camps and our own dedicated soldiers.
>
> But to admit those remaining in Guantanamo without doing something to deter new rafters risked unleashing a new, massive exodus of Cubans, many of whom would perish seeking to reach the United States.[41]

Justifying these operations publicly illustrates the spectacular staging of deterrence as humanitarian to this particular audience. In the lead-up to the one-year anniversary of Gatekeeper, Clinton advisor Tom Epstein e-mailed a strategic approach to legislative hearings on immigration to Stephen Warnath, a member of the White House Domestic Policy Council. Epstein suggested that the INS should use "graphic, provocative terms" to emphasize the "effectiveness of Operation Gatekeeper and the entire Southwest border strategy" in contrast with "the 12 years of neglect and the miserable condition of the federal border enforcement effort upon the arrival of the Clinton administration."[42] He further advised that the rhetorical framing should employ warlike terms to emphasize the strength of border enforcement:

Use strong language and military metaphors where appropriate (i.e., shut down the free-for-all at Imperial Beach, forced the aliens onto our terrain, using a pincer movement to squeeze them into easily apprehendable patterns, etc.). Articulate a clear vision of how we expect this to end—just a trickle of illegals, on the run, by the end of '95 or early '96.[43]

Where Clinton had reframed deterrence as a means to prevent the deaths of Cubans at sea, officials applauded the difficulties presented to migrants by the enforcement strategy—discussed in militarized terms—in the Southwest. U.S. Attorney for the Southern District of California, Alan Bersin, lauded the strictures: "The border is now harder to cross than at any time in modern history. Those who attempt illegal entry into the United States have been forced to take longer and more arduous routes through the mountains and deserts of southeastern California" (1996, 255). Efforts to deflect attention from the controversy surrounding Safe Haven and the harms of detention and deterrence for migrants in the Caribbean and to shore up the Clinton administration's toughness for the electorally important states of California and Florida were contradictory. Drawing on longstanding border narratives, officials would applaud the deadly effects of border fortification only in the United States–Mexico borderlands. These were conscious ideological efforts that further cemented the nativist issue of migration to the United States–Mexico borderlands and again legitimated the use of military force to secure sovereign territory.

ANTI-BLACKNESS AND THE CARCERAL ARCHIPELAGO

People remaining at Guantánamo and subject to military control would be all but forgotten amidst this deployment of force and military rhetoric to celebrate Gatekeeper's accomplishments. Operation Sea Signal ended quietly in 1996 (JTF-160 1996). Yet the anti-Black racism of transnational deterrence efforts continued. Even as Safe Haven was winding down, there were ongoing struggles to unite Haitian children, whom the United States had returned to Haiti from Guantánamo, with their families in the United States. As with the "wet foot, dry foot" policy, the racial inequities in the treatment of unaccompanied children were sharp. While Attorney General Reno announced that she would consider all Cuban children at GTMO for parole on December 2, 1994, over 350 Haitian children unaccompanied by family members were then being held at GTMO.[44] As at Krome, children found

FIGURE 10. A Haitian girl jumps rope while confined at Guantánamo Bay. This image was taken by a legal advocate for Haitian asylum seekers confined on Guantánamo. The snapshot depicts two boys swinging the jump rope for the younger girl on the military base tarmac. In the background are the fabric tents with cots inside. (Reprinted with permission of Americans for Immigrant Justice. Courtesy of Duke University, Rubenstein Library, Human Rights Archive.)

ways to play, even within the harsh conditions of the camp's barren tarmac (see figure 10).

In February 1995, the New York–based group Guantanamo Watch wrote to the Attorney General, urging her to allow all unaccompanied Haitian minors to join relatives in the United States. Guantanamo Watch was a high-profile group comprising Black freedom and cultural legends Harry Belafonte, Edwidge Danticat, Danny Glover, and Randall Robinson, and other prominent Hollywood actors, including Robert De Niro, Jonathan Demme, Michelle Pfeiffer, Tim Robbins, Julia Roberts, and Susan Sarandon (Pearcy and Little 1996, appendix C). The group cited "disturbing allegations that many of these children have suffered further abuse and terror at the hands of U.S. military personnel charged with their supervision at Guantanamo."[45] Indeed, the U.S. Atlantic Commander would admit that some of his soldiers had subjected Haitian children to "excessive force" and "verbal abuse" while they were confined at GTMO (2). In addition to this group's organizing, twenty-three members of the Congressional Black Caucus (CBC) wrote to the president, calling on him to "do the right thing" and to "mitigate what has already been a serious humanitarian tragedy—as well as to avoid the appearance of a double standard." Finally, the Dade County Public School Board passed a resolution supporting parole for the children (Appendix c).

Despite this concerted pressure, the United States began forcibly repatriating the remaining children on March 8, 1995, even *after* the UNHCR had condemned the repatriation of Haitians. By the end of April 1995 only twenty-three of the children had been granted parole (2). The Florida Immigrant Advocacy Center, which had been providing legal services at GTMO, attempted to find children who had been returned to Haiti. On a fact-finding mission to Haiti in August 1995, FIAC interviewed fifteen children and corresponded with the Repatriated Orphaned Children's Organization, a group that the young people and an advocate had founded.

FIAC learned that the physical and mental health of the children they visited had "deteriorated markedly" since their forcible return. They had virtually no access to medical care or education, and their daily needs could not be met by the caregivers whom the Red Cross had identified for them. At least forty of the children were homeless. FIAC also raised "serious concerns" about the procedures used by the Red Cross and Save the Children to assure the well-being of the children (5). Some relatives said they felt coerced into signing agreements. Other people who were not relatives signed agreements in exchange for money and then did not care for the children, while some relatives were not even contacted. These children did have family in the United States who were willing and able to sponsor them, but as of June 1995, Attorney General Reno had reunited only five whom the U.S. government cruelly had sent to Haiti.

Haitian asylum seekers had long identified and challenged their transnational experiences of state violence. Affidavits collected by FIAC between 1989 and 1991 document the consistently poor treatment that Haitian asylum seekers faced while in the Krome detention facility and jails in Louisiana and Texas. These included brutal encounters with capricious guards, lack of food, and arbitrary transfers. The following narrative from the affidavit of B. P., with which we began this chapter, is illustrative. While imprisoned in Texas, B. P. explains:

> I got fed better than some people, but it wasn't good. They had some kind of potatoes, smashed up and fried, with ketchup. With that, I had beans. Sometimes there were eggs, but they always stank. And the guards said they couldn't change the food, because there were orders from Miami that Haitians were to be treated that way. For the same reason, we couldn't see our relatives, either.

> When I got back [to Krome], I found that things were as bad as before: running through the food line, having to stand in bad weather, everything. They took us all out by section this morning just for spite, because it was cold. And they tell us we will never get out unless our parents are citizens. You know, they never even let us go to the bathroom when we need to—they just keep us standing through head counts, over and over, for spite.[46]

B. P. points to systemic violence in institutions where he was confined, from Miami (INS) to Texas. B. P.'s testimony suggests that the dehumanizing treatment across INS detention and jail space attaches to and follows Black bodies, nationality, and legal status. These conditions and treatment rested on the anti-Blackness of the U.S. carceral state, and created the conditions for asylum seekers' forcible return to Haiti. Indeed, these experiences led B. P. to conclude, "Maybe they will kill me in Haiti. The government doesn't forget anything there. But this is worse. This is no country for black people. I will never come back, no matter what."[47]

B. P. was not the only person who expected to be deported and concluded that he would never return to the United States. Indeed, a group of Haitian refugees confined in Louisiana wrote a letter of protest not so much disputing their confinement in a penal space, but explaining how this remote space would contribute to their abandonment: "Because this prison is a prison where they can forget about you."[48] If, as B. P. contended, the United States was no place for Black people, the U.S. government succeeded in extending this inhospitable terrain to forms of confinement offshore.

As the affidavits, open letters, and advocacy reports document, this process was not uncontested. Signs carried by Haitian protestors in Miami (as depicted earlier in figure 7) would work to counter the state's efforts to conceal Haitians through their remote, carceral dispersal. The U.S. policy of detention as a deterrent, then, rests on the carceral state's efforts to erase memories of Black asylum-seekers' presence in the United States, rendering Black social life as "ungeographic" (McKittrick 2006). This attempted erasure shows the U.S. state colluding with the Haitian government's refusal to forget dissidents. That is, the conditions of social death produced by the carceral state abet the political violence that led displaced people to flee their homes in the first place. Yet both the U.S. and Haitian states' practices of violence are displaced onto the figure of the criminal. Criminalization, thereby, shrinks the terms of asylum seeking. The ramifications would affect particular people's bodies and enable an expansion of militarized enforcement practices transnationally in particular regions—notably, in this case, across the Caribbean.

LESSONS NOT HEEDED: MIGRATION CONTROL
AND THE GEOPOLITICS OF CONTAINMENT

The outcome of safe haven as a deterrence strategy was known from the start. An unnamed talking-points memo regarding interagency debate about whether safe haven should continue for Haitians notes, "Whatever the outcome of the intervention, economic migration is likely to resume; safe haven is the only humane and broadly accepted disincentive we have found."[49] Yet by 1996, the last of the remaining Cubans eligible for parole at GTMO would be admitted to the United States. Almost 30,000 of the 32,784 Cubans processed through Sea Signal would reach the United States, while the "majority of Haitians were repatriated" (JTF-160 1996, EXSUM-1-5). Although the Caribbean border was effectively deprioritized in the 1994 Border Patrol policy, deterrence policies implemented in the Caribbean helped to produce a militarized border and detention landscape there and across U.S. mainland territory.

Deterrence practices create harsher conditions and greater risks for those seeking safety (or a livelihood). But border spectacles paint citizens as victims endangered by the very act of migration. This now-common discursive move shifts the harms of border enforcement away from state policies that make entry for asylum or livelihoods more difficult and instead situates migrants who endure treacherous trips across desert or sea and prolonged detention as criminalized threats. Border spectacles, thereby, operate to distract, distancing the burden of migrant deaths from the state policies that cause them (De Genova 2002; Nevins 2003; Andreas 2009; Andersson 2014). As Nevins and Aizeki (2008) have shown, in the United States–Mexico border region, the material effects of further border fortification on borderland communities and environments and on people's bodies would be significant. Yet the efforts to focus attention on the United States–Mexico border even as Cubans and Haitians were being confined offshore would also erase the suffering from and resistance to U.S. border deterrence in the Caribbean Basin.

As B. P.'s testimony and concerted efforts to contest Haitians' exclusion suggest, deterrence as a policy was never solely directed against external "threats," but also aimed to prevent migrants already in U.S. territory from remaining. The entwining of domestic and foreign policy and spaces is most evident in the local jails confining asylum seekers and government boats patrolling the seas. The U.S. strategy of relying on detention as deterrent clashed with its capacity to detain. Crises of capacity would recur as this commitment grew more entrenched institutionally. For example, the lengthy detention of asylum seekers, which varied considerably by nationality, contributed to the space the government needed for confinement. In 1990, people were detained for an average of 23 days, but Haitians were held at Krome for an average of 101 days, and Salvadorans between 21 and 92 days, a disparity that reflects the intertwining of racism and geopolitics (GAO 1992, 25, 27). Thus, the early discriminatory responses to Haitian asylum seekers in the form of the Haitian Program would persist for decades. They continue still—including the targeting of Haitians to prevent their entry into the United States from Mexicoand the spike in asylum claims made by Haitians crossing into Canada from the US in 2017—as we discuss in the coda.

As demonstrated in the previous chapter, legislation that criminalized migrants and required mandatory detention increased the number of people subjected to detention. Overcrowding in the jails and prisons relied upon by the INS to meet its confinement objectives meant that much of this space was unavailable for contract use. By the early 1990s, therefore, when a new set of asylum movements developed from Haiti, Cuba, and Central America, the U.S. commitment to detention as deterrent faced a significant crisis of capacity. The General Accounting Office (GAO) concluded that it was not "feasible to expand INS' detention capabilities sufficiently to solve the problems" (1992, 43).

Indeed, as we have shown in the controversy over safe haven, the United States sought to resolve its overcrowding problem onshore in part by shifting enforcement and detention offshore. This carceral space at sea—established in U.S. territorial and international waters—grew with the proliferation of spaces of confinement, from Coast Guard cutters to so-called safe havens. Therefore, the expansion of the U.S. carceral regime involved a transnational proliferation of spaces of confinement on land and sea, on mainland territory and offshore: a buffer zone at sea, "safe haven" on military bases, and the construction and repurposing of spaces on military bases on the mainland. The sustained reliance on imprisonment to deter Haitian asylum seekers built on existing national and geopolitical racial formations and associations between Blackness, poverty, and criminality. This became all the more important with the material expansion of the immigration-detention system and discursive tightening between criminality and illegality that would follow.

6

Onshore Expansion

Consolidating Deterrence through Criminalization and Expulsion

Crafting ideological connections between crime and migration proved an explicit and ongoing part of the Bill Clinton administration's strategy. Clinton advisor Rahm Emanuel explained that the administration's event in San Diego scheduled before the 1996 GOP convention would feature "the President and Attorney General, the sheriff and district attorney of San Diego, both big Republicans, [who] will make remarks about the decrease in crime."[1] "We want to make the point that once resources were available to law enforcement at the border, San Diego and other cities witnessed a significant drop in crime."[2] Ultimately, Emanuel continued, "We must remember this is a law enforcement event, not just an anti-immigration event."[3]

Emanuel had been concerned that Clinton's administration (and perhaps the Democratic Party as a whole) was perceived as "elitist and removed from their concerns on jobs and drugs."[4] In planning immigration legislation for 1995 with the Senate's Democratic Policy Committee, Emanuel again pushed for a focus on migration enforcement and "not on the smaller Education and HHS Medicaid assistance pieces [of legislation] because they may beg more difficult questions on why we don't do more instead."[5] What the administration and Congress did do instead was undermine welfare entitlements for citizens and permanent residents, while wielding enforcement as a tough remedy to real and perceived woes (Calavita 1996; Escobar 2016).

In this chapter, we tell the story of how mid-1990s migration and crime legislation fueled the expansion of migration detention and the transportation infrastructure it relied upon. Between 1985 and 1994, there had already been a "nearly 1,300 percent" increase in the deportation of "criminal aliens," from 1,699 to 21,992.[6] As we detail below, the provisions of the Anti-Terrorism and Effective Death Penalty Act (AEDPA) and the Illegal Immigration Reform and Immigrant Responsibility Act (IIRIRA) expanded the set of crimes that carried deportation consequences and expanded the use of mandatory detention. This moment is rightfully recognized for forcefully criminalizing migration and noncitizens. Yet wielding mandatory detention as a tool for expulsion was also the logical extension of mandatory detention for asylum seekers. Ongoing political crises over migration and crime dovetailed to cement detention into the landscape both materially and discursively.

Plans as they are recorded in writing rarely take the same shape in their operationalization. By the mid-1990s, Immigration and Naturalization Service (INS) officials had been scrambling to expand detention space for well over a decade. Yet out of this seemingly intractable situation, a vast and flexible detention infrastructure—comprising government-owned and -run facilities, local jails, and privately contracted facilities—would nonetheless become a reality. Criminal legislation passed in the mid-1980s to mid-1990s repeated the patterns established earlier in *Boats, Borders, and Bases:* the executive branch detains asylum seekers, then the president issues executive orders, and Congress passes legislation authorizing these practices. The established pattern of responses to migration crises eventually dovetailed with formal criminalization, but within the context of a much larger prison and detention system.

Amidst bipartisan struggles over the economy, welfare reform, and immigration, the Clinton administration would advance crime and enforcement as principle elements of its ideological battles and legislative strategy. Crime and border control were entwined legislatively and discursively from the time of the midterm 1994 elections to the 1996 presidential election. These include three significant bills—Violent Crime Control and Law Enforcement Act (Crime Act), AEDPA, and IIRIRA—that Clinton signed into law on September 13, 1994, April 24, 1996, and September 30, 1996, respectively.

As migration and criminal-justice policy became more closely entwined, this entanglement became the basis for expanding detention. As with the earlier treatment of "undesirable" Cubans and "bogus" Haitian asylum seekers, the figure of the criminal alien was consolidated and juxtaposed against notions of legal, "good," and contributing refugees and immigrants. Meanwhile, the use of detention as a tool of deterrence had clearly failed. People continued to arrive. Although a failed public policy, deterrence remained politically popular. Rather than concede defeat, new forms of criminalization were adopted to establish a more robust tool of punishment and expulsion and a correspondingly expansive material infrastructure to confine growing numbers of deportable people.

In order to understand the dramatic expansion of what Nancy Hiemstra (2013) refers to as "interlocking systems" of detention and deportation, we resume our account begun in chapter 4 of how the INS sought to expand onshore capacity by telling the story of how a small town near Attica, New York, came to be the site of a new facility. After discussing why a detention facility was built near the border with Canada, we pan out to explain the mid-1990s legislation that laid the basis of further detention expansion. We then turn to the development of the Justice Prisoner and Alien Transportation System (JPATS), the largest transport system of its kind, designed to move prisoners and detainees throughout the country. Finally, the chapter concludes with an exploration of the politics of prison expansion and privatization.

BATAVIA AND "THE NON-EXISTENCE OF PUBLIC OPPOSITION"

In her 1994 Border Patrol strategic plan, Attorney General Janet Reno suggested that migration policing and detention expansion would focus on the United States–Mexico borderlands. Instead, we find construction in curious places that have little direct connection with apprehension at the southern border per se. As one example, the Buffalo Federal Detention Facility is a men's detention facility built with a capacity for holding more than four hundred people. Despite its name, the facility is located in Batavia, New York, and was the closest federal facility to our homes in Syracuse, New York, when we began this project. We knew that the facility was not placed in close proximity to the Canadian border for purposes of deportation to Canada. But why *was* it located in this small town?

In many ways, this site illustrates the role of historical trajectories and local politics detailed thus far in this book. Like Florence, Arizona, Western New York has a long-standing prison economy. Generations of families in the area have worked in the prisons located there. The Western House of Refuge for Women at Albion was established by the

Laws of 1890, Chapter 238, and was expanded to become the Albion Correctional Facility in 1971.[7] A few dozen miles away, the prison in Attica, New York, was established by the Laws of 1927, Chapter 56, which appropriated funds for construction. The prison opened in 1931 and gained notoriety forty years later for the Attica Uprising of 1971.

The small town of Batavia is located between Buffalo and Rochester, an area of farms and wetlands, with a population of just over fifteen thousand (see map 9). Although the detention facility abuts Interstate 90, it is easy to miss when driving by because a grass-covered berm shields the single-story facility from sight. In fact, its proximity to I-90 made it an appealing location for ease of transportation—both by automobile and airplane, out of Buffalo Niagara International Airport and the smaller Niagara Falls International Airport, where flights carrying detainees fly quietly out of view of the larger airport in Buffalo. After a tour with architecture students from Syracuse University in 2010 that afforded some interior observations, we knew to look just beyond the billboards along the Thruway to the telltale row of tall bright lights that illuminate the uninhabited green field surrounding the facility.

The architectural design of the facility is panoptic in nature, with a central watchtower that houses a bank of video monitors and views onto people incarcerated in cells that open into common spaces, each arranged around diagonal nodes, or pods. While the building is surrounded by ample green space, people detained inside have little access to the yard. On the outside, the building's purpose is masked in plain sight; it presents as a banal, brown institution with the American flag flying out front. The building could be easily confused for a school or library. On a visit in 2012, signs of construction were evident. Prefabricated units spray-painted with bright orange lettering reading "SHU" suggested that additional solitary-confinement facilities were being installed.

The detention facility that would eventually be built here was being planned before the 1996 legislation that would drive even more expansion. Its construction was part of the earlier wave of expansion that the INS had embarked upon to meet its legislated obligations and policy of confining asylum seekers. A 1992 report by the General Accounting Office (GAO) had concluded that the "INS' planned expansion from 6,259 to 8,600 beds by 1996 will not significantly alleviate the shortage of detention space." Moreover, "detaining all such [deportable] aliens in current available facilities is impractical and cost prohibitive. On the other hand, detaining some but not all aliens may mean that aliens in similar circumstances are treated differently" (3). Indeed, while the

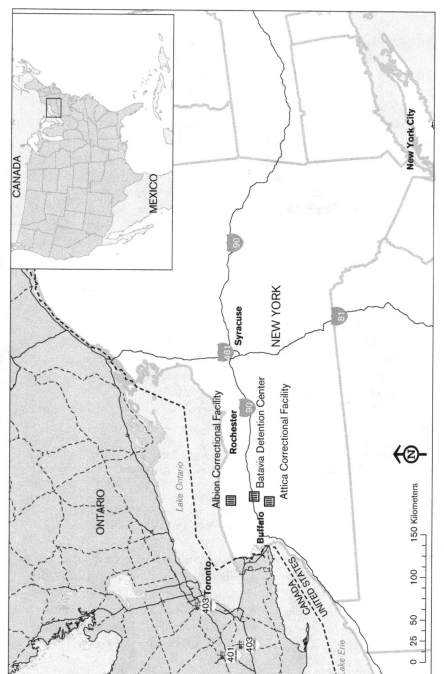

MAP 9. Situating Batavia, New York, and regional prisons. This map situates the small town of Batavia within the broader regional prison economy and regional Thruway infrastructure in Western New York.

average length of detention was 23 days, Haitian asylum seekers were held on average for 101 days. The availability of detention space also prolonged confinement; Chinese nationals who sought entry were confined for eleven days on average in New York City, but for an average of eighty-six days if they were transferred to the Denver facility (5).

In May 1993, Kathleen Hawk, director of the Bureau of Prisons (BOP), testified to Congress about the sentencing and other legislative changes driving prison overcrowding in order to justify appropriations for further construction.[8] She also discussed a new BOP–INS facility similar to Oakdale that was in the pipeline for Arizona and explained the request for $10.3 million to build a joint INS–U.S. Marshals Service (USMS) detention facility in Western New York. This latter facility would help to relieve limited pretrial detention capacity and enable the INS to engage in enforcement activity in the region, which had been hampered due to lack of detention space.

The House *Congressional Record* published on December 4, 1995, reporting on appropriations for 1996, indicated that $25 million had been appropriated to the INS for construction, with $11 million of this amount was allocated for the facility in Batavia, New York.[9] The February 21, 1996, *Federal Register* stated that the facility—originally constructed to provide 254 beds, with the possibility of expansion to 454 beds—would be built on 22.5 acres in Genesee County.[10]

The INS announced construction of the new facility in 1996, and explained how Batavia was selected over nearby Albion:

> After carefully evaluating more than 20 sites, Batavia was judged to be the best possible location. The Batavia site had all the needed utilities available at the property line and transportation access was superior in Batavia due to it's [sic] location adjacent to the New York Thruway, reducing travel time and expense over the years. In addition, the proposal to build a detention facility at Batavia has received strong support from the local community.[11]

The site was purchased from three different landowners for $281,250.

Given the INS's aversion to community opposition, it is unsurprising that the INS cites local support alongside efficiency and cost effectiveness in operations as rationales for selecting Batavia. As shown elsewhere in New York State, local economic-development specialists and politicians showed unbridled excitement for the construction and longer-term jobs that might be created (Norton 2015). According to Batavia Republican and chair of the Genesee County Legislature Carl Perkowski, "the economic impact can't be overstated. Existing businesses, like laundry and food service, will see a boost," and he noted that entry-level jobs at the prison would pay $30,000 to $35,000. "That's a good chunk of change."[12]

The *Batavia Daily News* reported on how design and perception of the facility helped to curb potential public opposition to the project: "That relatively short stay, combined with promises the detention center will be buffered by trees and not ringed with barbed wire, contributed to the non-existence of public opposition to the project."[13] As in Louisiana, the town government also invested in readying the site to attract the facility, including a $600,000 investment in water and sewer lines.[14] Far from benefitting from a federal economic-development infusion, towns with struggling economies would subsidize federal prison projects in the hopes of garnering steady federal salaries and benefits.

At its opening in 1998, facility director Terry Nelson lauded the site as a forward-looking development for the INS: "I think that we have finally evolved in terms of detention operations. I think that we are going to take the lead in where we take our detention program. It is a model facility. It has been outfitted to take us into the next century. This is our future in detention operations."[15] When asked about the reactions of local residents to the new facility, Nelson suggested that most were positive, but some expressed concerns about *who* would be detained. Here, the figure of the criminal alien made an appearance:

> We are a criminal facility as we've always said. I don't think we've ever hidden that fact. The facility was designed to hold criminal aliens. It was also designed to hold pretrial US Marshal's [sic] prisoners. We have 150 beds available for the US Marshal's [sic] Service. They're criminals. We don't expect to be holding non-criminal aliens.[16]

While officials routinely distinguish between administrative detention and criminal punishment, from the start this facility blended criminal legal and migration enforcement, segregated in separate areas of the facility. As in Oakdale, an immigration court is onsite, within the building.

This appearance of the criminal alien in this small Western New York town is one material part of how a nationwide *system* of detention and deportation expanded in the 1990s. A news release at the time of the opening of the Batavia facility announced that it would be linked to "not only the Buffalo area, but also our Cleveland, Detroit and Chicago Districts."[17] It would also be part of a nationwide project: "Batavia will be a valuable weapon in our arsenal to help remove criminal aliens from the United States."[18] As in earlier times in other places, facilities were built where there was little to no public opposition. If anything, public support for detention siting could be found in places that already rested on prison and military economies. For these reasons of local politics and economics—not proximity to the border or busy sites of apprehension—expansion was geographically uneven and featured the concentration of facilities in places that were often far from major cities.

CRIMINALIZATION AND THE LEGISLATIVE GROUNDWORK FOR EXPANSION

As Robyn Sampson (2013) suggests, the global growth of detention involves not only an increase in the number of countries that are detaining migrants, but also an expansion of their scope and capacity to detain. Nowhere was this expansion more acute than in the United States in the late 1990s and early 2000s. It was during this time that the seeds of enforcement-as-deterrence that had been planted earlier blossomed into the largest system of detention and expulsion in the world.

A ferocious driver of this rapid expansion of detention and deportation was the racialized process of criminalization (Miller 2003; Chacón 2007). In chapter 4, we detailed changes to immigration legislation in the mid-1980s to 1990 that laid the ideological and legislative groundwork for subsequent rounds of criminalization. In 1996, a new, more comprehensive round of crime and immigration legislation was built on the already existing figure of the criminal alien to fortify an expressly punitive stance toward immigrants. This move involved ramping up the dynamics of expulsion and criminalization that legislators and officials in the executive branch had set into play earlier.

The new round of criminalization enacted in 1996 featured a series of key changes. AEDPA expanded the web of incarceration fueled by mandatory detention of some asylum seekers by now requiring the "mandatory detention of non-citizens convicted of a wide range of offenses, including minor drug offenses."[19] IIRIRA further expanded this list of offenses, with Congress requiring detention of noncitizens with one or two "crimes of moral turpitude."[20] Congress also expanded the definition of "aggravated felonies" to include misdemeanors under state law. These provisions were also applied retroactively. That is, a noncitizen who committed an offense that was not grounds for deportation twenty years prior now could be subject to both mandatory detention and removal. The legislation manufactured an immediate increase in the number of noncitizens who could now be targets of migration enforcement.

The 1996 legislative changes, while sweeping, built on measures that were introduced years earlier. As discussed in chapter 4, the passage of the Anti-Drug Abuse Act (ADAA) in 1988 resulted in the creation of the Institutional Hearing Program (IHP). The INS worked with the BOP to centralize men who were subject to deportation in one facility: Oakdale. The program was expanded beyond Oakdale to other hearing sites, including Leavenworth, Kansas; La Tuna and Big Springs, Texas; Dublin, California; Lexington, Kentucky; and the newly contracted and jointly run BOP/INS contract facility in Eloy, Arizona.[21]

In response to the massive backlog in immigration courts, IIRIRA also paved the way for sweeping new "expedited removal" procedures. Expedited removal is a form of deportation without court proceedings. Expedited removal builds upon the "entry" doctrine and applies removal consequences (in distinction to a voluntary return) to foreign nationals who attempt entry to the United States without authorization or with documents that are suspected to be fraudulent. Expedited removal generally had been applied to undocumented immigrants who have been in the United States for less than fourteen days or if apprehended within one hundred miles of the U.S. border with Canada or Mexico (American Immigration Council 2017; Hallman 2017). Under IIRIRA, a person with an aggravated felony conviction was now subject to mandatory detention and expedited removal.

A September 1999 INS fact sheet announced a pilot program to test these new removal procedures at three detention centers in Texas (Big Spring, Eden, and Reeves County). The pilot program targeted those people convicted of illegal entry and present in the United States for less than two years.[22] This program crafted operational relationships between federal agencies through the ad hoc involvement of local authorities and experimentation with localized federal programs. This pilot program also created the groundwork for subsequent formalization and expansion in the form of Operation Streamline (summarized by Boyce and Launius 2013).

This was the institutional context within which the Batavia facility was built and the harsh 1996 legislation passed. For example, in August 1995, the INS—in collaboration with New York State Governor George Pataki—announced the deportation of eighty-six criminal aliens, the "largest single-country deportation of criminals in New York history."[23] The group was deported to Colombia, all for "non-violent" offenses, most of them drug charges. This high-profile action was the culmination of years of collaboration between the federal government and New York officials, who together constructed noncitizens apprehended in the drug trade as responsible for prison overcrowding.

By early 1996, the press and the INS favorably reported a steady increase in deportations. An editorial in the *Los Angeles Times,* for example, found "Encouraging Progress on Deportations: Statistics Support the Steady, Measured Approach of the INS."[24] Yet the implementation of IIRIRA and AEDPA created pressure to build even more detention space. In October 1996, INS Commissioner Dorris Meissner informed Congress that the INS "lacks sufficient detention facilities and personnel to implement the mandatory detention provisions of the new Act and of the AEDPA. *By operation of the law, the notification renders these mandatory provisions inoperative.*" She explained, "A new set of rules, called the Transition Period Custody Rules ('TPCR'), now applies to terrorist and most criminal aliens subject to deportation proceedings." These rules mandated detention, outlining circumstances for detention and release, and once again vastly increased the number of people detained and the need to move people among facilities.[25]

Attorney General Reno also spoke to the difficulties that the new legislation posed. In remarks drafted for a press conference on removals to be held on October 30, 1997, she wrote: "Several years ago, President Clinton set a goal for us to reverse years of neglect of our immigration laws and to dramatically increase the number of criminal and other illegal aliens that we put into formal exclusion or deportation proceedings each year."[26] She went on to explain that removal efforts were "part of this Administration's plan to create a seamless web of enforcement from the border to the workplace."[27] Reno summarized the push to deport: "Our message is simple. Those who immigrate legally are welcome, while those who do not abide by our laws are not welcome and will be removed in increasing numbers." The statistics bear out this shift. Fiscal year 1997 total removals of 111,000 far exceeded the target of 93,000.[28]

In 1999, hearings on House appropriations for fiscal year 2000 once again linked the TPCR to the vast expansion of the detention and transport systems:

> The INS's ability to remove aliens from the United States is directly linked to our ability to detain and transport them. Over the past few years, INS, pursuant to Congressional direction and funding, has rapidly expanded the number of detention beds used to detain removable aliens. While about 5,500 aliens were in detention in fiscal year 1994, more than 16,300 are detained today. The percentage of detainees with criminal records has also increased substantially during this period, from 60 percent in 1994 to more

than 90 percent today. Increases continued to occur during a period when custody decisions were governed by the INS's Transition Period Custody Rules (TPCR), structured regulations which mandated detention in many circumstances and outlined the factors to be considered in weighing release in other circumstances (US Congress 1999, 177).

In highlighting the increasing proportion of people with criminal records who were held in migration detention, this statement suggests that the INS was prioritizing the steady removal of dangerous individuals. While this statement naturalized the common sense of "criminality," it was also in tension with the mission of INS incarceration-supposedly of a civil, nonpunitive nature, and with the INS's frequent characterization of people within its custody as minimum security threats.

After the implementation of IIRIRA, which replaced TPCR with stricter mandatory detention provisions, federal narratives to the public and in private—in the archives—offer a variety of reasons for the expansion of detention, often tied to increasing criteria for detainability and deportability. A 1999 Department of Justice (DOJ)/INS fact sheet, for example, explains that the "rise of sophisticated smuggling operations, the increase in the number of criminal aliens, and effects of Hurricane Mitch" were responsible for the need for yet more detention space.[29] This explanation mixes enforcement operations and efforts to deter people seeking refuge from environmental devastation into a single trajectory from apprehension to detention to deportation. All amounted to increasing demands, if with distinct rationales, for the expansion of detention capacity.

A "SEAMLESS WEB OF ENFORCEMENT": THE CREATION OF A SYSTEM OF TRANSIT AND REMOVAL

The capacity to deport includes the ability to transport people out of the country and to detention spaces that are available elsewhere within the U.S. system. In 1995, the federal government launched the Justice Prisoner and Alien Transportation System (JPATS). Assistant Attorney General Stephen Colgate explained to the GAO that the launch of JPATS on October 1 would "complete continental US air capability" with an "increased number of regional hub-site locations."[30] The joint U.S. Marshals Service–INS transportation system once again illustrates the relationship between the expansion of the criminal legal and migration-detention systems.

Given its crucial role in carrying out detention, transfer, and deportation from the United States, little has been written about JPATS. JPATS makes occasional appearances in Hiemstra's (2013) writing on transnational geographies of detention and deportation experienced by Ecuadorian nationals. She asked interlocutors to describe where in the United States they had been confined between the time of apprehension and their return to Ecuador and then created maps, which illustrated the frequent transfers, via JPATS, within the U.S. detention system and the route back to Ecuador. Before that a piece of embedded, photographic journalism on JPATS, nicknamed "Con Air," was published in *Wired* in 2010. It provides some insights into the materiality of transfers organized by JPATS, "the biggest prison transport network in the world."[31] At the time in 2009, JPATS shuttled some 350,000 people around the country on its fleet of 10 planes. On the ground, a tactical team from the Bureau of Prisons supervised those being transported onto the plane. On flights, the *Wired* photographer witnessed up to fifteen guards, armed with tasers, overseeing prisoners traveling in handcuffs, shackles, and belly chains.

JPATS formalized and expanded what had operated previously as a less-organized series of regional flights that became more formal following the 1986 and 1988 drug laws. For example, Boston's Deportation Fugitive Unit used "Wanted" fliers and an enforcement program was filling airplanes leaving from Boston as early as 1992.[32] The Northern Region Detention and Deportation Program involved cooperation between local authorities and the Air National Guard to transport people convicted on narcotics charges.[33] Finally, a "special Northeast route" was established between Otisville, New York; New York City; Buffalo, New York; Lewisburg, Pennsylvania; and Salisbury, Maryland.[34] Notably, these routes would serve a mix of federal and state prisons and migration-detention facilities.

Since its creation, JPATS flight paths have been woven into the vast U.S. detention and prison system, and detainee routes through the system and out of the country reflect these hubs and networks. An April 1995 press release from the DOJ noted that the main hub would be located in Oklahoma City, and that a new 1,800-bed transfer facility would be built near El Reno, which had been considered a decade earlier for an INS detention facility.[35] Flight routes would link Oklahoma City to facilities in Arizona, Louisiana, and elsewhere throughout the country (see map 10).[36] Indeed, JPATS would grow out of military base realignment and the consolidation of federal facilities in places that had already welcomed them. The airfields in Arizona and Louisiana that became regional hubs for JPATS had been World War II (WWII) Air Force bases.

USMS/INS Air Transport Operations
National Transportation System

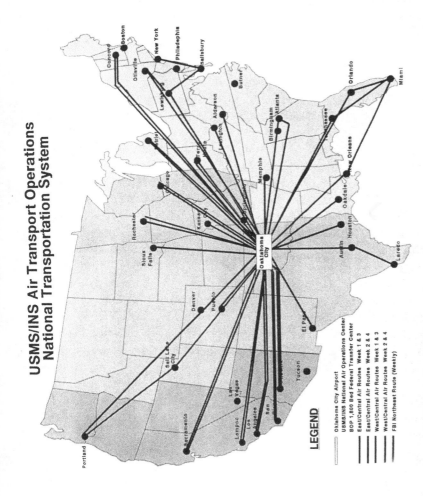

LEGEND

- ⬤ Oklahoma City Airport
- ⬤ USMS/INS National Air Operations Center
- ⬤ BOP 1,800 Bed Federal Transfer Center
- East/Central Air Routes Week 1 & 3
- East/Central Air Routes Week 2 & 4
- West/Central Air Routes Week 1 & 3
- West/Central Air Routes Week 2 & 4
- FBI Northeast Route (Weekly)

MAP 10. JPATS flight paths. Reproduced from the archives, this map illustrates c. 1995 infrastructure of JPATS flights designed to transport detainees among facilities within the United States and, ultimately, to deport them.

(Source: USCIS Library.)

Then FBI Director Louis Freeh had recommended the consolidation, using bureaucratic and logistical rationales to pool resources and create cost efficiencies.[37] The U.S. Marshals Service echoed these rationales:

> Given the number of administrative detainees and criminal aliens which need to be transported within the United States to detention centers and then deported from the United States, air transportation is more efficient than ground transportation, presents fewer security risks, and is less demanding on D&D [detention and deportation] staff.
>
> JPATS is already producing many benefits. Through increased air service and greater use of Department [of Justice]-wide resources, costs per alien deported are going down.[38]

The rapid increase in the overall number of trips and in the percentage counted as "criminal aliens" reflects the material effects of legislation that criminalized noncitizens. After one year of operations, JPATS could report an increase in the monthly average transport of criminal aliens nationwide, from 1,754 to 2,172.[39] At that point, criminal aliens (numbering 4,500) comprised 69 percent of "aliens" transported.[40] The Central and Western regions started a "regularly scheduled route from Seattle, WA, to the border, via Salt Lake City, UT. This flight is in addition to the Central Region weekly Denver, CO flight to the border."[41]

Reflecting the reliance of civilian agencies on military infrastructure, the INS and USMS were trained to work JPATS flights at Camp Beauregard, Louisiana. The U.S. Marshals Service also contracted with the U.S. Customs Service to provide transport. At the time, U.S. Customs owned King Aircraft based in Jacksonville, Florida, New Orleans, Louisiana, Tucson, Arizona, Albuquerque, New Mexico, Houston, Texas, San Angelo, Texas, and San Diego, California.[42] By 1996, an INS fact sheet shows the scope of flights operating from Oakdale Airport, with an agreement that there would be a maximum of "250 takeoffs, and 250 landings annually."[43]

Detention critics and administrators alike have observed how detention capacity drives both numbers of people who are confined and numbers who are deported ("If you build them, they will be filled."). As William Walters argues (2016), far less attention has been paid to the material infrastructure of transportation that undergirds deportation. The historical development of JPATS was necessary to support the expansion of detention and deportation. Changes in legislation and policy did not automatically result in the funding, infrastructure, or personnel to carry out new detention and deportation mandates. As federal agencies sought to grapple with criminalization and the carceral space that increased policing and prosecutions required, they experimented with a transportation system that would enable agencies to coordinate available space, schedule court dates, and also disrupt imprisoned people's organizing. In order to resolve shortages of space, transportation became all the more crucial to knit together a dispersed and growing network of federal, local jail, and privately contracted facilities.

SUBCONTRACTING AND PRIVATIZATION

The panoply of changes to legislation, policy, and detention practice between the early 1980s and mid-1990s that led to overcrowding and a vast expansion of carceral space soon collided with the realities of appropriations shortfalls, economic recession, and a bipartisan embrace of experiments to remake government. Three options were available to the federal government to expand its prisons: 1) turning mothballed military bases into new prisons; 2) renting detention space from local jails where sheriffs would supervise detainees; and 3) contracting with private firms to build and run detention facilities on behalf of the federal government. Local sheriffs and private security and prison firms would insert themselves into this uncertainty and turn crisis into opportunities to capture revenues.

Military Restructuring

The 1988 ADAA had required the INS to consider using surplus military space to expand its detention capacity. This was followed by the 1988 Base Realignment and Closure Commission (BRAC), which called for the consideration of repurposing military bases for prison use. By 1990, fourteen military properties had been acquired by local and state governments and turned into corrections facilities (President's Economic Adjustment Committee 1990). At least three other military bases had been turned over to the federal Bureau of Prisons by 1995 (GAO 1995).

Despite entreaties from Congress and the president, INS officials expressed misgivings about the utility of military bases for their use. This should not be surprising given the agency's difficulties with using or seeking use of military spaces in the early 1980s. By this time, INS's reasoning had shifted its emphasis on security. In a hearing before the

House Committee on the Judiciary in February 1994, DOJ Deputy Commissioner Chris Sale testified:

> We have concerns with the provision authorizing the use of closed military bases for criminal alien incarceration. In most cases, without prohibitively expensive conversion, military bases are appropriate only for confining minimum- to low-security offenders who present minimal risk to institutional and community safety.[44]

Sale cited the need for more secure space than could be created inexpensively at a former military facility, yet it is worth recalling that the GAO (1992) had found that the people who were confined the longest were often asylum seekers. The figure of the dangerous "Marielito" was being gradually replaced by the more abstract specter of the criminal alien.

Subcontracting

Subcontracting arrangements with local governments (intergovernmental agreements, or IGAs) and the private sector became the principal way in which the federal government resolved its crises of detention capacity. Much attention has been paid to the role that private prison firms, and their profit motives, play in the expansion and relative intransigence of migration detention. Yet it is important to recall that the private prison sector would not exist in the absence of government contracts and authorization. Understanding the political and economic dynamics that fueled federal subcontracting arrangements—with both private firms and local jails—provides a more complete understanding of U.S. migration detention as a public and publicly-funded private system, rather than exclusive focus on private firms.

The INS and USMS had long relied upon contracts with local jails for space to hold migrant and pretrial detainees, respectively. By the late 1980s, the USMS alone held 825 intergovernmental contracts with local jails, but overcrowding and legal challenges regarding jail conditions created additional pressures for federal agencies to find new spaces (Bureau of Justice Statistics 1988). As a result, the federal government created a Cooperative Agreement Program (not to be confused with the Criminal Alien Program), which provided capital funds to local governments for jail construction in exchange for a guaranteed use of that space. Between 1982 and 2005, the Cooperative Agreement Program spent $285 million on jail construction for 13,600 USMS detainees (Office of the Inspector General 2005).

Jails

The Cooperative Agreement Program is relevant to migration detention because it expanded local jail capacity that the INS also used. The case of Louisiana parish sheriffs and the jail systems they run is instructive.[45] In the midst of federal demands for temporary detention space, Louisiana parish sheriffs became skilled at using their strategic command of jail space to garner per diem revenues (rents) from federal (and state) agencies. Some sheriffs began to expand their facilities with the objective of fulfilling contracts with other jurisdictions. In the process, they, like the mayor of Oakdale years earlier, sought support from their elected officials to help pursue Cooperative Agreement Program grants.

Who would be held in Louisiana jails? While the courts had ruled since the early 1980s that the transfer of Haitian detainees out of Krome to remote locations would impede their legal counsel, transfers to Oakdale and parish jails in Louisiana continued (also see Masters 1996). Through the 1980s and 1990s, lawsuits, protests, prison riots, and escapes generated national media and congressional attention to the conditions of Louisiana jails where Haitian and Cuban nationals and asylum seekers from many other countries were held. These actions also brought federal investigation. In 1991, for example, the Department of Justice looked into allegations of abuse brought by Cuban detainees against Avoyelles Parish guards. As a result of its investigation, the INS ended (temporarily) its contract with the parish. Sheriff Billy Belt, described as the "scrappy sheriff" by *The State-Times,* defended his guards and indicated that he "was trying to secure other contracts to house out-of-state prisoners, including Cuban women, to replace the Cuban men that the INS plans to remove."[46] This entrepreneurial treatment of racialized and gendered people as interchangeable forms of revenue affirms the dehumanization of a system predicated not only on criminalization, but on their easy intersection with bureaucratization—as Conlon and Hiemstra (2017) show.

At the time of the DOJ's investigation, Belt was running four different jails to fulfill contracts to confine prisoners for the District of Columbia, the INS, the state of Louisiana, and his own parish.[47] The enterprising sheriff valued out-of-state contracts more than those from the state of Louisiana because they garnered a higher per diem. Belt explained to the *State-Times* that the "Cubans have generated an income of more than $3 million a year that helped Avoyelles Parish to pay for an ambulance service for the parish."[48]

In 1998, Sheriff Belt contacted Senator John Breaux's office "for help to get inmates."[49] Namely, Belt wanted "the Senator to stop INS from moving so many INS prisoners to other facilities."[50] By this time, the sheriff was operating five prisons and employing six hundred people, facts conveyed to the press to suggest the economic impact for his parish. On this occasion, the INS informed Senator Breaux's staff that the sheriff was "not doing anything wrong." Only a year before, however, detained Cuban nationals had gone on a hunger strike to protest the lack of air conditioning in Belt's jails (Human Rights Watch 1998). While the sheriff was expecting 275 to 280 federal inmates, the INS indicated that his parish had a cap of 200 prisoners, and other detainees had been transferred to the St. Martinville jail and the federal facility at Oakdale. St. Martinville soon would be at the center of the controversy over long-term and indefinite migration detention after a group of Cuban nationals held the facility hostage for six days in 1999.

Following the passage of the 1996 legislation, an already overcrowded immigration system became all the more so, increasing the INS's reliance on local jails and private facilities. Human Rights Watch (HRW) issued a report in 1998, *Locked Away,* reporting that the INS held contracts with 1,041 county jails and 18 private facilities across the country. While the INS maintained that its contract facilities should meet American Correctional Association standards, the senior counsel for the INS's Field Operations bluntly told HRW, "It's not in the INS's interest to force the jails to meet certain standards because we need the space."

By the late 1990s, reporting on migrants detained in county jails followed a naturalizing narrative analogizing the sheriff to a pragmatic farmer or benevolent plantation master. Revenues garnered by rural jailers were scripted as the equivalent of crop yields from industrial agriculture. The *New York Times,* for example, characterized "refugees" held in Louisiana jails as a new "cash crop" who were detained "170 miles from New Orleans in a sea of cotton and cornfields."[51] The *Times* interviewed Avoyelles Sheriff Belt, who reliably conveyed the "amenities" that federal revenues enabled him to provide for "this poor parish in the heart of French-speaking Louisiana." After the St. Martinville uprising, *Salon.com*'s reporting equated the INS to a colonial power: "Because the INS doesn't have space for its burgeoning inmate population, it has farmed them out. Its jails of choice are often in small towns and counties in Louisiana and Texas, where rents range between $30 and $55 a day, per prisoner."[52] These federal rates, in turn, created "a windfall that has helped stabilize or lower taxes in some areas and enabled several counties, including Comal County and Denton County [in Texas], to embark on major capital building projects."

In consistently equating revenues with profits, reporters and critics missed the material and historical basis of the sheriffs' power *and* their precariousness. Sheriffs were not in a position of tutelage (or sharecropping) as the colonial analogy and language of "windfalls" would suggest. To the contrary, their power was tied to their command over detention space, contracting their coercive powers to the federal government to secure monopoly rents. Yet this revenue stream remained contingent; it depended on other government authorities continuing to send them people, arrangements that were vulnerable to public scandals, legal challenges, and political organizing.

Private Prison Contractors

Presidents Ronald Reagan, George H. W. Bush, and Bill Clinton all supported privatization efforts, yet the privatization of prisons was never an obvious answer to prison overcrowding. Private firms initially gained a foothold in constructing and providing prison services through a contracting opportunity from the INS in 1983. Corrections Corporation of America (CCA) (now CoreCivic) received its first contract to build a detention facility in Houston, which it opened in 1984. That same year, the security firm Wackenhut (now GEO Group) opened a contract detention facility for the INS in Aurora, Colorado (Shull 2014a), and in 1985 the INS contracted with CCA to open a facility for children in Laredo, Texas (Kahn 1996, 117).[53]

The appeal of private prisons grew amidst the contradiction between bipartisan support for migration detention and persistent congressional reluctance to fund detention construction. Local jails and state prison officials had turned to the federal government for grants, voters to pass bond measures, or public authorities to issue bonds to finance construction (Bonds 2006; Gilmore 2007; Norton 2015). Private firms promised not only to build prisons, ostensibly providing a way around sticky budgeting and appropriations politics, but also to run them at less expense to the government. Yet key players, such as the Bureau of Prisons, opposed the privatization of prisons. The idea was unproven and controversial to many legislators and journalists as well. A *New York Times* article published in 1995 titled "Jail Business Shows Its Weakness" drew attention to the shaky position of private prison firms. The flexibility and lower costs that private security and prison firms promised to deliver efficiently to cash-strapped authorities actually depended on locking in a steady revenue stream. This was a decidedly uncompetitive deal for the government, and a source of persistent criticism, by the government and advocacy groups alike (GAO 1992; Office of the Inspector General 2001; Schriro 2009; Greene and Mazón 2012; ACLU 2014; National Immigrant Justice Center 2015; Office of the Inspector General 2016). Moreover, privatization projects exposed conflicts within the executive branch. While political figures could score ideological points for claiming to remake the government, officials charged with running the carceral state were skeptical about the concept. The *Times* reported that the White House and the Department of Justice had no studies demonstrating that privatization would save money; instead, some showed they would cost more. Indeed, the DOJ contended that privatization efforts were driven not so much by cost considerations as by efforts to shrink the federal workforce.[54]

A PUBLIC-PRIVATE DETENTION SYSTEM

The relentless push to criminalize and confine persistently outpaced prison capacity and political will to site or appropriate funds for imprisonment. Despite campaigning against migration into Florida, Governor Lawton Chiles, for example, made an arrangement with then INS head Meissner in 1998 that no long-term detention facilities would be built in the state.[55] The result for the migration-detention system as a whole was a mix of public and private facilities, often located in former military or existing prison towns, run by an equally complex mix of federal, local, and private agents. This system would be touted as flexible because, as we have seen, it relied upon the coordination of transfers to available spaces within the system.

The INS boasted of its ad hoc experiments as "creative and innovative strategies." For example, a c. 1994 INS "Public Affairs Backgrounder" highlighted its relationships with other federal agencies and the private sector to expand its facilities:

> INS has been a leader in contracting for private, turnkey detention facilities such as the new facility in Elizabeth, NJ designed to house excludable aliens arriving at international airports in the New York and New Jersey areas. INS also recently collaborated with the Bureau of Prisons on development of a 1,000-bed contract facility to house criminal aliens pending deportation. The Eloy facility recently opened and will centralize criminal aliens in order to more efficiently process them for removal from the United States. Criminal aliens are also centralized in Oakdale, LA.[56]

This statement shows not only the collusion of an array of public and private entities, but also the emerging geography of routes, transit hubs, and limbo stations scattered strategically as nodes to force migrant mobility and facilitate migration detention across the entire carceral landscape. It also demonstrates how administrative distinctions were used to sort differently categorized people through the system. Distinguishing "excludable aliens" from "criminal aliens" would also signal levels of security, further proliferating the construction of carceral spaces designated for particular categories of people.

Struggles over the Expansion of Arizona's Deportation Complex

The INS's "Public Affairs Backgrounder" also referenced the Institutional Hearing Program (IHP), developed to accelerate the removal of noncitizens convicted with deportable offenses. The IHP was not without criticism. A 1995 Senate investigation into the program railed that the INS's focus on so-called "quick deports"—"predominately [sic] Mexican or Central American nationals, who are in the U.S. illegally and have usually been convicted of drug offenses"—was a "sham" (18, 20).

> [I]nstead of removing (from the U.S.) the "worst of the worst" as the INS asserts, the program is actually a fast-track home for the "best of the worst" criminal aliens. Cases that may be difficult to complete before sentences expire are excluded from the program in favor of less complicated, uncontested cases (3).

By the late 1990s, the GAO had issued at least two reports finding that the INS's efforts to identify and remove criminal aliens were hampered by lack of staffing resources and detention capacity (GAO 1997; GAO 1999). This difficulty remained despite the fact that Oakdale had been made into a model for the Institutional Hearing Program some ten years earlier and that similar efforts to concentrate and efficiently remove criminal aliens were in place at facilities across the country. More space again was proffered as the solution, but there had just been a massive expansion of the detention and deportation complex in Florence and neighboring Eloy, Arizona (see figure 11). In 1994, two new contract facilities designed to hold two thousand people each, some designated expressly for criminal aliens, opened in these two towns. Within months of the facilities' opening, people being held in the Eloy prison had rioted on two different occasions regarding the conditions and delays in deportation hearings, which ostensibly had been speeded by criminal-alien legislation.[57]

FIGURE 11. Photograph of a privately owned and run migration-detention facility in Eloy, Arizona. This image taken at dusk shows the perimeter lights and surrounding agricultural fields. (Photo courtesy of Jenna M. Loyd.)

Yet another round of expansion began in 2000. In a major departure from its longstanding opposition to private contracting, the Bureau of Prisons issued a call for three new private prisons that would exclusively hold noncitizens serving their sentences under BOP jurisdiction. These new facilities would be called Criminal Alien Requirement (CAR) prisons. CCA signed the first two of these contracts for facilities in California City, California, and Cibola, New Mexico (Hammer-Tomizuka 2004, 75–76). The timing of these contracts was crucial for CCA. According to private prison analyst Judy Greene, CCA owed over $1 billion to creditors at the time, so the contract amounted to "a virtual bailout" to the firm (76).

The third CAR prison would be slated for the small town of Willcox in southern Arizona. Over the course of the next two years, a coalition of immigrant-rights, antiprison, labor, environmentalist, and other groups fought the construction of the prison (Hammer 2012). Zoe Hammer, who was involved in the campaign and documented its activities, recounts how activists raised the issue of the awful records that private prison firms had with their host communities. They also challenged the rationale that prisons were a form of economic development by pointing to Florence, Arizona. A town that was "home to five prisons[,] and no grocery store, was evidence that prisons do not grow local economies" (223). In 2002, the Bureau of Prisons withdrew its proposal for the Willcox site, once again affirming the significant role that local politics and political mobilization play in explaining the geography of migration detention in the United States.

Struggles over Expansion in Louisiana's Deportation Complex

The tenuous foothold that private prison firms held in the migration-detention and broader prison system is further illustrated by returning to Louisiana. By the early 2000s, scores of politicians and government officials had worked to build a federal prison complex in central Louisiana with a robust transport infrastructure and network of parish jails to support the short- and long-term confinement of INS, USMS, and BOP prisoners (Loyd forthcoming). This network of prisons and jails was not separate from, but interlinked with, the Louisiana state adult and juvenile prison systems. One of these juvenile prisons in Jena, located about 1.5 hours drive northeast of Oakdale, would soon become the site of an extended effort on the part of Wackenhut to insert itself into INS contracting in Louisiana.

Confronted with a Department of Justice lawsuit charging Wackenhut with abuse and neglect of minors, Wackenhut ceased its operations of the Jena youth prison. The firm then approached the BOP and the INS in May 2000 to gauge their interest in purchasing the facility. The BOP inspected the facility, but determined that its capacity of 275 was far smaller than the 1,000-plus capacity that it preferred for economy of scale. Moreover, the BOP indicated that the facility would not be suitable for confining women: "The majority of federal female offenders are from urban areas, particularly southern Florida, and the location of the Jena facility would make it difficult to provide the accessibility and support services needed."[58] The INS also turned down Wackenhut's request, indicating that it would have needed to improve security. Further, the INS had just opened a facility in Pennsylvania and already relied upon the Oakdale facility and intergovernmental contracts with eighteen Louisiana parishes.[59]

As we have seen in Sheriff Belt's discussion of seeking a different category of prisoners to confine, subcontracts rest on the promise of being able to make abstract equivalences among different groups, what Cynthia Bejarano, Maria Morales, and Said Saddiki refer to as "transferable bodies" (2012). In this moment, however, Wackenhut found that it could not simply replace juveniles with another group. A federal purchase of the facility seemed unlikely, but the federal response to September 11, 2001, represented a new opportunity for a former assistant to Senator Breaux who was now working as a prison lobbyist for Wackenhut. In an e-mail to Breaux's aide Johnny Broussard, Diane McRee suggested that the INS may be more receptive "in view of recent events which has resulted in a need to incarcerate or detain more people."[60] Indeed, the private prison firm had been facing tremendous private and governmental scrutiny over its operations, resulting in falling stock prices before 9/11 (Greene and Mazón 2012).

With the facility sitting empty, the state senator for the area also began pushing to get the prison filled. Yet other elected officials in the area were more concerned about ensuring that a BOP facility that was already in the pipeline would be built. In late January 2003, a Washington, D.C.–based staffer for Senator Breaux sent an e-mail to other of Breaux's aides, explaining the situation:

> As you probably know, the Senator's office has arranged a number of meetings with federal agencies in an effort to help Senator Ellington fill the LaSalle Parish Correctional Facility. Since no agencies want to place prisoners there at this time, Wackenhut, the owner of the prison, has apparently hired several lobbyists to insert language into a bill or report that would instruct the BOP to place some of their prisoners at the LaSalle Parish Correctional Facility.[61]

Indeed, Wackenhut lobbyists had approached Senator Breaux's office with drafts of committee-report language proposing three different policy options. The first would direct the Attorney General to "enter into good faith negotiations with Louisiana Parish Sheriffs for the utilization of available jail space and to enter into good faith negotiations to purchase for fair market value not to exceed $18,500,000, the 300 bed correctional facility located in the town of Jena."[62] The second option was the same as the first, but removed the $18.5 million cap, and offered Jena as among the facilities it could purchase. The final option directed the Attorney General to negotiate with parish sheriffs to utilize existing jail space and to enter into a long-term contract to confine at least three hundred federal prisoners in the Jena facility.

The options that Wackenhut proposed to the government decidedly favored the private firm. It would take several years following September

11 and the reorganization of the INS into Immigration and Customs Enforcement (ICE) within the Department of Homeland Security (DHS) for the facility to be reopened. In this case, a different kind of public-private contracting arrangement was developed, one that would be eligible to enter into an intergovernmental agreement with ICE. In 2006, the LaSalle Economic Development District signed an IGA with ICE, and the following year the district contracted with GEO Group (formerly Wackenhut). After the facility sat vacant for a half dozen years, GEO Group would expand it, more than doubling the capacity to over one thousand people.

This snapshot of efforts in Louisiana to try to prevent the entrance of private prison firms and then accommodate their presence illustrates how privatization is but one element of the overriding issue of intergovernmental and subcontracting arrangements and their intense bureaucratization (Hiemstra and Conlon 2017). Sheriffs played, and continue to play, an important role in providing the space and work of imprisoning migrants. Private firms did not drive the expansion of the system. Rather, they were able to gain a foothold only in the context of a persistent crisis over detention space, which was driven by criminalizing legislation and recurrent appeals to confine and expel noncitizens, dynamics only amplified after 9/11. As the scandal over juvenile imprisonment in Jena, Louisiana, and legislation passed by some states barring the use of private prisons (Bonds 2015) suggest, however, private firms remain subject to political pressure.

CONCLUSION

As legal scholar Angélica Cházaro writes in her challenge to what she calls "the criminal alien paradigm," by 2016, the "deportation of so-called 'criminal aliens' has become the driving force in U.S. immigration enforcement" (2016, 1). Put another way, the invention of the "criminal alien" facilitated the expansion of detention and grounds for removal for even longtime permanent residents. As we have shown, this dynamic of criminalization has its roots in earlier attempts to deter and remove unwanted asylum seekers. The desire to detain and expel Haitian and Afro-Cuban asylum seekers created the initial conditions for mandatory detention, which criminalization further consolidated.

This chapter has shown the iterative process wherein detention and deportation capacity was expanded massively through criminalization. The growth of detention spaces during the mid-1990s to early 2000s was always about expanding legal and material conditions for deportability.

Over time, criminalization became a more formal and ideologically rationalized set of tools used for responding to migration events. The entrenchment of criminalization and internal expulsion latches detention as a deterrent, specifically of Haitians (including those who were residing in the country), together with its more expansive target of deporting "'criminal aliens."

The ideological commitment to and subsequent legislated requirement for a detention infrastructure—including that of transportation—and the persistent scramble for space led to subcontracting and privatization arrangements. These were fueled and made possible by the expansion of the broader prison and jail systems. This history also demonstrates the contingent creation of federal infrastructures in spite of fiscal crises and through the forging of intergovernmental relationships. While the case of Batavia illustrates the embrace of another government-owned and -run prison in Western New York, expansion did not happen uniformly. Instead, there were battles over privatization and expansion plans, as illustrated by the cases in Louisiana and Arizona.

The past twenty years of legal research in the wake of these legislative changes saw introduction of the term "crimmigration" by legal scholars and criminologists (Stumpf 2006; Dowling and Inda 2013; Chacón 2015). The term is an expression of a phenomenon that was decades-in-the-making: policies that were tested on and disproportionately borne by Haitian migrants. Crimmigration as a term captures only one element of the forces driving the expansion of detention. Recalling the anti-Black racism informing concerted governmental efforts to deter asylum seekers is also crucial because these deterrent efforts failed. As we continue to explore in chapter 7, criminalization would become a one-size-fits-all policy answer, yet by design it is a tool that creates more of the problem that it sets out to solve.

Post-9/11 Policing

Back to the Future

While the massive scope of U.S. migration detention is often thought of as a post-9/11 development, *Boats, Borders, and Bases* shows how the roots of the transnational architecture of migration deterrence and policing had been established much earlier. This book has told decades-long histories of how efforts to deter and detain asylum seekers eventually dovetailed with policies and practices of mass, though still targeted, criminalization to result in the construction of the world's largest infrastructure for imprisonment and deportation. In this final chapter, we resume the discussion of how asylum, criminalization, and deterrence were intertwined leading up to and following the terrorist attacks on the United States on September 11, 2001. We draw out conclusions from this history, and explore their implications for the reorganization and expansion of migration policing and boundary fortification thereafter.

THE MEANING OF ASYLUM AFTER IIRIRA

Soon after the passage of the punitive Illegal Immigration Reform and Immigrant Responsibility Act (IIRIRA), officials in President Bill Clinton's White House debated what to do about long-term Central American residents who as a result might be subject to deportation. Prior to the bill's passage, an immigration judge could grant relief to a long-term resident for whom deportation would cause "extreme hardship." IIRIRA increased the amount of time one needed to be present continuously in the United States, raised the bar for what constituted hardship to "exceptional and extremely unusual," and capped the number of people who could be granted relief from deportation to four thousand per year.[1] By this time, some 40,000 Nicaraguan asylum seekers whom the Ronald Reagan administration had admitted, and 190,000 Salvadorans and 50,000 Guatemalans who were protected under the ABC settlement, were now vulnerable to deportation.[2]

The situation pointed both to the intricate connections between asylum and criminalization, and to the politics of which groups would be considered for presidential action and which—conversely—would be rendered more precarious through their "permanent temporariness" (Bailey et al. 2002). In July 1997 Phil Caplan, deputy staff secretary, sent President Clinton a memo penned by Sandy Berger and other members of the Domestic Policy Council (DPC) that charted a strategy to "provide relief to Central American migrants affected by the new immigration law." Their approach involved three courses of action—legislative, administrative, and executive action. They recommended that the president support legislation that would return these groups to their prior status, and have Attorney General Janet Reno announce temporary administrative steps she would take to prevent deportation for qualified groups. If these approaches were inadequate, the president could issue an executive action to grant Deferred Enforced Departure (DED), but this was the least preferable action because it was temporary and revocable.[3]

As expected, Congress passed the new legislation, the Nicaraguan Adjustment and Central American Relief Act (NACARA). Yet in so doing, Congress reproduced Cold War distinctions in treatment, allowing Nicaraguans to apply for permanent residency while making Salvadorans and Guatemalans eligible for a "special rule of cancellation" (Coutin 2011, 584). (Some former Soviet-bloc residents were also covered by the legislation.) Susan Coutin explains the tensions that ensued. While "the passage of NACARA and the drafting of its implementing regulations caused an immigrant group previously defined as economic migrants to be considered deserving of protection," the disparate treatment the bill enshrined meant that Salvadorans and Guatemalans under the act would not be eligible to apply for permanent residency until the early 2000s (585). Their effective asylum was made vulnerable by the combination of increased policing and a growing list of deportable offenses.

Haitians were not included in the NACARA legislation. At the time, some 105,000 Haitians were living in the United States without permanent residency, and this included the 12,000 people whom President

Bush paroled into the United States after the coup against Jean-Bertrand Aristide (a group some referred to as Guantanamo Haitians).[4] A memo prepared by the Immigration and Naturalization Service (INS) and Attorney General officials observed that Haitian advocates and the Congressional Black Caucus (CBC) were pushing for action that could result in permanent resident status for Haitians, yet these officials concluded, "Failing a legislative solution, there is no viable, long-term administrative solution for the Haitians."[5] A presidential order extending DED would be temporary only, and its use was "generally based on foreign policy interests."[6] While "the prospect of a Salvadoran, Guatemalan, and Nicaraguan mass return raised foreign policy concerns sufficiently serious," the implications for Haiti's "fragile economy and political infrastructure might similarly justify DED."[7]

Julie Fernandes, a civil-rights lawyer working in Clinton's Domestic Policy Council, wrote to Elena Kagan, director of the DPC, explaining that for the president to issue DED, "it would likely have to be for a group larger than the Guantanamos—it would be difficult to justify, for foreign policy reasons, deporting some Haitians and not others."[8] While expanding who would be covered by DED would be consistent with the foreign-policy rationale necessary for exercising this authority, Fernandes held it would also be "inconsistent with our limited goal of providing relief for the Guantanamo group."[9] Moreover, the option of the Attorney General exercising her discretion would make Reno "vulnerable to attack by Rep. Smith."[10]

Indeed, Lamar Smith (R-Texas), who chaired the subcommittee responsible for IIRIRA and introduced legislation to grant permanent residency for Nicaraguans, wrote to the White House following the passage of NACARA to challenge the rationale for extending relief to Haitians. Smith argued:

> Haitians have no similar claims against the government for unfair treatment. In fact, they have been treated better than individuals from most other countries. Haitians fleeing their country in the early 1990s—"the Guantanamo Haitians"—were paroled into the United States, where they received work authorization, were not subject to deportation, and were given the ability to pursue asylum claims. No other nationality group has received similar treatment. In fact, other aliens interdicted at sea during the same period were typically returned home with a less generous process for screening their asylum claims.[11]

His letter continued to claim that contrary to negative discrimination,

> Haitians have historically received very generous treatment from the United States. During the last 11 years, over 200,000 legal immigrants from Haiti

have been admitted. (This is a higher percentage of that country's population than almost any other country.) Clearly the United States does not discriminate against Haitians in its immigration policy. In fact, as described above, the U.S. has recently discriminated *in favor* of Haitians by having brought the Guantanamo Haitians into the U.S. to pursue their asylum claims.[12]

Smith ended his letter with an appeal to "emphasize healing rather than dividing."[13]

The representative's reading of history ignored governmental reports and court rulings on the record of discriminatory treatment of Haitian asylum seekers. He told a selective history of Guantánamo that erased the returns of Haitians and twisted detention into a virtual welcome for them. He sidestepped the simultaneous development of the "wet foot, dry foot" policy that, while not a wholesale refuge for Cubans, did nonetheless treat them better than Haitians. Smith also invoked a statistic intended to convey the United States's exceptional leniency toward Haitians. Yet the Haitian diaspora was not significantly larger than other diasporic populations in the world—or in the United States. According to United Nations figures, in 1990 some 7 percent of Haitians were living outside of Haiti as compared to 19 percent of Salvadorans, 7 percent of Cubans, 20 percent of Jamaicans, 4 percent of Guatemalans, and 10 percent of Nicaraguans.[14]

Clinton would authorize DED for a portion of the Haitians living in the United States, including the so-called "Guantanamo Haitians." The group that the White House made eligible for DED, nonetheless, was smaller than that pushed for by Representative Carrie Meek (D-Florida) and other Haitian advocates. Berger, Clinton's National Security Advisor, advised the president against providing relief for this larger number of individuals: "We believe granting DED to such a potentially large group, without regard for the reasons they came here, conflicts with our immigration enforcement efforts and would meet with significant opposition on the Hill."[15] Following the president's authorization issued just before Christmas, the *New York Times* reported that deportation hearings for Haitians were continuing. Smith called this resumption "common sense," while attorney Cheryl Little characterized the situation as yet another "double standard."[16]

This wrangling over legislation, entry, and exclusion by national origin once again sheds light on the entanglement of U.S. migration detention with Cold War politics. Administrative and legislative categories were not neutral bureaucratic terms, but were used to pit racialized and geopoliticized groups against one another, positing some as "deserving" and others as "undeserving." While asylum cases were supposed to be heard individually, legislative and administrative actions routinely were used to create a blanket resolution for groups. Yet with the increased bipartisan support for criminalization, a conviction for an expanding set of offenses could now serve to effectively exclude people from asylum. Indeed, both NACARA and Clinton's 1998 authorization of EVD for select Haitians excluded people with certain criminal convictions. Ironically, Smith later wrote to Attorney General Reno in 1999, prevailing upon her to exercise prosecutorial discretion with regard to permanent residents with family ties who had "committed a single crime at the lower end of the aggravated felony spectrum" (Macías-Rojas 2016, 66).

SEPTEMBER 11 AND THE CONSOLIDATION OF A TRANSNATIONAL CARCERAL STATE

While the political, ideological, and legislative conditions had been laid for continued expansion of the detention and deportation system, 9/11 served as the political occasion to consolidate these forces. Existing institutional momentum was accelerated with infusions of resources and renewed security rationales to increase interior policing, deepen collaborations between local and federal authorities, and further fortify the United States–Mexico borderlands. Republican George W. Bush, who ran against Democratic candidate Al Gore, had been in the White House since January of 2001. As governor of Texas, he had established more moderate relationships with Latinx people in the state and with the government of Mexico than fellow Republican governor Pete Wilson or other restrictionists in Congress. During his second term as president, he pursued a migration-reform proposal that would have created a guest-worker visa as a way to regularize the status of many unauthorized residents.[17]

Before Bush proposed these reforms, however, the White House massively restructured federal agencies. The scope of changes following 9/11 has been well documented (e.g., Coleman 2007a) and can only be summarized here. The first major step in this restructuring was the creation of the vast Department of Homeland Security (DHS), which was created two months after the terrorist attacks and operationalized on March 1, 2003. The DHS integrated twenty-two federal departments and agencies. The Immigration and Naturalization Service, previously under the Department of Justice (DOJ), was dismantled and its duties were separated into three new departments within the DHS: 1) U.S. Immigration and Customs Enforcement (ICE) was made responsible for interior policing; 2) Border Patrol was renamed U.S. Customs and Border Protection (CBP), and remained responsible for policing and inspections in border and entry points; and 3) U.S. Citizenship and Immigration Services (USCIS) was created to process visa and citizenship applications. Additionally, the Coast Guard (USCG) was placed under the DHS.

The folding of most functions of immigration policy and border enforcement into one of the largest federal departments named with the mandate of securing the homeland is a signal of the extent of criminalization that took place after 9/11 through the elision of "terrorist" and "criminal alien." Still, the developments that followed 9/11 were the continuation of historical cycles of political crises, expansion of confinement and policing, and contestation of these responses. Although the 9/11 attacks did not relate directly in any way to asylum, immigrants, asylum seekers, and refugees were subjected to more intensified criminalization and securitization as a result. On September 20, 2001, the DOJ and the INS changed detention procedures to allow for continued detention during times of emergency, a development that was soon followed by the even more troubling passage of the PATRIOT Act on October 26, 2001, which authorized the indefinite detention of noncitizens if the government had "reasonable grounds to believe" they had connections to terrorism. As a result of these expanded powers, the DOJ and the INS targeted the Arab and Muslim immigrant community and detained nearly ten thousand people, most of whom were men (Macías-Rojas 2016, 67). This response mirrored earlier enforcement responses we have detailed to perceived migration crises and once again advanced a toxic mix of race, geopolitics, and country of origin to rationalize discrimination and confinement.

Deterrence in a Post-9/11 World

On December 3, 2001, before the DHS restructuring, a boat named *Si M'ap Viv*, carrying 187 Haitian asylum seekers, ran aground offshore of Florida. According to an account of events that Senator Edward Kennedy (D-Massachusetts) detailed at the outset of an October 2002 Senate hearing, the Coast Guard rescued 167 persons and transferred them into the custody of the Department of Justice. (A subsequent press report indicates that eighteen people escaped and two presumably drowned.[18]) The INS deputy commissioner had quietly issued a new policy to field officers in Florida, which stated that "no Haitian should be paroled from detention without approval from Washington" (US Congress 2002, 1). Prior to the hearing, the Justice Department "confirmed their change in policy and explained their reasons for the change, that detention was needed to 'prevent against a potential mass migration to the United States'" (1–2). By the time of the hearing only 16 of the 167 detainees had been granted asylum, even though the majority of them had passed a credible-fear interview. The Justice Department, headed by Attorney General John Ashcroft, did not send officials to the hearing.

Despite claims of newness, this 2001 moment echoed the longstanding policies and practices we have recounted in this book. Soon after this Senate hearing, Bush issued an executive order that authorized the Attorney General (subsequently amended to read the Secretary of Homeland Security) to take custody of and screen noncitizens who were intercepted in the Caribbean. As Azadeh Dastyari (2015) observes, this was already policy, and interdiction practices had continued since the mid-1990s when significant attention had last been paid to the issue. Assistant Attorney General Daniel Bryant noted that several boats had been interdicted by the Coast Guard since November 2011, resulting in the apprehension of 1,391 Haitian people.[19] This uptick continued into the first quarter of 2002 when the Coast Guard intercepted another 1,354 Haitians.[20]

People who had been on board the *Si M'ap Viv* continued to be held in three different facilities in Florida: the men at Krome, the women in a maximum-security jail called Turner Guilford Knight Correctional Center (TGK), and families in a secure hotel in Miami.[21] Inside TGK, women reported that they were repeatedly strip-searched, not provided with menstrual pads or toothpaste, and not given adequate medical care. The women did not have access to a library or outdoor recreation and lived in cells rather than dormitory-style rooms.[22] A letter signed by fifty women held at TGK conveys the betrayal they felt:

> When we got here, we thought that the Americans would understand us because there are laws that protect victims of abuse and torture. We did not leave our homes because of lack of food, it was political problems that forced us to leave. What hurts us more is that everyone we've spoken to has told us that this is not the way Immigration usually treats asylum seekers.[23]

The Florida Immigrant Advocacy Center (FIAC) contended that the women held at TGK "face double discrimination in the custody of the INS, not only because of the policy targeting Haitians, but also on the basis of their gender."[24] The harshness of the conditions the women faced at TGK were made all the more egregious by the fact that the INS had begun holding women at TGK in December 2000 following allegations of sexual abuse at Krome.

Private reports about conditions at the secure hotel indicated that there had been a sharp increase in the numbers of people that the INS was holding there, from 29 in November 2001 to 113 in April 2002.[25] The FIAC, which provided legal representation for some of the people held at the hotel, knew of two families that had been transferred to the family-detention facility in Pennsylvania, despite their representation by FIAC and the fact that the father who was part of one of the families remained confined at Krome.[26] These transfers were alarming, as were the conditions at the hotel, where detainees had no access to Know Your Rights presentations and only limited access to their attorneys. In short, "the Hotel is completely inappropriate for detention. For example, the detainees at the Hotel, including children, have NO access to recreation, exercise or fresh air. They spend their days locked in their rooms, where they eat and sleep. Children have no access to education."[27]

These conditions of detention and the INS's exclusive focus on Haitian asylum seekers led Director of FIAC Cheryl Little, Ira Kurzban, and other attorneys to sue the INS in March 2002. The class-action lawsuit (*Moise v. Bulger*) contended that the asylum seekers' detention negatively affected their asylum cases and challenged the INS's contention that another mass boat migration was brewing. Little explained to the press, "This policy is not about saving Haitian lives."[28] Rather, "It's about keeping Haitians out."[29] The United Nations High Commissioner for Refugees (UNHCR) issued an advisory opinion on April 15, 2002, contending that the blanket detention policy violated international laws and norms.[30] Yet on May 17, 2002 a district court ruled against their class-action suit challenging the detention.

Legal and political challenges to ongoing detention continued after the court ruling. Senators Kennedy and Sam Brownback (R-Kansas) wrote to Attorney General Ashcroft, urging him to "reinstate the prior policy that treated Haitians consistently with other asylum seekers and to promptly release this vulnerable group of asylum seekers."[31] They concluded by reminding the Attorney General, "It is both unfair and violative of our own principles of refugee protection to discriminate against one nationality."[32] In early July 2002, Haitian asylum seekers detained at Krome began a hunger strike to protest their confinement. Their statement released a few days later reads in full:

We began a hunger strike at lunch time on Saturday, July 6, 2002. We feel that the humiliation we are experiencing is going too far. We came to the United States on December 3, 2001 to seek asylum because we encountered political persecution in our country. Since then, we have been detained at Krome. We are not criminals, we only ask for asylum because we will be persecuted again if we go back to Haiti. We have seen asylum seekers from other nationalities coming to Krome and released in a couple of days, while we have been kept for over seven months now.

We are asking for justice. We want to demonstrate peacefully by wearing pieces of cardboard around our necks, which have slogans on them such as: "Justice for the Haitians," "Freedom for All," "We Love America," "7 months in jail are not 7 weeks," "It's about time that we have justice." Captain Lao ordered us to remove the slogans because he stated that they are not part of the uniform provided by the facility. We complied with this order, but we are still searching for justice because we cannot go back to Haiti. We are not going to eat until we hear something positive from INS.[33]

As in past crises, electoral season politics came into the mix. Florida Governor Jeb Bush, brother of the president, was running against Democratic candidate Bill McBride. The *Wall Street Journal* reported that critics regarded the exclusionary efforts as a way to "insulate" the governor.[34] On October 29, 2002, another boat carrying some two hundred Haitians reached shore near Key Biscayne. The detention policy remained in effect, and some residents of Miami immediately mobilized to protest in the streets and outside of Krome. By this time, in a de facto return to the Haitian Program, 90 percent of the asylum seekers held from December 2001 had had their requests denied.[35]

The political cartoon in figure 12 depicts the distinctly racialized narratives about migration and detention circulating at the time. The artist criticizes the hypocrisy and inequity of a migration system that would confine Haitian men en masse while issuing a student visa to a person who would later be suspected in the World Trade Center attack. Yet in drawing attention to the distinct fates of these different groups of men, the artist would also obscure the fate of Haitian women, Haitian children, and the Arab and Muslim men who themselves were arbitrarily confined, like Haitians, following September 11.

Criminalization after 9/11

President Bush used his 2007 State of the Union address to make a case for comprehensive immigration reform. He reminded the nation that funding for border security had increased from $4.6 billion in 2001 to

FIGURE 12. Political cartoon, 2002. (*Miami Herald.*)

$10.4 billion in fiscal year 2007, and that the number of Border Patrol agents would double during his two terms in office.[36] Among the security advances he highlighted was the Secure Border Initiative (SBI), which the White House touted as a comprehensive approach to securing the border using drones, "tactical infrastructure," and other state-of-the art technologies. A few months earlier, Bush had signed the Secure Fence Act of 2006. Joe Nevins observes that this law "outbid" the 2005 James Sensenbrenner (R-Wisconsin) bill, which called for seven hundred miles of "security fencing" (2010, 212). The Secure Fence Act ordered 850 miles of "reinforced fencing" and patrols.

Other measures that the president highlighted used charged political terms that naturalized migration detention. Funding to increase detention capacity to 27,500 bed spaces ended the previous practice of so-called "catch and release." Collaboration between the federal government and local law enforcement—through programs such as 287(g), in which local law-enforcement agents are deputized to serve as ICE agents, and the Criminal Alien Program (CAP)—also were bolstered. Even as the president invoked these tough measures to make the case for legislative reform, he also noted that "walls and patrols alone cannot stop" migration.[37] Yet the expansionist dynamics of criminalization set in place between the late 1980s and mid-1990s had an ideological and material inertia, which had only been entrenched with the creation of the Department of Homeland Security. Indeed, in 2008 the DHS would launch the Secure Communities program, through which local authorities transmit identity information to ICE, which can then issue a "hold" requesting that the local jail detain the individual.

Soaring imprisonment and deportation numbers resulting from these programs and those like Operation Streamline, launched in 2005 to criminally prosecute, imprison, and then deport unauthorized migrants, created a veritable deportation diaspora (Burridge 2009; Kanstroom 2012; Boyce and Launius 2013). Sociologist Tanya Golash-Boza reports that there was a thirtyfold increase in the budget for interior enforcement between 2004 and 2011. CAP was the program responsible for 50 percent of removals between 2010 and 2012 (2015, 177). Within the context of racially targeted patterns of policing, there is also a racialized pattern of deportation. "Proportionally speaking, Jamaicans and Dominicans were the LPRs [legal permanent residents] most likely to be deported" (142), revealing the tight connection between the war on drugs, stop-and-frisk policing, and the deportation machinery.

Patrisia Macías-Rojas's (2016) ethnographic study of "criminal alien removals" in Arizona explains that the detention-space shortage owing to IIRIRA created the conditions for criminal prosecution in the borderlands. Many legal permanent residents had lost their status due to changes in the law that applied retroactively, in turn filling detention centers. As a result, "This left fewer beds to detain unauthorized border crossers without convictions. Mexican nationals could be removed through voluntary departure, and they were. But the cases of Central American migrants apprehended at the border were more complicated and were more likely to result in detention." In turn, Macías-Rojas argues, "DHS expanded criminal prosecution in order to minimize the practice of paroling eligible, mostly Central American, migrants from detention and to reduce a backlog of removal cases in the immigration courts" (69). Effectively, this move to institute the criminal prosecution of unauthorized border-crossers, such as through Streamline and its predecessor Safeguard, would act as a way of circumventing the rights to asylum that had been established through years of concerted advocacy.

Restrictionist legislators, in turn, reframed due-process rights and administrative discretion as "catch and release." The analogy suggested that migration and border agents were successful at "netting fish," but were unjustly prohibited from keeping them due to arbitrary bureaucratic forces. This imagery once more naturalized the use of state force and provided another necessary rationale for further expansion. In 2009, soon after Dora Schriro (2009) issued her report calling for reform of the detention system, Congress instituted a "bed mandate," which required ICE to maintain a minimum capacity of 33,400 beds (Macías-Rojas 2016, 73). Moreover, the Bureau of Prisons (BOP) was expanding its Criminal Alien Requirement (CAR) prisons, all of which were run by private firms. The expansion of CAR prisons hinged on the federal prosecution of noncitizens on entry and reentry charges. Mass trials conducted as part of Operation Streamline, as described by Burridge (2009), Boyce and Launius (2013), and Macías-Rojas (2016), of individuals facing these charges led to felony convictions, prison time, and deportation. A deportation or removal order together with a felony conviction creates a virtually insurmountable barrier to future authorized entry. The effects would be vast: between 2005 and 2015, nearly 750,000 people had been prosecuted and imprisoned on unauthorized entry or reentry charges (Greene, Carson, and Black 2016, viii). Between the Clinton and Obama administrations, the overall pattern of migration operations had become increasingly criminalized, shifting from large numbers of returns under Bill Clinton, to interior enforcement under George W. Bush, to criminal prosecution and removal in the borderlands (Chishti, Pierce, and Bolter 2017).

ANTI-BLACKNESS AND THE TRANSNATIONAL CRIMINALIZATION OF ASYLUM SEEKERS

Commonsense understandings equating criminality, confinement, and Blackness continued to inform the treatment of unwanted asylum seekers, discursively rendering them confineable and punishable (James 1996; Miller 2003; Rodríguez 2008; Muhammad 2010). The fact of confinement—accompanied by the circulation of images of incarceration, barbed wire, prison clothing, shackles, and handcuffs—effectively becomes the mark of criminality, regardless of criminal conviction (Mountz 2010; Loyd 2015). We have shown how this discursive and practical elision between confinement and criminality *preceded* the criminalization of noncitizens in the formal legislative process. The failure of deterrent projects together with broader criminalization dynamics created the conditions for trying to use criminal prosecutions and imprisonment as an escalated means of deterrence.

Boats, Borders, and Bases has established that the detention of Haitian asylum seekers three decades earlier established the grounds for the expansion of detention for all noncitizens, a condition of detainability that was subsequently entrenched by legislation criminalizing noncitizens. It is important to return to these roots of criminalization and transnational detention to reveal areas for further political mobilization and further research. The early targeting of Haitian asylum seekers as a detainable population planted seeds not only for the contemporary detention system, but also for aggressive contemporary racialized practices of deportation. The histories of deterrence and expulsion of asylum seekers we have documented hold net-widening momentum with important implications for others, as the production of one deportable population is readily expanded to another.

The longer histories we have documented in this book reveal, importantly, that governmental efforts have both amplified and naturalized the United States–Mexico boundary as the site for border fortification, even as deterrence efforts in the Caribbean were entrenched, but with much less spectacular attention. Remembering this Caribbean history of imprisonment and deterrence is important because it speaks to the fundamental, if widely forgotten, dimension of anti-Blackness foundational to the design of U.S. border and immigration policy. Moreover, this history also speaks to the capacity of regional racial projects to become part of national and international policy in apparently race-neutral terms (Loyd 2015).

Safe Haven from the Cold War to the Post-911 World

International law professor Guy Goodwin-Gill called President Reagan's 1981 Executive Order 12324, on the "Interdiction of Illegal Aliens," "the model, perhaps, for all that has followed." At the time, Goodwin-Gill was working for the UNHCR, and he recalls being "struck by the incongruity, the inconsistency, between this measure and the resolute stand taken by the United States on the protection of Indochinese refugees in South East Asia, for whom first asylum, non-discrimination and at least temporary admission were considered the essential minimum" (2011, 443).

Indeed, the proximate roots of detention as a form of deterrence were entangled with U.S. imperial relations and built on the "humane deterrence" policy that Thailand, a U.S. ally, implemented in 1981 to constrain refugee movements from Laos.[38] Notably, Thai policy amounted to sending asylum seekers to "austerity" camps that did not provide a path to resettlement in a third country. Thus, even as the United States extended refugee status to some survivors of its war in Southeast Asia, it simultaneously used detention within a different regional geopolitical context to deter the arrival of unwanted refugees from Haiti and Cuba. As Yến Lê Espiritu writes, the refugee status of Vietnamese refugees has "continued to serve as a stage for the (re)production of American identities and for the shoring up of militarism" in ways that "naturalize and buttress the self-appointed US role as rescuer" (2006, 412). This imperial ideology of rescue promises the "gift of freedom" to Vietnamese subjects who are determined as needing care (Nguyen 2012). Presidents George H. W. Bush and Clinton deployed this rhetoric of care and rescue to refugees at sea in the Caribbean in ways that similarly erased violent U.S. military and geoeconomic policies. Yet what differed is that this rhetoric of rescue was at odds with the persistent disavowal of Haitians as rescuable (that is to say, "assimilable" in terms of patriarchal forms of protection and subjection [Young 2003; Enloe 2014]). Likewise, the discursive and practical shift to treating Cuban refugees as unwanted, unruly, criminal subjects undermined the imperial deployments of humanitarianism.

While there were great hopes for the fall of walls at the end of the Cold War, deterrent ideologies and practices would be reworked. In the midst of the 1992 Bush-Clinton presidential election debates, former INS head Doris Meissner criticized the Bush administration's return policy, but offered her support of so-called safe havens. In a *Los Angeles Times* editorial, she contended, "A policy of safety requires places to put people."[39] As we have discussed, the establishment of internationally monitored "safe havens" located within regions in conflict—rather than permanent resettlement—was part of a broader trend following the end of the Cold War (Hyndman and Giles 2017). While the United States or European nations portrayed such "safe havens" as humanitarian measures, law professor Joan Fitzpatrick argues that a safe haven "instead constitutes one more device to constrict access to asylum" (1994, 413; see also Chimni 1995; Hyndman 2003).

Attorney Harold Koh (1994a) recalls that the safe-haven camps differed from other forms of detention carried out simultaneously by the United States in a few important ways. First, those who were detained at Guantánamo and other camps were intercepted on the high seas, a strategy of deterrence designed to prevent their arrival on sovereign territory. Second, they were detained offshore indefinitely, without regard for the status of their claims for political asylum. And third, the U.S. government treated offshore locations as "'rights-free zones,' where refugees lack any legal rights cognizable under U.S. law and American citizens lack First Amendment rights to communicate with them" (1994a, 141).

These practices would continue after September 11 at Guantánamo. As many legal and cultural scholars have detailed (e.g., Butler 2004; Kaplan 2005; Gregory 2007; Lipman 2008; Dastyari 2015; Paik 2016), Guantánamo Bay's history as a site of U.S. imperialism and intervention laid the foundation for the repurposing of colonial relations to carry out sovereign projects of exclusion and confinement. During the United States–led "global war on terror," the Bush administration set up Camp X-ray, a high-security site for the indefinite detention of "foreign enemy combatants." This label was significant, as was the geographical location of the U.S. base. Both placed the detainees beyond the protections of international human-rights law, which would have applied had they been deemed prisoners of war or located on U.S. sovereign territory. This moment not only repurposed Guantánamo Bay's historical role as a site of confinement and human-rights abuses (Slahi 2015), but set in motion an unending scenario in which those detained might never be released or returned home. Although Barack Obama campaigned for president on a promise to end the detention of foreign enemy combatants of the global War on Terror at Guantánamo, and although he transferred many to other countries, by the end of his administration and at the time of writing forty-one people remained.[40]

These practices of creating buffer zones and offshore detention would also travel globally. In the mid-1990s, human-rights observer Bill Frelick noted that, even as the United States was pursuing its interdiction policy in the Caribbean, Italy and Hong Kong were also forcibly repatriating asylum seekers attempting to arrive by sea. "These developments on the international front might have occurred with or without the United States precedent," Frelick concluded; however, the "United States is now in no moral position to protest the treatment of refugees and asylum seekers by other governments, even when the United States thinks it is wrong" (1993, 691).

Tracing this offshoring from our historical analysis to the present shows that transnational carceral regimes are neither new nor isolated. Rather, state authorities think and act transnationally to control human mobility, and carceral regimes must be understood in these broader geopolitical contexts. Since this time, buffer zones and spatial strategies to offshore, distance, and otherwise control asylum-seeking and seekers through remote control, interception, and detention have become well-rehearsed practices around the world (Mountz 2010; Mountz forthcoming). Australia and the European Union (EU) set up their own buffer zones with interception at sea and use of islands to detain people closer to their regions of origin and sites of interception. As Violeta Moreno-Lax and Efthymios Papastavridis observe, growing indifference and hostility to migrants attempting to reach the EU by sea resulted in twenty-thousand fatalities between 1993 and 2015 (2017, 3; also see Goodwin-Gill 2017).

The specter of U.S. bilateral arrangements to police mobility and asylum-seeking in the Caribbean can now be recognized in similar regional arrangements around the globe. Australia, for example, beginning in the late 1990s and early 2000s, took the lead for bilateral agreements for return with source countries. EU member states also led in this arena, a situation particularly acute in southern states that are the first points of landing for those seeking to enter the EU by boat. Bilateral arrangements between Italy and Libya, for example, enable the wealthier, gatekeeping country to "assist" with the policing of territorial waters (Bialawicz 2012). Such bilateral arrangements also fund, or sanction, the racialized policing of migration by less wealthy states (Andersson 2014).

The Globality of U.S. Migration Policing and Detention

The history of U.S. detention we trace demonstrates the entanglements between remoteness, preemptive exclusion, and offshore expansion, and thereby underscores the importance of shifting the scale of analysis beyond national territory for a more complete view of U.S. deterrence practices. The broader transnational framing shows not only how far practices of remote enforcement and detention could reach, but how geopolitics would frame and facilitate this expansion and exclusion. The expansion of the U.S. carceral regime involved a transnational proliferation of spaces of confinement on land and sea, on mainland territory and offshore: the buffer zone at sea, the safe haven on military bases, and the construction and repurposing of spaces on military bases on the mainland. This buffer zone challenges "landed" ontologies of geography, shifting attention to fights over jurisdiction, access to rights, and constructions of jurisdiction at sea (Steinberg 2001; Benton 2010; Loyd et al. 2015).

This transnational analysis of U.S. geopolitical maneuvers to detain onshore and offshore sheds light on another set of dynamics. First, the production of remoteness, or relative isolation, of detention facilities, transpires across transnational, interlocking networks of spaces of confinement and associated policies. In some ways, this panoply of sites resembles Agamben's (1998) space of exception: zones in the borderlands where people are at once inside and outside of sovereign territory. In this case, the U.S. government exercises power to control territory, mobility, and access while operating beyond its jurisdictional space. Boats function as islands of law (Benton 2005) and carceral spaces (Pickering 2014) as they move through these jurisdictionally ambiguous spaces of exception.

Of course, the "exceptionality" of these spaces is not so exceptional, as they become the norm. Legally, politically, and morally questionable practices of offshore detention or indefinite detention were routinized to capture other people in different places (Kaplan 2005; Gregory 2007; Hernández 2016), underscoring what critical ethnic-studies scholar Dylan Rodríguez (2008) calls the globality of U.S. imprisonment. Opposition to these practices was challenging because these spaces rested both on imperial claims to space in other sovereign territories (militarily and through influence and aid) and on racialized carceral logics establishing the normalcy and legitimacy of confining Black and Brown people. As David M. Hernández argues, "Internationally the dispersion of detention operations in the war on terror has also created a sense of havoc, wherein apprehension, interrogation, and punishment are unstandardized and the absence of accountability and training fosters abuse and deflects responsibility" (2016, 317).

Second, the dominance of the Southern border narrative to explain detention and deterrence obscures the racialized dynamics of migration and the Cold War geopolitics in the Caribbean that set the institutional stage for the amplification of deterrence policy on the United States–Mexico boundary in the mid-1990s. Preventing Haitian arrivals expanded the government's reliance on detention for *all* groups of noncitizens, extending racialized carceral responses to mobility. Thus, migration detention builds upon both what Kelly Lytle Hernández (2010) calls anti-Mexican Brown racism, which would be extended unevenly to Central Americans, and the anti-Black racism undergirding *both* the criminal-justice system *and* asylum policy. This finding contributes to interrelated histories of racism and xenophobia that have implications for building interracial coalitions against criminalization (Simon 1998; Cacho 2012; Loyd et al. 2012; Márquez 2013; Escobar 2016).

Third, the problem of *remote* detention is tied to mandatory detention, and the *expansion* of a *transnational* detention system. The dynamics of the expansion of the U.S. detention system that we discovered are not tethered exclusively to border spaces or sites of apprehension, but linked to the contingent politics of space and local economies. While government-controlled spaces like military bases might be imagined as politically expedient, we found that even ad hoc, temporary use of these spaces was subject to tremendous political opposition. The INS, like the Bureau of Prisons, worked to avoid controversy and selected sites where the agency found community support. The geography of detention would therefore be notably different if sites like Fort Drum in upstate New York had been selected or if Florida residents and politicians had not opposed prison construction so vocally. Countless rounds of political opposition to the use of some places, together with support and lobbying from others, would further consolidate prison agglomeration in Western New York, central Arizona, and central Louisiana, among other states like Texas. Although not detailed comprehensively in this book, Texas and other states also featured struggles over the repurposing of military spaces and the agglomeration of carceral infrastructures in some places rather than others.

Deportation, detention, and deterrence more broadly are always transnational in scope, never simply involving arrangements between two countries, but rather a set of practices involving multiple countries working in coordinated fashion. The transnational (Mountz and Loyd 2014) and geopolitical (Coleman 2007) scope of criminalization, policing, detention, and deportation reverberate at local and intimate scales within and far beyond the United States (De Genova and Peutz 2010; Golash-Boza 2012, 2015; Hiemstra 2012; Kanstroom 2007, 2012; Martin 2012; Escobar 2016; Macías-Rojas 2016). The very remoteness of migration control offshore has enabled the erasure—or strategic forgetting—of a long history of racialized and geopoliticized enforcement. It is important, therefore, not only to ask *Where is remote?*—as we did in our introduction – but also, *What is happening remotely?*

Overlooking offshore enforcement histories minimizes and even legitimizes violent and racist histories of exclusion. This past foreshadowed the present. Its silence now haunts the contemporary rounds of investment in exclusion offshore in Mexico and Central and South America and the 2017 departure of Haitians from the United States to cross into Canada in search of safe haven. Offshore, it becomes easier to produce the appearance of compliance with international law, providing large groups of people with thin forms of justice—whether it be blanket or mass representation, or schemes for expedited screening, processing, and return. Once again, detached forms of detention mediate access to territory, rights, and life itself through practices made legitimate, if just barely so, by virtue of the geopolitical and geoeconomic might of the United States.

Coda

In 2014, a Border Patrol training facility in Artesia, New Mexico—a three-hour drive from the nearest cities of Albuquerque, New Mexico, or El Paso, Texas—became one of the sites across the United States where thousands of women and their children fleeing violence in Central America were confined.[1] That year, the United States apprehended upwards of 68,000 children along the United States–Mexico border, and President Barack Obama declared the mass migration an "urgent humanitarian situation."[2] He ordered the Department of Homeland Security (DHS) and the Federal Emergency Management Agency (FEMA) to coordinate their responses, which would entail:

> fulfilling our legal and moral obligation to make sure we appropriately care for unaccompanied children who are apprehended, while taking aggressive steps to surge resources to our Southwest border to deter both adults and children from this dangerous journey, increase capacity for enforcement and removal proceedings, and quickly return unlawful migrants to their home countries.[3]

As in previous moments described in this book when large numbers of people sought entry into and protection from the United States, the framing of asylum-seeking as crisis stoked polarized responses from U.S. residents. This framing of crisis proved a reliable fuel to bolster enforcement-oriented responses in the forms of detention and the off-shoring of asylum (Mountz and Hiemstra 2013). Residents in some places, like Syracuse, New York, organized public acts of welcome for the children. In other places, residents invoked "not in my backyard" arguments to reject provision of refuge.

The framing of crisis fit a pattern we have seen repeated many times. Narratives of dangerous crisis were stoked and could gain traction in an election-year spectacle produced by self-interested government agencies, elected officials, anti-immigrant groups, and media outlets. Transnational labor writer David Bacon observed that the Breitbart website, media home to a nationalist, racist, hard right political formation, published the first photos of children in detention, and then took responsibility for creating the desired political hysteria that ensued.[4]

Others on the Right also painted the crisis as manufactured, but not by the forces of xenophobia and law enforcement that critics on the Left identified. According to some, the White House itself had manufactured this crisis. In one version of the story, Obama was motivated to support the "invasion" so that pregnant women could give birth on U.S. soil where their children would automatically become citizens.[5] Needless to say, this conspiracy theory rested on racist and sexist narratives about Latina immigrants and the racist "birther" charge that President Obama was not really a U.S. citizen. This was not a marginal phenomenon. Senator Jeff Sessions (R-Alabama), who would become Attorney General under President Donald J. Trump, asserted that President Obama was "responsible for this calamity" because he was "incentivizing youth and their families to undertake these perilous treks."[6] Such charges obscure empirical facts, namely that the United States had tripled the number of Border Patrol agents between 2004 and 2012 and also appropriated significant funds to transnational policing efforts designed to deter migration (Slack et al. 2016, 8; Seelke and Finklea 2017).

While some sought to de-escalate the child migration crisis, the resulting spiral was predictable enough.[7] The invocation of crisis entrenched the common sense of detention, border fortification, and migration policing as deterrents to migration. Once again, the government scrambled to find space, using military facilities such as Fort Sill, Oklahoma, and issued new contracts to build still more detention space. Immigration attorneys from across the country also scrambled to provide legal services to people being confined in Artesia and elsewhere through efforts organized by the National Immigration Law Center (NILC) and the American Immigration Lawyers Association (AILA)— American Immigration Council Pro Bono Project. The early 1980s case, *Orantes-Hernandez v. Smith,* which required the government to inform Salvadoran asylum seekers of their rights, afforded the NILC standing to represent Salvadorans held in detention. The NILC's lead attorney explained what they found in Artesia:

> Many of the women reported to us what I would describe as "a culture of no." They were being told by government officials, "No one who's here, who gets to Artesia, gets to stay. This is the place where we hold folks for deportation." Or, "no one with those kind of claims"—meaning, you know, fears and threats from the gangs—["]gets to stay in this country."[8]

Such pressure, of course, violates the terms of *Orantes-Hernandez v. Smith* and international humanitarian law. Geographer Elizabeth Kennedy analyzed press reports and was able to identify the deaths of at least eighty-three people whom the United States deported at this time and who were killed upon their return to El Salvador, Guatemala, or Honduras. As Kennedy observes, "These figures tell us that the US is returning people to their deaths in violation of national and international law. Most of the individuals reported to have been murdered lived in some of the most violent towns in some of the most violent countries in the world—suggesting strongly that is why they fled."[9]

The "culture of no" at Artesia was cultivated by White House officials.[10] Before Artesia opened, Vice President Joe Biden traveled to the Northern Triangle countries of El Salvador, Guatemala, and Honduras to discuss the youth migration. He also used the occasion to announce the establishment of *Plan Frontera Sur,* discussed more fully below. Despite acknowledging the violence there that fueled mothers and children to leave, Biden sent an unvarnished message to stay home. The Department of Justice (DOJ) and Homeland Security were:

> enhancing the enforcement and removal proceedings because those who are pondering risking their lives to reach the United States should be aware of what awaits them. It will not be open arms. It will not be come on—it will be, we're going to hold hearings with our judges consistent with international law and American law, and we're going to send the vast majority of you back.[11]

Indeed, Secretary of Homeland Security Jeh Johnson reiterated this message, assuring Congress that he "personally witnessed a flight of repatriated adults returning home."[12] Moreover, "within the last several months, we have dramatically reduced the removal time of many of these migrants. Within the law, we are sending this group back, and we are sending them back quicker." To AILA attorneys working at Artesia, the message was, "Velocity mattered."[13] "*Everyone* was supposed to be deported—not *almost* everyone."[14]

This most recent nationalist panic about a surge in asylum-seeking repeats the historical patterns identified in this book. At each of these moments since 1980, the U.S. response has involved massive investments in detention infrastructure and enforcement agents onshore and offshore, and on former military bases. Each "crisis" has also occasioned new siting wars. As a result of the 2014 asylum crisis, for example, the administration sought to build new detention facilities. It issued a four-year, $1 billion, no-bid contract to Corrections Corporation of America (CCA) to run a new 2,400-bed family-detention facility in Dilley, Texas, while GEO Group would run a 532-person facility in Karnes City, Texas.[15] Unsurprisingly, acting in crisis mode results in wildly unfavorable agreements for the government. Under the contract terms, CCA would be paid for 100 percent occupancy even if the facility was not filled to capacity. Dilley, previously a camp for oil workers, provided 14 percent of CCA's revenue for 2015. But in June 2016, a state district judge ruled that the Texas Department of Family and Protective Services could not license an immigration-detention facility as a child-care center.[16]

Despite great hopes for comprehensive immigration reform when Obama took office in 2009, the machinery of migration enforcement and removal did not diminish, earning him the moniker "Deporter in Chief." During his two terms in office, the executive actions and administrative reforms that Obama oversaw morphed and entrenched the system he inherited . While Obama moved away from workplace raids, he also naturalized the criminalization of migration through programs like Secure Communities that facilitate the interface between local and federal police agents and through the federal prosecution of unauthorized entrants, such as in Operation Streamline (Chishti, Pierce, and Bolter 2017). This emphasis further solidified the discursive associations between "the border," unauthorized migration, and criminality, and undermined possibilities for asylum.

Racialized patterns of detention and deportation that affect Black migrants continue to be overlooked. For example, Garifuna people— descendants of African and indigenous Arawak peoples, inhabiting the coast of Honduras—also were part of the mass 2014 migration. A combination of racial discrimination, land grabs, and narco violence fueled their flight. Yet once in the United States, many ended up in detention or paroled on ankle monitors.[17] The Black Alliance for Just Immigration (BAJI) and New York University Law School's Immigrant Rights Clinic report that while Black immigrants are 7 percent of the total immigrant population, they comprise over 10 percent of the people who were in removal proceedings between 2003 and 2015, and over 20 percent of noncitizens facing removal on criminal grounds (Morgan-Trostle, Zheng, and Lipscombe 2016).

TRANSNATIONAL DETERRENCE, DETENTION, AND DEPORTATION REGIMES

In August 2016, the bodies of eight people were found on the southern shore of Lake Nicaragua. Officials in Nicaragua said, "They died by drowning. We believe they were Africans going by the color of their skin." An official in Costa Rica conjectured, "The odds are the drowned migrants are Haitians."[18] Two questions immediately surface. Why would migrants thought to be from Haiti or the African continent find themselves in a boat crossing a freshwater lake located just north of the land border between Nicaragua and Costa Rica? And what does it mean that the racialization of people of African descent would result in people from such distant and different places having to take such great risks to save their and their loved ones' lives?

Just as African migrants are displaced multiple times—from home and then from the Mediterranean crossing into the European Union (EU) or to Central America, en route to North America—anti-Black racism and practices of criminalization and exclusion ricochet transnationally across regions and national borders, manifesting in tougher asylum procedures and increasingly fortified borderlands. The U.S. Coast Guard (USCG), Bahamian, and other governments' patrols in the Caribbean are linked to patrols in the Mediterranean and EU-based refugee deterrence. The steady refusal on the part of the U.S. government to recognize asylum claims made by Haitians is echoed by the difficulty of many African asylum seekers of having their claims recognized in Europe. Some EU nation-states claim that asylum seekers from some African nations are economic migrants and not "bona fide" refugees. For example, in Italy in the first part of 2015, some 90 percent of Syrians and Eritreans were granted some form of asylum, while over 70 percent of Nigerians and Malians were denied on their first application.[19] Afghan asylum seekers also face great difficulty in having their claims recognized. The point, then, is that anti-Black racism is one of the dynamics which has ripple effects for other groups, fueling global apartheid (Sharma 2005; Nevins and Aizeki 2008; Nevins 2012; Loyd 2015). Governments' selective filtering of different groups of people is simultaneously geopolitical and informed by political pressure brought to bear by diasporic communities and their supporters. The intertwined dynamics of race and geopolitics around the world result in distressing forms of exclusion that parallel and advance the racialized taxonomies we found documented in the U.S. presidential archives and materialized in the U.S. migration-detention system.

Global apartheid should not be thought of as an easy or singular division between global North and South. Rather, global apartheid is a transnational phenomenon with multiple borders, checkpoints, state agents, private actors, and island detentions. The United States as a dominant player in the Americas and global hegemon has spent decades brokering agreements with other countries in North America, the Caribbean, Central America, and South America; it has also been directly involved in other nation-states' border-patrol activities and has influenced enforcement practices in states around the world. Journalist Todd Miller reports in *Border Patrol Nation* (2014, 177–208) that the United States helped the Dominican Republic to establish its Land Border Security Special Forces Unit, known as CESFRONT, in 2006 to patrol its land border with Haiti. In addition, U.S. Customs and Border Protection (CBP) has organized trainings in more than one hundred countries for some fifteen thousand people. Border Patrol's tactical special forces unit, Border Patrol Tactical Unit (BORTAC), has also trained border guards in Guatemala and Honduras. According to Reuters, the Department of Homeland Security has sent "mentor" teams to unnamed countries in Central and South America to "professionalize" agents from those countries.[20] In other cases, third parties such as the International Organization for Migration (IOM) play the role of facilitating training, knowledge-sharing, and bilateral arrangements, in a macabre version of Peck and Theodore's (2015) "fast policy transfer."

The United States is not simply training the border forces of foreign governments, but also deploying its own migration operatives abroad to conduct joint work and gather intelligence. Reuters reported in August 2016 that CBP officers are stationed at a Mexican detention facility located on the border with Guatemala where they are training Mexican agents and using U.S. criminal databases to investigate detainees' backgrounds. CBP has also begun a similar program in Panama. Nancy Hiemstra (2012) has documented Immigration and Customs Enforcement's (ICE) presence in Ecuador. Wherever we look around the world, we find the United States involved in global policing (Andreas and

Nadelmann 2008), directly influencing the infrastructural design of global apartheid through the racialized containment of human mobility.

The deterrence efforts created by the United States are bolstered by the proliferation of border patrols in Central and South America, safe third-country agreements, as with Canada, and stricter visa policies. For example, Suriname announced that as of September 15, 2016, Haitian nationals must have a visa to visit, a travel restriction instituted apparently as the result of the French government's complaints that Haitians were transiting through Suriname to French Guinea, where they have been applying for asylum.[21] As routes to asylum in Europe have become increasingly difficult, people from across the world have been making their way to South and Central America in their search for safety and livelihood. Costa Rica has become one of the corridors that asylum seekers from the Caribbean, Africa, and Asia—among them people from Haiti, Cuba, Eritrea, Ghana, Nigeria, Pakistan, Afghanistan, and India—attempt to traverse en route to the United States.

The multiplication of border patrols and migration raids across Central America creates a cascade of barriers that makes their travels more dangerous. Before the boat tragedy on Lake Nicaragua in the late summer of 2016, the Nicaraguan government had increased border patrols with Costa Rica. Soon thereafter, Costa Rica announced that it would increase policing along its southern border with Panama. This is now affecting Haitians who had sought refuge in Brazil following the 2010 earthquake in Haiti. Following the earthquake, the United States immediately began flying over the island, broadcasting a message that if they tried to get to the United States by boat, they would be intercepted and returned (Miller 2014, 197). Brazil, with its relatively favorable visa regime, became a destination for Haitians compelled to leave their home country.[22] But with the 2015 downturn in Brazil's economy, many Haitians living in Brazil sought to move on from there to the United States.[23] In 2017, the Trump administration's intensification of enforcement and its moves to end Temporary Protected Status for Haitians and Central Americans set in motion yet another movement of Haitians and Central Americans in search of asylum in Canada.

The ripple of border policing in Central America has essentially trapped people on the move, at least temporarily (Brigden 2016). For example, Cubans avoiding patrols in the Straits of Florida have begun migrating to Central and South America to make their way to the United States across the Mexican border. Besides the U.S. Coast Guard, the Royal Bahamas Defence Force in September 2016 apprehended Cuban nationals on Cay Lobos, the atoll we discussed in chapter 1.[24] But following Panama's decision to increase patrols of its border with Colombia, Cubans found themselves stuck in limbo in the border town Turbo. Some even posted a makeshift sign pointing to the historically Cuban Miami neighborhood, Calle Ocho, to not lose sight of their ultimate destination.[25] In August 2016, Colombian authorities deported some eight hundred Cubans who had been waiting in Turbo; many others sought to make their way through the additional barriers that governments had constructed to halt their movement.[26] The Mexican government also stepped up deportations of Cubans in the summer of 2016, increasing the time and distance that it would take Cuban nationals to reach the United States if they were to try again.[27]

The fluidity of border patrols, interior policing, and asylum practices in different countries and the imperfection of migration controls make it difficult to say how many people are on the move through the region at any one time. In July 2016, the IOM estimated that two thousand "extra-continental" migrants (those from outside of the Americas and the Caribbean) were present in Costa Rica. Some 10 percent of this group hailed from Pakistan and Afghanistan.[28] According to *The Guardian*, "7,882 Africans and Asians presented themselves at Mexican immigration in the first seven months of this year [2016]—86% higher than in the whole of 2015 and more than four times the number registered in 2014."[29] Mexico currently does not have deportation agreements with many of these countries—as it does with Central American states—so the temporary travel documents that some "extra-continental" migrants can procure from the Mexican government ostensibly enable them to travel more freely to the U.S. border.[30] Not everyone manages to pass through the increasingly fortified borders and treacherous terrain or survive violence at the hands of the state, *coyotes* (smugglers or guides), or robbers. A Somali asylum seeker who, once in South America, had made his way from Colombia to Mexico en route to the United States told a journalist: "There are many who die in the jungle, but noone [sic] to count them."[31]

While these "extra-continental" patterns of movement through the Americas illustrate the effects of deterrence activities undertaken in other regions of the world, the U.S. and Mexican governments focus their policing resources on migrants from the Northern Triangle (Brigden 2016). The IOM estimates that four hundred thousand Central American nationals cross without authorization into southern Mexico.[32] A 2016 report by International Crisis Group (ICG) documents the harmful effects of the recent uptick in deportations of Central Americans and calls for more robust asylum protections by Mexico; in 2015, 92 percent of asylum claims in Mexico were made by Central American nationals. The ICG called for the United States to extend Temporary Protected Status (TPS) to Central American youth. In 2015, the United States deported 75,000 people from Central America, and Mexico deported 165,000 (2016, 4).

Violence is a main driver of migration from the Northern Triangle (Swanson et al. 2015). The vast majority of Central American and Mexican women interviewed by the UN cited incidents and threats of gang and police violence as their reasons for seeking asylum in the United States (ICG 2016, 9). Murder rates in Central America and Mexico have increased significantly; in 2015 El Salvador's murder rate was 103 per 100,000, Honduras's was 57 per 100,000, and Guatemala's was 30 per 100,000 (i). By comparison, the rate in 2015 for the United States was 4.88 homicides per 100,000, and Canada 1.68 per 100,000.[33] (The Peace Corps ceased its programs in El Salvador due to the escalation in violence.)[34] Such steep rates of violence can be attributed, most proximately, to organized crime and drug syndicates, in turn creating the rationale for further investments in policing and military responses. Yet organized violence in the region, including that perpetrated by authorities, is part of a longer history of civil war and economic restructuring supported openly and clandestinely by the U.S. government. In the case of El Salvador, the transnational gang network *Mara Salvatrucha* formed in the aftermath of war, displacement, and criminalization. Many members had witnessed violence and lost loved ones during the war. While living in the United States, these same individuals faced targeted policing and the escalation of deportation consequences for criminal activity (Coutin 2010; Zilberg 2011). Deportation, in turn, fueled the transnationalization of violence, amid the continuum of state violence experienced by individuals and households displaced in both directions, across generations between El Salvador and the United States.

In 2007, the United States spearheaded a transnational security and aid project with Mexico, Central American states, Haiti, and the Dominican Republic to target organized crime. Known as the Mérida Initiative, this project focused its spending and efforts on intelligence, police training and equipment upgrades, and the creation of the "21st century border," supported by U.S. congressional appropriations of $2.5 billion between fiscal years 2008 and 2015 (Seelke and Finklea 2017, 1). In Mexico, the increase in violence since 2007 is the result of the Mexican government's escalation of its war on drugs, bolstered in part by the Mérida Initiative (Boyce, Banister, and Slack 2015). During President Felipe Calderón's term in office alone, the United States spent more than $146 million to train police and border agents and over $870 million to purchase equipment (such as surveillance aircraft and helicopters)—all through the Mérida Initiative (Seelke and Finklea 2017, 8). Most of the 121,000 homicides documented in Mexico between 2007 and 2012 were of men under the age of 30. The UN special rapporteur on torture found that torture by police agents was widespread (he backed down from calling it "systematic") and rarely investigated (Boyce et al. 2015, 10). Sexual violence, particularly against women and LGBT people on the part of state and illicit actors, has also been widely documented.[35]

As part of the Mérida Initiative, the United States and Mexico established the 21st Century Border Bilateral Executive Steering Committee to bolster information-sharing, build new screening facilities and pedestrian bridges, and establish bilateral customs enforcement. The work of the U.S. Border Patrol alongside Mexican agents on the Mexican side of the boundary was enabled by Mexico's passage of a law authorizing U.S. customs and immigration agents to carry arms in Mexico (Seelke and Finklea 2017, 14).

In 2014 President Enrique Peña Nieto announced the establishment of *Plan Frontera Sur* to fortify Mexico's southern border. According to the Congressional Research Office, Mexico has established twelve naval bases and extended three "security cordons" spanning one hundred miles along its river and land borders with Guatemala and Belize (15–16). Mexican agents are also patrolling known migration routes. For its part, the U.S. State Department has provided equipment and training for migration officials (including canine units), and the Department of Defense (DOD) has provided equipment and training to the Mexican military (16). Since the establishment of *Plan Frontera Sur,* Mexican deportations of Central Americans now outpace those of the United States. Furthermore, Mexico deported almost 80 percent of the minors apprehended by the Mexican and U.S. governments between 2010 and 2014, according to the Migration Policy Institute (Dominguez Villegas and Rietig 2015, 1).

Activists and migration scholars have been documenting the violence and trauma endured by Central Americans and other foreign nationals from Latin America, Asia, and the African continent as they traverse Mexico. While the notorious train routes of *La Bestia*—the beast— have become known sites of terror where travelers are targeted and particularly vulnerable, other locations such as migrant shelters set up across the country have become precarious places because migrants are known to gather there (Vogt 2013; Brigden 2016).

The escalation of state and nonstate violence has led state authorities to "double-down on a given policy, often through militaristic escalation, rather than reconsider faulty premises or harmful outcomes" (Boyce et al. 2015, 3). Governments seeking to deflect such criticisms have also responded with "soft power" and development initiatives to prevent migration. Yet these responses generally amount to minimal investments, when compared to ongoing investments in the policing of migration and border security. Such preventive spending also fails to dismantle the transnational deterrence regimes that amplify violent conditions for people on the move (see Andersson 2014; Swanson et al. 2015). For example, days before President Obama declared a "humanitarian situation" in 2014, his administration, together with the governments of El Salvador, Guatemala, and Honduras, announced the formation of the Alliance for Prosperity, meant to spur economic development and reforms to criminal justice in the Northern Triangle (ICG 2016, 23). The U.S. Congress appropriated $750 million for FY 2015, while the Central American governments pledged $2.6 billion, a small amount only in the context of a $19 billion immigration-enforcement budget.

The safe-haven plan from the mid-1990s has also been rejuvenated. In July 2016, Costa Rica and the United States announced that Costa Rica would host two hundred Central Americans at a time for six months. Other partners involved in the agreement were the United Nations High Commissioner for Refugees (UNHCR) and the IOM. Under the protection transfer arrangement (PTA), the U.S. government, through the UNHCR and the IOM, would prescreen people within their countries of origin (El Salvador, Guatemala, and Honduras). If deemed eligible, they would then be allowed to travel to Costa Rica for further refugee processing.[36] People from these nations already present within Costa Rica would not be eligible for the program, nor would people from Africa, Asia, or Haiti.[37] We were unable to learn the cost for the program. Also repeating its past, the United States announced an expansion of in-country processing for Central American minors (CAM). Under the CAM refugee program, "qualifying parents" are those who legally reside in the United States, who may petition for the admission of their unmarried child (under twenty-one years of age) through the U.S. Refugee Admissions Program. Since its inception in

2014, 9,500 applications have been submitted, but only 144 minors have entered the United States.[38]

Deterrence—and the centrality of detention and deportation in deterrence efforts—must be seen as part of this transnational escalation of state violence. States consider detention, deportation, and border patrols as sovereign prerogatives and routinely paint them as humanitarian (Ticktin 2011; Andersson 2014; Williams 2014). Yet the legality (if not legitimacy) of these practices within the nation-state system does not compensate for or erase the violence they inflict through migration policing and detention, the generation of more dangerous conditions for people on the move, and their exposure to violence and criminalization when deported. Indeed, a director of a migrant shelter in Mexico interviewed by ICG noted that increased policing had not deterred migration, but it did "make migrants more vulnerable, more invisible, more trafficked" (2016, 6).

THE FUTURE OF U.S. ENFORCEMENT

We finished writing this book in the midst of a presidential election season. As Secretary of State in the Obama administration, Democratic presidential candidate Hillary Clinton largely continued the interagency responses set in motion under her husband's presidential administration, which blossomed under George W. Bush, post 9/11, and continued under Obama. When asked in an interview in 2014 what should happen to Central American minors who had claimed asylum in the United States that summer, Clinton responded that the United States should do more to support Mexico in enforcing its southern border and that the minors should be returned: "They should be sent back as soon as it can be determined who responsible adults in their families are."[39] Republican candidate Trump promised repeatedly to build a wall along the border between Mexico and the United States, and extract funds for its construction from Mexico. Trump also promised a dedicated and sizable deportation police, and a ban on migration from countries with sizable Muslim populations. Although these plans met considerable resistance and numerous court challenges in the early months of his administration, Trump succeeded in unleashing a culture of impunity in the Department of Homeland Security—to "take the shackles off of ICE agents" in the words of then Press Secretary Sean Spicer. The administration's statements and actions sowed conditions of uncertainty and terror in communities and households where people held liminal status.

Of course, there are already walls built between Mexico and the United States. In fact, there is an extensive system of walls and border patrols, biometric checks, visa authorizations, and surveillance that enmeshes the world and sifts people into governmental categories (Heyman 2004). The United States is but one powerful, hegemonic participant in the advancement a system of global apartheid that is constructed, carried out, and contested every day. Each new president inherits a system that is not totally within the administration's control. But so too does each new president hold power to advance construction of a global system of surveillance, policing, and war-making that produces so many refugees.

As the number of displaced people globally reached its highest number since World War II (WWII), nation-states retreated from global perspectives and open borders, as evidenced by the rebordering of Europe in response to the mass migration of Syrian asylum seekers in 2015, to Trump's taste for walling. Trump's new administration immediately worsened the landscape for people seeking asylum in the United States. With a rapid series of executive orders, he wrought havoc on landscapes of enforcement and protection and on transnational families and communities. Trump's first two executive orders intensified interior and border enforcement with additional resources and Border Patrol employees; these investments disproportionately affected asylum seekers (Harvard Immigration and Refugee Clinical Program 2017). Trump's third and most notorious executive order—"Protecting the Nation from Foreign Terrorist Entry into the United States" (suspended in repeated court challenges)—was the infamous "travel ban" immediately banning all foreign nationals without U.S. citizenship (including permanent residents) from entering or reentering the country if they were from a list of seven Muslim-majority countries of origin. The order also suspended all refugee resettlement for four months and the resettlement of Syrian refugees indefinitely.

In the most recent round in the cycle of repeated crises, Trump immediately expanded many of the enforcement and criminalizing programs detailed in this book. Following Trump's executive order on Border Security and Immigration Enforcement Improvements, the DHS Secretary John Kelly issued a guidance memo that expanded the targets for expedited removal by extending its geographic reach beyond its previous enforcement within one hundred miles of the U.S. border to anywhere in the United States and its temporal reach beyond fourteen days to within two years of continuous presence (Hallman 2017; Kelly 2017). This memo further stated that it would use laws prohibiting human trafficking to prosecute parents of unaccompanied minors who entered the United States. Trump also made it more difficult to pass credible-fear screenings, and moved to detain and separate families with more draconian detention and deportation practices. The travel ban reduced chances for parole (Harvard Immigration and Refugee Clinical Program 2017). As legal scholar Deborah Anker points out, the executive orders also set the stage for massive expansion of detention: "It will take billions of dollars to accommodate this kind of mass incarceration" (Harvard Law Today 2017). Read together, these provisions extend trends of expanding the net of detention and removal by stripping due-process protections and targeting people who have been fleeing violence.

As Hiemstra (2013) argues in the context of Ecuador, U.S. immigration and border-enforcement policies reverberate far beyond U.S. borders. Detention and deportation remove livelihoods and fragment families and households living across borders. Inhumane policies further displace the displaced in all directions. One immediate effect of Trump's executive orders was to push asylum seekers and people with liminal status from the United States to Canada. Due to the Safe Third Country Agreement (STCA) between Canada and the United States, which prevents making a claim at port of entry at a border crossing, asylum seekers had to cross frigid, isolated terrain between ports of entry to evade authorities. Beginning in February 2017, there were reports of people—primarily from the African continent—suffering hypothermia and losing digits as they made their way into Quebec and Manitoba. These arrivals reignited a campaign to persuade the Canadian government to repeal the STCA (unsuccessful as this book goes to print). In May 2017, authorities found the body of fifty-seven-year-old Mavis Otuteye, a Ghanaian national reportedly entering Canada to reunite with her daughter. Mavis was discovered in a field a half mile from Canada, where she died of hypothermia. For many residents of Canada, she embodied the first border death, bringing home the simultaneously proximate and transnational implications of Trump's policies—what Pratt and Rosner (2006) would call the global intimate. By summer, a new route had opened up from upstate New York into Quebec. Approximately 44 percent of several thousand people who made refugee claims in Canada after crossing the land border from the United States during the summer of 2017 were Haitians; a total of 6,304 Haitians made refugee claims in Canada between February and October 2017, with approximately 10 percent of those adjudicated being accepted as of

November 2017.[40] Among approximately 15,100 crossings over the land border as of October 20, 2017, 69 percent of those adjudicated received asylum in Canada.

As exemplified by the 2016 presidential candidates, and subsequently by the newly elected President Trump, U.S. popular and political narratives continue to address migration as a threat to the national social body; but a transnational perspective disrupts this hollow rhetoric. As we have shown, during the late and immediate post–Cold War, the United States amplified its border-deterrence efforts and created a transnational system of detention, deterrence, and expulsion. Well over three decades of bipartisan commitment to deterrence and criminalization led to a robust policing and detention infrastructure that resists oversight and reform and harms groups of people who were already vulnerable. Countless people have been separated from their families and struggle to repay debts from migration and make a living in economies that have undergone neoliberal capitalist restructuring. Further, U.S. war-making and support of war-making is responsible for many of the dislocations for which most politicians (and their supporters) refuse to take responsibility. Criminalization, likewise, exceeds national boundaries as policing and associated displacement from the United States is increasingly, if unevenly, transnational. People who have been deported do not escape the criminal sentences they have served, but instead face further criminalization and policing as easy targets on whom governments can pin the violence and unrest fueled by decimated safety nets and economies.

Current offshore enforcement efforts continue to mix narratives of humanitarian rescue with militarized border-enforcement operations designed to thwart human mobility and access to rights and protections. Today, the United States continues its historical treatment of refugees as geopolitical pawns, particularly in congressional and presidential election seasons. States, too, have entered the game, some in 2015 refusing to allow the resettlement of Syrian refugees. Pulitzer Prize–winning novelist and self-described refugee Viet Thanh Nguyen places this refusal to welcome refugees in contrast with the celebration of U.S. historical narratives of being 'a nation of immigrants':

> Immigrants are more reassuring than refugees because there is an endpoint to their story; however they arrive, whether they are documented or not, their desires for a new life can be absorbed into the American dream or into the European narrative of civilization. By contrast, refugees are the zombies of the world, the undead who rise from dying states to march or swim toward our borders in endless waves.[41]

As this book goes to press, Congress debated whether to cut the U.S. annual intake of refugees by half, to return to the quota of fifty thousand set by Jimmy Carter when he codified refugees into domestic law more than three decades ago. But the world is a different place, with far more displaced people and far fewer legal paths to protection and survival.

We find hope in the continuation of resistance to the exclusionary moves detailed in this book, with activism forged at every scale, from local blockades to stop deportations and disrupt mass immigration hearings, to well-known authors such as Edwidge Danticat and Junot Díaz speaking out against the Dominican Republic's threat to deport Haitian people, even if they were born in the Dominican Republic.[42] A new round of research is also targeting offshore deterrence and detention practices, as well as documenting the deaths offshore that result from state practices (e.g., Last et al. 2017). Mothers confined with their children at the Berks family-detention facility in Pennsylvania went on hunger strike, and their children said that they will refuse to go to school until their release.[43] Mass popular resistance across the United States arose in response to President Trump's executive orders, and most notably his proposed travel ban, which prompted new forms and geographies of resistance, such as the spontaneous occupation of airports across the United States (Kocher 2017).

People whom the United States has deported also continue to organize for the right to family and the right to return, using social media as part of their organizing strategies (e.g., the #Right2Family and the #Right-2Return). They offer an analysis of the forces and ties between U.S. warmaking and criminalization that must both be challenged in order to end deterrence and detention. Members of the Khmer-American group, 1Love, who had been deported to Cambodia, wrote in April 2016:

> We were adopted children of war—refugees—to the US, resettled with a history of trauma into unjust systems and surroundings that led us to make mistakes that would forever label us "Criminal Aliens" by the US government and subject to permanent deportation. We are not perfect—we are human. We recognize the harm we have caused, and we live to amend that harm everyday because we believe in healing and accountability for our actions. We also believe in our human ability to change and be better people in the world for ourselves, our families, and our communities.[44]

In this book, we have focused on the role of boats, borders, and bases in the U.S. deterrence of people in search of safe haven. Over time, ad hoc responses offshore and piloted programs onshore repeatedly became institutionalized, resulting in the contemporary morass that is the transnational U.S. detention system. This material infrastructure emerged out of the contingent politics of asylum, migration, and their criminalization. People on the move need actual legal and material paths to safety, not humanitarian euphemisms and infrastructure repurposed for imprisonment, criminalization, and deportation. Transnational forms of racialized exclusion will continue to proliferate as long as the United States continues to deploy this tripartite infrastructure in its relentless pursuit of mythic border perfection and global dominance. Undoing this infrastructure will require attending to all of these strands of criminalization, militarization, and bordering, restoring meaningful or "thick" access to asylum, and challenging the ideological and material capacity to confine.

Notes

ARCHIVES AND ABBREVIATIONS

Entries for archival records are cited in the following way: For correspondence, the author to recipients names are cited. For memos or other materials, we list the author and title or the title of the document alone. Following the document is the date (if known or estimated), box number, file name and/or number, collection, and archive. For individuals' records that are part of a broader record group or office (e.g., Rudolph Giuliani [RG]), the record group or office (e.g., RG60) is not included in the citation; information about the associated record group or office can be ascertained by referring to the listing below. Collection names and archives are indicated using the abbreviations below. Collections that resulted from FOIA or mandatory review requests are listed by the FOIA number or Appeal number, unless otherwise noted. Digital archives are publicly available via the internet.

Arizona Historical Society (AHS), Tucson, AZ

 Ephemeral Files (EF)

Arizona State University Libraries (ASUL), Tempe, AZ

 Arizona Collection (AC):

  Ephemeral Files (EF)

  Fm Mss. 1: Personal and Political Papers of Senator Barry M. Goldwater (BMG)

  Mss. 1: Carl T. Hayden Papers (CTH)

  Mss. 2: Papers of Senator Paul J. Fannin, 1958–1977 (PJF)

Delta State University Library Archives (DSUL), Cleveland, MS

> Collection M040: Lower Mississippi Delta Development Commission Papers (LMDDC)

George Bush Presidential Library (GBPL) and Museum, College Station, TX

> FOIA Request 2005-0995-F: Bush Presidential Files on Cuba: Cabinet Affairs, Michael P. Jackson Files (MPJ)

> George H.W. Bush Vice Presidential Records, Office of the Chief of Staff to the Vice President, Philip D. Brady Files (PDB)

Jimmy Carter Library (JCL), Atlanta, GA

> Domestic Policy Staff (DPS):

>> Annie Gutierrez's Subject Files (AG)

>> Stuart Eizenstat's Subject Files (SE)

>> Frank White's Subject Files (FW)

> Office of the Assistant to the President: Louis Martin's Files (LM)

> Office of the National Security Advisor (NSA):

>> Previously withdrawn records partially or fully released and scanned for Remote Archives Capture (RAC) project

>> Staff Material—North/South Files (NSA 24) (NSA24)

> Record Group 220: Cuban-Haitian Task Force (CHTF)

> White House Central Files (WHORM): Subject Files:

>> Immigration-Naturalization (IM)

>> National Security-Defense (ND)

> White House Staff Offices: Office of the Cabinet Secretary, Jack Watson (JW)

William J. Clinton Presidential Library (WJCL), Little Rock, AR

> Appeal 2014-0868-A (appeal to restriction b(7)(e) in FOIA 2011-1044-F)

> FOIA 2006-0187-F (Haiti)

> FOIA 2011-1045-F (Haiti Safe Haven)

> Clinton Digital Library (CDL):

>> Declassified Documents concerning National Security Council (NSC)

>> FOIA 2009-1006-F (Elena Kagan Collection) (EKC)

>> FOIA 2011-0376-F (Operation Gatekeeper)

>> FOIA 2011-1044-F (Records on Immigrant Detention Policy)

>> FOIA 2011-1045-F (Haiti Safe Haven)

Duke University, Rubenstein Library, Human Rights Archive (Duke), Durham, NC

> Americans for Immigrant Justice records, (formerly Florida Immigrant Advocacy Center) (AIJ)

Genesee County History Department (GCHD), Batavia, NY

GovernmentAttic.org Digital Archive (GADA)

> FOIA request AG/03-R0320 (Federal Mass Immigration Emergency Plan, Operation Distant Shore), 1991–1995 (ODS)

Louisiana State University (LSUL) Libraries Special Collections, Baton Rouge, LA

> Mss. 4922: John B. Breaux Papers (JBB)
>
>> US Senate Subgroup, Senate Office Files Series:
>>
>>> Department and Independent Agency Files (DIA)
>>>
>>> Legislative Assistants' Files: Johnny Broussard, Project Director (JB)
>>>
>>> Legislative Correspondents' Files: Spiller for Hawes (LC)
>>>
>>> Louisiana State Affairs Files (LSA)
>>>
>>> Personal Office Files (PO)
>
> Mss. 4473: J. Bennett Johnston Papers (JBJ)
>
>> US Senate Series, Senate Office Files, Louisiana Grants and Projects (LGP)

National Archives Building (NARA), Washington, D.C.

> Record Group 26: US Coast Guard (RG26)
>
>> Search and Rescue Division—Flag Pilot Staff, Search and Rescue Case Files, 1965–66 and 1969–80, Special Cases, 1976–77 (SRC)

National Archives at College Park (NARAII), College Park, MD

> Record Group 60 (RG60): General Records of the Department of Justice:
>
>> Office of the Associate Attorney General Rudolph Giuliani (RG)
>>
>> Office of the Attorney General William French Smith (WFS)
>>
>> Office of the Attorney General Richard Thornburgh (RT)
>
> Record Group 389 (RG389): Office of the Provost Marshal General:
>
>> Administrative Division, Mail & Records Branch (M&RB)

Pinal County Historical Society (PCHS), Florence, AZ

Ronald Reagan Presidential Library (RRPL), Simi Valley, CA

> National Security Council, Latin American Affairs Directorate: Roger W. Fontaine's Files (RWF)
>
> Office of Cabinet Affairs: Kenneth T. Cribb, Jr. Subject Files (KTC)
>
> Office of the Chief of Staff:
>
>> Francis (Frank) S.M. Hodsoll: Subject Files (FSMH)
>>
>> Francis (Frank) S.M. Hodsoll: President's Task Force on Immigration and Refugee Policy (PTFIRP)
>>
>> James W. Cicconi Files (JWC)
>>
>> Kate Moore's Files (KM)

Office of Intergovernmental Affairs: Richard S. Williamson's Files (RSW)

White House Office Records Management Central Files (WHORM): Subject Files:

Immigration/Naturalization (IM)

White House Staff:

John G. Roberts, Jr. Files (JGR)

Edwin G. Meese, III Files (EGM)

University of Arkansas Libraries Special Collections (UALCL), Fayetteville, AR

Vertical Files (VF)

US Citizenship and Immigration Services Library (USCIS), Washington, D.C.

Vertical Files (VF)

INTRODUCTION

1. ICE. 2017 (10 February). "FY 2016 ICE Immigration Removals," *U.S. Immigration and Customs Enforcement,* https://www.ice.gov/removal-statistics /2016/, last accessed 28 October 2017.

2. Jennifer Chen. 2017 (13 January), "Immigration Detention Bed Quota Timeline," *National Immigrant Justice Center,* http://www.immigrantjustice.org /staff/blog/immigration-detention-bed-quota-timeline, last accessed 31 October 2017. Detention Watch Network and Center for Constitutional Rights, 2016 (16 June), *Banking on Detention: 2016 Update,* http://www.detentionwatch network.org/sites/default/files/reports/Banking%20on%20Detention%20 2016%20Update_DWN,%20CCR.pdf, last accessed 31 October 2017.

3. TRAC, 2016 (12 April), "New Data on 637 Detention Facilities Used by ICE in FY 2015." *TRAC,* http://trac.syr.edu/immigration/reports/422/, last accessed 31 October 2017.

CHAPTER 1. "AMERICA'S 'BOAT PEOPLE'"

1. *NBC Evening News,* "Bahamas/Haitians evicted," 13 November 1980. Available from Vanderbilt Television News Archive: http://tvnews.vanderbilt .edu/program.pl?ID=507844.

2. "Marooned Haitians Finally Give Up and Board Bahama Transport Ship," *Sarasota Herald-Tribune,* 13 November 1980.

3. Coast Guard log, 20 October 1980, Box 189, "Haitians stranded at Cay Lobos 1268-80" Folder, SRC, RG26.

4. Secretary of State to Coast Guard, 19 October 1980, Box 189, "Haitians stranded at Cay Lobos 1268-80" Folder, SRC, RG26.

5. Ibid.

6. Secretary of State to Coast Guard, 7 November 1980, Box 189, "Haitians stranded at Cay Lobos 1268-80" Folder, SRC, RG26.

7. Coast Guard to U.S. Embassy in Nassau, 8 November 1980, Box 189, "Haitians stranded at Cay Lobos 1268-80" Folder, SRC, RG26.

8. A "credible fear interview" refers to preliminary interviews conducted to determine whether a person is submitting an asylum claim that they face a "well founded fear of persecution" if they were returned home, based on the terms of the 1951 *Convention Relating to the Status of Refugees.*

9. Coast Guard log, 12 November 1980, Box 189, "Haitians stranded at Cay Lobos 1268-80" Folder, SRC, RG26.

10. Coast Guard log, 13 November 1980, Box 189, "Haitians stranded at Cay Lobos 1268-80" Folder, SRC, RG26.

11. "Refugees Forced on Boat to Haiti," *New York Times,* 13 November 1980, A20. "Four Missing on Helicopter Covering Bahamian Eviction of Haitians," *New York Times,* 14 November 1980, A15. Jo Thomas, "Sadly, the Marooned Haitians Return Home," *New York Times,* 17 November 1980, A3.

12. "Bahamians Agree to Rescue 102 Haitians Marooned for a Month," *New York Times,* 9 November 1980. Cited in Shull 2014a, 40.

13. Lauralee Peters to Robert Pastor, 31 August 1978, Box 2, "Bahamas, 6/77–12/78" Folder, Pastor Country File, NSA24, JCL.

14. Ibid.

15. International Issues Division of the Office of Regional and Political Analysis CIA Directorate for Intelligence, 31 August 1977, Declassified RAC document NLC-17-29-8-3-1, JCL. In her memo to Pastor, Peters writes regarding negotiations over the military-facilities agreement: "They appear to be hoping for just a massive check." Peters to Pastor, 31 August 1978.

16. "Bahamas Asks U.N. or America to Accept 202 Fleeing Haitians," *New York Times,* 16 November 1980, 31.

17. Gene Eidenberg and Jack Watson to The President, 1 October 1980, Box 34, "Haiti & Refugees" Folder, JW, JCL.

18. Zbigniew Brzezinski and Stu Eizenstat to Jimmy Carter, 27 February 1978, Box 31, "Refugee Policy [O/A 8110] [1]" Folder, AG, JCL.

19. Cyrus Vance to Jimmy Carter, n.d., attached to confidential memo from Zbigniew Brzezinski to Jimmy Carter, 24 February 1978, Box 31, "Refugee Policy [O/A 8110] [1]" Folder, AG, JCL.

20. Ibid.

21. Cyrus Vance to The President, 23 June 1977, Box 267, "Refugees [2]" Folder, SE, JCL.

22. Zbigniew Brzezinski to The President, 1 July 1977, Box 267, "Refugees [2]" Folder, SE, JCL. Annie Gutierrez to Stu Eizenstat, 16 February 1978, Box 31, "Refugee Policy [O/A 8110] [1]" Folder, AG, JCL. Zbigniew Brzezinski to Jimmy Carter, 24 February 1978, Box 31, AG, JCL.

23. Brzezinski and Eizenstat to Carter, 27 February 1978.

24. Ibid.

25. Gutierrez to Eizenstat, 16 February 1978.

26. Stuart Eizenstat and Annie M. Gutierrez to The President, 27 February 1978, Box 31, "Refugee Policy [O/A 8110] [1]" Folder, AG, JCL.

27. Shirley Chisholm et al. to Jimmy Carter, 2 April 1980, Box 23, "Refugees—Cubans & Haitians [7]" Folder, FW, JCL. Emphasis in original.

28. James L. Carlin to Edward T. Sweeney, 19 April 1978, Box 23, "Refugees—Cubans & Haitians [10]" Folder, FW, JCL.

29. D. Binder, "101 Haitian Refugees Pose Painful Problem for U.S.," *New York Times,* 1 September 1977, 3.

30. Following Ambassador Young's visit, Haiti indicated that it would "not oppose openly U.S. human rights policies and will welcome the OAS commission on human rights," but "Duvalier does not intend to introduce any significant reforms or to refrain from using arrests or the threats of arrests to remove people he views as political threats." The Situation Room to Zbigniew Brzezinski, 8 September 1977, RAC document NLC 1-3-6-27-2, JCL.

31. Robert Pastor to Zbigniew Brzezinski through Madeline Albright, 20 December 1979, Box 44, "ND 16/CO 64 Executive 1/20/77–4/30/80 [Haiti]" Folder, ND 16, JCL.

32. Zbigniew Brzezinski to Shirley Chisholm, 16 January 1980, Box 44, "ND 16/CO 64 Executive 1/20/77–4/30/80 [Haiti]" Folder, ND 16, JCL.

33. Henry Owen to Shirley A. Chisholm, 19 February 1980, Box 44, "ND 16/CO 64 Executive 1/20/77–4/30/80 [Haiti]" Folder, ND 16, JCL.

34. Ibid.

35. Congressional Black Caucus, Press Statement on United States Relationship with Haiti and Haitian Asylum Claimants for The Honorable Cardiss Collins, 19 July 1979, Box 43, "Haiti" Folder, LM, JCL.

36. Robert Pastor to Zbigniew Brzezinski, 15 April 1980, RAC document NLC 24-55-1-15-8, JCL.

37. Lincoln P. Bloomfield to Zbigniew Brzezinski, 24 April 1980, Box IM-3, "IM 3/26/80–6/13/80" Folder, IM, JCL.

38. Roger C. Adams to Christian R. Holmes, 12 August 1980, Box 7, "Reference Notebook [2]" Folder, CHTF, JCL.

39. Doris M. Meissner to Louis E. Martin, 8 January 1980, Box 44, "ND 16/CO 64 Executive 1/20/77–4/30/80 [Haiti]" Folder, ND 16, JCL.

40. Peters to Pastor, 31 August 1978.

CHAPTER 2. MILITARIZING MIGRATION

1. Donna Alvarado to Frank Hodsoll, Ed Gray, and Ken Starr, 27 February 1981, Box 12, "Immigration and Refugees Task Force (2)" Folder, FSMH, RRPL.

2. David Crosland to David Hiller, 19 May 1981, Box 51, "INS—Detention Facilities" Folder, RG, NARAII.

3. Immigration and Naturalization Service Policy Cable, 8 September 1980, Box 22, "Homosexuals [File No. 2]" Folder, CHTF, JCL.

4. Carolyn Pollan to Jimmy Carter, 30 July 1980, Box 4, "Fort Chaffee #2" Folder, CHTF, JCL.

5. Joe Ghougassian to Ed Meese and Ed Thomas, 15 July 1981, Box 12, "Immigration and Refugees General (19)" Folder, FSMH, RRPL.

6. Frank White to James Baker, 27 August 1981, Box 1, "Immigration (8)" Folder, FSMH, RRPL.

7. Frank Hodsoll memorandum, 17 February 1981, Box 12, "Immigration and Refugees Task Force (2)" Folder, FSMH, RRPL.

8. Benjamin R. Civiletti to the President, 13 January 1981, Box 225, "Refugees 1981" Folder, WFS, NARAII.

9. Charles B. Renfrew to William French Smith, 14 February 1981, Box 225, "Refugees 1981" Folder, WFS, NARAII.

10. Phillip N. Hawkes to Doris Misner *[sic]*, 19 June 1981, Box 6, "New Entrant Processing Center (New Sites)" Folder, CHTF, JCL.

11. Attorney General to the President, 6 July 1981, Box 51, "INS—Detention Facilities" Folder, RG, NARAII.

12. Frank White to Stu Eizenstat, 6 June 1980, Box 178, "Cuban refugees [1]" Folder, SE, JCL. Secretary of Defense to James Baker III, 7 July 1981, Box 8, "Detention Center and Chaffee Working (2)" Folder, PTFIRP, RRPL. Thomas O. Enders to Frank Hodsoll et al., 22 July 1981, with declassified report attached entitled, "Resettling the Mariel Undesirables, If Only Provisionally, in a Third Country Pending Cuban Repatriation," Box 8, "Detention Center and Chaffee Working (5)" Folder, PTFIRP, RRPL.

13. Attorney General to the President, 6 July 1981.

14. Ibid.

15. Immigration Detention Policy [n.a], 14 September 1981, Box 2, "Cuban-Haitian (5)" Folder, KM, RRPL.

16. "Ellington as Refugee Center Draws Fire," *Port Arthur News,* 21 June 1981.

17. Johnny Isbell to Frank Hodsoll, 19 June 1981, Box 3, "Frank Hodsoll (1)" Folder, KM, RRPL.

18. Paul F. Strain to James G. Gigante, 14 July 1981, Box 8, "Detention Center and Chaffee Working (3)" Folder, PTFIRP, RRPL.

19. Frank Hodsoll to Ed Meese, Jim Baker, and Mike Deaver, 14 July 1981, Box 8, "Detention Center and Chaffee Working (4)" Folder, PTFIRP, RRPL.

20. "Bainbridge Alien Center Could Cost $41 Million," *The Sun,* 12 July 1981, Box 8, "Detention Center and Chaffee Working (4)" Folder, PTFIRP, RRPL.

21. Hodsoll to Meese, Baker, and Deaver, 14 July 1981.

22. "Bainbridge Alien Center Could Cost $41 Million," *The Sun.*

23. Hodsoll to Meese, Baker, and Deaver, 14 July 1981.

24. Carol [Williams] to Renée [Szybala], [n.d.], handwritten note attached to Larry L. Simms to Associate Attorney General, 27 October 1981, Box 52, "INS—Guantanamo" Folder, RG, NARAII.

25. [Caspar Weinberger] to William French Smith, 5 June 1981, "File 90120 Cuba Refugees (2)" Folder, RWF, RRPL.

26. Ibid.

27. Kate Moore to Frank Hodsoll, 28 July 1981, Box 8, "Detention Center and Chaffee Working (4)" Folder, PTFIRP, RRPL.

28. Ibid.

29. John E. Cannon to Kate Moore, 28 July 1981, Box 8, "Detention Center and Chaffee Working (4)" Folder, PTFIRP, RRPL.

30. Caspar Weinberger to James Baker, III, 7 July 1981, with attached working paper from Perry J. Fliakas to Mr. Nelson, Box 8, "Detention Center and Chaffee Working (2)" Folder, PTFIRP, RRPL.

31. Alan C. Nelson and Philip N. Hawkes to Rudolph W. Giuliani, 15 December 1981, Box 225, "Refugees 1981" Folder, WFS, NARAII.

32. Hodsoll to Meese, Baker, and Deaver, 14 July 1981.

33. Ibid.
34. Ibid.
35. Moore to Hodsoll, 28 July 1981.
36. Renee L. Szybala to Carol E. Dinkins, 14 September 1981, Box 52, "INS—Glasgow" Folder, RG, NARAII.
37. Kathryn A. Oberly to David Crosland, 21 September 1981, Box 52, "INS—Glasgow" Folder, RG, NARAII.
38. Kate Moore to Frank Hodsoll, 5 October 1981, Box 8, "Detention Center and Chaffee Working (6)" Folder, PTFIRP, RRPL.
39. There appears to be some dispute, or confusion in the least, about when the INS took lead on the Glasgow project. Frank Hodsoll noted that the INS took over negotiations for Glasgow from HHS in September 1981, whereas the Deputy Attorney General explained that while the INS had been working with HHS, the OMB had decided in late December to transfer the entire project to the INS. Shull (2014, 170) explains that the OMB had made the "eleventh hour" decision to transfer the Glasgow project to the INS after the possibility of using Fort Drum in New York was no longer an option. Frank Hodsoll to Jim Baker, 6 October 1981, Box 1, "Cuban-Haitian (1)" Folder, KM, RRPL. Edward C. Schmults to James A. Baker III, 8 January 1982, Box 52, "INS—Glasgow" Folder, RG, NARAII.
40. Hodsoll to Baker, 6 October 1981.
41. Ibid.
42. Ibid.
43. Mike Horowitz to Ed Harper, Glenn Schlede, and Annelise Anderson, 16 September 1981, "Immigration Control [2 of 3]" Folder, KTC, RRPL.
44. Peter R. Steenland and David C. Shilton to Rudoph W. Giuliani, 25 August 1981, Box 52, "Fort Allen—INS" Folder, RG, NARAII. Alan C. Nelson to William French Smith, 13 January 1983, Box 52, "Fort Allen—INS" Folder, RG, NARAII.
45. Attorney General to the President, 6 July 1981, Box 51, "INS—Detention Facilities" Folder, RG, NARAII.
46. USCIS. "Voluntary departure." Available from: https://www.uscis.gov/tools/glossary/voluntary-departure, last accessed 30 October 2017.
47. [Bob Graham] to William French Smith, 15 July 1981, Box 52, "Krome—INS" Folder, RG, NARAII.
48. "White House Announces Plan to Stem Refugee Flow, Aid Fla.," *Washington Post,* 19 September 1980, Box 22, "Refugees—Cubans & Haitians [1]" Folder, FW, JCL.
49. Dade County Department of Public Health to James Gigante, 8 September 1980, Box 5, "Krome South [1]" Folder, CHTF, JCL.
50. William Swarm to John Cannon, 19 February 1981, Box 5, "Krome South [1]" Folder, CHTF, JCL.
51. Rick Neal to Rich Williamson, 21 July 1981, Box 1, "Immigration (4)" Folder, FSMH, RRPL.
52. Rudolph W. Giuliani to Frederick Richmond, 31 July 1981, Box 52, "Fort Allen—INS" Folder, RG, NARAII.

53. Frank Hodsoll to Mike Deaver and Bill Clark, 27 July 1981, Box 14, "Immigration Fact Sheet & Statement—Comments (5)" Folder, FSMH, RRPL.

54. Alan C. Nelson to William French Smith, 13 January 1983, Box 52, "Fort Allen—INS" Folder, RG, NARAII.

55. Robert J. Schmidt, Inspection Report—Fort Allen, Puerto Rico, 27 August 1981, Box 52, "Fort Allen—INS" Folder, RG, NARAII.

56. Raymond Bonner, "U.S. Transfers 120 Haitians to Prison in New York State," *New York Times,* 5 September 1981. Gregory Jaynes, "Haitian Refugees Still Languishing at Facility near Everglades," *New York Times,* 23 September 1981.

57. Whereas interdiction is a legal term for stopping people en route, interception is the more operational terminology that applies broadly to stopping boats at sea. In most archival materials we reviewed, U.S. government officials used the term *interdiction* in referring to Caribbean Basin operations at sea.

58. "Bodies on the Beach," *New York Times,* 28 October 1981, http://www.nytimes.com/1981/10/28/opinion/bodies-on-the-beach.html, last accessed 25 May 2017.

59. "Use Carrier Clinton Says," *Arkansas Gazette,* 14 May 1980 clipping, "Refugees, Cuban" VF, UALCL.

60. Zbigniew Brzezinski and Eugene Eidenberg to Secretary of State, 2 October 1980, Box 44, "ND 16/CO 64 Confidential 1/20/77-1/20/81 [Haiti]" Folder, ND 16, JCL.

61. U.S. Embassy in Port au Prince Embassy to State Department, 3 August 1981, [previously confidential cable], "Case 03341 (1 of 4)" Folder, IM, RRPL.

62. Ibid.

63. Fred F. Fielding to Richard G. Darman, 22 September 1981, "Case 03341 (2 of 4)" Folder, IM, RRPL.

64. Ibid.

65. Yet, "because immigration has historically been regarded as an area over which Congress has plenary authority and because the extent of the President's independent authority over immigration is not clear, opponents may contend that the President is acting where he has the least authority and that such acts constitute a usurpation of Congressional power." Ibid.

66. Walter E. Fauntroy to Ronald Reagan, 13 August 1981, Box 1, "Immigration (6)" Folder, FSMH, RRPL.

67. Gregory Jaynes, "33 Haitians Drown as Boat Capsizes off of Florida," *New York Times,* 27 October 1981.

68. Stuart Taylor Jr. "Deciding How to Stop Haitians—and Why," *New York Times,* 1 November 1981.

69. Gregory Jaynes, "Aides Say That Sea Patrol Has Slowed Haitian Entries," *New York Times,* 6 December 1981.

70. The White House Office of the Press Secretary, Press release, 10 November 1981, Box 2, "Cuban-Haitian (5)" Folder, KM, RRPL.

71. "U.S. Decision to Move Refugees to Fort Drum Draws Racism Charge," *Arkansas Gazette,* 12 November 1981, news clipping in "Refugees, Cuban" VF, UALCL.

72. Ibid.

73. Ibid.

74. On Weinberger's request, Perry Fliakas, the Deputy Assistant Secretary of Defense responsible for installations and housing, produced a list of "other than excess military bases" that could be used for a refugee-relocation center. For a nine hundred–person detention facility, Fliakas flagged five spaces: the abandoned Naval Disciplinary Facility within the Navy Complex at Portsmouth, New Hampshire; the partially used Navy Hospital in Philadelphia, Pennsylvania; a former Air Force station at Lockport, New York; the Fort Dix confinement facility in New Jersey; and the Richards Gebaur Air Force Base in Missouri. In addition, Fliakas listed seven other bases that could be used for a large refugee-relocation center, some of which had been considered for Vietnamese refugees [and the Mariel crisis/contingency planning]: Hamilton Air Force Base in northern California; Westover Air Force Base in Massachusetts; Rickenbacker Air Force Base in Ohio; Camp Parks in Livermore, California; Camp Atterbury in Indiana; the Navy facility at Imperial Beach, California; and Ramey Air Force Base in Puerto Rico. Caspar Weinberger to James Baker III, 7 July 1981, with attached working paper from Perry J. Fliakas to Mr. Nelson, Box 8, "Detention Center and Chaffee Working (2)" Folder, PTFIRP, RRPL.

75. Kate L. Moore to James A. Baker III, 4 November 1981, Box 8, "Detention Center and Chaffee Working (9)" Folder, PTFIRP, RRPL. Emphasis in original.

76. [Kate Moore] to Frank [Hodsoll], [n.d.], Box 8, "Detention Center and Chaffee Working (9)" Folder, PTFIRP, RRPL.

77. Kate L. Moore to James A. Baker III, 6 November 1981, Box 8, "Detention Center and Chaffee Working (9)" Folder, PTFIRP, RRPL.

78. Kate Moore and Kathy Collins to James A. Baker III and Edwin Meese III, 3 November 1981, Box 1, "Cuban-Haitian (2)" Folder, KM, RRPL. Moore to Baker, 6 November 1981.

79. James A. Baker to [Ronald Reagan], 9 November 1981, Box 8, "Detention Center and Chaffee Working (9)" Folder, PTFIRP, RRPL.

80. Gregory Jaynes, "Haitian Refugees Still Languishing at Facility near Everglades," New York Times, 23 September 1981.

81. Nelson and Hawkes to Giuliani, 15 December 1981.

82. "A Haitian Freeze," New York Times, 18 December 1981.

83. Ibid.

84. Ibid.

85. Jaynes, "Haitian Refugees Still Languishing."

86. "Preventing Another Mariel" [n.d., n.a.] [previously secret report], Box 4, "Refugees (1)" Folder, FSMH, RRPL. Alexander Haig Jr. and William French Smith to the President, [n.d.], Box 4, "Refugees (1)" Folder, FSMH, RRPL.

87. Tom Enders to The Secretary [of State], [n.d.], [previously secret], Box 4, "Refugees (1)" Folder, FSMH, RRPL.

88. Edward Schmults and David Crosland, 6 March 1981, Box 5, "Justice, Dept of (2)" Folder, CHTF, JCL.

89. Attorney General Smith touted the results of the program as "dramatic." In the first three months of the program, the Coast Guard stopped forty vessels carrying migrants and drugs. In the first month of the program, forty-seven

Haitians were apprehended in Florida as compared to one thousand in the same month the previous year. Alan C. Nelson to William French Smith, 4 January 1982, Box 154, "INS (1982) 1 of 3" Folder, WFS, NARAII.

90. Eve Baskowitz to Craig Fuller, 6 May 1982, "Immigrants/Refugees (OA 5666) (2)" Folder, RSW, RRPL.

91. Jaynes, "Aides Say That Sea Patrol Has Slowed Haitian Entries."

CHAPTER 3. "NOT A PRISON"

1. Edwin L. Harper to Stanley E. Morris, 20 February 1982, Box 159, "Refugees 1982" Folder, WFS, NARAII.

2. Maurice C. Inman to Alan C. Nelson, 8 July 1982, Box 51, "INS—Detention Rules" Folder, RG, NARAII.

3. Kevin D. Rooney to The Associate Attorney General, 18 March 1982, Box 51, "INS—Detention BOP" Folder, RG, NARAII.

4. Eve Baskowitz to Craig Fuller, 6 May 1982, "Immigrants/Refugees (OA 5666) (2)" Folder, RSW, RRPL.

5. Howell Raines, "New York Centers to House Haitians," *New York Times,* 18 July 1981. Also see Gwynn 1986, note 63.

6. These included the Haitian Refugee Center together with the NECLC), the NCC, and the ACLU.

7. Harper to Morris, 20 February 1982.

8. Ibid.

9. Edward C. Schmults to James A. Baker, III, 26 February 1982, Box 159, "Refugees 1982" Folder, WFS, NARAII.

10. Harper to Morris, 20 February 1982.

11. Ibid.

12. Ibid.

13. Annelise Anderson to Jim Cicconi, 9 March 1982, Box 10, "Immigration Policy: Cubans and Haitians" Folder, JWC, RRPL.

14. Ibid.

15. Ibid.

16. Schmults to Baker, 26 February 1982.

17. Renee L. Szybala to Rudolph W. Giuliani, 26 March 1982, Box 51, "INS—Detention BOP" Folder, RG, NARAII.

18. Ibid.

19. US Department of Justice, "Issue Paper—Detention Options," 18 March 1982, Box 51, "INS—Detention BOP" Folder, RG, NARAII.

20. Ibid.

21. Ibid.

22. Szybala to Giuliani, 26 March, 1982.

23. Norman A. Carlson to David Crosland, 5 March 1981, Box 5, "Justice, Dept of (2)" Folder, CHTF, JCL.

24. David Crosland to Edward C. Schmults, 6 March 1981, Box 5, "Justice, Dept of (2)" Folder, CHTF, JCL.

25. Ibid.

26. Ibid.

27. David Hiller to Wilford J. Forbush, 13 April 1981, Box 5, "Justice, Dept of (2)" Folder, CHTF, JCL.

28. Norman A. Carlson and Alan C. Nelson to Rudolph W. Giuliani, 30 April 1982, Box 51, "INS—Detention Facilities" Folder, RG, NARAII.

29. Max Friedersdorf to Jim Baker, Ed Meese, Mike Deaver, Frank Hodsoll, and Craig Fuller, 21 July 1981, Box 8, "Detention Center and Chaffee Working (4)" Folder, PTFIRP, RRPL.

30. John W. Warner, Jr., Harry F. Byrd, Jr., and Robert W. Daniel, Jr. to William French Smith, 26 July 1982, Box 51, "INS—El Reno/Petersburg" Folder, RG, NARAII.

31. Ibid.

32. Ibid.

33. Frank Harbin to William French Smith, 28 December 1981, Box 159, "Refugees 1982" Folder, WFS, NARAII.

34. Carlson and Nelson to Giuliani, 30 April 1982.

35. Don Nickles to William French Smith, 16 December 1982, Box 51, "INS—El Reno/Petersburg" Folder, RG, NARAII.

36. Carlson and Nelson to Giuliani, 30 April 1982.

37. The Lower Mississippi Delta Development Commission Hearing, 23 January 1990, 52, Box 1, Folder 21, LMDDC, DSUL.

38. Kris Kirkpatrick to Dave Batt, Wayne Smith, and Carson Killen, 12 March 1982, Box 372, "Oakdale-Alien Detention Center File 005" Folder, LGP, JBJ, LSUL.

39. Lower Mississippi Delta Development Commission Hearing, 23 January 1990, 50.

40. J. Bennett Johnston and Russell B. Long to William French Smith, 17 March 1982, Box 372, "Oakdale-Alien Detention Center File 005" Folder, LGP, JBJ, LSUL.

41. Sacred Heart Catholic Church and St. Francis of Rome Mission bulletin, c. 1982, Box 372, "Oakdale-Alien Detention Center File 005" Folder, LGP, JBJ, LSUL.

42. Skip to JBJ [J. Bennett Johnston], 27 April [1982], Box 372, "Oakdale-Alien Detention Center File 005" Folder, LGP, JBJ. LJ to JBJ [J. Bennett Johnston], 25 March 1982, Box 372, "Oakdale-Alien Detention Center File 005" Folder, LGP, JBJ, LSUL.

43. LJ to JBJ [J. Bennett Johnston], DB, and SW, 10 May 1982, Box 372, "Oakdale-Alien Detention Center File 005" Folder, LGP, JBJ, LSUL.

44. Carlson and Nelson to Giuliani, 30 April 1982.

45. Rudolph W. Giuliani to William French Smith, 5 May 1982, Box 51, "INS—Detention Facilities" Folder, RG, NARAII.

46. Rudolph W. Giuliani to J. Bennett Johnston, 1 June 1982, Box 372, "Oakdale-Alien Detention Center File 005" Folder, LGP, JBJ, LSUL.

47. Ibid.

48. LJ to JBJ [J. Bennett Johnston], SW, DB, and WN, 21 May 1982, Box 372, "Oakdale-Alien Detention Center File 005" Folder, LGP, JBJ, LSUL.

49. LJ to JBJ [J. Bennett Johnston], 25 March 1982, Box 372, "Oakdale-Alien Detention Center File 005" Folder, LGP, JBJ, LSUL.

50. Robert A. McConnell to J. Bennett Johnston, 31 March 1982, Box 372, "Oakdale-Alien Detention Center File 005" Folder, LGP, JBJ, LSUL.

51. LJ to JBJ [J. Bennett Johnston], SW, DB, 11 August 1982, Box 372, "Oakdale-Alien Detention Center File 005" Folder, LGP, JBJ, LSUL.

52. Russell B. Long, Gillis Long, J. Bennett Johnston, and John Breaux to Ronald Reagan, 28 May 1982, Box 372, "Oakdale-Alien Detention Center File 005" Folder, LGP, JBJ, LSUL.

53. Senator Johnston, speaking on Supplemental Appropriations Act, 1982, 97th Cong., 2nd. sess., *Congressional Record – Senate* (August 11, 1982): p. S10223. Box 372, "Oakdale-Alien Detention Center File 005" Folder, LGP, JBJ, LSUL.

54. Jim Leggett, "Officials Seeking Alien Center Site Greeted Enthusiastically in Oakdale," *Alexandria Daily Town Talk,* 5 March 1982.

55. "Aliens Don't Bother Town," c. 1982, Box 372, "Oakdale-Alien Detention Center File 005" Folder, LGP, JBJ, LSUL.

56. Ibid.

57. J. Bennett Johnston news release, 11 August 1982, Box 372, "Oakdale-Alien Detention Center File 005" Folder, LGP, JBJ, LSUL.

58. Mary Gail to Tony Garrett, 4 August 1982, Box 372, "Oakdale-Alien Detention Center File 005" Folder, LGP, JBJ, LSUL.

59. Sacred Heart Catholic Church and St. Francis of Rome Mission bulletin.

60. Ibid.

61. David Hiller to The Attorney General [William French Smith], 8 February 1982, Box 159, "Refugees 1982" Folder, WFS, NARAII.

62. Eric Alterman, "An Actual War Criminal May Become Our Second-ranking Diplomat," *The Nation,* 2 February 2017, https://www.thenation.com/article/an-actual-american-war-criminal-may-become-our-second-ranking-diplomat/.

63. Hiller to The Attorney General [Smith], 8 February 1982.

64. "Additional background for the House/Senate conferees on the need for two detention centers," c. 1982, Box 51, "INS—El Reno/Petersburg" Folder, RG, NARAII.

65. U.S. Department of Justice, *Site Selection Analysis for the Alien Detention Center,* [1983], Box 177, "INS 1983 (1 of 3)" Folder, WFS, NARAII.

66. Issue paper, c. 1982, Box 51, "INS—Detention Facilities" Folder, RG, NARAII.

67. City of Oakdale, Fact Sheet on Proposed Alien Center, c. 1982, Box 372,"Oakdale-Alien Detention Center File 006" Folder, LGP, JBJ, LSUL. Kris Kirkpatrick to Members of the Louisiana Delegation, 28 September 1982, Box 372,"Oakdale-Alien Detention Center File 006" Folder, LGP, JBJ, LSUL.

68. Kirkpatrick to Louisiana Delegation, 28 September 1982.

69. City of Oakdale, Fact Sheet on Proposed Alien Center.

70. U.S. Department of Justice, *Site Selection Analysis for the Alien Detention Center.*

71. Ibid.

72. [Ken] to Attorney General [William French Smith], 21 January 1983, Box 177, "INS 1983 (1 of 3)" Folder, WFS, NARAII.

73. Rudolph W. Giuliani to The Attorney General [William French Smith], 10 January 1983, Box 177, "INS 1983 (1 of 3)" Folder, WFS, NARAII.

74. Wade Houk to Renee Szybala, 3 February 1983, Box 177, "INS 1983 (1 of 3)" Folder, RG, NARAII. Resolution Endorsing Location of Alien Detention Center in Oakdale, Louisiana, 2 February 1983, Box 53, "INS—Oakdale" Folder, RG, NARAII.

75. Associate Attorney General [Rudolph Giuliani] to Attorney General [William French Smith], 7 February 1983, Box 177, "INS 1983 (1 of 3)" Folder, RG, NARAII.

76. Draft Environmental Impact Statement Proposed Alien Detention Center, 8 April 1983, 10, 26, Box 372,"Oakdale-Alien Detention Center File 006" Folder, LGP, JBJ, LSUL.

77. U.S. Department of Justice, *Site Selection Analysis for the Alien Detention Center.*

78. Note to Files, 10 December 1983, Box 372,"Oakdale-Alien Detention Center File 006" Folder, LGP, JBJ, LSUL. Executive Summary: A Report to the Attorney General, 1 February 1988, Box 523, "State Affairs: Justice: Oakdale uprising folder 11," LSA, JBB, LSUL.

79. Clifford May, "Immigration Enforcement Is Assailed," *New York Times,* 28 July 1986.

80. J. Bennett Johnston, Russell B. Long, John B. Breaux, and Gillis Long to Hugh Brian, 19 March 1984, Box 372, "Oakdale-Alien Detention Center File 007" Folder, LGP, JBJ, LSUL.

81. Russell Long, J. Bennett Johnston, John B. Breaux, and Gillis W. Long to Paul Galis, 18 December 1984, Box 372, "Oakdale-Alien Detention Center File 007" Folder, LGP, JBJ, LSUL.

82. Paul L. Galis to George B. Mowad, 17 September 1984, Box 372, "Oakdale-Alien Detention Center File 007" Folder, LGP, JBJ, LSUL.

83. C. Paul Phelps to George B. Mowad, 1 May 1995, Box 372, "Oakdale-Alien Detention Center File 007" Folder, LGP, JBJ, LSUL.

84. D. Lowell Jensen to The Attorney General [William French Smith], 21 April 1983, Box 176, "INS 1983 (2 of 3)" Folder, WFS, NARAII.

85. Edmund S. Muskie to The President [Jimmy Carter], 9 January 1981, NLC 15-89-3-8-7, JCL.

86. Dick Thornburgh to George Bush, 26 January 1990, "Marielitos [OA/ID 02719]" Folder, MPJ, GBPL.

87. John G. Roberts to Fred F. Fielding, 12 March 1985, Box 28, "Immigration & Naturalization Folder 7," JGR, RRPL.

88. Jeb Bush to Edwin Meese, 25 June 1986, "Cuban/Nicaraguan Immigration (5) [OA/ID 14831]" Folder, PDB, GBPL.

89. Earle E. Morris, Jr. to George Bush, 29 January 1988, "Cuban/Nicaraguan Immigration (1) [OA/ID 14831]" Folder, PDB, GBPL.

90. Federal Correctional Institution, Oakdale, LA, 13 March 2002, Box 373, "St. Affairs: Oakdale, LA/Bureau of Prisons (BOP) Facilities 2002 file 140," LSA, JBB, LSUL. Nacci 1988, 8.

91. Robert Pears, "Behind the Prison Riots: Precautions Not Taken," *New York Times,* 6 December 1987. Nacci 1988, 9.

92. Art Harris, "Meese Offers to Delay Cuban Deportations," *Washington Post,* 23 November 1987.

93. Thomas Boyd to Robert W. Kastenmeier, 29 April 1988, Box 523, "State Affairs: Justice: Oakdale uprising folder 11," LSA, JBB, LSUL.

94. Pears, "Behind the Prison Riots."

95. Ibid.

96. Executive Summary: A Report to the Attorney General, 1 February 1988, Box 523, "State Affairs: Justice: Oakdale uprising folder 11," LSA, JBB, LSUL.

97. Boyd to Kastenmeier, 29 April 1988. Emphasis in original.

98. George B. Mowad to John Breaux, 3 March 1988, Box 286, "Bureau of the Prisons: Oakdale Detention Center, Folder 16," DIA, JBB, LSUL.

99. George B. Mowad to Paul Galis, 9 April 1988, Box 372, "Oakdale Airport—Allen Parish File 009" Folder, LGP, JBJ, LSUL. George B. Mowad to Paul Galis, 31 January 1990, Box 372, "Oakdale Airport—Allen Parish File 009" Folder, LGP, JBJ, LSUL.

100. Joan C. Higgins to Paul L. Galis, 27 February 1990, Box 372, "Oakdale Airport—Allen Parish File 009" Folder, LGP, JBJ, LSUL.

CHAPTER 4. "UNCLE SAM HAS A LONG ARM"

1. "Arizona: Life Is Great in Florence," n.a., n.d., "CE EPH DTO-FLORENCE.17 Historical writings on Florence Arizona" Folder, EF, AC, ASUL.

2. David Hiller to Craig Fuller, 19 May 1982, "Immigrants/Refugees (OA 5666) (2)" Folder, RSW, RRPL.

3. Norman Carlson to Rudolph W. Giuliani, 15 December 1982, Box 51, "INS—Detention Facilities" Folder, RG, NARAII.

4. Fred Gibson to Carl Hayden, 17 February 1942, Box "408 P/W Camps—Florence," "254 Florence, Ariz." Folder, "P/W Camps—Beauregard to Carson, Unclassified Decimal file," M&RB, RG389, NARAII.

5. E. G. Dentzer to Carl Hayden, 20 February 1942, Box "408 P/W Camps—Florence," "254 Florence, Ariz." Folder, "P/W Camps—Beauregard to Carson, Unclassified Decimal file," M&RB, RG389, NARAII.

6. The Provost Marshal General kept detailed daily and quarterly records about labor time, crops, and crop prices, which are available at NARAII.

7. Paul L. Allen, "Florence, 1942: Former POW Guard Has Fond Memories of Italians, Germans," *Tucson Citizen,* 3 January 1989, "Prisoner of War Camps—Arizona—Florence ephemera" Folder, AHS. Lowell Parker, "Eloy Trying to Live Down 'Toughest Town' Reputation," c. 1976, "DTO-Eloy Newsclippings" Folder, EF, AC, ASUL.

8. Parker, "Eloy Trying to Live Down 'Toughest Town' Reputation."

9. Walter Douglas to [Carl Hayden], 8 February 1951, Box 182, Folder 26, CTH, AC, ASUL.

10. Edmund F. Mansure to Carl Hayden, 28 October 1954, Box 182, Folder 26, CTH, AC, ASUL.

11. "Former Prisoner of War Camp to House Modern School for First Offenders," [3 October 1947], "POW Camp, Post—articles" Folder, PCHS.

12. Internal Security Act of 1950, Public Law 8-831, U.S. Statutes at Large 64 (1950): 987–1031.

13. "U.S. Explains Why Stockades Being Installed in Arizona," *Arizona Republic,* 6 January 1952, "Prisoner of War Camps—Arizona—Florence ephemera" Folder, AHS.

14. "Federal Camp near Florence Has Neither Guns nor Guards," *Arizona Republic,* 4 January 1953, "EPH DTO-FLORENCE, Florence Newsclippings; 1950–" Folder, EF, AC, ASUL.

15. Ibid.

16. Carl Hayden to Perry W. Morton, 17 February 1956, Box 182, Folder 26, CTH, AC, ASUL.

17. Jerry Poole, "U.S., Arizona May Go to Court over Status of Ex-prison Camp," *Arizona Republic,* [20 September 1954], Box 182, Folder 26, CTH, AC, ASUL.

18. Frank E. Fraser to Barry M. Goldwater, 17 February 1954, Box 182, Folder 26, CTH, AC, ASUL.

19. Hayden to Morton, 17 February 1956.

20. James Bennett to Carl Hayden, 6 March 1956, Box 182, Folder 26, CTH, AC, ASUL.

21. H. G. Moeller to Paul Fannin, 22 December 1966, "Cabinet Departments—Justice Dept: Bureau of Prisons, 1966" Folder, PJF, AC, ASUL.

22. Ibid.

23. Ibid.

24. Leslie A. Wakefield to Paul Fannin, 16 November 1966, "Cabinet Departments—Justice Dept: Bureau of Prisons, 1966" Folder, PJF, AC, ASUL.

25. Robert R. Bean to Paul Fannin, 2 December 1966, "Cabinet Departments—Justice Dept: Bureau of Prisons, 1966" Folder, PJF, AC, ASUL.

26. Craig E. Davids to Jack Williams, 8 December 1967, "323 Microfilm: Pending Cases 1970," Box 017, Reel 015_004, BMG, AC, ASUL.

27. Bean to Fannin, 2 December 1966.

28. Florence Community Development Corporation, "Five Area Development Proposal," c. 1967, "323 Microfilm: Pending Cases 1970," Box 017, Reel 015_004, BMG, AC, ASUL.

29. Ibid.

30. Ibid.

31. Ibid.

32. Ibid.

33. Jack Williams to G. E. McNamara, 19 July 1968, "323 Microfilm: Pending Cases 1970," Box 017, Reel 015_004, BMG, AC, ASUL.

34. C. R. Hagan to Norval C. Jesperson, 19 March 1969, "323 Microfilm: Pending Cases 1970," Box 017, Reel 015_004, BMG, AC, ASUL.

35. Allen Cook and Norval C. Jesperson to Jack Williams, 25 March 1969, "323 Microfilm: Pending Cases 1970," Box 017, Reel 015_004, BMG, AC, ASUL.

36. Ibid.

37. Ibid.

38. Ibid.

39. Mary Leonhard, "Sun Living," *The Arizona Republic*, 10 January 1971, "EPH DTO-FLORENCE, Florence Newsclippings; 1950–" Folder, EF, AC, ASUL. "Consolidated's Growth Means Population Boom in Florence," *Central Arizona Progress,* November 1983, "DTO Eloy 7" Folder, EF, AC, ASUL.

40. Steve Yozwiak, "'Powder Keg' Pops; Cubans Ruin Prison," *Arizona Republic,* 23 August 1985, "Prisons-state-Arizona-Florence-1985-1999 ephemera" Folder, EF, AHS.

41. Chris Limberis, "116 Mariel Cubans Producing Some Unease in Florence," *The Arizona Daily Star,* 24 August 1986, "Prisons-state-Arizona-Florence-1985-1999 ephemera" Folder, EF, AHS.

42. Ibid.

43. Limberis, "116 Mariel Cubans Producing Some Unease."

44. Ibid.

45. United Press International [untitled], 7 February 1981, Box 8, "Florida file," PTFIRP, RRPL.

46. Bob Graham to Ronald Reagan, 9 September 1982, "Case 097544," IM, RRPL.

47. United Press International, [untitled].

48. Graham to Reagan, 9 September 1982.

49. Michael M. Uhlmann to Edwin Meese, III, 24 May 1983, "Immigration and Refugee Matters (1)" Folder, EGM, RRPL.

50. Ibid., emphasis in original.

51. ACLU, "Analysis of Immigration Detention Policies." www.aclu.org/other/analysis-immigration-detention-policies?redirect=immigrants-rights/analysis-immigration-detention-policies. Accessed 3 June 2017.

52. Immigration and Naturalization Service, *Special Report: Hold the Line,* 30 June 1989, Box 465, "Immigration Central America—Closed 1989" Folder, RT, NARAII.

53. Ibid.

54. Alan Nelson to Dick Thornburgh, 31 January 1989, Box 465, "Immigration Central America—Closed 1989" Folder, RT, NARAII.

55. E.M. Trominski to Luis del Rio, 26 January 1989, Box 465, "Immigration Central America—Closed 1989" Folder, RT, NARAII.

56. Immigration and Naturalization Service, *Special Report: Hold the Line.*

57. Joe D. Whitley to Dick Thornburgh, 17 February 1989, Box 465, "Immigration Central America—Closed 1989" Folder, RT, NARAII.

58. Immigration and Naturalization Service, *Enhancement Plan for the Southern Border,* 16 February 1989, Box 465, "Immigration Central America—Closed 1989" Folder, RT, NARAII.

59. Immigration and Naturalization Service, *Special Report: Hold the Line.* Immigration and Naturalization Service, *Enhancement Plan for the Southern Border.*

60. Immigration and Naturalization Service, *Enhancement Plan for the Southern Border.*

61. In still longer historical perspective, criminal legal sanctions to police the mobility of working-class people can be found in postbellum regulations of formerly enslaved people in the United States. The much longer history of regu-

lating "vagrancy" and "incorrigibility" fundamentally stretches to the long history of capitalism (Walters 2010b; Melossi 2013).

62. Office of the General Counsel to Jack Shaw [draft], c. January 1989, "Detention and Deportation" VF, USCIS.

CHAPTER 5. SAFE HAVEN

1. Affidavit no. 47 (B. P.), 20 October 1989, Box 4, "Abuses at Krome 1989" Folder, AIJ, Duke.

2. Ibid.

3. Elaine Sciolino, "Clinton Says U.S. Will Continue Ban on Haitian Exodus," *New York Times*, 15 January 1993.

4. The Haiti Commission, Report from Fact Finding Mission to Guantanamo, 20 March 1993, Box 17, "Immigration-Haitians, Articles, letters to politicians etc (1 of 5) 1990–1991" Folder, AIJ, Duke.

5. Haitian Refugee Center, press release, 2 June 1992, Box 9, "Krome 1992" Folder, AIJ, Duke.

6. Anthony Lake and Samuel Berger to the President, 16 April 1993, FOIA 2011-1044-F, CDL.

7. Ibid.

8. Ibid.

9. Ibid.

10. Lawton Chiles to Janet Reno, 9 December 1993, ODS, GADA.

11. Ibid.

12. Porter Goss to Bill Clinton, 3 March 1994, NSC Records Management (Haiti and Lake) 9406327, Box 2, FOIA 2006-0187-F, WJCL. Porter J. Goss, "Supply a 'Safe Haven' in Haiti," *Christian Science Monitor*, 23 November 1993.

13. Goss to Clinton, 3 March 1994.

14. Summary of Conclusions of Meeting of the NSC Deputies Committee, 10 May 1994, NSC, CDL.

15. Ibid.

16. Ibid.

17. Phyllis Coven to Robert Perito, 20 October 1993, ODS, GADA.

18. Meeting of the NSC Deputies Committee, 10 May 1994.

19. Ibid.

20. Ibid.

21. Summary of Conclusions of Meeting of the NSC Deputies Committee, 5 July 1994, NSC, CDL.

22. Jeanne Butterfield to Carol Wolchok et al., 25 July 1994, Box 1, "General information" Folder, AIJ, Duke.

23. Ibid.

24. Ibid.

25. WORLD RELIEF, press release, 1 September 1994, Box 2, "Memos, reports, Ltrs on Regulations and policy in GTMO" Folder, AIJ, Duke.

26. Ibid.

27. Ibid.

28. Bill Frelick, Observations on Safe Haven for Haitian Refugees, 27 July 1994, Box 1, "General—GTMO reports (Background, etc)" Folder, AIJ, Duke.

29. Conversation with Bonn Lander, 26 September 1995, Box 2, "Memos, reports, Ltrs on Regulations and policy in GTMO" Folder, AIJ Duke.

30. Ibid.

31. Frelick, Observations on Safe Haven.

32. Ibid.

33. Ibid.

34. Ibid., emphasis in original.

35. Lawton Chiles to Janet Reno, 6 May 1994, ODS, GADA.

36. Lawton Chiles to Janet Reno, 18 August 1994, ODS, GADA.

37. Clemence Fiagome, "Cuban Americans Shift on Refugees," *The Christian Science Monitor,* 13 October 1994. Rebecca Kaplan, "Jeb Bush and the Perils of Immigration," *CBS News,* 17 December 2014.

38. POTUS to Simon Ferro, attached to Robert Malley to Morton H. Halperin, 17 May 1995, FOIA 2011-1044-F, CDL.

39. Ibid.

40. Ibid.

41. William J. Clinton, "Remarks to the Cuban-American Community," 27 June 1995, The American Presidency Project http://www.presidency.ucsb.edu/ws/?pid=51547.

42. Thomas S. Epstein to Stephen C. Warnath, 23 February 1995, FOIA 2011-0376-F, CDL.

43. Ibid.

44. FIAC believed the number was much higher because many unaccompanied minors had not been placed, and thereby counted, in Camp 9 (Pearcy and Little 1996, 2).

45. Guantanamo Watch to Janet Reno, 16 February 1995, Box 1, "National Security Council—Multilateral & Humanitarian Affairs (Schwarz, Eric) Haiti Safe Haven, 1994–1995 (1)" Folder, FOIA 2011-1045-F, WJCL.

46. Affidavit no. 47 (B. P.).

47. Ibid.

48. Affidavit no. 54, Letter addressed to "All Haitians living in Miami, Florida," 20 February 1989, Box 4, "Abuses at Krome 1989" Folder, AIJ, Duke.

49. "Safe Haven for Haitian boat people," c. 14 September 1995, FOIA 2011-1045-F, CDL.

CHAPTER 6. ONSHORE EXPANSION

1. Rahm Emanuel to Chief of Staff, 7 June 1996, FOIA 2011-0376-F, CDL.

2. Ibid.

3. Ibid.

4. Rahm Emanuel to Chief of Staff and President, 13 October 1995, FOIA 2011-0376-F, CDL.

5. Christopher F. Edley et al. to Jeremy Benami et al., 31 January 1995, FOIA 2011-0376-F, CDL.

6. Stephen Colgate to GAO, 31 March 1995, "Expedited Removal" VF, USCIS Library.

7. "Guide to Records of the Department of Correctional Services," New York State Archives, 1992, accessed 6 June 2017, http://www.archives.nysed.gov/common/archives/files/res_topics_legal_corrections.pdf.

8. Kathleen Hawk, statement before the Subcommittee on Intellectual Property and Judicial Administration, House Judiciary Committee, 12 May 1993, Box 129, "Prison-Pollock (2 of 3) Folder 019," JB, JBB, LSU.

9. Conference report and statement on the bill (H.R. 2076), 104th Cong. 1st Sess., 1995. *Congressional Record* 141 (4 December 1995): H 104-378, p. 23.

10. "Notice of Final Environmental Impact Statement," *Federal Register* 61, no. 35 (21 February 1996): 6658.

11. INS, "Batavia, New York selected as site of new federal detention facility," 13 February 1996, "Detention and Deportation Service Processing Centers—New York—Batavia" VF, USCIS.

12. Kevin Savaille, "Genesee Wins Out; Designated Site for New Detention Center," *Batavia Daily News,* 7 December 1995, GCHD.

13. Ibid.

14. Ibid.

15. "Detention Center Director Proud of the New Facility," *Daily Batavia News,* 3 March 1998, GCHD.

16. Ibid.

17. INS, "Batavia Federal Detention Center opens," 11 March 1998, "Detention and Deportation Service Processing Centers—Batavia" VF, USCIS.

18. Ibid.

19. ACLU, "Analysis of Immigration Detention Policies," [nd], accessed 3 June 2017, www.aclu.org/other/analysis-immigration-detention-policies?redirect=immigrants-rights/analysis-immigration-detention-policies.

20. Ibid.

21. Institutional Hearing Program (IHP), September 1994, "Detention and Deportation" VF, USCIS.

22. INS, "Pilot of Expedited Removal Procedures at Three Institutional Removal Program Sites," 20 September 1999, "Detention and Deportation" VF, USCIS.

23. INS News Release, "INS and New York State set to deport 86 criminal aliens; action is largest single-country deportation of criminals in New York history," 28 August 1995, "Expedited Removal" VF, USCIS.

24. "Encouraging Progress on Deportations; Statistics Support the Steady, Measured Approach of the INS," *Los Angeles Times,* 2 January 1996. "Expedited Removal" VF, USCIS.

25. Office of the Deputy Commissioner to Management Team et al., 29 October 1996, "Expedited Removal" VF, USCIS.

26. Janet Reno draft remarks for Removals News Conference, 30 October 1997, "Expedited Removal" VF, USCIS.

27. Ibid.

28. Ibid.

29. INS, "INS Improves Management of Detention Program," 8 June 1999, "Detention and Deportation" VF, USCIS.

30. Stephen Colgate to GAO, 31 March 1995.

31. L. Graves. "Relocating Prisoners: The Cross-country Inmate Transfer." *Wired,* 24 May 2010, last accessed 10 October 2016, https://www.wired .com/2010/05/process_prisoners/.

32. Memo: "Boston's Deportation Fugitive Unit," c. 1992, "Detention and Deportation" VF, USCIS.

33. Tim Counts and Roger Lindo, "The Northern Region Detention and Deportation Program," 17 April 1992, "Detention and Deportation" VF, USCIS.

34. Department of Justice, "Justice Department consolidates air fleets to transport federal prisoners and criminal aliens," 6 April 1995, "Detention and Deportation Justice Prisoner and Alien Transport System (JPATS)" VF, USCIS.

35. Ibid.

36. "U.S. Marshals Service Position on Oakdale airport," n.d., Box 372, "Oakdale Airport—Allen Parish File 009" Folder, LGP, JBJ.

37. Department of Justice, "Justice Department consolidates air fleets."

38. "U.S. Marshals Service Position," n.d.

39. Detention and Deportation Division (HQDDP) to Distribution, 19 April 1996, "Detention and Deportation Vertical File. Justice Prisoner and Alien Transport System (JPATS)" VF, USCIS.

40. Ibid.

41. Ibid.

42. Ibid.

43. [INS], Fact Sheet: Oakdale Airport (Allen Parish, LA), 19 January 1996, Box 372, "Oakdale Airport—Allen Parish File 009" Folder, LGP, JBJ.

44. Chris Sale, Testimony for hearing before the House Committee on the Judiciary, 23 February 1994, "Detention and Deportation" VF, USCIS.

45. A Louisiana parish is the jurisdictional equivalent to a county in other states.

46. Frank Main, "[Illegible] Pleads Guilty on Assault on Cuban," *State-Times,* 16 September 1991, Box 336, "Avoyelles—Prison—U.S. Immigration and Naturalization Service" Folder 10, LGP, JBJ.

47. Avoyelles Parish fax, 26 August 1991, Box 336, "Avoyelles—Prison—U.S. Immigration and Naturalization Service" Folder 10, LGP, JBJ.

48. Main, "[Illegible] Pleads Guilty."

49. Unknown author, handwritten notes re. Avoyelles Sherriff's Office, 29 September 1998 and 7 October 1998, Box 086, Folder 007, JB, JBB.

50. Johnny Broussard to Judy Siegel and Tommy Hudson, 24 September 1998, Box 086, Folder 007, JB, JBB.

51. "In Rural Jails, Haitians Suffer from Isolation," *New York Times,* 28 June 1993.

52. Robert Bryce and Lisa Tozzi, "The Roots of a Hostage Crisis," *Salon. com,* 20 December 1999, Box 046, "Pers. Office: Research: Cuban Prisoners—Cuban Detainees" Folder 033, PO, JBB.

53. See Shull (2014a) for a comprehensive history of the role of private firms in migration detention.

54. Jeff Gerth and Stephen Labaton, "Jail Business Shows Its Weaknesses: Prisons for Profit," *New York Times,* 24 November 1995.

55. Intel Daily e-mail, 20 October 1998, Appeal 2014-0868-A, WJCL.

56. "Public Affairs Backgrounder," c. 1994, "Detention and Deportation" VF, USCIS.

57. Miriam Davidson, "Do Private Prisons Work?: Arizona Riots Raise Doubts," *Christian Science Monitor,* 29 December 1994.

58. Kathleen Hawk Sawyer to John Breaux, 30 August 2001, Box 128, "Pollock Prison (2 of 2) Folder 53," JB, JBB.

59. Memo re. conversation between Johnny [Broussard] and Kathleen Hawk Sawyer re. Jena, Pollock Prison, 7 August 2001, Box 128, Pollock Prison "(2 of 2) Folder 53," JB, JBB. Bob Mann to Johnny Broussard, 22 August 2002, Box 223, "LaSalle Parish Prison Folder 063," LC, JBB.

60. Diane McRee to Johnny Broussard, 21 October 2001, Box 223, "LaSalle Parish Prison Folder 063," JB, JBB.

61. Scott Kirkpatrick et al. to Fred Hatfield, 27 January 2003, Box 116, "LaSalle Parish-Wackenhut Prison" Folder, JB, JBB.

62. Attachment to e-mail from Wesley Bizzell forwarded from Lindsay Spiller to Johnny Broussard, 14 January 2003, Box 116, "LaSalle Parish-Wackenhut Prison" Folder, JB, JBB.

CHAPTER 7. POST-9/11 POLICING

1. Ingrid Schroeder to Distribution List, 10 July 1997, Box 32, "Immigration-Deportation Rules [1]" Folder 8, EKC, CDL.

2. Phil Caplan to the President, 8 July 1997, Box 32, "Immigration-Deportation Rules [1]" Folder 8, EKC, CDL.

3. Ibid.

4. Philip Bartz, John Morton, David Martin, Allen Erenbaum, and H. Bradford Glassman to the Attorney General, 7 November 1997, Box 32, "Immigration-Deportation Rules [1]" Folder 8, EKC, CDL.

5. Ibid.

6. Ibid.

7. Ibid.

8. Julie Fernandes to Elena Kagan, 19 November 1997, Box 32, "Immigration-Deportation Rules [1]" Folder 8, EKC, CDL.

9. Ibid.

10. Ibid.

11. Lamar Smith to John Hilley, 17 November 1997, Box 32, "Immigration-Haitians" Folder 16, EKC, CDL. Emphasis in original.

12. Ibid.

13. Ibid.

14. By 2000, those figures were 9 percent of Haitians, 8 percent of Cubans, 25 percent of Jamaicans, 5 percent of Guatemalans, and 9 percent of Nicaraguans living outside of their country of origin. International Migrants by Country, Pew Research Center, 10 November 2016, accessed 7 June 2017, available at: http://www.pewglobal.org/interactives/migration-tables/.

15. Samuel Berger to the President, 20 December 1997, Box 32, "Immigration-Haitians" Folder 16, EKC, CDL.

16. Eric Schmitt, "U.S. Pursues Deportation of Haitians," *New York Times,* 9 January 1998.

17. Jim Yardley, "Hispanics Give Attentive Bush Mixed Reviews," *New York Times,* 27 August 2000. Maia Jachimowicz, "Bush Proposes New Temporary Guest Worker Program," *Migration Policy Institute,* 1 February 2004, accessed 8 June 2017, http://www.migrationpolicy.org/article/bush-proposes-new-temporary-worker-program.

18. Catherine Wilson, "US Changes Detention Policy to Discourage Haitian Refugees," *Naples Daily News,* 20 March 2002, Box 17, "Articles 2001–2002 (Haitian boat people, 12-03-01 (2 of 2)" Folder, AIJ, Duke.

19. "Senate Subcommittee Explores Detention of Haitian Asylum Seekers as DOJ Outlines Policy," *Interpreter Releases,* 7 October 2002, Box 17, "Articles 2001-2002 (Haitian boat people, 12-03-01 (1 of 2)" Folder, AIJ, Duke.

20. Ibid.

21. Honeymag.com, "Shipwrecked," August 2002, Box 17, "Articles 2001–2002 (Haitian boat people, 12-03-01 (1 of 2)" Folder, AIJ, Duke.

22. Ibid.

23. Florida Immigrant Advocacy Center, "No justice for Haitian asylum seekers," June 2002, Box 21, "Haitian Asylum seekers 2002" Folder, AIJ, Duke.

24. Florida Immigrant Advocacy Center, "Treatment of Haitian women seeking asylum in south Florida," June 2002, Box 21, "Haitian Asylum seekers 2002" Folder, AIJ, Duke.

25. Charu Newhouse Al-Sahli to Cheryl Little, 2 May 2002, Box 21, "Haitian Asylum seekers 2002" Folder, AIJ, Duke.

26. Ibid.

27. Ibid., emphasis in original.

28. Honeymag.com, "Shipwrecked."

29. Ibid.

30. Florida Immigrant Advocacy Center, "No justice for Haitian asylum seekers."

31. Edward Kennedy and Sam Brownback to John Ashcroft, 19 June 2002, Box 21, "Haitian Asylum seekers 2002" Folder, AIJ, Duke.

32. Ibid.

33. Statement of detained Haitian asylum seekers on hunger strike at Krome, 9 July 2002, Box 21, "Haitian Asylum seekers 2002" Folder, AIJ, Duke.

34. "Protecting Jeb?" *Wall Street Journal,* 26 April 2002, Box 21, "Haitian Asylum seekers 2003 (1 of 3)" Folder, AIJ, Duke.

35. "Protesters: Free the 200 Haitians Detained on the Coast of Florida," *The Militant,* 18 November 2002, http://www.themilitant.com/2002/6643/664350.html.

36. President's plan for comprehensive immigration reform, c. 23 January 2007, *The White House,* https://georgewbush-whitehouse.archives.gov/stateoftheunion/2007/initiatives/immigration.html.

37. Ibid.

38. On Thai policy, see Suhrke (1983); Simon (1998, 583). B. Ryan writes: "Probably the first case of systematic enforcement action at sea against irregular

migration was taken by the British against unauthorized Jewish arrival to Palestine in the late 1930s and between 1945 and 1948" (2010, 23).

39. Doris Meissner, "Yes, They're Poor—and Persecuted, Too: Haitians: Refugees Can Be Given Safe Haven without Being Brought to U.S. Territory," *Los Angeles Times,* 31 July 1992.

40. "The Guantánamo Docket," *New York Times,* https://www.nytimes .com/interactive/projects/guantanamo. Last accessed 29 December 2017.

CODA

1. Dara Lind, "Inside the Remote, Secretive Detention Center for Migrant Families," *Vox,* 24 July 2014, accessed 29 December 2017, http://www.vox .com/2014/7/24/5932023/inside-the-remote-secretive-detention-center-for -migrant-families.

2. Kate Swanson, Rebecca Torres, Amy Thompson, Sarah Blue, and Óscar Misael Hernández Hernández, "A Year after Obama Declared a 'Humanitarian Situation' at the Border, Child Migration Continues," *NACLA,* 27 August 2015, accessed 29 December 2017, https://nacla.org/news/2015/08/27/year -after-obama-declared-"humanitarian-situation"-border-child-migration-con tinues.

3. The White House, "Letter from the President—Efforts to Address the Humanitarian Situation in the Rio Grande Valley Areas of Our Nation's Southwest Border," *The White House,* 30 June 2014, accessed 29 December 2017, https://obamawhitehouse.archives.gov/the-press-office/2014/06/30/letter- president-efforts-address-humanitarian-situation-rio-grande-valle.

4. David Bacon, "Tea Party and Border Patrol Spin the Story of Children in Detention," *Counterpunch,* 26 June 2014, accessed 4 November 2017, http:// www.counterpunch.org/2014/06/26/tea-party-and-border-patrol-spin-the -story-of-children-in-detention/.

5. Bethany Stotts, "Obama's Manufactured Border Crisis," *Accuracy in Media,* 20 June 2014, accessed 29 December 2017, http://www.aim.org/aim -column/obamas-manufactured-border-crisis/.

6. Jeff Sessions, "Sessions: President Obama Is Personally Responsible for 'Rising Crisis' at Border," *Jeff Sessions: United States Senator for Alabama,* 3 June 2014, accessed 9 September 2016, http://www.sessions.senate.gov/public /index.cfm/news-releases?ID=78815d9b-40f6-4c2c-88e8-b119271ae845.

7. Veronica Escobar, "Why the Border Crisis Is a Myth," *New York Times,* 25 July 2014, accessed 29 December 2017, http://www.nytimes.com/2014/07/26 /opinion/why-the-border-crisis-is-a-myth.html.

8. Lind, "Inside the Remote, Secretive Detention Center."

9. Sibylla Brodzinsky and Ed Pilkington, "US Government Deporting Central American Migrants to Their Deaths," *The Guardian,* 12 October 2015, accessed 29 December 2017, https://www.theguardian.com/us-news/2015 /oct/12/obama-immigration-deportations-central-america.

10. Stephen W. Manning, *Ending Artesia: The Report,* 2014, accessed 29 December 2017, https://innovationlawlab.org/the-artesia-report-story/.

11. The White House, "Remarks to the Press with Q&A by Vice President Joe Biden in Guatemala," *The White House,* 20 June 2014, accessed 29 December 2017, https://obamawhitehouse.archives.gov/the-press-office/2014/06/20/remarks-press-qa-vice-president-joe-biden-guatemala.

12. Jeh Johnson, "Statement by Secretary of Homeland Security Jeh Johnson before the Senate Committee on Appropriations," *US Department of Homeland Security,* 10 July 2014, accessed 29 December 2017, https://www.dhs.gov/news/2014/07/10/statement-secretary-homeland-security-jeh-johnson-senate-committee-appropriations.

13. Manning, *Ending Artesia.*

14. Ibid., emphasis in original.

15. Chico Harlan, "Inside the Administration's $1 Billion Deal to Detain Central American Asylum Seekers," *Washington Post,* 14 August 2016, accessed 29 December 2017, https://www.washingtonpost.com/business/economy/inside-the-administrations-1-billion-deal-to-detain-central-american-asylum-seekers/2016/08/14/e47f1960-5819-11e6-9aee-8075993d73a2_story.html.

16. Julián Aguilar, "Judge Blocks License for Immigration Detention Facility," *The Texas Tribune,* 1 June 2016, accessed 29 December 2017, https://www.texastribune.org/2016/06/01/judge-blocks-state-licensing-detention-facility-ch/.

17. Kyle Barron and Cinthya Santos Briones, "No Alternative: Ankle Monitors Expand the Reach of Immigration Detention," *NACLA,* 6 January 2015, accessed 29 December 2017, http://nacla.org/news/2015/01/06/no-alternative-ankle-monitors-expand-reach-immigration-detention. Marlon Bishop, "The Garifuna Exodus," *Latino USA,* 23 January 2015, accessed 29 December 2017, http://latinousa.org/2015/01/23/garifuna-exodus/.

18. AFP, "Update: 10 US-Bound Migrants Drown in Southern Nicaragua," *Tico Times,* 3 August 2016, accessed 29 December 2017, http://www.ticotimes.net/2016/08/03/eight-us-bound-migrants-drown-southern-nicaragua.

19. Kavitha Surana, "Italy Quietly Rejects Asylum Seekers by Nationality, Advocates Say," *Al Jazeera America,* 19 October 2015, accessed 29 December 2017, http://america.aljazeera.com/articles/2015/10/19/italy-quietly-rejects-asylum-seekers-based-on-nationality-advocates-say.html.

20. Julia Edwards, "U.S. Seeks Latin American Help Amid Rise in Asian, African Migrants," *Reuters,* 24 August 2016, accessed 29 December 2017, http://www.reuters.com/article/us-usa-immigration-mexico-exclusive-idUSKCN10RoDD.

21. "Suriname Clamping Down on Illegal Haitian Travel," *Jamaica Observer,* 7 September 2016, accessed 29 December 2017, http://www.jamaicaobserver.com/news/Suriname-clamping-down-on-illegal-Haitian-travel.

22. Emily Gogolak, "Haitian Migrants Turn toward Brazil," *The New Yorker,* 20 August 2014, accessed 29 December 2017, http://www.newyorker.com/news/news-desk/haitian-migrants-turn-toward-brazil.

23. Gage Norris, "San Diego Church Working to Transition Thousands of Haitian Migrants Fleeing Brazil," *The Haitian Times* 24 August 2016, accessed 29 December 2017, http://haitiantimes.com/san-diego-church-working-to-transition-thousands-of-haitian-migrants-fleeing-brazil-15279/.

24. "RBDF Apprehends Undocumented Cuban and Haitian Nationals," *The Eleutheran,* 9 September 2016, accessed 29 December 2017, http://www.eleutheranews.com/permalink/5474.html.

25. Alina Dieste, "There Are Many Who Die in the Jungle," *AFP.com,* 8 September 2016, accessed 29 December 2017, https://correspondent.afp.com/there-are-many-who-die-jungle.

26. Jim Wyss, "Colombia Deports 1,350 Travelers Amid Crackdown on Cuban Migrants," *Miami Herald,* 9 August 2016, accessed 29 December 2017, http://www.miamiherald.com/latest-news/article94548632.html.

27. Ibid. Nina Lakhani, "Passage through Mexico: The Global Migration to the US," *The Guardian,* 6 September 2016, accessed 29 December 2017, https://www.theguardian.com/global-development/2016/sep/06/mexico-african-asian-migration-us-exit-permit.

28. "Tougher Europe Borders Push More Migrants towards US," *The Express Tribune,* 23 July 2016, accessed 29 December 2017, http://tribune.com.pk/story/1147547/tougher-europe-borders-push-migrants-towards-us/.

29. Lakhani, "Passage through Mexico."

30. Ibid.

31. Dieste, "There Are Many Who Die in the Jungle."

32. Nina Lakhani, "US and Mexico's Mass Deportations Have Fueled Humanitarian Crisis, Report Says," *The Guardian,* 27 July 2016, accessed 29 December 2017, https://www.theguardian.com/world/2016/jul/27/us-mexico-mass-deportations-refugees-central-america.

33. UNODC Statistics. "Homicide counts and rates (2000-2015)," United Nations Office on Drugs and Crime, accessed 26 October 2017, https://data.unodc.org/#state:1.

34. Nina Lakhani, "Surge in Central American Migrants at US Border Threatens Repeat of 2014 Crisis," *The Guardian,* 13 January 2016, accessed 29 December 2017, https://www.theguardian.com/us-news/2016/jan/13/central-american-migration-family-children-detention-at-us-border.

35. Stephanie Nolen, "Southern Exposure: The Costly Border Plan Mexico Won't Discuss," *The Globe and Mail,* 31 August 2016, accessed 17 September 2016, http://www.theglobeandmail.com/news/world/the-costly-border-mexico-wont-discuss-migration/article30397720/.

36. Amanda Holpuch, "US Partners with Costa Rica to Protect Central American Refugees," *The Guardian,* 26 July 2016, accessed 29 December 2017, https://www.theguardian.com/world/2016/jul/26/central-american-refugees-costa-rica-obama-administration. Carrie Kahn, "Costa Rica Strains to Handle Central Americans Fleeing Violence," *NPR Morning Edition,* 22 August 2016, accessed 29 December 2017, http://www.npr.org/2016/08/22/490895595/costa-rica-strains-to-handle-central-americans-fleeing-violence.

37. Zach Dyer, "Costa Rica to Host Central Americans Seeking Asylum in US," *Tico Times,* 26 July 2016, accessed 29 December 2017, http://www.ticotimes.net/2016/07/26/costa-rica-to-host-central-americans-seeking-asylum-in-usa.

38. Lazaro Zamora, "Administration Attempts to Adapt as Central American Flow Continues," *Bipartisan Policy Center,* 23 August 2016, accessed 29

December 2017, http://bipartisanpolicy.org/blog/administration-attempts-to
-adapt-to-central-american-flow/.

39. "Hillary Clinton: Unaccompanied Child Migrants 'Should Be Sent Back'
to Central America," *Fox News,* 18 June 2014, accessed 29 December 2017,
http://www.foxnews.com/politics/2014/06/18/hillary-clinton-unaccompanied
-child-migrants-should-be-sent-back-home.html.

40. Kathleen Harris. Nearly half of illegal border-crossers into Canada are
from Haiti. CBC News, 22 November 2017, accessed 30 December 2017. http://
www.cbc.ca/news/politics/haiti-border-crossers-canada-irregular-1.4414781.
Nicholas Keung, "New data show 69% of illegal border-crossers are being
granted asylum." *The Toronto Star,* 19 October 2017, accessed 30 December
2017. https://www.thestar.com/news/canada/2017/10/19/new-data-show-69-of
-illegal-border-crossers-are-being-granted-asylum.html.

41. Viet Thanh Nguyen, "The Hidden Scars All Refugees Carry," *The New
York Times,* 2 September 2016, accessed 29 December 2017, http://www
.nytimes.com/2016/09/03/opinion/the-hidden-scars-all-refugees-carry.html.

42. Daniel Rivero, "Junot Diaz and Edwidge Danticat Jointly Speak Out
against Dominican Republic Refugee Crisis," *Splinter* 25 June 2015, accessed
29 December 2017, https://splinternews.com/junot-diaz-and-edwidge-danticat-
jointly-speak-out-again-1793848659.

43. "Children Held at Berks Threaten School Strike Amid Parents' Hunger
Strike," *Democracy Now!,* 8 September 2016, accessed 29 December 2017,
http://www.democracynow.org/2016/9/8/headlines/children_held_at_berks
_threaten_school_strike_amid_parents_hunger_strike.

44. 1Love Cambodia, "Open Letter from Cambodian Deportees to Our
Community in the United States," *1LoveMovement,* 21 April 2016, accessed 29
December 2017, https://1lovemovement.wordpress.com/2016/04/21/statement
-from-cambodian-deportees/.

References

Agambem, G. 1998. *Homo Sacer: Sovereign Power and Bare Life.* Stanford: Stanford University Press.

Agnew, J. 1994. "The Territorial Trap: The Geographical Assumptions of International Relations Theory." *Review of International Political Economy* 1 (1): 53–80.

Allspach, A. 2010. "Landscapes of (Neo-)liberal Control: The Transcarceral Spaces of Federally Sentenced Women in Canada." *Gender Place and Culture* 17: 705–23.

American Civil Liberties Union. 2014. *Warehoused and Forgotten: Immigrants Trapped in Our Shadow Private Prison System.* New York: ACLU and ACLU of Texas. Available from: https://www.aclu.org/sites/default/files/assets /060614-aclu-car-reportonline.pdf. Last accessed: 28 October 2017.

American Immigration Council. 2015. "Border Patrol 'Hieleras'—Background and Legal Action." Available from: https://www.americanimmigrationcouncil .org/sites/default/files/other_litigation_documents/border_patrol_hieleras _-_background_and_legal_action.pdf. Last accessed: 28 October 2017.

———. 2017. "A Primer on Expedited Removal." Available from: https:// www.americanimmigrationcouncil.org/research/primer-expedited-removal. Last accessed: 28 October 2017.

Andersson, R. 2014. *Illegality, Inc.: Clandestine Migration and the Business of Bordering Europe.* Oakland: University of California Press.

Andreas, P. 2009. *Border Games: Policing the U.S.-Mexico Divide.* 2nd ed. Ithaca: Cornell University Press.

Andreas, P., and E. Nadelmann. 2008. *Policing the Globe: Criminalization and Crime Control in International Relations.* New York: Oxford University Press.

Ashutosh, I., and A. Mountz. 2012. "The Geopolitics of Migrant Mobility: Tracing State Relations through Refugee Claims, Boats, and Discourses." *Geopolitics* 17: 335–54.

Bailey, A., R. Wright, A. Mountz, and I. Miyares. 2002. "(Re)Producing Salvadoran Transnational Geographies." *Annals of the Association of American Geographers* 92 (1): 125–44.

Bejarano, C., C. Morales, and S. Saddiki. 2012. "Understanding Conquest through a Border Lens: A Comparative Analysis of the Mexico-U.S. and Morocco-Spain Regions." In *Beyond Walls and Cages: Prisons, Borders and Global Crisis*, edited by J.M. Loyd, M. Mitchelson, and A. Burridge, 27–41. Athens: University of Georgia Press.

Benton, L. 2010. *A Search for Sovereignty: Law and Geography in European Empires, 1400–1900.* Cambridge: Cambridge University Press.

Bersin, A.D. 1996. "Reinventing Immigration Law Enforcement in the Southern District of California." *Federal Sentencing Reporter* 8 (5): 254–58.

Bialawicz, L. 2012. "Off-shoring and Out-sourcing the Borders of Europe: Libya and EU Border Work in the Mediterranean." *Geopolitics* 17 (4): 843–66.

Blum, C.P. 1991. "The Settlement of *American Baptist Churches v. Thornburgh*: Landmark Victory for Central American Asylum-seekers." *International Journal of Refugee Law* 3: 347–56.

Bonds, A. 2006. "Profit from Punishment?: The Politics of Prisons, Poverty and Neoliberal Restructuring in the Rural American Northwest." *Antipode* 38: 174–77.

———. 2009. "Discipline and Devolution: Constructions of Poverty, Race, and Criminality in the Politics of Rural Prison Development." *Antipode* 41: 416–38.

———. 2015. "From Private to Public: Examining the Political Economy of Wisconsin's Private Prison Experiment." In *The Historical Geography of Jails and Prisons*, edited by K. Morin & D. Moran, 205–18. New York and London: Routledge.

Bon Tempo, C. 2008. *Americans at the Gate: The United States and Refugees during the Cold War.* Princeton, NJ, and Oxford: Princeton University Press.

Boswell, T.D. 1983. "In the Eye of the Storm: The Context of Haitian Migration to Miami, Florida." *Southeastern Geographer* 23 (2): 57–77.

Bosworth, M. 2009. *Explaining U.S. Imprisonment.* Thousand Oaks, CA: SAGE Publications.

———. 2014. *Inside Immigration Detention.* Oxford: Oxford University Press.

Bosworth, M., and E. Kaufman. 2011. "Foreigners in a Carceral Age: Immigration and Imprisonment in the United States." *Stanford Law & Policy Review* 22 (2): 429–54.

Boyce, G., and S. Launius. 2013. "Warehousing the Poor: How Federal Prosecution Initiatives like 'Operation Streamline' Hurt Immigrants, Drive Mass Incarceration and Damage U.S. Communities." *Different Take* 82 (Fall): 1–4.

Boyce, G.A., J.M. Banister, and J. Slack. 2015. "You and What Army? Violence, the State, and Mexico's War on Drugs." *Territory, Politics, Governance* 3: 446–68.

Brathwaite, K. 2007. *DS (2): Dreamstories 2*. New York: New Directions Publishing.

Brigden, N.K. 2016. "Improvised Transnationalism: Clandestine Migration at the Border of Anthropology and International Relations." *International Studies Quarterly* 60 (2): 343–54.

Bryan, J. 2015. "War without End?: Military Humanitarianism and the Limits of Biopolitical Approaches to Security in Central America and the Caribbean." *Political Geography* 47: 33–42.

Buff, R.I. 2008. "The Deportation Terror." *American Quarterly* 60 (3): 523–51.

Bureau of Justice Statistics. 1988. *Our Crowded Jails: A National Plight*. Washington, D.C.: Department of Justice.

Burnett, C.D. 2005. "The Edges of Empire and Limits of Sovereignty: American Guano Islands." *American Quarterly* 57 (3): 779–803.

Burridge, A. 2009. "Differential Criminalization under Operation Streamline: Challenges to Freedom of Movement and Humanitarian Aid Provision in the Mexico-US Borderlands." *Refuge: Canada's Journal on Refugees* 26 (2): 78–91.

Butler, J. 2004. *Precarious Life: The Powers of Mourning and Violence*. New York: Verso.

Cacho, L.M. 2012. *Social Death: Racialized Rightlessness and the Criminalization of the Unprotected*. New York: New York University Press.

Calavita, K. 1992. *Inside the State: The Bracero Program, Immigration, and the I.N.S.* New York: Routledge.

———. 1996. "The New Politics of Immigration: 'Balanced-budget Conservatism' and the Symbolism of Proposition 187." *Social Problems* 43 (3): 284–305.

Camacho, K.L. 2012. "After 9/11: Militarized Borders and Social Movements in the Mariana Islands." *American Quarterly* 64 (4): 685–713.

Camp, J.T., and C. Heatherton. 2016. *Policing the Planet: Why Policing the Crisis Led to Black Lives Matter*. London: Verso.

Canaday, M. 2009. *The Straight State: Sexuality and Citizenship in Twentieth-Century America*. Princeton, NJ: Princeton University Press.

Chacón, J.M. 2007. "Unsecured Borders, Crime Control and National Security." *Connecticut Law Review* 39 (5): 1827–91.

———. 2009. "Managing Migration through Crime." *Columbia Law Review* 109: 135–48.

———. 2015. "Producing Legal Liminality." *Denver University Law Review* 92 (4): 709–67.

Chávez, K. 2012. "ACT UP, Haitian Migrants, and Alternative Memories of HIV/AIDS." *Quarterly Journal of Speech* 98: 63–68.

Cházaro, A. 2016. "Challenging the 'Criminal Alien' Paradigm." *UCLA Law Review* 63: 594–664.

Chazkel, A., M. Pappademos, and K. Sotiropoulos. 2013. "Editors' Introduction: Haitian Lives/Global Perspectives." *Radical History Review* 115: 1–9. doi:10.1215/01636545-1724679.

Cheng, W. 2013. *The Changs Next Door to the Díazes: Remapping Race in Suburban California*. Minneapolis: University of Minnesota Press.

Chimni, B.S. 1995. "The Incarceration of Victims: Deconstructing Safety Zones." In *International Legal Issues Arising under the United Nations Decade of International Law, Proceedings of the Qatar International Law Conference 1994,* edited by N. Al Nauimi and R. Meese, 823–54. Boston: Martinus Nijhoff.

Chishti, M., S. Pierce, and J. Bolter. 2017. "The Obama Record on Deportations: Deporter in Chief or Not?" *Migration Policy Institute.* Available from: https://www.migrationpolicy.org/article/obama-record-deportations -deporter-chief-or-not, Last accessed 31 October 2017.

Coddington, K.R., T. Catania, J. Loyd, E. Mitchell-Eaton, and A. Mountz. 2012. "Embodied Possibilities, Sovereign Geographies, and Island Detention: Negotiating the 'Right to Have Rights' on Guam, Lampedusa, and Christmas Island." *Shima* 6 (2): 27–48.

Coleman, M. 2007a. "A Geopolitics of Engagement: Neoliberalism, the War on Terrorism, and the Reconfiguration of US Immigration Enforcement." *Geopolitics* 12: 607–34.

———. 2007b. "Immigration Geopolitics beyond the Mexico-US Border." *Antipode* 39: 54–76.

———. 2008. "US Immigration Law and Its Geographies of Social Control: Lessons from Homosexual Exclusion during the Cold War." *Environment and Planning D: Society & Space* 26: 1096–114.

Conlon, D., and N. Hiemstra, eds. 2017. Intimate Economies of Immigration Detention: Critical perspectives. New York: Routledge.

Cotter, C.P., and J.M. Smith. 1957. "An American Paradox: The Emergency Detention Act of 1950." *The Journal of Politics* 19: 20–33.

Coutin, S.B. 2000. "Denationalization, Inclusion, and Exclusion: Negotiating the Boundaries of Belonging." *Indiana Journal of Global Legal Studies* 7: 585–91.

———. 2003. *Legalizing Moves: Salvadoran Immigrants' Struggle for US Residency.* Ann Arbor: University of Michigan Press.

———.2010. "Exiled by Law: Deportation and the Inviability of Life." In *The Deportation Regime: Sovereignty, Space, and the Freedom of Movement,* edited by N. De Genova and N. Peutz, 351–71. Durham, NC: Duke University Press.

———. 2011. "Falling Outside: Excavating the History of Central American Asylum Seekers." *Law & Social Inquiry* 26: 569–96.

D'Amato, A.M. 1983. "Aliens in Prison—The Federal Response to a New Criminal Justice Emergency." *Detroit College of Law Review* 4: 1162–69.

Danticat, E. 2007. *Brother, I'm Dying.* New York: Vintage Books.

Dastyari, A. 2015. *United States Migrant Interdiction and the Detention of Refugees in Guantánamo Bay.* New York: Cambridge University Press.

Davis, S. 2011. "The US Military Base Network and Contemporary Colonialism: Power Projection, Resistance and the Quest for Operational Unilateralism." *Political Geography* 30 (4): 215–24.

———. 2015. *The Empire's Edge: Militarization, Resistance, and Transcending Hegemony in the Pacific.* Athens and London: University of Georgia Press.

Debord, G. (1967) 1994. *The Society of the Spectacle.* New York: Zone Books.

De Genova, N. 2002. "Migrant 'Illegality' and Deportability in Everyday Life." *Annual Review of Anthropology* 31: 419–47.

De Genova, N., and N. Peutz, eds. 2010. *The Deportation Regime: Sovereignty, Space, and the Freedom of Movement.* Durham, NC: Duke University Press.

Department of the Army. 1982 *Task Force Resettlement Operation After Action Report—Fort Chaffee, Arkansas, 7 May 1980–19 February 1982.* Fort Sill, Oklahoma: Department of the Army.

Department of the Army, Operations and Readiness Directorate. 1977. *After Action Report: Operations New Life/New Arrivals US Army Support to the Indochinese Refugee Program, 1 April 1975–1 June 1976.* Washington, D.C.: Department of the Army Office of the Deputy Chief of Staff for Operations and Plans.

Dominguez Villegas, R., and V. Rietig. 2015. *Migrants Deported from the United States and Mexico to the Northern Triangle: A Statistical and Socioeconomic Profile.* Washington, D.C.: Migration Policy Institute. http://www.migrationpolicy.org/research/migrants-deported-united-states-and-mexico-northern-triangle-statistical-and-socioeconomic. Last accessed: 27 October 2017.

Dow, M. 2004. *American Gulag: Inside US Immigration Prisons.* Berkeley: University of California Press.

Dowling, J.A., and J.X. Inda, eds. 2013. *Governing Immigration through Crime: A Reader.* Stanford, CA: Stanford Social Sciences.

Dubois, L. 2012. *Haiti: The Aftershocks of History.* New York: Picador.

Dunn, T.J. 1996. *The Militarization of the US-Mexico Border, 1978–1992: Low-Intensity Conflict Doctrine Comes Home.* Austin: CMAS Books, University of Texas at Austin.

Eagly, I.V., and S. Shafer. 2015. "A National Study of Access to Counsel in Immigration Court." *University of Pennsylvania Law Review* 164 (1): 1–91.

Enloe, C. 2014. *Bananas, Beaches, and Bases,* revised and updated ed. Berkeley: University of California Press.

Escobar, M.D. 2016. *Captivity Beyond Prisons: Criminalization Experiences of Latina (Im)migrants.* Austin: University of Texas Press.

Espiritu, Y.L. 2006. "Toward a Critical Refugee Study: The Vietnamese Refugee Subject in US Scholarship." *Journal of Vietnamese Studies* 1: 410–33.

———. 2014. *Body Counts: The Vietnam War and Militarized Refugees.* Berkeley: University of California Press.

Farmer, P. 2006 (1992). *AIDS and Accusation: Haiti and the Geography of Blame.* Berkeley: University of California Press.

———. 2004. *Pathologies of Power: Health, Human Rights, and the New War on the Poor.* Berkeley: University of California Press.

Fassin, D., and R. Rechtman. 2009. *The Empire of Trauma: An Inquiry into the Condition of Victimhood.* Princeton, NJ: Princeton University Press.

Feldman, C.H. 1993. "The Immigration Act of 1990: Congress Continues to Aggravate the Criminal Alien." *Seton Hall Legislative Journal* 17: 201–33.

Ferrer, A. 2016. "History and the Idea of Hispanic Caribbean Studies." *Small Axe* 20 (3) 51: 49–64. doi:0.1215/07990537-3726854.

Fitzpatrick, J. 1994. "Flight from Asylum: Trends toward Temporary 'Refuge' and Local Responses to Forced Migrations." *Virginia Journal of International Law* 35: 13–70.

Foley, N. 2007. "'God Bless the Law, He Is White': Legal, Local, and International Politics of Latina/o and Black Desegregation Cases in Post–World War II California and Texas." In *A Companion to Latina/o Studies,* edited by J. Flores and R. Resaldo, 297–312. Malden, MA: Blackwell.

Foucault M. (1978) 1995. *Discipline and Punish: The Birth of the Prison.* New York: Vintage Books.

Frelick, B. 1989. *Refugees at Our Border: The U.S. Response to Asylum Seekers, The U.S. Committee for Refugees Issue Brief.* Washington, D.C.: U.S. Committee for Refugees, American Council for Nationalities Service.

———. 1993. "Haitian Boat Interdiction and Return: First Asylum and First Principles of Refugee Protection." *Cornell International Law Journal* 26: 675–94.

———. 1994. "U.S. Safe Haven Camps in Cuba and Panama—A Study in Contrasts." *Refugee Reports* 15: 14–19.

Frenzen, N. 2010. "US Migrant Interdiction: Practices in International and Territorial Waters." In *Extraterritorial Immigration Control: Legal Challenges,* edited by B. Ryan and V. Mitsilegas, 375–96. Leiden, Netherlands: Brill.

García Hernández, C.C. 2011. "Due Process and Immigrant Detainee Prison Transfers: Moving LPRs to Isolated Prisons Violates Their Right to Counsel." *Berkeley La Raza Law Journal* 21: 17–60.

Garcilazo, J.M. 2001. "McCarthyism, Mexican Americans, and the Los Angeles Committee for the Protection of the Foreign Born, 1950–1954." *Western Historical Quarterly* 32: 273–95.

Gati, C., ed. 2013. *Zbig: The Strategy and Statecraft of Zbigniew Brzezinski.* Baltimore: The Johns Hopkins University Press.

General Accounting Office. 1983. *Detention Policies Affecting Haitian Nationals.* Washington, D.C.: Government Printing Office.

———. 1989. *Criminal Aliens: INS Enforcement.* Washington, D.C.: Government Printing Office.

———. 1992. *Immigration Control: Immigration Policies Affect INS Detention Efforts.* Washington, D.C.: Government Printing Office.

———. 1995. *Military Bases: Case Studies on Selected Bases Closed in 1988 and 1991.* Washington, D.C.: Government Printing Office.

———. 1997. *Criminal Aliens: INS' Efforts to Identify and Remove Imprisoned Aliens Need to Be Improved.* Washington, D.C.: Government Printing Office.

———. 1999. *Criminal Aliens: INS' Efforts to Identify and Remove Imprisoned Aliens Continue to Need Improvement.* Washington, D.C.: Government Printing Office.

Gilmore, R. W. 2002. "Race and Globalization." In *Geographies of Global Change: Remapping the World,* 2nd ed., edited by R. J. Johnston, P. J. Taylor, and M. J. Watts, 261–274. Malden, MA: Blackwell.

———. 2007. *Golden Gulag: Labor, Land, State, and Opposition in Globalizing California.* Berkeley: University of California Press.

Goffman, E. 1961. *Asylums: Essays on the Social Situation of Mental Patients and Other Inmates.* New York: Anchor Books.

Golash-Boza, T.M. 2012. *Immigration Nation: Raids, Detention, and Deportations in Post-9/11 America.* Boulder, CO: Paradigm Press.

———. 2015. *Deported: Immigration Policing, Disposable Labor, and Global Capitalism.* New York: New York University Press.

Golden, R., and M. McConnell. 1986. *Sanctuary: The New Underground Railroad.* Maryknoll, NY: Orbis Books.

Gollobin, I. 1978. "Foreign Born: Dragnets and Amnesty." *Bill of Rights Journal* 11: 18–19.

Goodwin-Gill, G.S. 2011. "The Right to Seek Asylum: Interception at Sea and the Principle of *Non-Refoulement.*" *International Journal of Refugee Law* 23 (3): 443–57.

———. 2017. "Setting the Scene: Refugees, Asylum Seekers, and Migrants at Sea—The Need for a Long-term, Protection Centered Vision." In *"Boat Refugees" and Migrants at Sea: A Comprehensive Approach,* edited by V. Lax-Moreno and E. Papastavridis, 17–31. Leiden, Netherlands: Brill.

Greene, J., B. Carson, and A. Black. 2016. *Indefensible: A Decade of Mass Incarceration of Migrants Prosecuted for Crossing the Border.* Austin, TX, and Brooklyn, NY: Grassroots Leadership and Justice Strategies. Available from: https://grassrootsleadership.org/reports/indefensible-decade-mass-incarceration-migrants-prosecuted-crossing-border. Last accessed: 28 October 2017.

Greene, J., and A. Mazón. 2012. *Privately Operated Federal Prisons for Immigrants: Expensive, Unsafe, Unnecessary.* Brooklyn, NY: Justice Strategies. Available from: https://www.justicestrategies.net/publications/2012/privately-operated-federal-prisons-immigrants-expensive-unsafe-unnecessary. Last accessed: 28 October 2017.

Gregory, D. 2004. *The Colonial Present.* Malden, MA: Blackwell.

———. 2007. "Vanishing Points: Law, Violence, and Exception in the Global War Prison." In *Violent Geographies,* edited by D. Gregory and A. Pred, 205–36. New York: Routledge.

Grosfoguel, R., N. Maldonado-Torres, and J.D. Saldívar. 2005. *Latin@s in the World-System: Decolonization Struggles in the 21st Century U.S. Empire.* Boulder, CO: Paradigm Publishers.

Guerrero, P.M. 2016. "Yellow Peril in Arkansas: War, Christianity, and the Regional Racialization of Vietnamese Refugees." *Kalfou: A Journal of Comparative and Relational Ethnic Studies* 3 (2): 230–52.

Gwynn, E.B. 1986. "Immigration Law—Race and National Origin Discrimination and the Haitian Detainees—*Jean v. Nelson,* 105 S. Ct. 2992 (1985)." *Florida State University Law Review* 14: 333–57.

Hahamovitch, C. 2011. *No Man's Land: Jamaican Guestworkers in America and the Global History of Deportable Labor.* Princeton, NJ: Princeton University Press.

Haitian Refugee Center v. Civiletti. 1980. 503 F. Supp. 442 (S.D. Fla. 1980).

Haley, S. 2016. *No Mercy Here: Gender, Punishment, and the Making of Jim Crow Modernity.* Chapel Hill: The University of North Carolina Press.

Hall, S., C. Critcher, T. Jefferson, J. Clarke, and B. Roberts. 1978. *Policing the Crisis: Mugging, the State, and Law and Order.* New York: Holmes & Meier Publishers, Inc.

Hallman, H. 2017. "Deportation Without a Hearing: A Primer." *Bipartisan Policy Center,* https://bipartisanpolicy.org/blog/deportation-without-a-hearing-a-primer/. Accessed 31 October 2017.

Hamlin, R. 2012. "Illegal Refugees: Competing Policy Ideas and the Rise of the Regime of Deterrence in American Asylum Politics." *Refugee Survey Quarterly* 31 (2): 33–53.

Hamann, J. 2005. *On American Soil: How Justice Became a Casualty of World War II.* Seattle: University of Washington Press.

Hammer, Z. "Community, Identity, and Political Struggle: Challenging Immigrant Prisons in Arizona." In *Beyond Walls and Cages: Prisons, Borders and Global Crisis,* edited by J.M. Loyd, M. Mitchelson, and A. Burridge, 215–27. Athens: University of Georgia Press.

Hammer-Tomizuka, Z. 2004. *Criminal Alienation: Arizona Prison Expansion, 1993–2003.* PhD dissertation, University of Arizona.

Harvard Immigration and Refugee Clinical Program. 2017. "The Impact of President Trump's Executive Orders on Asylum Seekers." https://today.law.harvard.edu/wp-content/uploads/2017/02/Report-Impact-of-Trump-Executive-Orders-on-Asylum-Seekers.pdf. Accessed 14 November 2017.

Harvard Law Today. 2017. "Harvard releases report on effect of Trump's executive orders on asylum seekers," 8 February. https://today.law.harvard.edu/harvard-releases-first-report-effect-trumps-executive-orders-asylum-seekers/. Accessed 30 December 2017.

Hawk, K.D., R. Villela, A.L. de Varona, and K. Cifers. 2014. *Florida and the Mariel Boatlift of 1980: The First Twenty Days.* Tuscaloosa: The University of Alabama Press.

Heisler, B.S. 2007. "The 'Other Braceros': Temporary Labor and German Prisoners of War in the United States, 1943–1946." *Social Science History* 31 (2): 239–71.

Helton, A.C. 1986. "The Legality of Detaining Refugees in the United States." *New York University Review of Law & Social Change* 14: 353–81.

Hernández, D.M. 2008. "Pursuant to Deportation: Latinos and Immigrant Detention." *Latino Studies* 6: 35–63.

———. 2013. "A Place Reeking with Rottenness: The Valente Detention Home and Contemporary Private Detention." Paper presented at American Studies Association, Washington, D.C.

———. 2016. "Surrogates and Subcontractors: Flexibility and Obscurity in U.S. Immigrant Detention." In *Critical Ethnic Studies: A Reader,* edited by N. Elia, D.M. Hernández, J. Kim, S. Redmond, D. Rodríguez, and S.E. See, 303–25. Durham, NC: Duke University Press.

Hernández, K.L. 2010. *Migra!: A History of the US Border Patrol.* Berkeley: University of California Press.

Heyman, J. 2004. "Ports of Entry as Nodes in the World System." *Identities: Global Studies in Culture and Power* 11 (3): 303–27.

Hiemstra, N. 2012. "Geopolitical Reverberations of U.S. Migrant Detention and Deportation: The View from Ecuador." *Geopolitics* 17 (2): 293–311.

———. 2013. "'You Don't Even Know Where You Are': Chaotic Geographies of U.S. Migrant Detention and Deportation." In *Carceral Spaces: Mobility and Agency in Imprisonment and Migrant Detention,* edited by D. Moran, N. Gill, and D. Conlon, 57–75. Surrey, England: Ashgate.

Hiemstra, N., and D. Conlon. 2017. "Beyond privatization: spatialities of immigration detention expansion." Territory, Politics, Governance 5(3): 252–268.

Hodge, P. 2015. "A Grievable Life? The Criminalisation and Securing of Asylum Seeker Bodies in the 'Violent Frames' of Australia's *Operation Sovereign Borders*." *Geoforum* 58: 122–31.

Hooks, G., C. Mosher, S. Genter, T. Rotolo, and L. Lobao. 2010. "Revisiting the Impact of Prison Building on Job Growth: Education, Incarceration, and County- Level Employment, 1976–2004." *Social Science Quarterly* 91 (1): 228–44.

Huling, T. 2003. "Building a Prison Economy in Rural America." In *Invisible Punishment: The Collateral Consequences of Mass Imprisonment,* edited by M. Chesney-Lind and M. Mauer, 197–213. New York: The New Press.

Human Rights Watch. 1998. *Locked Away: Immigration Detainees in Jails in the United States.* Available from: http://www.hrw.org/legacy/reports98/us-immig/. Last accessed: 28 October 2017.

———. 2009. *Locked Up Far Away: The Transfer of Immigrants to Remote Detention Centers in the United States.* Available from: https://www.hrw.org/sites/default/files/reports/us1209webwcover.pdf. Last accessed: 28 October 2017.

Hyndman, J. 2000. *Managing Displacement: Refugees and the Politics of Humanitarianism.* Minneapolis: University of Minnesota Press.

———. 2003. "Preventive, Palliative, or Punitive? Safe Spaces in Bosnia-Herzegovina, Somalia, and Sri Lanka." *Journal of Refugee Studies* 16 (2): 167–85.

———. 2007. "The Securitization of Fear in Post-Tsunami Sri Lanka." *Annals of the Association of American Geographers* 97 (2): 361–72.

Hyndman, J., and W. Giles. 2017. *Refugees in Extended Exile: Living on the Edge.* New York: Routledge.

Hyndman, J., and A. Mountz. 2008. "Another brick in the wall? 'Neo-refoulement' and the externalisation of asylum in Australia and Europe." *Government and Opposition* 43(2): 249–269.

Inda, J. X. 2013. "Subject to Deportation: IRCA, 'Criminal Aliens,' and the Policing of Immigration." *Migration Studies* 1 (3): 292–310.

International Crisis Group. 2016. *Easy Prey: Criminal Violence and Central American Migration.* Available from: https://www.crisisgroup.org/latin-america-caribbean/central-america/easy-prey-criminal-violence-and-central-american-migration. Last accessed: 28 October 2017.

James, J. 1996. *Resisting State Violence: Radicalism, Gender, and Race in U.S. Culture.* Minneapolis: University of Minnesota Press.

Joint Task Force 160. 1996. *Operation Sea Signal: Joint Task Force 160: After Action Report: 17 May 1994–2 February 1996, Guantanamo Bay, Cuba.* Fort Monroe, VA: Joint Warfighting Center.

Kahn, J. S. 2013. *Islands of Sovereignty: Haitian Migration and the Borders of Empire.* Ph.D. dissertation, The University of Chicago.

Kahn, R. S. 1996. *Other People's Blood: U.S. Immigration Prisons in the Reagan Decade.* Boulder, CO: Westview Press.

Kanstroom, D. 2007. *Deportation Nation: Outsiders in American History.* Cambridge, MA: Harvard University Press.

———. 2012. *Aftermath: Deportation Law and the New American Diaspora.* Oxford: Oxford University Press.

Kaplan, A. 2005. "Where Is Guantánamo?" *American Quarterly* 57 (3): 831–58.

Karacki, L. 1989. "Serious Prison Infractions: Differences between the 70's and 80's." *Federal Prisons Journal* 1: 31–35.

Kelly, J. 2017. "Implementing the President's Border Security and Immigration Enforcement Improvements Policies." Department of Homeland Security, https://www.dhs.gov/sites/default/files/publications/17_0220_S1_Implementing -the-Presidents-Border-Security-Immigration-Enforcement-Improvement -Policies.pdf. Accessed 31 October 2017.

Kennedy, R., dir. 2014. *Last Days in Vietnam.* PBS.

Kim, C. J. 1999. "The Racial Triangulation of Asian Americans." *Politics & Society* 27 (1): 105–38.

Kim, C., and J. M. Loyd. 2008. "Is Riding the Bus a Ticket to Jail?" *ColorLines,* 12 June.

Kocher, A. 2017. "The New Resistance: Immigrant Rights Mobilization in an Era of Trump." *Journal of Latin American Geography* 16(2): 165–171.

Koh, H. H. 1994a. "America's Offshore Refugee Camps." *University of Richmond Law Review* 29 (1): 139–73.

———. 1994b. "The 'Haiti Paradigm' in United States Human Rights Policy." *The Yale Law Journal* 103 (8): 2391–435.

———. 1994c. "Reflections on *Refoulement* and *Haitian Centers Council.*" *Harvard International Law Journal* 35 (1): 1–20.

Koh, H. H., and M. J. Wishnie. 2009. "The Story of *Sale v. Haitian Centers Council:* Guantánamo and *Refoulement.*" In *Human Rights Advocacy Stories,* edited by D. R. Hurwitz and M. Satterthwitte, 385–432. St. Paul, MN: Foundation Press.

Krammer, A. 1996. *Nazi Prisoners of War in America.* Lanham, MD: Scarborough House.

Krupar, S. R. 2013. *Hot Spotter's Report: Military Fables of Toxic Waste.* Minneapolis: University of Minnesota Press.

Kurzban, I. J. 1983–1984. "'Long and Perilous Journey': The *Nelson* Decision." *Human Rights* 11: 41–44.

Lao-Montes, A. 2007. "Decolonial Moves: Trans-locating African Diaspora Spaces." *Cultural Studies* 21 (2–3): 209–338.

Last, T., G. Mirto, O. Ulusoy, I. Urquijo, J. Harte, N. Bami, M. P. Pérez, F. Macias Delgado, A. Tapella, A. Michalaki, E. Michalitsi, E. Latsoudi, N. Tselepi, M. Chatziprokopiou, and T. Spijkerboer. 2017. "Deaths at the

Borders Database: Evidence of Deceased Migrants' Bodies Found along the Southern External Borders of the European Union." *Journal of Ethnic and Migration Studies* 43 (5): 693–712.

Lipman, J. 2008. *Guantánamo: A Working-Class History between Empire and Revolution*. Berkeley: University of California Press.

Lipman, J.K. 2012. "'Give Us a Ship': The Vietnamese Repatriate Movement on Guam, 1975." *American Quarterly* 64 (1): 1–31.

———. 2013. "'The Fish Trusts the Water, and It Is in the Water That It Is Cooked': The Caribbean Origins of the Krome Detention Center." *Radical History Review* 115: 115–41.

———. 2014. "A Refugee Camp in America: Fort Chaffee and Vietnamese and Cuban Refugees, 1975–1982." *Journal of American Ethnic History* 33 (2): 57–87.

Loescher, G. and J. Scanlan. 1984. "Human Rights, U.S. Foreign Policy, and Haitian Refugees." *Journal of Interamerican Studies and World Affairs* 26 (3): 313–56.

Loescher, G., and J.A. Scanlan. 1986. *Calculated Kindness: Refugees and America's Half-Open Door, 1945–Present*. New York: The Free Press.

Louis v. Meissner. 1981. 530 F. Supp. 924 (S.D. Fla. 1981).

Loyd, J.M. 2015. "Carceral Citizenship in an Age of Global Apartheid." *Occasion* 8: 1–15.

———. Forthcoming. "'This Wack(yhut) Idea!!!': The Plantation Bloc and Political Economy of Prison Expansion in Louisiana." In *Geographies of Power,* edited by M. Coleman and J. Agnew. Northampton, MA: Edward Elgar Publishing.

Loyd, J.M., E. Mitchell-Eaton, and A. Mountz. 2015. "The Militarization of Islands and Migration: Tracing Human Mobility through US Bases in the Caribbean and the Pacific." *Political Geography* 53: 66–75. doi:10.1016/j.polgeo.2015.11.006.

Loyd, J.M., M. Mitchelson, and A. Burridge, eds. 2012. *Beyond Walls and Cages: Prisons, Borders and Global Crisis*. Athens: University of Georgia Press.

Luibhéid, E. 2015. *Entry Denied: Controlling Sexuality at the Border*. Minneapolis: University of Minnesota Press.

Lutz, C. 2009. *The Bases of Empire: The Global Struggle against U.S. Military Posts*. New York: New York University Press.

Lynch, M. 2010. *Sunbelt Justice: Arizona and the Transformation of American Punishment*. Stanford, CA: Stanford Law Books.

Macías-Rojas, P. 2016. *From Deportation to Prison: The Politics of Immigration Enforcement in Post–Civil Rights America*. New York: New York University Press.

Maddux, T.R. 2005. "Ronald Reagan and the Task Force on Immigration." *Pacific Historical Review* 74 (2): 195–236.

Márquez, J.D. 2013. *Black-Brown Solidarity: Racial Politics in the New Gulf South*. Austin: University of Texas Press.

Martin, L.L. 2012. "'Catch and Remove': Detention, Deterrence, and Discipline in US Noncitizen Family Detention Practice." *Geopolitics* 17 (2): 312–34.

Martin, L. L., and M. L. Mitchelson. 2009. "Geographies of Detention and Imprisonment: Interrogating Spatial Practices of Confinement, Discipline, Law, and State Power." *Geography Compass* 3 (1): 459–77.

Masters, A. 1996. "Is Procedural Due Process in a Remote Processing Center a Contradiction in Terms—*Gandarillas-Zambrana v. Board of Immigration Appeals*." *Ohio State Law Journal* 57 (3): 999–1025.

Mayes, A., Y. C. Martín, C. U. Decena, K. Jayaram, and Y. Alexis. 2013. "Transnational Hispaniola: Toward New Paradigms in Haitian and Dominican Studies." *Radical History Review* 115: 26–32. doi:10.1215/01636545-1724679.

McKittrick, K. 2006. *Demonic Grounds: Black Women and the Cartographies of Struggle*. Minneapolis: University of Minnesota Press.

———. 2013. "Plantation Futures." *Small Axe* 17 (3) 42: 1–15. doi:10.1215/07990537-2378892.

Melossi, D. 2013. "People on the Move: From the Countryside to the Factory/Prison." In *The Borders of Punishment: Migration, Citizenship, and Social Exclusion*, edited by K. F. Aas and M. Bosworth, 273–90. Oxford: Oxford University Press.

Menjívar, C. 2006. "Liminal Legality: Salvadoran and Guatemalan Immigrants' Lives in the United States." *American Journal of Sociology* 111 (4): 999–1003.

Milian, C. 2013. *Latining America: Black-Brown Passages and the Coloring of Latino/a Studies*. Athens: University of Georgia Press.

Miller, J. C. 1984. *The Plight of Haitian Refugees*. New York: Praeger Publishers.

———. 2006. "International Concern for Haitians in the Diaspora." *The Western Journal of Black Studies* 30 (1): 35–45.

Miller, T. 2014. *Border Patrol Nation: Dispatches from the Front Lines of Homeland Security*. San Francisco: City Lights Books.

Miller, T. A. 2003. "Citizenship & Severity: Recent Immigration Reforms and the New Penology." *Georgetown Immigration Law Journal* 17 (4): 611–66.

Minnesota Lawyers International Human Rights Committee. 1987. *Oakdale Detention Center: The First Year of Operation*. Minneapolis: Minnesota Lawyers International Human Rights Committee.

Minnesota Lawyers International Human Rights Committee and Physicians for Human Rights. 1991. *Hidden from View: Human Rights Conditions in the Krome Detention Center*. Minneapolis: Minnesota Lawyers International Human Rights Committee.

Mitchell, C. 1994. "U.S. Policy toward Haitian Boat People, 1972–93." *Annals of the American Academy of Political and Social Science* 54: 69–80.

Molloy, J., and J. Simeon. 2016. "Introduction: The Indochinese Refugee Movement and the Launch of Canada's Sponsorship Program." *Refuge* 32 (2): 2–8.

Moloney, D. M. 2012. *National Insecurities: Immigrants and U.S. Deportation Policy since 1882*. Chapel Hill: University of North Carolina Press.

Moran, D. 2013. "Leaving Behind the 'Total Institution'? Teeth, Transcarceral Spaces and (Re)Inscription of the Formerly Incarcerated Body." *Gender Place & Culture* 21 (1): 35–51. doi:10.1080/0966369X.2012.759906.

Moran, D., N. Gill, and D. Conlon, eds. 2013. *Carceral Spaces: Mobility and Agency in Imprisonment and Migrant Detention*. Surrey, England: Ashgate.

Moran, D., L. Piacentini, and J. Pallot. 2013. "Liminal Transcarceral Space: Prison Transportation for Women in the Russian Federation." In *Carceral Spaces: Mobility and Agency in Imprisonment and Migrant Detention,* edited by D. Moran, N. Gill, and D. Conlon, 109–24. Surrey, England: Ashgate.

Moreno-Lax, V., and E. Papastavridis. 2017. "Tracing the Bases of an Integrated Paradigm for Maritime Security and Human Rights at Sea." In *"Boat Refugees" and Migrants at Sea: A Comprehensive Approach,* edited by V. Moreno-Lax and E. Papastavridis, 1–16. Leiden, Netherlands: Brill.

Morgan-Trostle, J., K. Zheng, and C. Lipscombe. 2016. *The State of Black Immigrants.* New York: New York University Law School Immigrant Rights Clinic and Black Alliance for Just Immigration. Available from: http://www.stateofblackimmigrants.com/. Last accessed: 28 October 2017.

Mountz, A. Forthcoming. *The Enforcement Archipelago: hidden geographies and the death of asylum.* Minneapolis: University of Minnesota Press.

Mountz, A. 2010. *Seeking Asylum: Human Smuggling and Bureaucracy at the Border.* Minneapolis: University of Minnesota Press.

———. 2011a. "The Enforcement Archipelago: Detention, Haunting, and Asylum on Islands." *Political Geography* 30 (3): 118–28.

———. 2011b. "Specters at the Port of Entry: Understanding State Mobilities through an Ontology of Exclusion." *Mobilities* 6 (3): 317–34.

——— and N. Hiemstra. 2013. "Chaos and crisis: dissecting the spatio-temporal logics of contemporary migrations and state practices." *Annals of the Association of American Geographers* 104(2): 382–390.

———., and J. Loyd. 2014. "Transnational Productions of Remoteness: Building Onshore and Offshore Carceral Regimes across Borders." *Geographica Helvetica.* doi:10.5194/gh-69-389-2014.

———., R. Wright, I. Miyares, A. Bailey. 2002. Lives in limbo: Temporary Protected Status and immigrant identities. *Global Networks* 2(4): 335–356.

Muhammad, K. G. 2010. *The Condemnation of Blackness: Race, Crime, and the Making of Modern Urban America.* Cambridge, MA: Harvard University Press.

Murakawa, N. 2014. *The First Civil Right: How Liberals Built Prison America.* New York: Oxford University Press.

Nacci, P. L. 1988. "The Oakdale-Atlanta Prison Disturbances: The Events, the Results." *Federal Probation* 52: 3–12.

National Immigrant Justice Center. 2010. *Isolated in Detention: Limited Access to Legal Counsel in Immigration Detention Facilities Jeopardizes a Fair Day in Court.* Available from: https://www.immigrantjustice.org/isolatedindetention. Last accessed: 27 October 2017.

———. 2015. *The Immigration Detention Transparency & Human Rights Project.* Available from: http://immigrantjustice.org/immigration-detention-transparency-and-human-rights-project-august-2015-report. Last accessed: 28 October 2017.

Neocleous, M. 2014. *War Power, Police Power.* Edinburgh: Edinburgh University Press.

Nevins, J. 2003. "Thinking Out of Bounds: A Critical Analysis of Academic and Human Rights Writings on Migrant Deaths in the US-Mexico Border Region." *Migraciones Internacionales* 2 (2): 171–91.

————. 2010. *Operation Gatekeeper and Beyond: The War on "Illegals" and the Remaking of the U.S.-Mexico Boundary*. New York: Routledge.

————. 2012. "Policing Mobility, Maintaining Global Apartheid—from South Africa to the United States." In *Beyond Walls and Cages: Prisons, Borders and Global Crisis*, edited by J. M. Loyd, M. Mitchelson, and A. Burridge, 19–26. Athens: University of Georgia Press.

Nevins, J., and M. Aizeki. 2008. *Dying to Live: A Story of U.S. Immigration in an Age of Global Apartheid*. San Francisco: City Lights Books.

New York Civil Liberties Union, with Families for Freedom and New York University School of Law. 2011. *Justice Derailed: What Raids on New York's Trains and Buses Reveal about Border Patrol's Interior Enforcement Practices*. Available from: https://www.nyclu.org/sites/default/files/publications /NYCLU_justicederailedweb_0.pdf. Last accessed: 27 October 2017.

Ngai, M. 2008. *Impossible Subjects: Illegal Aliens and the Making of Modern America*. Princeton, NJ: Princeton University Press.

Nguyen, M. T. 2012. *The Gift of Freedom: War, Debt, and Other Refugee Passages*. Durham, NC, and London: Duke University Press.

Noble, D. L. 2011. *The U.S. Coast Guard's War on Human Smuggling*. Gainesville: University Press of Florida.

Norton, J. 2015. "Little Siberia, Star of the North: The Political Economy of Prison Dreams in the Adirondacks." In *The Historical Geography of Jails and Prisons*, edited by K. Morin & D. Moran, 168–84. New York and London: Routledge.

Office of the Inspector General. 2001. *The Department of Justice's Reliance on Private Contractors for Prison Services*. Washington, D.C.: Department of Justice.

————. 2005. *The United States Marshals Service's Cooperative Agreement Program*. Washington, D.C.: Department of Justice.

————. 2016. *Review of the Federal Bureau of Prisons' Monitoring of Contract Prisons*. Washington, D.C.: Department of Justice.

Paik, A. N. 2013. "Carceral Quarantine at Guantánamo: Legacies of US Imprisonment of Haitian Refugees, 1991–1994." *Radical History Review* 115: 142–68.

————. 2016. *Rightlessness: Testimony and Redress in U.S. Prison Camps since World War II*. Chapel Hill: The University of North Carolina Press.

Pain, R., and L. Staeheli. 2014. "Introduction: intimacy-geopolitics and violence." *Area* 46(4): 344–360.

Pearcy, K., and C. Little. 1996. *Unaccompanied Haitian Children Repatriated from Guantánamo: Stories of Trauma and Despair*. Miami: Florida Immigrant Advocacy Center.

Peck, J., and N. Theodore. 2015. *Fast Policy Transfer: Experimental Statecraft at the Thresholds of Neoliberalism*. Minneapolis: University of Minnesota Press.

Pickering, S. 2014. "Floating Carceral Spaces: Border Enforcement and Gender on the High Seas." *Punishment and Society* 16 (2): 187–205.

Pratt, G., and V. Rosner. 2006. "The Global & the Intimate." *Women's Studies Quarterly* 34 (1/2): 13–24.

President's Economic Adjustment Committee. 1990. *Using Former Military Installations as Correctional Facilities.* Washington, D.C.: Office of the Secretary of Defense.

Pulido, L. 2006. *Black, Brown, Yellow, and Left: Radical Activism in Los Angeles.* Berkeley: University of California Press.

Rivera-Rideau, P. R., J. A. Jones, and T. S. Paschel. 2016. "Introduction: Theorizing Afrolatinidades." In *Afro-Latin@s in Movement: Critical Approaches to Blackness and Transnationalism in the Americas,* edited by P. R. Rivera-Rideau, J. A. Jones, and T. S. Paschel, 1–29. New York: Palgrave Macmillan.

Rodríguez, D. 2008. "'I Would Wish Death on You ...': Race, Gender, and Immigration in the Globality of the US Prison Regime." *Scholar & Feminist Online* 6. Available from: http://sfonline.barnard.edu/immigration/drodriguez_01.htm. Last accessed 27 October 2017.

Roshan v. Smith. 1985. 615 F. Supp. 901 (D.D.C 1985).

Rouse, R. 1991. "Mexican Migration and the Social Space of Postmodernism." *Diaspora* 1 (1): 8–23.

Rusin, S., J. Zong, and J. Batalova. 2015. "Cuban Immigrants in the United States." Migration Policy Institute. https://www.migrationpolicy.org/article/cuban-immigrants-united-states. Last accessed: 27 October 2017.

Ryan, B. 2010. "Extraterritorial Immigration Control: What Role for Legal Guarantees?" In *Extraterritorial Immigration Control: Legal Challenges,* edited by B. Ryan and V. Mitsilegas, 1–37. Leiden, Netherlands: Brill.

Sampson, R. 2013. "Embodied borders: Biopolitics, knowledge mobilisation and alternatives to immigration detention," PhD dissertation, Swinburne University of Technology.

Sartori, M. E. 2001. "The Cuban Migration Dilemma: An Examination of the United States' Policy of Temporary Protection in Offshore Safe Havens." *Georgetown Immigration Law Journal* 15 (2): 319–55.

Schoultz, L. 1992. "Central America and the Politicization of U.S. Immigration Policy." In *Western Hemisphere Immigration and United States Foreign Policy,* edited by C. Mitchell, 157–219. University Park: The Pennsylvania State University Press.

Schrecker, E. 1996. "Immigration and Internal Security: Political Deportations during the McCarthy Era." *Science & Society* 60 (4): 393–426.

Schriro, D. 2009. *Immigration Detention Overview and Recommendations.* Washington, D.C.: Department of Homeland Security, Immigration and Customs Enforcement. Available from: https://www.ice.gov/doclib/about/offices/odpp/pdf/ice-detention-rpt.pdf. Last accessed: 27 October 2017.

Schuck, P. H. 2013. "Immigrant Criminals in Overcrowded Prisons: Rethinking an Anachronistic Policy." *Georgetown Immigration Law Journal* 27: 597–661.

Schuck, P. H., and J. Williams. 1999. "Removing Criminal Aliens: The Pitfalls and Promises of Federalism." *Harvard Journal of Law & Public Policy* 22 (2): 367–463.

Scott, J. C. 1998. *Seeing Like a State: How Certain Schemes to Improve the Human Condition Have Failed.* New Haven, CT: Yale University Press.

Seelke, C. R., and K. Finklea. 2017. *U.S.-Mexican Security Cooperation: The Mérida Initiative and Beyond.* Washington, D.C.: Congressional Research Service. http://fas.org/sgp/crs/row/R41349.pdf. Last accessed: 27 October 2017.

Sharma, N. 2005. "Anti-Trafficking Rhetoric and the Making of Global Apartheid." *NWSA Journal* 17 (3): 88–111.

Shemak, A. A. 2011. *Asylum Speakers: Caribbean Refugees and Testimonial Discourse.* New York: Fordham University Press.

Shull, K. K. 2014a. *"Nobody Wants These People": Reagan's Immigration Crisis and America's First Private Prisons.* PhD thesis, University of California, Irvine.

———. 2014b. "'Nobody Wants These People': Reagan's Immigration Crisis and the Containment of Foreign Bodies." In *Body and Nation: The Global Realm of U.S. Body Politics in the Twentieth Century,* edited by E. S. Rosenberg and S. Fitzpatrick, 241–63. Durham, NC: Duke University Press.

Simon, J. 1998. "Refugees in a Carceral Age: The Rebirth of Immigration Prisons in the United States." *Public Culture* 10: 577–607.

———. 2007. *Governing through Crime: How the War on Crime Transformed American Democracy and Created a Culture of Fear.* New York: Oxford University Press.

Slack, J., D. E. Martínez, A. E. Lee, and S. Whiteford. 2016. "The Geography of Border Militarization: Violence, Death and Health and the United States." *Journal of Latin American Geography* 15 (1): 7–32.

Slahi, M. O. 2015. *Guantánamo Diary.* New York: Little, Brown & Company.

Spidle, J. W. 1975. "Axis Prisoners of War in the United States, 1942–1946: A Bibliographical Essay." *Military Affairs* 39 (2): 61–6.

Stein, B. 1979. "Geneva Conferences and the Indochinese Refugee Crisis." *International Migration Review* 13 (4): 716–23.

Steinberg, P. 2001. *The Social Construction of the Ocean.* New York: Cambridge University Press.

Stepick, A. 1982. "Haitian Boat People: A Study in the Conflicting Forces Shaping U.S. Immigration Policy." *Law and Contemporary Problems* 45 (2): 163–96.

———. (1982) 1986. *Haitian Refugees in the U.S.* The Minority Rights Group, report no. 52. London: Minority Rights Group.

———. 1992. "Unintended Consequences: Rejecting Haitian Boat People and Destabilizing Duvalier." In *Western Hemisphere Immigration and United States Foreign Policy,* edited by C. Mitchell, 125–55. University Park: The Pennsylvania State University Press.

Stierl, M. 2017. "A Fleet of Mediterranean Border Humanitarians." *Antipode.* doi:10.1111/anti.12320.

Stoler, A. 2011. "Colony." *Political Concepts: A Critical Lexicon.* http://www.politicalconcepts.org/issue1/colony/. Last accessed: 27 October 2017.

Stumpf, J. 2006. "The Crimmigration Crisis: Immigration, Crime, and Sovereign Power." *American University Law Review* 56 (2): 367–419.

———. 2013. "The Process Is the Punishment in Crimmigration Law." In *The Borders of Punishment: Migration, Citizenship, and Social Exclusion,* edited by K. F. Aas and M. Bosworth, 58–75. Oxford: Oxford University Press.

Sudbury, J. 2005. "'Mules,' 'Yardies,' and Other Folk Devils: Mapping Cross-border Imprisonment in Britain." In *Global Lockdown,* edited by J. Sudbury, 167–84 New York: Routledge.

Suhrke, A. 1983. "Indochinese Refugees: The Law and Politics of First Asylum." *Annals of the American Academy of Political and Social Science* 467: 102–15.

Swanson, K., R. Torres, Amy Thompson, S. Blue, and Ó.M. Hernández Hernández. 2015. "A Year after Obama Declared a 'Humanitarian Situation' at the Border, Child Migration Continues." NACLA, 27 August. https://nacla.org/news/2015/08/27/year-after-obama-declared-"humanitarian-situation"-border-child-migration-continues. Accessed 30 December 2017.

Taylor, M.H. 1995. "Detained Aliens Challenging Conditions of Confinement and the Porous Border of the Plenary Power Doctrine." *Hastings Constitutional Law Quarterly* 22 (4): 1088–158.

Ticktin, M. 2011. *Casualties of Care: Immigration and the Politics of Humanitarianism in France.* Berkeley: University of California Press.

U.S. Border Patrol. 1994. *Border Patrol Strategic Plan: 1994 and Beyond.* Washington, D.C.: U.S. Border Patrol.

U.S. Congress, House Committee on the Judiciary. 1982a. *Detention of Aliens in Bureau of Prisons Facilities: Hearing before the Subcommittee on Courts, Civil Liberties and the Administration of Justice.* 97th Cong., 2nd sess. 23 June 1982.

U.S. Congress, House Subcommittee of the Committee on Government Operations. 1982b. *Proposal for Detention Center for Illegal Aliens in El Reno, Okla.* 97th Cong., 2nd sess. 8 July 1982.

U.S. Congress, Senate Committee on Appropriations. 1999. *Departments of Commerce, Justice, and State, the Judiciary, and Related Agencies Appropriations for Fiscal Year 2000* (HR 2670/S 217). 106th Cong., 1st sess. 9 March, 11 March, 16 March, 19 March, 22 March, 24 March, and 25 March 1999.

U.S. Congress, Senate Committee on the Judiciary. 2002. *The Detention and Treatment of Haitian Asylum Seekers: Hearing before the Subcommittee on Immigration.* 107th Cong., 2nd sess. 1 October 2002.

U.S. Congress, Senate Permanent Subcommittee on Investigations of the Committee on Governmental Affairs. 1995. *Criminal Aliens in the United States.* 104th Cong., 1st sess. 7 April 1995.

Villiers, J.D. 1994. "Closed Borders, Closed Ports: The Plight of Haitians Seeking Political Asylum in the United States." *Brooklyn Law Review* 60 (3): 841–928.

Vine, D. 2009. *Island of Shame: The Secret History of the U.S. Military Base on Diego Garcia.* Princeton, NJ: Princeton University Press.

———. 2012. "The Lily-pad Strategy." TomDispatch.com. http://www.tomdispatch.com/archive/175568/. Last accessed: 27 October 2017.

Vogt, W. 2013. "Crossing Mexico: Structural violence and the commodification of Central American migrants." *American Ethnologist* 40(4): 746–780.

Walters, W. 2008. "Bordering the Sea: Shipping Industries and the Policing of Stowaways." *Borderlands E-Journal* 7 (3): 1–25.

———. 2010a. "Foucault and Frontiers: Notes on the Birth of the Humanitarian Border." In *Governmentality: Current Issues and Future Challenges,* edited by U. Brockling, B. Krasmann, and T. Lemke, 138–64. New York: Routledge.

————. 2010b. "Deportation, Expulsion, and the International Police of Aliens." In *The Deportation Regime: Sovereignty, Space, and the Freedom of Movement,* edited by N. De Genova and N. Peutz, 69–100. Durham, NC: Duke University Press.

————. 2016. "The Flight of the Deported: Aircraft, Deportation, and Politics." *Geopolitics* 21 (2): 435–58.

Weinberg, S. A. 1984–1985. "*Jean v. Nelson:* Expansion of the 'Entry Doctrine' Fiction." *Southwestern University Law Review* 15 (3): 575–614.

Welch, M. 2000. "The Role of the Immigration and Naturalization Service in the Prison-Industrial Complex." *Social Justice* 27 (3): 73–88.

————. 2004. *Detained: Immigration Laws and the Expanding I.N.S. Jail Complex.* Philadelphia: Temple University Press.

Williams, J. M. 2014. "The Safety/Security Nexus and the Humanitarianisation of Border Enforcement." *Geographical Journal* 182 (1): 27–37. doi:10.1111/geoj.12119.

————. 2015. "From Humanitarian Exceptionalism to Contingent Care: Care and Enforcement at the Humanitarian Border." *Political Geography* 47: 11–20.

Wimmer, A., and N. Glick Schiller. 2002. "Methodological Nationalism and Beyond: Nation-state Building, Migration, and the Social Sciences." *Global Networks* 2 (4): 301–34.

Wynter, S. 1995. "1492: A New World View." In *Race, Discourse, and the Origin of the Americas,* edited by V. L. Hyatt and R. Nettleford, 5–57. Washington, D.C.: Smithsonian Institution Press.

Yates, J., T. A. Collins, and G. J. Chin. 2005. "A War on Drugs or a War on Immigrants?: Expanding the Definition of 'Drug Trafficking' in Determining Aggravated Felon Status for Noncitizens." *Maryland Law Review* 64 (3): 875–909.

Young, I. M. 2003. "The Logic of Masculinist Protection: Reflections on the National Security State." *Signs* 29 (1): 1–25.

Zilberg, E. 2011. *Spaces of Detention: The Making of a Transnational Gang Crisis between Los Angeles and San Salvador.* Durham, NC: Duke University Press.

Zucker, N. F. 1983. "The Haitians versus the United States: The Courts as Last Resort." *The Annals of the American Academy of Political and Social Science* 467: 151–62.

Zucker, N. L. 1983. "Refugee Resettlement in the United States: Policy and Problems." *The Annals of the American Academy of Political and Social Science* 467: 172–86.

Zucker, N. L., and N. F. Zucker. 1996. *Desperate Crossings: Seeking Refuge in America.* Armonk, NY: M. E. Sharpe.

Index

ABC case *(American Baptist Churches v. Thornburgh)*, 136, 140–41, 202
Abrams, Elliot, 105
ACLU. *See* American Civil Liberties Union (ACLU)
ACT-UP, 155
ADAA (Anti-Drug Abuse Act) (1988), 133–35, 144, 183, 189
Adams, Roger, 50–51
Administrative Procedures Act, 88
AEDPA (Anti-Terrorism and Effective Death Penalty Act) (1996), 176, 182, 184
Afrolatinidade, 18–19
aggravated felony, 133–34, 141, 182–84, 205. *See also* criminalization of migration
agricultural labor, history of, 121–22, 142
AIDS. *See* detention, confinement of HIV positive Haitian refugees
air travel: detainee transport, 63, 100, 111, 142, 178; Justice Prisoner and Alien Transportation System (JPATS), 185–89, 187*map*; refugee transport, 38–39
Albright, Madeline, 49
Alcatraz, California, 64
alien, use of term, 5, 17. *See also* criminal alien
Alien Criminal Apprehension Program (ACAP), 132–35. *See also* Institutional Hearing Program (IHP)

Allenwood, Pennsylvania, 123
Alliance for Prosperity, 230
Almaden Air Force Station, California, 64
Alvarado, Donna, 55
American Baptist Churches v. Thornburgh (ABC case), 136, 140–41, 202
American Civil Liberties Union (ACLU): *Jean v. Meissner* (1981), 73; opposition to Oakdale, Louisiana facility, 109–15; opposition to private prisons, 194
Andreas, Peter, 164
Anti-Drug Abuse Act (ADAA) (1988), 133–34, 183
Anti-Terrorism and Effective Death Penalty Act (AEDPA), 176, 182, 184
apartheid, global, 224–25
Arab immigrants: September 11, 2001 and consolidation of carceral state, 206, 209, 210*fig*; Trump administration, 232–33
Arizona: as "border" state, 13, 26, 118, 141; Clinton administration Border Patrol policy, 2; Cold War internal security detention camps, 123; Department of Corrections, 117, 126–27; Eloy, detention facility, 13, 26, 118, 119*map*, 183, 194–97, 196*fig*; WWII POW camps, 26; sanctuary movement, 135–41. *See also* Florence, Arizona

U.S. Navy: Operation Sea Signal (1994–
1996), 158–60
U.S. Refugee Admissions Program, 230–31
U.S. Supreme Court: *HRC v. Baker*, 151;
Jean v. Nelson, 109; *Louis v. Nelson*,
89–90; on mandatory detention of
"aliens," 72; *Plyler v. Doe*, 98; *Sale v.
Haitian Centers Council (HCC-II)*,
152–54, 156–57

V.A. Medical Center, Augusta, Georgia, 64
Vance, Cyrus, 41
Vietnam and Vietnamese refugees, 33,
36–42, 213–14
Vietnam War, 36
violence, Northern Triangle, 227–31
violence, state, 24, 171, 228–31
Violent Crime Control and Law
Enforcement Act (Crime Act), 176
Virginia, politics of detention center
location decisions, 96–101
Voice of America, 160
voluntary departure, and detention, 105–06;
Anti-Drug Abuse Act (ADAA) (1988),
133–34; use of term, 72–73. *See also
Orantes-Hernández v. Smith*
voluntary repatriation, 163

Wackenhut, 193–94, 197–99
walrus courts, 77
Walters, William, 188
War Assets Administration, 122
Warnath, Stephen, 168
Warner, John W., 98, 102
war on drugs: criminal alien deportation
efforts, 130, 132–35; militarization of

migration, 23–24; Northern Triangle
violence, 228–31
war on terror, 215, 217
Watson, Jack, 55
Webb County Detention Center, Laredo,
Texas, 139–40, 147–48
Weinberger, Caspar, 68, 80
Westover Air Force Base, Massachusetts, 80
West Virginia: transfer of Haitians from
Krome, 89–92, 91*map*
wetback, use of term, 124, 127–28
wet foot, dry foot policy, 160–64, 161*fig*,
167
White, Frank, 60
Whitley, Joe, 139
Wickenburg, Arizona, 123
Williams, Jack, 126–27
Wilson, Pete, 135, 166, 168
Windward Passage, 76–79, 78*map*
Wisconsin: Fort McCoy, 59–60
women: from Central America (2014),
220–24; crimes involving moral
turpitude, 130; at Fort Chaffee, 63;
HIV-positive Haitians, 154; hunger
strike at Guantánamo Bay, 155; hunger
strike at Krome, 84; mistreatment in
detention, 76; Northern Triangle, migra-
tion from, 227–31; Operation Hold the
Line (1989), 139; Operation Safe Haven
(1994), 148; sex workers, 57; at Turner
Guilford Knight (TGK) Center, 207–8
WORLD RELIEF, 162

Young, Andrew, 42, 48

Zucker, Naomi, 52